itakdalee/iStock • mauro_grigollo/iStock (top)

THE MICHELIN AWARDS FOR GOOD FOOD

STARS

Our famous One ✿, Two ✿✿ and Three ✿✿✿ Stars identify establishments serving the highest quality cuisine – taking into account the quality of ingredients, the mastery of techniques and flavours, the levels of creativity and, of course, consistency.

✿✿✿ **Exceptional cuisine, worth a special journey!**

Our highest award is given for the superlative cooking of chefs at the peak of their profession. The ingredients are exemplary, the cooking is elevated to an art form and their dishes are often destined to become classics.

✿✿ **Excellent cuisine, worth a detour!**

The personality and talent of the chef and their team is evident in the expertly crafted dishes, which are refined, inspired and sometimes original.

✿ **High quality cooking, worth a stop!**

Using top quality ingredients, dishes with distinct flavours are carefully prepared to a consistently high standard.

BIB GOURMAND

Good quality, good value cooking.

'Bibs' are awarded for simple yet skilful cooking, with 3 courses costing £28 or less.

PLATE

Good cooking.

Fresh ingredients, capably prepared: simply a good meal.

DEAR READER,

We are delighted to present the 2018 edition of the Michelin Guide to London. All the restaurants within this guide have been chosen first and foremost for the quality of their cooking. You'll find comprehensive information on over 500 dining establishments, ranging from gastropubs and neighbourhood brasseries to internationally renowned restaurants. The diverse and varied selection bears testament to the rich and buoyant dining scene in London, with the city enjoying a worldwide reputation for the range and quality of its restaurants.

Our most famous awards are our Michelin Stars but look out too for the Bib Gourmands. These are restaurants where the cooking is still carefully prepared but in a simpler style and, priced at under £28 for three courses, they represent excellent value for money. The rest of the restaurants in our selection are then identified by a new symbol: The Michelin Plate 🍽. Being chosen by the Michelin Inspectors for inclusion in the guide is a guarantee of quality in itself and the plate symbol highlights restaurants where you will have a good meal.

We are committed to remaining at the forefront of the culinary world and to meeting the demands of our readers. Please don't hesitate to contact us, as your contributions are invaluable in directing our work and improving the quality of the information that we provide.

Thank you for your support and happy travelling with the 2018 edition of the Michelin Guide to London.

Consult the Michelin Guide at
www.viamichelin.co.uk
and write to us at
themichelinguide-gbirl@michelin.com

CONTENTS

INDEXES 402

A CULINARY HISTORY OF LONDON

London, influenced by worldwide produce arriving via the Thames, has always enjoyed a close association with its food, though most of the time the vast majority of its people have looked much closer to home for their sustenance.

Even as far back as the 2nd century AD, meat was on the menu: the profusion of wildlife in the woods and forests around London turned it into a carnivore's paradise, thereby setting the tone and the template. Large stoves were employed to cook everything from pork and beef to goose and deer. The Saxons added the likes of garlic, leeks, radishes and turnips to the pot, while eels became a popular staple in later years.

What a lark!

By the 13th century, the taste for fish had evolved to the more exotic porpoise, lamprey and sturgeon, with saffron and spices perking up the common-or-garden meat dish. Not that medieval tastes would have been considered mundane to the average 21st century diner: Londoners of the time would think nothing about devouring roasted thrush or lark from the cook's stalls dotted around the city streets. And you'd have been unlikely to hear the cry "Eat your greens!" In the 15th century, the vegetable diet, such as it was, seemed to run mainly to herbs such as rosemary, fennel, borage and thyme.

As commercial and maritime success burgeoned in the age of the Tudors, so tables began to groan under the weight of London's penchant for feasting. No excess was spared, as oxen, sheep, boars and pigs were put to the griddle; these would have been accompanied by newly arrived yams and sweet

potatoes from America and 'washed down' with rhubarb from Asia. People on the streets could 'feast-lite': by the 17th century hawkers were offering all sorts of goodies on the hoof.

Full of Beans

All of this eating was of course accompanied by a lot of drinking. Though much of it took place in the alehouses and taverns - which ran into the thousands - by the 18th century coffee houses had become extraordinarily popular. These were places to do business as well as being convenient 'for passing evenings socially at a very small charge'.

Perhaps the biggest revolution in eating habits came midway through the 19th century when the first cavernous dining halls and restaurants appeared. These 'freed' diners from the communal benches of the cook-house and gave them, for the first time, the chance for a bit of seclusion at separate tables. This private dining experience was an egalitarian movement: plutocrats may have had their posh hotels, but the less well-off were buttering teacakes and scones served by 'nippies' at the local Lyons Corner House.

Influenced by post World War II flavours brought in by immigrants from Asia, the Caribbean and Africa – and, more recently, from Eastern Bloc Countries – Londoners now enjoy an unparalleled cuisine alive with global flavours. We're also more confident about waving the flag for Britain these days, with pop-ups, pubs and high end eateries helping us rediscover and celebrate our own culinary heritage.

A. Spatari/Moment/Getty Images (left) • C. Crespo/age fotostock (right)

Xsandra/iStock (left) • sinarp2/iStock (right)

CENTRAL LONDON

fotoVoyager/iStock (bottom) • olaser/iStock (top)

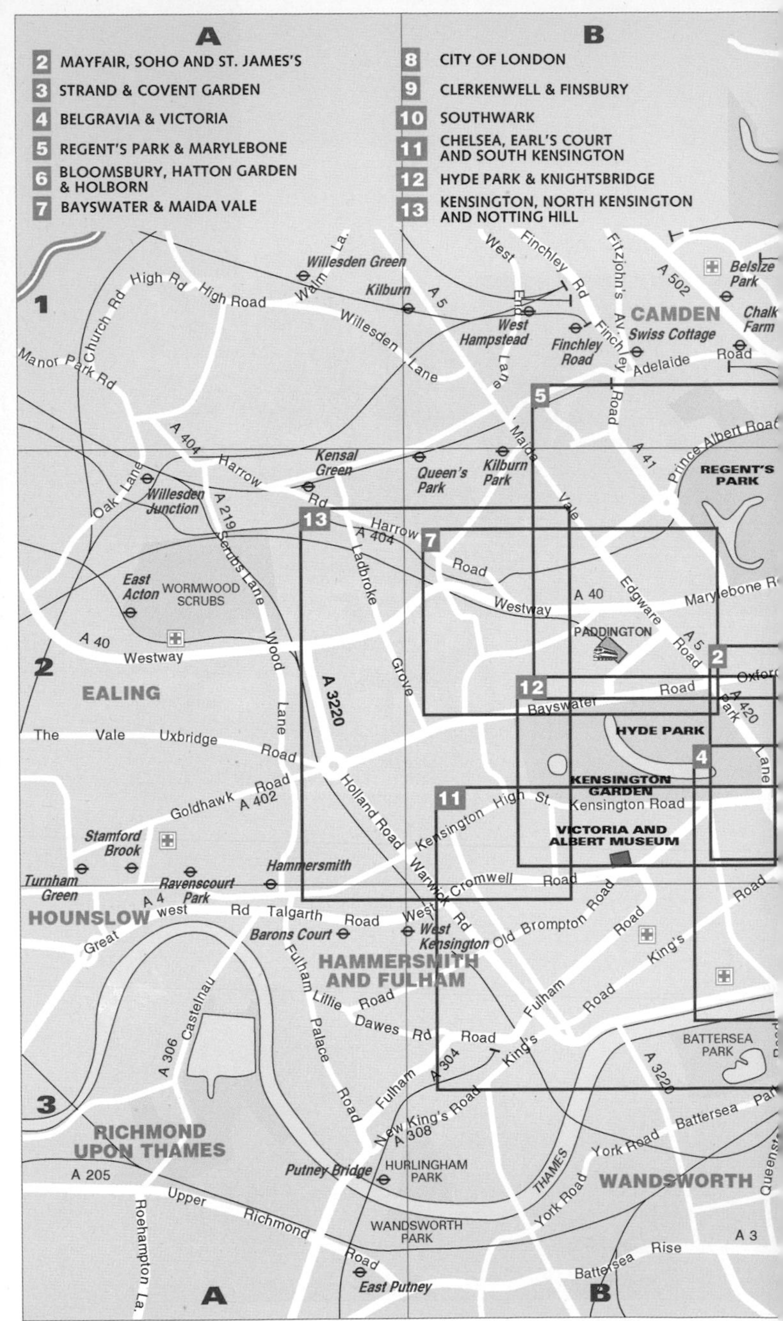
A
B
2 MAYFAIR, SOHO AND ST. JAMES'S
3 STRAND & COVENT GARDEN
4 BELGRAVIA & VICTORIA
5 REGENT'S PARK & MARYLEBONE
6 BLOOMSBURY, HATTON GARDEN & HOLBORN
7 BAYSWATER & MAIDA VALE
8 CITY OF LONDON
9 CLERKENWELL & FINSBURY
10 SOUTHWARK
11 CHELSEA, EARL'S COURT AND SOUTH KENSINGTON
12 HYDE PARK & KNIGHTSBRIDGE
13 KENSINGTON, NORTH KENSINGTON AND NOTTING HILL
CAMDEN
REGENT'S PARK
PADDINGTON
HYDE PARK
KENSINGTON GARDEN
VICTORIA AND ALBERT MUSEUM
WORMWOOD SCRUBS
EALING
HOUNSLOW
HAMMERSMITH AND FULHAM
RICHMOND UPON THAMES
WANDSWORTH
BATTERSEA PARK
HURLINGHAM PARK
WANDSWORTH PARK
THAMES
Willesden Green
Kilburn
West Hampstead
Finchley Road
Swiss Cottage
Belsize Park
Chalk Farm
Kensal Green
Queen's Park
Kilburn Park
Willesden Junction
East Acton
Stamford Brook
Turnham Green
Ravenscourt Park
Hammersmith
Barons Court
West Kensington
Putney Bridge
East Putney
1
2
3

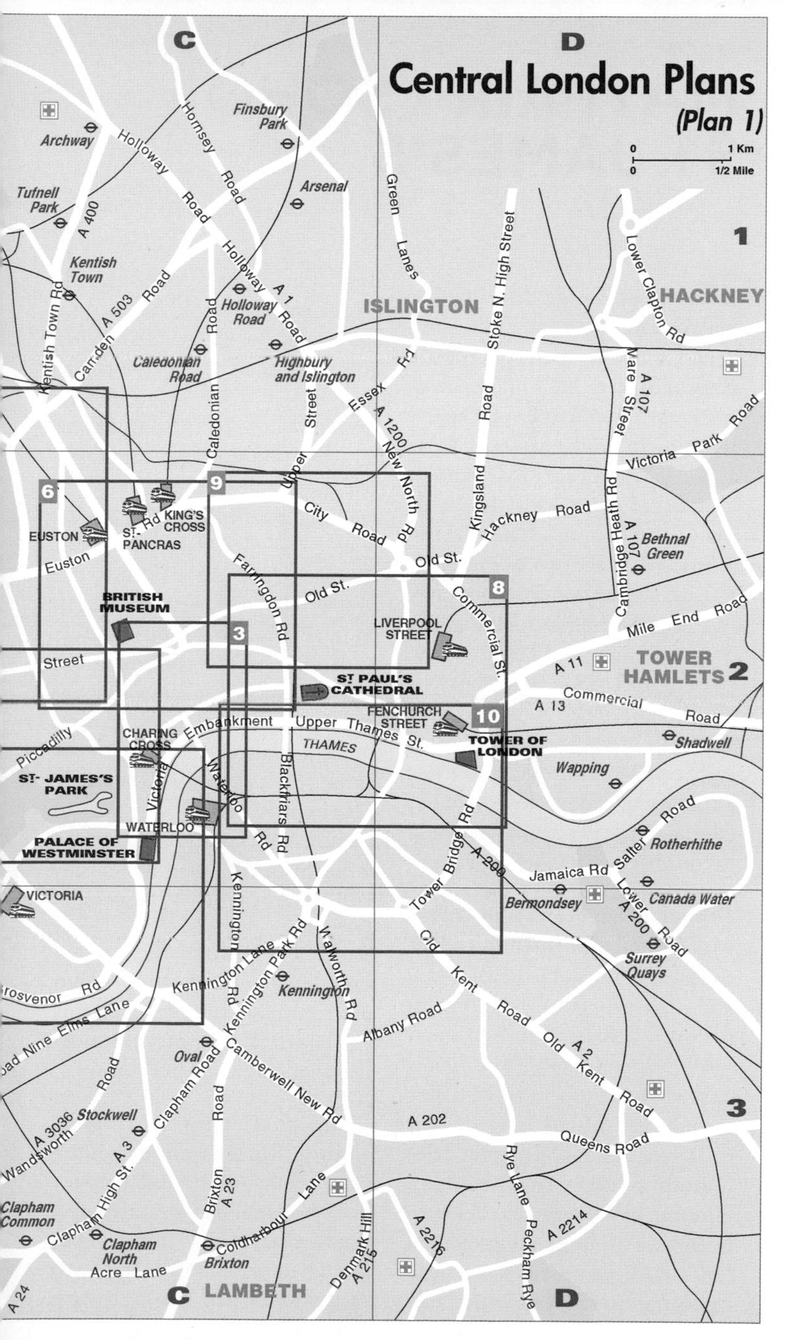
Central London Plans
(Plan 1)
0 1 Km
0 1/2 Mile
C
D
1
2
3
Archway
Holloway Road
Hornsey Road
Finsbury Park
Arsenal
Tufnell Park
A 400
Kentish Town
Kentish Town Rd
A 503
Camden Road
Holloway
Holloway Road
A 1
Caledonian Road
Highbury and Islington
ISLINGTON
Green Lanes
Stoke N. High Street
Lower Clapton Rd
HACKNEY
Mare Street
A 107
Essex Rd
A 1200
New North Rd
Upper Street
Kingsland Road
Victoria Park Road
Hackney Road
City Road
Cambridge Heath Rd
A 107
Bethnal Green
Old St.
EUSTON
ST. PANCRAS
KING'S CROSS
Euston Rd
BRITISH MUSEUM
Farringdon Rd
LIVERPOOL STREET
Commercial St.
Mile End Road
A 11
TOWER HAMLETS
Street
ST. PAUL'S CATHEDRAL
Commercial Road
A 13
FENCHURCH STREET
TOWER OF LONDON
Upper Thames St.
Embankment
THAMES
Shadwell
Wapping
Piccadilly
CHARING CROSS
ST. JAMES'S PARK
Victoria
Waterloo Rd
Blackfriars Rd
WATERLOO
PALACE OF WESTMINSTER
Tower Bridge Rd
A 200
Salter Road
Rotherhithe
Jamaica Rd
Bermondsey
Canada Water
Lower Road
A 200
Surrey Quays
VICTORIA
Kennington Rd
Kennington Lane
Kennington Park Rd
Walworth Rd
Kennington
Old Kent Road
Grosvenor Rd
Nine Elms Lane
Albany Road
Oval
Clapham Road
Camberwell New Rd
A 2
Stockwell
A 3036
Wandsworth
A 3
Clapham High St.
Brixton Road
A 23
A 202
Queens Road
Rye Lane
Peckham Rye
A 2214
A 2216
Denmark Hill
A 215
Coldharbour Lane
Clapham Common
Clapham North
Brixton
Acre Lane
A 24
LAMBETH
8
9
6
3
10

MAYFAIR · SOHO · ST JAMES'S

There's one elegant dividing line between Mayfair and Soho - the broad and imposing sweep of **Regent Street** - but mindsets and price tags keep them a world apart. It's usual to think of easterly Soho as the wild and sleazy half of these ill-matched twins, with Mayfair to the west the more sedate and sophisticated of the two. Sometimes, though, the natural order of things runs awry: why was rock's legendary wild man Jimi Hendrix, the embodiment of Soho decadence, living in the rarefied air of Mayfair's smart 23 Brook Street? And what induced Vivienne Westwood, punk queen and fashionista to the edgy, to settle her sewing machine in the uber-smart Conduit Street?

Mayfair has been synonymous with elegance for three and a half centuries, ever since the Berkeley and Grosvenor families bought up the local fields and turned them into posh real estate. The area is named after the annual May fair introduced in 1686, but suffice it to say that a raucous street celebration would be frowned upon big time by twenty-first century inhabitants. The grand residential boulevards can seem frosty and imposing, and even induce feelings of inadequacy to the humble passer-by but should he become the proud owner of a glistening gold card, then hey ho, doors will open wide. Claridge's is an art deco wonder, while **New Bond Street** is London's number one thoroughfare for the most chi-chi names in retailing. **Savile Row** may sound a little 'passé' these days, but it's still the place to go for the sharpest cut in town, before sashaying over to compact **Cork Street** to indulge in the purchase of a piece of art at one of its superb galleries. Science and music can also be found here, and at a relatively cheap price: the Faraday Museum in **Albemarle Street** explores 200 years of science, and Handel & Hendrix in Brook Street enables you not only to visit the beautifully presented

home of the German composer and view his musical scores but also to explore the flat belonging to Hendrix, his 'future' next door neighbour, as it was in 1968-69.

Soho challenges the City as London's most famous square mile. It may not have the money of its brash easterly rival, but it sure has the buzz. It's always been fast and loose, since the days when hunters charged through with their cries of 'So-ho!' Its narrow jumbled streets throng with humanity, from the tourist to the tipsy, the libertine to the louche. A lot of the fun is centred round the streets just south of **Soho Square,** where area legends like The Coach & Horses ('Norman's Bar'), Ronnie Scott's and Bar Italia cluster in close proximity. There's 80s favourite, the Groucho Club. The tightest t-shirts in town are found in **Old Compton Street,** where the pink pound jangles the registers of gay-friendly bars and restaurants. To get a feel of the 'real' Soho, where old engraved signs enliven the shop fronts and the market stall cries echo back to the 1700s, a jaunt along **Berwick Street** is always in vogue, taking in a pint at the eternally popular Blue Posts, an unchanging street corner stalwart that still announces 'Watney's Ales' on its stencilled windows.

Not a lot of Watney's ale was ever drunk in **St James's;** not a lot of ale of any kind for that matter. Champagne and port is more the style here, in the hushed and reverential gentlemen's clubs where discretion is the key, and change is measured in centuries rather than years. The sheer class of the area is typified by **Pall Mall's** Reform Club, where Phileas Fogg wagered that he could zip round the world in eighty days, and the adjacent **St James's Square,** which was the most fashionable address in London in the late seventeenth century, when dukes and earls aplenty got their satin shoes under the silver bedecked tables.

Shahaira/iStock

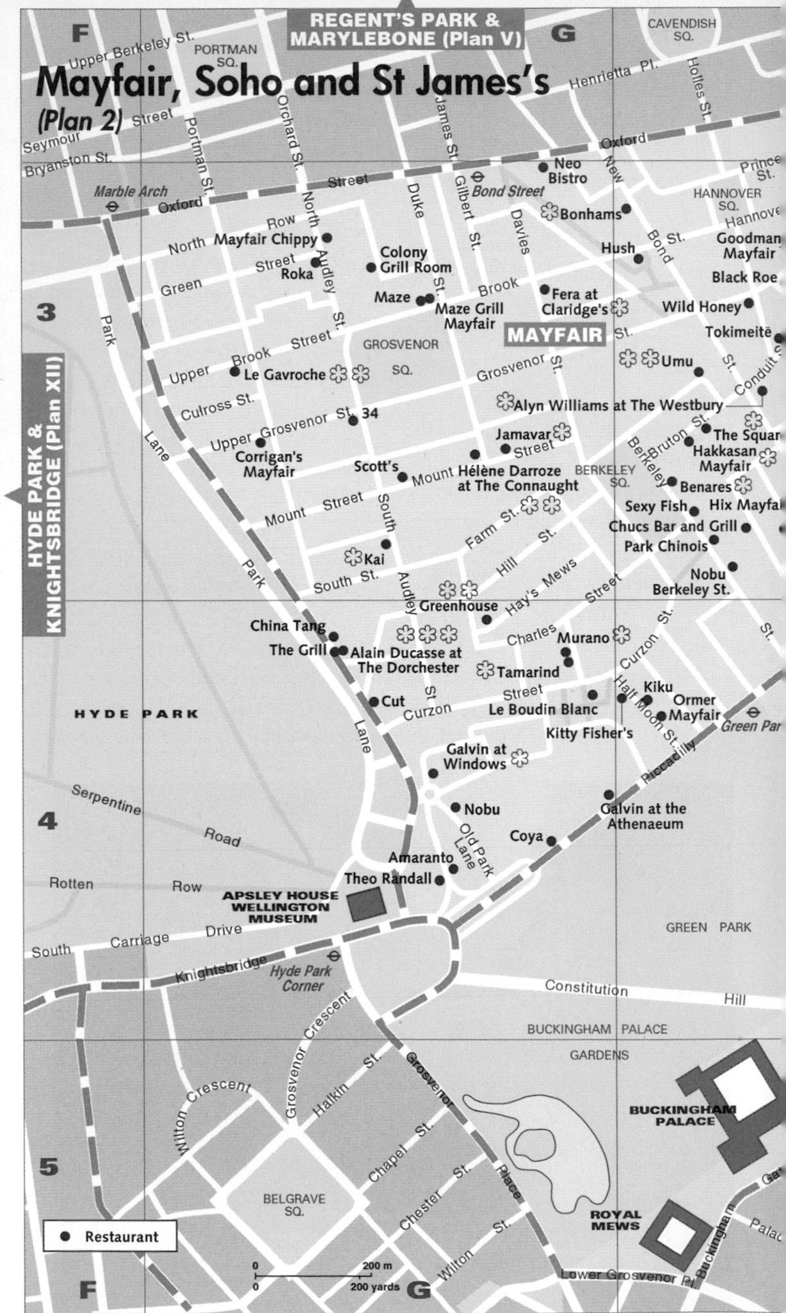
Mayfair, Soho and St James's
(Plan 2)
REGENT'S PARK & MARYLEBONE (Plan V)
HYDE PARK & KNIGHTSBRIDGE (Plan XII)
F
G
3
4
5
Upper Berkeley St.
PORTMAN SQ.
CAVENDISH SQ.
Henrietta Pl.
Holles St.
Seymour Street
Bryanston St.
Portman St.
Orchard St.
James St.
Oxford Street
Marble Arch
Bond Street
Neo Bistro
New Bond St.
Prince St.
HANNOVER SQ.
Hannover
Duke St.
Gilbert St.
Davies St.
Bonhams
North Row
North Mayfair Chippy
North Audley St.
Green Street
Roka
Colony Grill Room
Hush
Goodman Mayfair
Black Roe
Maze
Maze Grill Mayfair
Brook St.
Fera at Claridge's
Wild Honey
Park Lane
GROSVENOR SQ.
MAYFAIR
Tokimeitē
Upper Brook Street
Le Gavroche
Grosvenor St.
Umu
Conduit St.
Culross St.
Alyn Williams at The Westbury
Upper Grosvenor St.
34
The Square
Corrigan's Mayfair
Jamavar
Bruton St.
Hakkasan Mayfair
Scott's
Mount Street
Hélène Darroze at The Connaught
BERKELEY SQ.
Berkeley St.
Benares
South Audley St.
Sexy Fish
Hix Mayfair
Farm St.
Chucs Bar and Grill
Park Chinois
Hill St.
Kai
South St.
Hay's Mews
Nobu Berkeley St.
Greenhouse
China Tang
Charles Street
Murano
The Grill
Alain Ducasse at The Dorchester
Tamarind
Curzon St.
Kiku
Cut
Curzon Street
Le Boudin Blanc
Half Moon St.
Ormer Mayfair
HYDE PARK
Kitty Fisher's
Green Park
Galvin at Windows
Piccadilly
Serpentine Road
Nobu
Galvin at the Athenaeum
Old Park Lane
Coya
Amaranto
Theo Randall
Rotten Row
APSLEY HOUSE WELLINGTON MUSEUM
South Carriage Drive
GREEN PARK
Knightsbridge
Hyde Park Corner
Constitution Hill
BUCKINGHAM PALACE GARDENS
Grosvenor Crescent
Wilton Crescent
Halkin St.
Grosvenor Place
BUCKINGHAM PALACE
Chapel St.
BELGRAVE SQ.
Chester St.
ROYAL MEWS
Wilton St.
Palace
Buckingham
Lower Grosvenor Pl.
Restaurant
0
200 m
200 yards

BLOOMSBURY, HATTON GARDEN & HOLBORN (Plan VI)
Vasco and Piero's Pavilion
Zelman Meats
Barrafina
Ember Yard
100 Wardour St
Bibigo
Blanchette
Tamarind Kitchen
Quo Vadis
Oliver Maki
Yauatcha Soho
Copita
Duck & Rice
Red Fort
Refuel
Social Eating House
Little Social
Sketch (The Gallery)
Dehesa
Antidote
Temper
Dean Street Townhouse Restaurant
Ceviche Soho
Hoppers
Koya Bar
Bao
Jinjuu
Sketch (The Lecture Room & Library)
Polpo Soho
Bone Daddies
Cây Tre
Tonkotsu
Barshu
Gauthier-Soho
Polpetto
Spuntino
Nopi
Bob Bob Ricard
Mele e Pere
Rosa's Soho
Haozhan
The Araki
Sakagura
Cinnamon Soho
Casita Andina
Bocca di Lupo
Baozi Inn
Momo
Kiln
Ham Yard
Plum Valley
Imperial China
Hix
MASH
Palomar
Beijing Dumpling
Peyote
Brasserie Zédel
Heddon Street Kitchen
Hawksmoor
Veeraswamy
Bentley's
Kricket
Aquavit
Keeper's House
Veneta
Shoryu
Chop Shop
Milos
Portrait
Gymkhana
Ritz Restaurant
Al Duca
Brumus
Franco's
45 Jermyn St
The Wolseley
Quaglino's
Café Murano
Sake No Hana
Ginza Onodera
Le Caprice
Seven Park Place
Avenue
Chutney Mary
Boulestin
Oxford Circus
Tottenham Court Road
Covent Garden
Leicester Square
Piccadilly
Westminster
St James's Park
SOHO
ST JAMES'S
PICCADILLY CIRCUS
SOHO SQ.
GOLDEN SQ.
LEICESTER SQ.
ST JAMES'S SQ.
BURLINGTON HOUSE
THEATRE ROYAL
NATIONAL GALLERY
ST MARTIN-IN-THE-FIELDS
TRAFALGAR SQUARE
CHARING CROSS
CARLTON HOUSE TERRACE
OLD ADMIRALTY
HORSE GUARDS
BANQUETING HOUSE
SPENCER HOUSE
QUEEN'S CHAPEL
ST JAMES'S PALACE
LANCASTER HOUSE
ST JAMES'S PARK
St James's Park Lake
PALACE OF WESTMINSTER
ST MARGARET'S
WESTMINSTER ABBEY
STRAND & COVENT GARDEN (Plan III)
BELGRAVIA & VICTORIA (Plan IV)
Oxford St.
New Oxford St.
St Giles High St.
Charing Cross Rd
Shaftesbury Ave
Endell St.
Neal St.
Shorts Gardens
Earlham St.
Long Acre
St. Martins Lane
Strand
Regent St.
Great Marlborough St.
Poland St.
Dean St.
Greek St.
Frith St.
Broadwick St.
Wardour St.
Lisle St.
Brewer St.
Savile Row
Burlington Arcade
Piccadilly
Jermyn St
Haymarket
Regent St.
King St.
Pall Mall
The Mall
Whitehall
Whitehall Place
Whitehall Court
Horse Guards Ave
Horse Guards Road
Richmond Terrace
Parliament St.
Birdcage Walk
Storey's Gate
Tothill St.
Buckingham Gate
Petty France
Victoria Street
Abingdon Street
H
I
2
3
4
5

AL DUCA

Italian • Friendly

MAP: 2-H4

Al Duca has become as much a part of the fabric of St James's as many of the shirt makers who have made neighbouring Jermyn Street home over the years. It is also one of those restaurants that manages the trick of appearing quiet one minute and full to the rafters the next without anyone noticing and this ensures that the atmosphere is never less than spirited. The serving team are a young, confident bunch and the manager knows who his regulars are. The menu is priced per course, there is plenty of choice, and the cooking is crisp and confident, with plenty of well-priced bottles to match. The rib-eye with porcini mushrooms is a highlight. Prices are also pretty keen, especially for a restaurant in this neck of the woods.

- 4-5 Duke of York St SW1Y 6LA
  020 7839 3090 — **www**.alduca-restaurant.co.uk
  Piccadilly Circus
- Menu £17 (dinner) - Carte £26/45
  Closed Easter, 25-26 December, 1 January, Sunday and bank holidays

AMARANTO

Italian • Fashionable

MAP: 2-G4

The Four Seasons hotel emerged from its last refurbishment programme with a restaurant all about flexibility. Amaranto is a bar, a lounge and a dining room, and the idea is that you can have what you want, where you want it, from a largely Italian-inspired menu that covers all bases. That means you can enjoy some crab cakes with your drink in the smart bar, share a plate of charcuterie with friends in the comfortable lounge or order a full 3 course meal with business clients in the handsome dining room. No expense was spared on the decoration - the space is full of the colours of the plant after which it is named and there's lots of lacquered wood. Unusually for hotels on Park Lane, there is also a fine terrace attached.

- Four Seasons Hotel, Hamilton Pl, Park Ln W1J 7DR
  020 7319 5206 — **www**.fourseasons.com/london/dining
  Hyde Park Corner
- Carte £38/78

ALAIN DUCASSE AT THE DORCHESTER ✿✿✿

French • Elegant

XXXXX ♿ A/C ⊡ |♈ ✿ 🚗 **MAP:** 2-G4

Alain Ducasse at The Dorchester

FIRST COURSE: Dorset crab, celeriac and caviar. • Confit duck foie gras with cherry and basil.

MAIN COURSE: Dry-aged beef, artichoke and bone marrow. • Fillet of turbot with clams à la marinière.

DESSERT: 'Baba like in Monte Carlo'. • Cointreau soufflé with ginger granité.

Elegance, luxury and attention to detail are the hallmarks of Alain Ducasse's outpost at The Dorchester Hotel. Formality never crosses the line into starchiness however: service is attentive without being overbearing and the atmosphere is warm and relaxed. The best tables are in the main part of the room, as those on the raised dais by the window can feel a little separated from the action; luminaries should plump for the 'Table Lumière' with its shimmering curtain for an opulent semi-private dining experience. The kitchen uses the best seasonal produce, whether British or French, to create superbly crafted, visually striking dishes, including several which showcase the flavours of the South of France. Some of the dishes remain long in the memory, with the accompaniments adding to the experience, from the champagne trolley to the theatre of the rum baba and the preparation of a herbal infusion at the end of the meal. The wine list is exemplary, with a particularly impressive selection of Domaine de la Romanée Conti and Château d'Yquem.

■ Dorchester Hotel, Park Ln ✉ W1K 1QA
✆ 020 7629 8866 — **www**.alainducasse-dorchester.com
⊖ Hyde Park Corner

■ Menu £65/105
Closed 3 weeks August, first week January, 26-30 December, Easter, Saturday lunch, Sunday and Monday - booking essential

ALYN WILLIAMS AT THE WESTBURY ✿

Modern cuisine • Design

XXXX ♿ A/C ⌂ 🍷 ✿ **MAP:** 2-H3

Michelin

FIRST COURSE: Roast lobster with guacamole and green gazpacho. • Glazed veal sweetbreads with peas, caramelised black olives and morels.

MAIN COURSE: Herdwick lamb with preserved green walnut and borage. • Cornish sea bream with fennel compote, grapefruit and sea urchin velouté.

DESSERT: Strawberry pavlova with sweet cicely. • Salted caramel tart with baked apple curd ice cream.

Peep inside this restaurant within the Westbury Hotel and the impression you get is one of considerable formality but the good news is that it's a long way from being one of those whispering shrines to gastronomy. Granted, it's a very comfortable room, with rosewood panelling and well-spaced, smartly laid tables but the reason the atmosphere never strays into terminal seriousness is largely down to the staff who exude a warmth and sincerity that one all too rarely sees these days. Their willingness to please can also take one by surprise – for instance, they'll willingly let you mix and match the à la carte with the weekend tasting menu. The other reason for its appeal is the relative value for money when one considers the quality of the ingredients and the skill of the kitchen. Alyn Williams is a man with an innate understanding of flavours; his dishes are colourful and quite elaborate constructions but the combinations of textures and tastes marry happily together. Sourcing of ingredients is key and he displays his foraged herbs in glass pots by the kitchen.

- Westbury Hotel, 37 Conduit St ✉ W1S 2YF
  ✆ 020 7183 6426 — **www.**alynwilliams.com
  ⊖ Bond Street
- Menu £30/80
  Closed first 2 weeks January, last 2 weeks August, Sunday and Monday

ANTIDOTE

Modern cuisine • Intimate

MAP: 2-H3

As an antidote to big, brash restaurants, this cute little wine bar-cum-restaurant works a treat. On the ground floor it's all about biodynamic and organic French wines, accompanied by plates of charcuterie, cheese and assorted nibbles - it's always busy, noisy and fun. If you want slightly less cramped surroundings, then head upstairs to the restaurant. Here you'll find an à la carte menu that is a fairly fluid affair - its dish sizes lie somewhere between a starter and a main course and can easily be shared if that's your thing. The kitchen displays an appealing confidence and keeps the influences from largely within Europe. Natural flavours are allowed the space to shine and dishes are colourful and appealing.

■ 12a Newburgh St ✉ W1F 7RR
020 7287 8488 — **www**.antidotewinebar.com
Oxford Circus

■ Carte £25/38
Closed Sunday and bank holidays - booking advisable

AVENUE

Modern cuisine • Elegant

MAP: 2-H4

Mayfair meets Manhattan - albeit with a smidgen of St James's restraint - at this buzzing, all-American restaurant with a light, bright interior designed by Russell Sage; so in a street that once epitomised the very essence of Britishness, you can now enjoy a stack of buttermilk pancakes at brunch, monkfish with Old Bay spice for lunch, and a shared Boston butt for dinner. As the cascading wine 'chandelier' suggests, wine is also a feature, with US and French wines fighting for supremacy - you can choose the winner by trying some great names by the glass. As you'd expect from anywhere influenced by NYC, the cocktails are very good; the craft beers are also worth trying, and the long, lively bar is a destination in itself.

■ 7-9 St James's St. ✉ SW1A 1EE
020 7321 2111 — **www**.avenue-restaurant.co.uk
Green Park

■ Menu £25 - Carte £32/80
Closed Sunday dinner and bank holidays

Ⓝ AQUAVIT ✿

MAP: 2-13

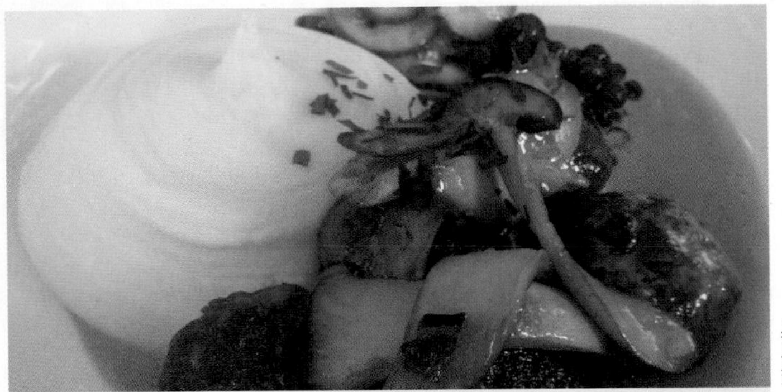

Michelin

FIRST COURSE: Smoked eel with charred spring cabbage. • Beef tartare with blueberries, lingonberries and juniper.

MAIN COURSE: Boned trout, dill, almond and capers. • Duck breast with liquorice, carrots and garlic.

DESSERT: Arctic bird's nest. • Warm chocolate cake with tarragon ice cream.

The original Aquavit has been a luminous feature of the New York dining scene for over twenty years but the owners sensibly decided to resist the temptation of making their London outpost a carbon copy. Instead, they created a large brasserie with plenty of marble, wood and leather that's much more informal and accessible. Open from breakfast, the place has real warmth, which is more than you can say for the redeveloped and erroneously named St James's Market. The cooking is also different: instead of tasting menus full of intricate dishes, you can expect a menu of more familiar Scandinavian influences – and it's all immensely appealing. Kick things off by heading straight to the smörgåsbord section and some wonderful herring or shrimp; follow up with venison tartare or smoked eel and then for a main course consider fish again: the whole trout will make you forget all the heinous culinary crimes committed in its name over the years. The ingredients are exemplary and there's a vitality to the food that leaves you feeling good about life.

■ St James's Market, 1 Carlton St ✉ SW1Y 4QQ
✆ 020 7024 9848 — **www**.aquavitrestaurants.com
⊖ Piccadilly Circus

■ Menu £29 (lunch) - Carte £26/67
Closed 24-26 December and 1 January

THE ARAKI ✿✿✿

Japanese • Intimate

XX A/C

MAP: 2-H3

Michelin

FIRST COURSE: Cornish squid with albino caviar. • Mackerel sushi with sesame and yuzu.

MAIN COURSE: Salmon roe with seaweed. • Sea bream sashimi with wasabi and ponzu sauce.

DESSERT: Japanese rice cake with red bean paste and macadamia.

When Mitsuhiro Araki, one of Japan's great Sushi Masters, was looking for a new challenge he wanted to do more than simply relocate. So when he packed up his Three Star sushi restaurant in Tokyo's Ginza district and sailed for London, he also set himself the challenge of using largely European fish and shellfish when he got there, instead of merely importing it from Tsukiji fish market. He spent time adjusting his Edomae methods and techniques to suit these different fish and the results are extraordinary – so now, here at his 9 seater counter, you can expect to find, for example, tuna and mackerel from Spanish waters, salmon from Scotland and caviar from Cornwall. His nigiri comes in manageable sizes and the rice, which is grown by his father-in-law and the one thing that is from Japan, is exemplary: it is near body temperature and every grain is discernible in the mouth. There are two sittings in the evening, at 18.00 and 20.30, and payment is taken in advance. The omakase does not come cheap, but the best things in life rarely do.

■ 12 New Burlington St ✉ W1S 3BF
✆ 020 7287 2481 – **www**.the-araki.com
⊖ Oxford Circus

■ Menu £300
Closed August, Christmas-first week January and Monday – booking essential – (dinner only) – (tasting menu only)

BAO

Asian • Simple

MAP: 2-H3

Bao's instant success was no accident because the three founders spent time perfecting their art through a series of pop-ups. Taiwanese street food is the draw – in particular the eponymous steamed buns. There are usually about five varieties on offer; the best are the classic bao with braised pork and peanut powder and the confit pork bao with tender pork belly. The 'small eats' are also good, like the trotter nuggets and fried chicken. Be prepared to queue – while you're standing there you'll be given a menu which doubles as an order form for you to fill in. Prices are ridiculously low so you can afford to tick enthusiastically, but in the unlikely event that you realise you've under-ordered, extra dishes can be whipped up quite quickly. There's also another Bao in Windmill St.

53 Lexington St ✉ W1F 9AS
020 3011 1632 — **www**.baolondon.com
Tottenham Court Road

Carte £17/27
Closed 23 December-3 January and Sunday – bookings not accepted

BAOZI INN

Chinese • Rustic

MAP: 2-I3

It's camouflaged on the street by the humdrum and the ordinary, so blink and you'll miss this loud, buzzy little place that's great for a quick bite. Granted, the laminated photographs of the dishes in the window don't necessarily inspire confidence but if you like pork buns and big, steaming bowls of noodles along with a hit of Sichuan fire then you won't be disappointed. Only beer, water and tea are on offer but frankly that's all you need; tables are so close together they're almost communal and you can't order too much straight away – not because you won't be able to eat it, but because the dishes simply won't all fit on your table. But who cares? You'll leave feeling energised and rejuvenated without having spent much money.

25-26 Newport Court ✉ WC2H 7JS
020 7287 6877
Leicester Square

Carte £15/22
Closed 24-25 December – bookings not accepted

BARRAFINA ✿

Spanish • Tapas bar

MAP: 2-13

Michelin

FIRST COURSE: Pluma Iberica with confit potatoes. • Tuna tartar with sesame.

MAIN COURSE: Rump of milk-fed lamb. • Salt cod à la Romana.

DESSERT: Santiago tart. • Conference pears in red wine.

At the end of 2016 the original Barrafina packed up and shipped out from Frith Street to new premises in Dean Street, a five minute stroll away. The owners – the Hart brothers – sliced their Quo Vadis restaurant into two to accommodate it and, apart from it now sitting beneath one of the famous neon signs of this Soho landmark, you can't see the join. This new site is brighter and roomier, although the number of seats at the L-shaped counter is actually the same as before, and the queues are still here if you don't arrive early enough. The menu is also reassuringly familiar and supplemented by an appealing little blackboard menu of the day's best produce – from which it's well worth ordering a few dishes like crisp anchovies or octopus with capers. The dishes burst with flavour, leave a lasting impression and are easy to share, although you'll find yourself ordering more when you look around and see what your neighbours are having. As well as hiring delightful staff, another thing they get right here is that once you've got your seats you won't be hurried out of them too quickly.

- 26-27 Dean St ✉ W1D 3LL
  ✆ 020 7440 1456 — **www.**barrafina.co.uk
  ⊖ Tottenham Court Road
- Carte £18/44
  Closed bank holidays - bookings not accepted

BARSHU

Chinese • Exotic décor

MAP: 2-13

Those who like their food with a kick won't be disappointed by Barshu as it features the fiery flavours of China's Sichuan province. The menu, which looks more like a brochure, features a photo of each dish along with a chilli rating - a useful aid, as the staff can be a little reluctant to engage with customers. But it's not all mouth-numbingly hot and some of the dishes do display a more subtle balance of flavours. The legendary chillies and peppers are imported directly from China and, with the chef coming from the province too, authenticity is assured, particularly with the 'Five colour appetiser platter', which includes duck tongues and pig intestines. Lots of carved wood and lanterns decorate the place; larger groups should head downstairs.

28 Frith St. W1D 5LF
020 7287 8822 — **www**.barshurestaurant.co.uk
Leicester Square

Carte £26/58
Closed 24-25 December - booking advisable

BEIJING DUMPLING

Chinese • Neighbourhood

MAP: 2-13

Flashing neon or hanging roast ducks in the window appear to be the popular Chinatown method of attracting passers-by; this little restaurant catches their attention by showing its chefs hard at work preparing dumplings. It's also a lot less frenzied than many of its more excitable neighbours and a cut above the norm with its food. It serves freshly prepared dumplings of both Beijing and Shanghai styles and, although the range is not quite as comprehensive as the restaurant's name would suggest, they are still the highlight, especially varieties of the famed Siu Lung Bao. The rest of the menu has a wide base but its worth exploring the specials which include the occasional Taiwanese offering like spicy chicken.

23 Lisle St. WC2H 7BA
020 7287 6888
Leicester Square

Menu £18 - Carte £10/40
Closed 24-25 December

BENARES ✿

Indian • Chic

XXX A/C ⊡ 🍷 ✿ **MAP:** 2-H3

Benares

FIRST COURSE: Chilli, lime and ginger marinated mackerel with gem lettuce salad, garlic and tomato raita. • Stir-fried prawns, scallops, squid and razor clams with onion and tomato.

MAIN COURSE: Venison with sorrel, oyster mushrooms and chocolate curry. • Guinea fowl tikka with sweet and sour smoked beetroot.

DESSERT: Peanut butter parfait with almond cake, cumin marshmallow and jaggery ice cream. • Dark chocolate mousse with blackcurrant yoghurt ice cream.

No Indian restaurant in London enjoys a more commanding location or expansive interior than Benares. You'll be greeted at the foot of the stairs before being escorted up past the flower-filled pool and busy bar into the cleverly textured and warmly lit main restaurant - you won't even notice the lack of windows. But what really sets this restaurant apart is the cooking. Atul Kochhar has lived in the east, north and south of India and his influences are many and varied. His use of British ingredients like Scottish scallops and New Forest venison is to be applauded and there is certainly no doubting his skill at spicing: flavours are judiciously layered and expertly balanced. Presentation isn't as elaborate or ornate as it once was and the dishes are all the better for it. The lunch menu offers good value and there is an evening tasting menu but the kitchen's strength lies with the à la carte. If you're coming in a large group consider booking the Chef's Table; its large window provides close-up views of all the action in the kitchen.

- 12a Berkeley Square House, Berkeley Sq. ✉ W1J 6BS
  ☎ 020 7629 8886 — **www**.benaresrestaurant.com
  ⊖ Green Park
- Menu £25 (lunch and early dinner)/98 - Carte £52/68
  Closed 25 December, 1 January and Sunday lunch

BENTLEY'S

Seafood • Traditional décor

MAP: 2-H3

This much-loved seafood institution is over one hundred years old and, under the aegis of Richard Corrigan, remains as popular as ever. Upstairs is the Grill, a smartly dressed restaurant with formal service and a clubby feel, which is popular with the corporate-minded and those entertaining the in-laws. The menu is extensive and includes seafood classics and some grilled meats. On the ground floor is the Oyster Bar, where the atmosphere is a little more louche and considerably more fun. Here you'll find most of the regulars perched at the bar watching the white-jacketed staff shuck oysters; they also do a good fish pie. Bentley's familiar green neon sign looks set to shine brightly on Swallow Street for a few more years yet.

11-15 Swallow St. W1B 4DG
020 7734 4756 — **www**.bentleys.org
Piccadilly Circus

Menu £25 (weekday lunch) - Carte £35/72
Closed 25 December, 1 January, Saturday lunch and Sunday

BIBIGO

Korean • Friendly

MAP: 2-H2

Bibigo represents the first foray into the UK market from Korea's largest food company, 'CJ'. With a little help from Psy, Korea's other famous non-electronic export, their mission is to bring healthy staples such as bibimbap - bowls of rice, vegetables, seeds and nuts finished with a hot pepper paste (gochujang) - to a wider public. Start with a soju-based cocktail then watch the kitchen behind the glass send forth dishes such as kimchi, Bossam (simmered pork belly) and hot stone galbi (chargrilled short ribs). Dishes have been adapted slightly for Western tastes and the place may feel a little chainy - you can even buy the sauces at reception on the way out - but it's enthusiastically run and won't break the bank.

58-59 Great Marlborough St W1F 7JY
020 7042 5225 — **www**.bibigouk.com
Oxford Circus

Menu £13 - Carte £18/27
Closed 25 December and 1 January

Ⓝ BLACK ROE

World cuisine • Trendy

MAP: 2-H3

Whenever a new food trend appears, one usually wonders why no one else thought of it first. Poke – bowls of marinated, cubed tuna served over sushi rice – was made famous in Hawaii and its popularity is now going rapidly global. Here there are a number of choices, from traditional ahi poke to more adventurous choices like scallop and braised octopus, or prawn and mussel. Other options on the menu, based on a loose collection of cuisines found on the Pacific Rim, include pot stickers (gyoza by any other name), ramen, and more substantial dishes cooked on a Kiawe wood grill like Cajun-style blackened sea bass or smoky lamb rack. Add in a buzzy atmosphere and decent cocktails and you have all the elements for a fun night out.

- 4 Mill St ✉ W1S 2AX
  020 3794 8448 – **www**.blackroe.com
  Oxford Circus
- Carte £26/66

BLANCHETTE

French • Simple

MAP: 2-H3

Opened by three frères – and named after their mother – Blanchette takes classic French bistro food and gives it the 'small plates' treatment. Start with a mini croque monsieur or some bite-sized cheese beignets and then try creamy smoked haddock Arnold Bennett or ox cheek Bourguignon which is made to mother Blanche's own recipe – this is the sort of food guaranteed to raise the spirits. The charcuterie is sliced in front of you, the veg section shouldn't be ignored, and the wine list offers an interesting variety of styles and a decent selection by the carafe. There are just nine tables, one of which is communal, and the place has an appealing rustic look, with lots of tiles and exposed brick – the counter is a good place to sit.

- 9 D'Arblay St ✉ W1F 8DR
  020 7439 8100 – **www**.blanchettesoho.co.uk
  Oxford Circus
- Menu £15 (lunch) - Carte £14/28
  Booking essential

BOB BOB RICARD

Modern cuisine • Vintage

MAP: 2-H3

Everyone needs a little glamour now and again and Bob Bob Ricard is one place that can provide it. This is a restaurant where diners still dress up a little and there's a feeling of exclusivity in the air. Start with a cocktail in their terrific basement bar then snare one of the booths in the restaurant. The room may be quite small but it clearly sees itself as a grand salon and is shiny, plush and elegant - you even get a button to push if you require more champagne. The menu is all encompassing, although the presence of caviar and vodka are clues as to the owner's nationality. For lighter eaters there are oysters, salads and grilled fish; those with heartier appetites can choose beef Wellington, a venison burger or chicken Kiev.

■ 1 Upper James St ✉ W1F 9DF
020 3145 1000 — **www.**bobbobricard.com
Oxford Circus
■ Carte £37/90

BOCCA DI LUPO

Italian • Tapas bar

MAP: 2-I3

Deservedly busy from the day it opened, Bocca di Lupo is one of the best things to have arrived in Soho since the espresso bar. Be sure to sit at the marble counter in front of the chefs rather than at one of the faux-distressed tables at the back - not only is the atmosphere here more fun but the food is often better as it hasn't hung around the waiters' station waiting to be delivered. Each item has its region of origin within Italy noted on the menu and is available in a large or smaller size. The flavours don't hang back and over-ordering in all the excitement is very hard to resist. Highlights include the veal and pork agnolotti, the poussin in bread, and the tripe; leave room for dessert or visit their gelato shop opposite.

■ 12 Archer St ✉ WID 7BB
020 7734 2223 — **www.**boccadilupo.com
Piccadilly Circus
■ Carte £26/45
Closed 25 December and 1 January - booking essential

BONE DADDIES

Asian • Fashionable

A/C **MAP:** 2-I3

Maybe ramen is the new rock 'n' roll. Bone Daddies' charismatic young Aussie chef-owner feels that we've only just begun to appreciate the potential of this Japanese speciality; he believes that anything can go into these warming, comforting bowls and that the combinations are endless. Along with the ramen, you'll find other dishes - such as yellowtail sashimi with ponzu and chilli - that owe their influence to the time he spent at Nobu. The staff are a confident, hospitable bunch and the shared tables add to the community spirit. You may have to queue but throughput is apparently quicker than at some of the top floor services offered close by. Those over 30, who probably don't like standing in line, at least get to recognise the music.

- 31 Peter St ✉ W1F OAR
  020 7287 8581 — **www**.bonedaddies.com
  Piccadilly Circus
- Carte £17/27
  Closed 25 December - bookings not accepted

LE BOUDIN BLANC

French • Rustic

A/C **MAP:** 2-G4

Cries of "Bonjour!" and "Bon appétit!" will soon alert even the most limited linguist that they've wandered into a little bit of France here in Shepherd Market. The terrific atmosphere hits you as soon as you sit down - it's warm, lively and contagious, thanks largely to the ebullient service team, and is also helped by the closeness of the tables - but do ask for the ground floor rather than upstairs: The large menu is unapologetically classical and very comforting; French onion soup, steak frites and of course boudin blanc are omnipresent, while daily fish or game specials are explained at the table. Even the most nationalistic of customers will find it hard not to be swept along by the very Frenchness of it all.

- 5 Trebeck St ✉ W1J 7LT
  020 7499 3292 — **www**.boudinblanc.co.uk
  Green Park
- Menu £19 (lunch) - Carte £28/55
  Closed 24-26 December and 1 January

BONHAMS ✿

Modern cuisine • Minimalist

MAP: 2-H3

Bonhams

FIRST COURSE: Scallops, smoked roe, peas and endive. • Caramelised veal sweetbreads with baby gem, apple and wild garlic velouté.

MAIN COURSE: Lamb with ratatouille, olive and anchovy. • Turbot with peas, onions, girolles, radish and vin jaune.

DESSERT: Chocolate sabayon tart with vanilla ice cream and sour cherry. • Oakchurch strawberries with rose ice cream and matcha tea meringue.

Established in 1793, Bonhams is one of the world's largest auctioneers of fine art and antiques. Following a recent £30m renovation, it includes this modern, crisply decorated restaurant with floor to ceiling windows, which is tucked away at the back of the building. The succinct lunch menu with four choices per course is an appealing document governed by what's in season. The dishes are elegantly presented and quite delicate in appearance yet there's real clarity to the flavours thanks to their French base being combined with Scandic-style simplicity. The menu is accompanied by a very thoughtful wine list, which is no surprise when you find that it is compiled by Bonhams' own wine department. It includes some terrific older vintages and some of the finest wines at quite generous prices, including by the glass and carafe. Service is assured and professional and while the restaurant can get busy on sales days, it provides a relaxing environment. It's now also open for 3 dinners a week, when it offers a set menu.

101 New Bond St ✉ W1S 1SR
✆ 020 7468 5868 — **www**.bonhamsrestaurant.com
⊖ Bond Street

Carte £47/59
Closed 2 weeks Christmas, 2 weeks mid August, Saturday, Sunday, dinner Monday-Tuesday and bank holidays – booking advisable

BOULESTIN

French • Elegant

MAP: 2-H4

St James's is one of the most elegant and distinguished parts of London and Boulestin is a perfect fit for the neighbourhood. Nearly a century after Xavier Marcel Boulestin opened his eponymous restaurant showcasing 'Simple French Cooking for English Homes', his spirit was resurrected by another name synonymous with the capital's dining scene – Joel Kissin. Behind the 17C bay windows, you'll find an elegant, light-filled brasserie with mirrors and antique lighting, which just oozes fin de siècle French charm. It also comes with a lovely courtyard terrace. The seasonal menu of classic, unfussy and flavoursome dishes like oeuf en gelée, duck confit and crème brulée pays homage to M. Boulestin's original offerings.

- 5 St James's St ✉ SW1A 1EF
  020 7930 2030 — **www**.boulestin.com
  Green Park
- Menu £30 - Carte £40/61
  Closed Sunday and bank holidays

BRASSERIE ZÉDEL

French • Brasserie

MAP: 2-H3

In many cities, the closer one gets to its centre, the more elusive good value restaurants become. Bucking this trend in London is this grand French brasserie, courtesy of Chris Corbin and Jeremy King – its prices are almost ridiculously friendly, especially for somewhere that can provide such a glamorous night out just a few paces from Piccadilly Circus. The bustling subterranean space has been restored to its original art deco splendour and the large menu includes all the classic French dishes you'd want to find, from cassoulet and boudin noir to Îles flottantes and tarte au citron – the 'formule' menu is a real steal. There's also a bar, a cabaret theatre and, on the ground floor, a small café.

- 20 Sherwood St ✉ W1F 7ED
  020 7734 4888 — **www**.brasseriezedel.com
  Piccadilly Circus
- Menu £13/20 - Carte £18/44
  Closed 25 December – booking advisable

BRUMUS

Modern cuisine • Fashionable

MAP: 2-I4

Brumus has always benefitted from its great location – pre-theatre dining is an altogether less frenzied activity when you can actually see the theatre from your table – but it also makes genuine efforts to appeal to a wide variety of customer. It's a modern yet elegant space, with switched-on staff adding to the appeal. It's also open from breakfast until late and usually has something to suit the time of day whether that's a shepherd's pie, burger or Dover sole. If you veer away from the set menus, prices can start to rise quite quickly – although the 'dish of the day' on the à la carte is often the way to go, followed by one of their sundaes. Alternatively, you can share a platter in the busy bar.

- Haymarket Hotel, 1 Suffolk Pl ✉ SW1Y 4HX
  020 7470 4000 — **www**.haymarkethotel.com
  Piccadilly Circus
- Menu £20 - Carte £24/62

CAFE MURANO

Italian • Fashionable

MAP: 2-H4

How satisfying it must have been for Angela Hartnett when she took over this site, considering she worked here over a decade ago when it was Pétrus. True to her roots she has put together, along with her chef, a menu of delicious North Italian delicacies with built-in flexibility so you can create your own meal according to the relative sizes of your appetite and wallet; try the truffle arancini with your prosecco while you choose. The lunch and pre/post theatre menu is good value and those who like to eat free from the tyranny of set meal times will appreciate the light selection of antipasti served mid-afternoon. The word 'café' was presumably adopted to imply accessibility but the place has proved so popular that pre-booking is essential.

- 33 St. James's St ✉ SW1A 1HD
  020 3371 5559 — **www**.cafemurano.co.uk
  Green Park
- Menu £23 (lunch and early dinner) - Carte £26/43
  Closed Sunday dinner - booking essential

LE CAPRICE

Modern cuisine • Fashionable

MAP: 2-H4

There are two types of customer at Le Caprice: those who are regulars and those who wish they were. This is one of those glamorous restaurants where the atmosphere is effortlessly sophisticated; the live pianist brings a bygone elegance to proceedings and the clientele are confident and urbane. The kitchen is well-practised and capable and the menu has something for everyone, whether that's a salad, their famous burger or a more ambitious offering like a well-judged game dish or Asian-spiced fish. From the moment you call to make a reservation to the time they bid you goodbye, the suited staff are reassuringly efficient - and it's not hard to see why this has been one of the capital's busiest restaurants for more than 35 years.

- Arlington House, Arlington St. ✉ SW1A 1RJ
  020 7629 2239 — **www**.le-caprice.co.uk
  Green Park
- Menu £25 (lunch and early dinner) - Carte £33/64
  Closed 24-26 December

N CASITA ANDINA

Peruvian • Rustic

MAP: 2-I3

Respect is paid to the home-style cooking of the Andes at this Peruvian picantería, which comes from the people behind the Ceviche restaurants. The menu is divided into nibbles, hot kitchen, ceviche & raw bar, and desserts. Start by ordering pork and liver croquetas and some papas ocopa - crispy potatoes - along with one of their excellent pisco sours. Other highlights include salmon tiradito with tiger's milk, pork shambar, and free-range chicken with Amarillo chillies. Dishes are gluten-free and as colourful as the decorations in this narrow 200 year old house - the room upstairs is the best place to sit. Prices allow for over-ordering and the staff are a friendly bunch, willing to offer sensible advice.

- 31 Great Windmill St ✉ W1D 7LP
  020 3327 9464 — **www**.andinalondon.com/casita
  Piccadilly Circus
- Carte £13/25

CÂY TRE

Vietnamese • Minimalist

MAP: 2-13

The West End could do with having plenty more Vietnamese restaurants, so hopefully others will follow the lead of Cây Tre. The bright and sleek surroundings of this Soho branch are smarter than the original in Hoxton and the bustling environment provides plenty of atmosphere. Staff know their menu and go about their business with determined efficiency. Dishes are made for sharing and influences cover all points from north to south. Standouts include Cha La lot (spicy ground pork wrapped in betel leaves) and the fragrant slow-cooked Mekong catfish, with its well-judged sweet and spicy sauce. Pho (noodle soup) is available in six different versions and represents good value; the set menu is a great starting point for neophytes.

42-43 Dean St W1D 4PZ
020 7317 9118 – **www**.caytresoho.co.uk
Tottenham Court Road

Menu £25 - Carte £23/32
Booking advisable

CEVICHE SOHO

Peruvian • Friendly

MAP: 2-13

Based on a Lima Pisco bar, Ceviche is as loud as it is fun and a great place to pop into for cocktails with a difference and some light dishes to share with friends. The long narrow room has a busy bar specialising in deliriously addictive drinks based on the Peruvian spirit pisco, a grape brandy, and beyond it you'll find tightly packed tables, posters and photos of 1950s Peru, and waiting staff struggling to keep up. As the name suggests, ceviche, marinated in lime and chilli, is the star of the show, whether that's the sea bass or the Alianza Lima – a mix of prawns, squid and octopus. 3 dishes per person plus perhaps an anticuchos skewer should be enough; they arrive in a random order so ask if you want the ceviche before any hot dish.

17 Frith St W1D 4RG
020 7292 2040 – **www**.cevicheuk.com/soho
Tottenham Court Road

Carte £18/26
Booking essential

CHINA TANG

Chinese • Fashionable

MAP: 2-G4

Sir David Tang's atmospheric, art deco inspired Chinese restaurant at The Dorchester Hotel is always a blur of activity, with noise spilling out from the large tables in the centre; regulars head for the library side, from where one can take in the whole room. In contrast to the sleek and decorative surroundings, the kitchen is a model of conservatism and rightly sticks to what it does best, namely classic Cantonese cooking. Peking duck and roasted meats are the highlights, but check out the chef's recommendations at the back of the menu too. The standard is good considering the numbers of customers and you can even have the full menu in the striking bar at lunch or dinner. Apart from the set lunch menu, it may not be cheap - but it is fun.

- Dorchester Hotel, Park Ln ✉ W1K 1QA
  020 7629 9988 — **www**.chinatanglondon.co.uk
  Hyde Park Corner
- Menu £30 (lunch) - Carte £28/79
  Closed 24-25 December

CHOP SHOP

Meats and grills • Simple

MAP: 2-I3

Things have certainly changed down at Haymarket and the huge redevelopment has created opportunities for new restaurants to give the established chains a run for their money. One of the first off the mark was Chop Shop from New York's Altamarea Group. Spread over two floors and using reclaimed materials for that ersatz-industrial look, it would not look out of place in Manhattan's Meatpacking district. The menu too takes its influences from both sides of the Atlantic: start with 'jars' of mousses, 'crocks' of meatballs or 'planks' of cheese - or simply order a cocktail and head straight for the main event: the steaks and chops. Perfectly matured meats from Cumbria, along with Creekstone USDA steaks, are expertly cooked and hit the spot.

- 66 Haymarket ✉ SW1Y 4RF
  020 7842 8501 — **www**.chopshopuk.com
  Piccadilly Circus
- Menu £22 (lunch and early dinner) - Carte £21/50

CHUCS BAR AND GRILL

Italian • Elegant

MAP: 2-H3

Rather like the clothes shop to which it is attached, Chucs Bar and Grill caters for those who know their way around the Riviera and are not afraid of showing it. The interior, with just 6 tables and some seats at the bar, is decked out like a yacht, with blond wood, brass handrails and navy banquettes; there are also sepia pictures of Positano on the walls and Murano glass chandeliers above. While there is something a little disconcerting about sitting in a restaurant where all your fellow diners seem to know each other, the staff – kitted out in linen mess jackets – have a charming swagger that makes you feel included. The succinct and not inexpensive menu offers satisfying, classic Mediterranean dishes with a focus on flavour.

■ 30b Dover St. ✉ W1S 4NB
020 3763 2013 — **www**.chucsrestaurant.com
Green Park

■ Carte £40/71
Closed 25-26 and dinner 24 and 31 December, 1 January and bank holidays – booking essential

CHUTNEY MARY

Indian • Elegant

MAP: 2-H4

In the heart of St James's is one of London's pioneering Indian restaurants; first opened in Chelsea back in 1990. It's a busy spot popular with businesspeople, who come for its modern take on traditional Indian dishes; enjoyed in elegant surroundings which feature bold art and plenty of Indian artefacts, as well as a smart bar. The menu suffers a little from having too many headings, which include Indian grills, slow-cooked dishes, and small plates which are actually just starters by another name – but there's no denying that the cooking is good. There is a subtlety to the spicing; the classics are done well; and some of the regional dishes have been successfully updated. Come at the weekend for brunch and live jazz.

■ 73 St James's St ✉ SW1A 1PH
020 7629 6688 — **www**.chutneymary.com
Green Park

■ Menu £28 (weekday lunch) - Carte £34/77
Closed 25 December

CINNAMON SOHO

Indian • Friendly

MAP: 2-H3

Don't be put off by the slightly branded feel of the place because this younger sister to the more formal Cinnamon Club in Victoria is good fun and offers a great selection of classic and contemporary Indian dishes. Let the very charming staff guide you through the meal – they run the place really well and cope effortlessly with the numbers. Along with the familiar dishes like king prawns with coconut come more quirky offerings like Rogan Josh shepherd's pie and their signature dish 'Balls!': deep-fried balls of various flavours which could include crab, quail or lamb – these are good to share. High Chai is offered in the afternoon and their pre-theatre menu is a steal. Just avoid the lower floor where the acoustics are hellish.

- 5 Kingly St ✉ W1B 5PF
  020 7437 1664 — **www**.cinnamonsoho.com
  Oxford Circus
- Menu £15 (lunch and early dinner) - Carte £16/32

COLONY GRILL ROOM

Traditional British • Brasserie

MAP: 2-G3

When restaurateurs Chris Corbin and Jeremy King opened The Beaumont, their first hotel, it was always going to include a restaurant where everyone wanted to get a table. Based on traditional 1920s grills seen in London and New York, it comes with perfectly burnished leather booths, striking age-of-speed art deco murals and clever lighting, so that you hardly notice the absence of windows. Ironically, by making the room and style of service so defiantly old fashioned, they have created somewhere effortlessly chic. The wide-ranging menu criss-crosses the Atlantic, offering shrimp cocktail alongside omelette Arnold Bennett, a pastrami Reubens next to shepherd's pie, and trifle and sundaes to finish – satisfying food without fuss or fanfare.

- The Beaumont Hotel, Brown Hart Gdns. ✉ W1K 6TF
  020 7499 9499 — **www**.colonygrillroom.com
  Bond Street
- Carte £28/68
  Booking essential

COPITA

Spanish • Tapas bar

MAP: 2-H3

It may not occupy a prime Soho spot but that doesn't stop this tapas bar, a sister to Barrica, from being packed most nights. A no-bookings policy means your best bet is to come before 7pm or else try your luck at lunch when there are fewer drinkers; then simply perch yourself on one of the high stools or stay standing and get stuck in. The daily menu offers a colourful array of diminutive dishes like croquetas de champiñones, pluma Ibérica with romesco sauce or duck egg with patata a lo pobre, and you'll find it hard to stop ordering – even the delicate custard tart is delightfully moreish. Staff add to the lively atmosphere and everything on the thoughtfully compiled Spanish wine list is available by the glass or copita.

■ 27 D'Arblay St ✉ W1F 8EP
020 7287 7797 — **www**.copita.co.uk
Oxford Circus

■ Carte £19/32
Closed Sunday and bank holidays - bookings not accepted - (bookings not accepted at dinner)

CORRIGAN'S MAYFAIR

Modern British • Elegant

MAP: 2-G3

There's something undeniably clubby but also quite glamorous about Richard Corrigan's flagship restaurant. You do get the feeling that many of the customers know one another and that this is a place where deals are sealed. Martin Brudnizki's design includes some playful features, such as the feather-covered lamps that give a nod to the restaurant's forte which is game. The menu is lengthy and the food largely a celebration of British and Irish cooking. It is also fiercely seasonal, which makes the day's special always a worthwhile choice. This relatively straightforward style of cooking still requires care and precise timing. Service is smooth and well-organised but the anachronistic cover charge is an unwelcome sight.

■ 28 Upper Grosvenor St. ✉ W1K 7EH
020 7499 9943 — **www**.corrigansmayfair.com
Marble Arch

■ Menu £28 (weekday lunch) - Carte £48/81
Closed 25-30 December, Saturday lunch and bank holidays

COYA

Peruvian • Friendly

MAP: 2-G4

It didn't take long for the people behind Roka and Zuma to act upon the realisation that the Next Big Thing on the London restaurant scene was Peruvian food. Their loud and enthusiastically run basement restaurant on Piccadilly provides a lively spot in which to discover this fresh and zesty cuisine. Add in the live music at weekends and it also represents a great night out, especially when fuelled by the deliriously addictive pisco sours. Prepared in one of the three kitchens – the main room, the charcoal grill or the ceviche bar – the food is a mix of the authentic, the refined and the more contemporary; ordering a sharp, refreshing ceviche is a must and consider too the huge tiger prawns cooked in the Josper oven.

- 118 Piccadilly ✉ W1J 7NW
  020 7042 7118 — **www**.coyarestaurant.com
  Hyde Park Corner
- Menu £31 (weekday lunch) - Carte £27/66
  Closed 24-26 December and 1 January - booking advisable

CUT

Meats and grills • Design

MAP: 2-G4

Cut is the first European venture from Wolfgang Puck, the US-based Austrian chef whose level of celebrity makes our lot look positively anonymous. Teaming up with the Dorchester's 45 Park Lane hotel, he has created a slick, stylish and sexy room where glamorous people come to eat meat. The steaks – from Kansas, Chile, Australia and Devon – are first presented raw with a few words about their heritage and then cooked over hardwood and charcoal and finished off in a broiler. Sides are as good as the steaks, especially the fries and the macaroni cheese. Artery hardening continues with dessert which eschews the much-needed citrus in favour of lots of cream. You'll leave eminently satisfied, if slightly heavier in weight and lighter in pocket.

- 45 Park Lane Hotel, 45 Park Ln ✉ W1K 1PN
  020 7493 4545 — **www**.dorchestercollection.com
  Hyde Park Corner
- Menu £45 (weekday lunch) - Carte £55/185
  Booking essential

DEAN STREET TOWNHOUSE RESTAURANT

Modern British • Brasserie

MAP: 2-I3

A restaurant for every occasion - even shouty ones, as you're hit by a cacophony of sound as soon as you open the heavy door of this attractive Georgian house. It's also a place to be seen, or perhaps not - a ban on flash photography means it's ideal for illicit trysts too. The classic brasserie aesthetic makes it look like it's been here for years and the heartwarming British comfort food fits these surroundings well. There's Dover sole and Porterhouse steaks but also plenty more proletariat fare on offer, like faggots with cabbage or mince and potatoes. The salads, such as trout with truffled potato or smoked pigeon with scotch egg are noteworthy - and who can resist kipper pâté for afternoon tea?

- Dean Street Townhouse Hotel, 69-71 Dean St. W1D 3SE
  020 7434 1775 — **www**.deanstreettownhouse.com
  Piccadilly Circus
- Menu £29 - Carte £29/44
  Booking essential

DEHESA

Mediterranean cuisine • Tapas bar

MAP: 2-H3

The menu is not an exact copy of Salt Yard, its sister restaurant a few streets away, but the bestsellers on the menu of Spanish and Italian tapas all feature: the pork belly with cannellini beans; courgette flowers with Monte Enebro and honey; and the soft chocolate cake with Frangelico ice cream. They recommend 2-3 plates per person and the prices are generous enough to allow for enthusiastic ordering. Between 3pm and 5pm the kitchen takes a breather so the choice becomes ham on or off the bone, charcuterie and cheese - and considering the restaurant is named after a wooded area that's home to the Ibérico pigs who produce such great ham, it'll be worth having. The drinks list is worthy of a visit in itself.

- 25 Ganton St W1F 9BP
  020 7949 4170 — **www**.dehesa.co.uk
  Oxford Circus
- Carte £14/36
  Closed 25 December

DUCK & RICE

Chinese • Intimate

MAP: 2-I3

Alan Yau is one of the most innovative restaurateurs around and with Duck & Rice he has once again created something a little different – a converted pub with a Chinese kitchen. The ground floor is the most 'pubby' part of the operation – the clue is in the four huge copper tanks of Pilsner Urquell – where the snacks and nibbles are served to complement your beer rather than the other way round. The real action, though, takes place in an intimate space upstairs which has a vague Victorian vibe thanks to the booths and fireplaces. Here the menu focuses on Chinese favourites and comforting classics such as Kung Po chicken and crispy shredded beef. The duck is, appropriately enough, the standout – whether crispy aromatic or Cantonese roast.

- 90 Berwick St ✉ WIF 0QB
  020 3327 7888 — **www**.theduckandrice.com
  Tottenham Court Road
- Carte £18/31
  Closed 25 December

EMBER YARD

Mediterranean cuisine • Tapas bar

MAP: 2-H2

Those familiar with the Salt Yard Group will recognise the Spanish and Italian themed menus at this fun and sprightly restaurant spread over two floors. But, as the name suggests, there is one major difference between this and the other three outlets – and that's the focus on cooking over charcoal or wood which imparts such an individual flavour to each dish. Start with the terrific smoked chorizo skewers, then share hot-smoked Gloucester Old Spot pork belly or chargrilled Cornish mackerel – even a gratin of root vegetables comes with some smoked ricotta. It's not just the ingredients that are seasonal – the wood, which could be hazel or silver birch, changes over the year – and even some of the cocktails come with a seductive smokiness.

- 60 Berwick St ✉ W1F 8DX
  020 7439 8057 — **www**.emberyard.co.uk
  Oxford Circus
- Carte £14/25
  Closed 25-26 December and 1 January – booking advisable

FERA AT CLARIDGE'S ✿

Creative British • Elegant

XXXX ♿ A/C ⛀ ⓥ ✿ **MAP:** 2-G3

Michelin

FIRST COURSE: White asparagus with veal sweetbread, curd and smoked egg. • Flamed mackerel with Isle of Wight tomatoes, almond and beetroot.

MAIN COURSE: Belted Galloway beef with globe artichoke, tomato and sea greens. • Roast monkfish with Fowey mussels, courgette and lemon balm.

DESSERT: Chocolate and sweet clover mousse with goat's cheese and apricot. • Frozen apple with fennel, white chocolate and puffed barley.

Fera is set in one of the most striking rooms in the capital, in the delightful and ever-so-British surroundings of Claridge's Hotel. Muted tones of green give it an almost herbaceous feel which is juxtaposed by touches of art deco and magnificent detailing, yet the grandeur of the room is tempered by the refreshing lack of pomposity or mannered formality in the service. The 'wild' of Fera may refer to the influence of nature but this is intricately planned and highly refined cuisine. Matt Starling continues to follow the principles put in place by Simon Rogan: there's an impressive purity and a natural, unforced style to the cooking that is evident on the plate, yet the wonderfully well-balanced and textured dishes deliver multi-dimensional layers of flavours. Lesser-known ingredients might include hyssop, mead, meadowsweet and pickled pine; choose the tasting menu to best appreciate the kitchen's skills. Arrive early to take in the ambience over a craft beer or a cocktail; the weighty wine list offers an intelligent mix of the classic and the more esoteric.

■ Claridge's Hotel, Brook St ✉ W1K 4HR
✆ 020 7107 8888 – **www.**feraatclaridges.co.uk
⊖ Bond Street

■ Menu £42/110 (lunch) - Carte £61/83
Booking advisable

45 JERMYN ST

Modern British • *Brasserie*

MAP: 2-H4

In 2015 Fortnum & Mason bade farewell to their 60-year old Fountain restaurant and, in its stead, created this contemporary brasserie for the modern age. The art deco inspired room is bright and colourful – most customers want the booths but others are happy to perch at the long marble-topped bar. Its previous incarnation isn't forgotten as tribute is paid in the form of sodas, coupes and floats, while the main menu has a strong British element running through it, with several dishes being modern interpretations of classics. Prices can get a little steep – and not just when you opt for their caviar – but, in contrast, the well-chosen wine list comes with very restrained mark-ups and offers some great value.

- 45 Jermyn St. SW1 6DN
  020 7205 4545 — **www**.45jermynst.com
  Piccadilly Circus
- Menu £30 (weekday dinner) - Carte £24/67
  Closed 25-26 December

FRANCO'S

Italian • *Traditional décor*

MAP: 2-H4

There can be few things more English than afternoon tea or the sound of Alan Bennett reading from The Wind in the Willows and, surprisingly enough, both can be enjoyed here at Franco's, one of London's oldest Italian restaurants that was relaunched in the mid-noughties. Open from breakfast onwards, it attracts a largely well-groomed clientele as befits its Jermyn Street address and boasts a clubby feel. Indeed, if you're not a regular visitor, you may find yourself with time to admire the service being enjoyed by other tables. The chef hails from Northern Italy but his menu covers all parts. There is a popular grill section, along with classics like beef Rossini – ideal accompaniment for one of those big Tuscan reds on the wine list.

- 61 Jermyn St SW1Y 6LX
  020 7499 2211 — **www**.francoslondon.com
  Green Park
- Menu £26/36 - Carte £28/66
  Closed Sunday and bank holidays - booking essential

GALVIN AT THE ATHENAEUM

Modern cuisine • Brasserie

MAP: 2-G4

The Athenaeum has always been one of the more enthusiastically run hotels in Mayfair and this eagerness to please has been successfully transplanted to the ground floor restaurant, which is now part of the Galvin brothers' growing empire. It's kitted out in a comfortable, unthreatening way and, although the name badges and the turgid music remind you that you're eating in a hotel, the payoff is the courteous, attentive service and the quality of the cooking. The menu purports to be more British than the Galvins' usual French leanings – the ingredients are certainly more from this side of the Channel – but the best dishes are often those with a Gallic heritage, such as the cassoulet and the Floating Island.

- Athenaeum Hotel,116 Piccadilly W1J 7BJ
  020 7640 3333 — **www**.athenaeumhotel.com
  Hyde Park Corner
- Menu £25 - Carte £22/48

GAME BIRD

Modern British • Classic décor

MAP: 2-H4

There is nowhere more fitting to wave the flag for our own culinary heritage than in a classic British hotel in that most traditional of London districts – St James's. Nestling in a delightful mews, The Stafford has long been one of its most discreet addresses and it boasts a dining room that is equally British and well-mannered. All the classics are here, from Dover sole to fish pie, liver and bacon to steak and ale suet pudding – even chicken Kiev is resurrected. The trolley of smoked and cured salmon is a highlight and the kitchen really shows what it can do with its seasonal game dishes. Dining in a hotel restaurant is not for everyone but the warmth of the service and the appealing menu make this a worthwhile choice.

- Stafford Hotel, 16-18 St James's Pl. SW1A 1NJ
  020 7493 0111 — **www**.thestaffordlondon.com
  Green Park
- Menu £25 - Carte £32/72

GALVIN AT WINDOWS ✿

Modern cuisine • *Friendly*

XXX ⋞ ♿ A/C 🍸 **MAP:** 2-G4

Galvin at Windows

FIRST COURSE: Raw scallop with nori emulsion, blood orange, sweet soy and shiso. • Kimchi risotto with slow-cooked egg, spring onion and sesame.

MAIN COURSE: Beef fillet with foie gras, mushrooms and truffle. • Fillet of brill with cauliflower purée, endive, pine nuts and shellfish & curry oil.

DESSERT: Pistachio and chocolate éclair, poached pear and vanilla ice cream. • Banana soufflé with peanut ice cream.

The lift may take time to drop off its cargo of Hilton Hotel residents as it makes its way up to the 28th floor but the wait will be worth it as the views from up here are spectacular – and it's certainly worth arriving early for a drink in the busy adjacent bar. The restaurant has been cleverly laid out to make the most of the three sides of views and, if you can't secure a window table, the elevated section in the middle of the room is a good compromise. Service is relaxed and friendly which softens some of the formality of the room, although a little more passion would dispel some of the corporate blandness that pervades the atmosphere. It is the food, however, that provides worthy competition to the views. British ingredients like Cornish lamb, Cumbrian beef and Dorset crab proudly feature on the various menus on offer – the Menu du Jour draws in plenty of customers at lunch as it's a steal for this postcode. There's a classical base to the boldly flavoured dishes, which come with a pleasing degree of flair and innovation.

- London Hilton Hotel, 22 Park Ln (28th floor) ✉ W1K 1BE
  ✆ 020 7208 4021 — **www**.galvinatwindows.com
  ⊖ Hyde Park Corner
- Menu £37 (weekday lunch)/82
  Closed Saturday lunch and Sunday dinner

GAUTHIER - SOHO

French • Intimate

MAP: 2-I3

Alexis Gauthier's restaurant occupies a charming Georgian townhouse that seems at odds with Soho's increasingly rowdy reputation. Dining is spread over three floors, with the ground floor often the most animated, the first floor used more for the special occasion diner and the top floor consisting of two private dining rooms. The main menu allows you to virtually construct your own meal: it's divided into five sections or 'plats' and you can order any combination of meat, fish or vegetarian dishes that suits you. The cooking is skilled and the kitchen is not afraid of adding some innovative touches to classic combinations. The enthusiastic sommeliers, in turn, also come up with some refreshingly original recommendations.

- 21 Romilly St ✉ W1D 5AF
  020 7494 3111 — **www**.gauthiersoho.co.uk
  Leicester Square
- Menu £24/75
  Closed Monday, Sunday and bank holidays except Good Friday

GINZA ONODERA

Japanese • Elegant

MAP: 2-H4

Matsuri, which specialised in teppanyaki, occupied this spot for over 20 years but eventually ran out of steam. After an impressive refit, it re-opened in 2017 as part of the Onodera Group, who run an international portfolio of restaurants. A staircase leads you down to the main space, where there is table seating and three counters – for sushi, teppanyaki and the robata grill. In contrast to the plethora of places reinterpreting Japanese cuisine, things here are kept unapologetically traditional, with an emphasis on top-quality ingredients – this is reflected in the prices, as is the fact that this comfortable, well-run and discreet restaurant occupies an impressive amount of prime real estate.

- 15 Bury St ✉ SW1Y 6AL
  020 7839 1101 — **www**.onodera-group.com
  Green Park
- Menu £23 (lunch) - Carte £25/70
  Closed 25 December and 1 January

LE GAVROCHE ꕥꕥ

French • Intimate

XXXX A/C ⊡ ꕥ **MAP:** 2-G3

Michelin

FIRST COURSE: Lobster mousse with champagne and caviar butter sauce. • Black pudding with crumbled egg, crackling, asparagus and spicy tomato chutney.

MAIN COURSE: Loin and cheek of Dingley Dell pork with heritage beetroot and confit lemon. • Roast 'T' bone of turbot with carrots, radish and chive butter sauce.

DESSERT: Bitter chocolate and praline with gold leaf. • Strawberry shortbread and sorbet with Madagascan vanilla cream.

A little indulgence never did anyone any harm and Le Gavroche is all about indulgence. Michel Roux and head chef Rachel Humphrey's unapologetically extravagant French dishes are an exhilarating riposte to all those hectoring health-conscious calorie-counters. The menu is a roll-call of luxury ingredients, the sauces are sublime and the cooking is accompanied by one of London's best wine lists. There are oohs and aahs as trolleys are brought forward and carving knives sharpened; regulars mingle with newcomers and the atmosphere is refreshingly unstuffy, helped along by there being more of a female presence to the service these days. Anyone with an interest in Britain's post-war culinary adventures should be aware of Le Gavroche's significance, not just because of its celebration of, and dedication to, the art of French cuisine but also because of all those chefs who have benefitted from passing through its kitchen. Just avoid sitting too close to the stairs by asking for a table in the main body of this historic restaurant.

■ 43 Upper Brook St ✉ W1K 7QR
✆ 020 7408 0881 — **www**.le-gavroche.co.uk
⊖ Marble Arch

■ Menu £67/160 **s** - Carte £67/197 **s**
Closed 2 weeks Christmas, Saturday lunch, Tuesday lunch, Sunday, Monday and bank holidays - booking essential

GOODMAN MAYFAIR ꟾO

Meats and grills • *Brasserie*

XX A/C

MAP: 2-H3

Goodman is a Russian-owned New York steakhouse in Mayfair, which sounds like a sketch from the UN's Christmas party. Wood and leather give it an authentic feel and it has captured that macho swagger that often seems to accompany the eating of red meat. Tables are usually full of guffawing men, with their jackets thrown over the back of their chairs and their sleeves rolled up. The American and Irish beef is mostly grain-fed and either dry or wet aged in-house – Australian beef is an option at lunch. It is cooked in a Josper oven using a blend of three types of charcoal and offered with a choice of four sauces. While the steaks, especially the rib-eye, are certainly worth coming for, side dishes tend to be more variable in quality.

■ 26 Maddox St ✉ W1S 1QH
✆ 020 7499 3776 — **www.**goodmanrestaurants.com
⊖ Oxford Circus

■ Carte £28/89
Closed Sunday and bank holidays – booking essential

THE GRILL ꟾO

French • *Elegant*

XXX ♿ A/C

MAP: 2-G4

In a hotel as magnificent as The Dorchester, a restaurant needs to be able to hold its own, and there are no doubts that The Grill can do just that. With a hand-blown Murano glass chandelier as its striking centrepiece, strips of reflective gold on the walls, leather banquettes and an abundance of copperware on display, it has all the glitz and glamour one would expect. Such surroundings could easily lead to stuffiness, but the bar, the well-spaced tables and an agreeable team adept at putting diners at ease mean that the atmosphere is far from formal. Grill favourites sit alongside modern day classics on the menu; sharing dishes are a good choice, as are the speciality soufflés, which get a section all to themselves.

■ Dorchester Hotel, Park Ln ✉ W1K 1QA
✆ 020 7317 6531 — **www.**dorchestercollection.com
⊖ Hyde Park Corner

■ Menu £40 (weekday lunch) – Carte £38/87
Booking advisable

GREENHOUSE ✿✿

Creative • Fashionable

XXX A/C MAP: 2-G4

Michelin

FIRST COURSE: Native lobster with Green Chartreuse, rhubarb and puntarella. • Veal sweetbreads with ginger and sea beets.

MAIN COURSE: Welsh lamb with aubergine, gomasio, harissa and soya. • Dover sole with potato, parsley, capers and black garlic.

DESSERT: Garrigue honey with gavotte biscuit and Greek yoghurt. • Lychee soufflé with champagne and hibiscus.

One of the many charms of The Greenhouse is its setting. You enter via the Mews, through a little bamboo garden, and this pastoral theme continues inside with a pale green colour scheme and leaf-etched glass; it's bright and airy during the day, and warm and intimate by night. Chef Arnaud Bignon offers a set lunch menu, a 6 course tasting menu, a 'Discovery' menu for those who don't mind surprises, and the main à la carte; descriptions are fashionably pithy so don't be afraid to seek help from the staff. He has sourced terrific produce from the UK – seafood from Scotland, fish from Cornwall, and lamb and venison from Wales, although he will look to Europe for certain ingredients. His cooking is highly innovative, light, balanced and rendered with exceptional skill – he's a chef who not only understands flavour but knows when to back off. The wine list features the good and the great and the breadth of vintages is exceptional: Château Lafite back to 1870, Château Latour to 1900, Château Haut Brion to 1945, 15 vintages of La Tâche and 37 of Penfolds Grange.

- 27a Hay's Mews ✉ W1J 5NY
  ✆ 020 7499 3331 — **www**.greenhouserestaurant.co.uk
  ⊖ Hyde Park Corner
- Menu £40/100
  Closed Saturday lunch, Sunday and bank holidays

GYMKHANA

Indian • Intimate

MAP: 2-H4

Michelin

FIRST COURSE: Dosa, Chettinad duck and coconut. • Amritsari shrimp and queenies with dill raita.

MAIN COURSE: Wild muntjac biryani with pomegranate and mint raita. • Peanut and green mango fish tikka with cucumber.

DESSERT: Mango kheer. • Saffron and pistachio kulfi.

If you enjoy Trishna then you'll love Karam Sethi's Gymkhana – that's if you can get a table. Inspired by Colonial India's gymkhana clubs, the interior is full of wonderful detail and plenty of wry touches, from the hunting trophies and ceiling fans to the glass wall lamps and Grandma Sethi's barometer. If you're on the ground floor ask for one of the booths but it's worth a little persistence to ensure you're seated downstairs, where the beaten brass topped tables, leather banquettes and the dimmest of lighting add to the intimate atmosphere. In such charming surroundings it would be easy for the food to play second fiddle but far from it. There's an array of dishes inspired by the flavours of North India – don't procrastinate, just go straight for the 6 courser; included could be wild tiger prawns that show what a charcoal grill can do; kid goat methi keema with a pleasing richness and well-judged spicing; suckling pig vindaloo with complex flavours; or wild muntjac biryani, a triumph of flaky pastry.

■ 42 Albemarle St ✉ W1S 4JH
✆ 020 3011 5900 — **www**.gymkhanalondon.com
⊖ Green Park

■ Menu £25 (weekday lunch) - Carte £25/71
Closed 1-3 January, 25-27 December and Sunday - booking essential

HAKKASAN MAYFAIR ✿

Chinese • Minimalist

MAP: 2-H3

Hakkasan Mayfair

FIRST COURSE: Supreme dim sum platter. • Golden-fried soft shell crab with curry leaf and red chilli.

MAIN COURSE: Black pepper rib-eye beef with merlot. • Stir-fried lobster in black bean sauce.

DESSERT: Banana and caramel délice. • Chocolate and olive oil ganache with raspberry sorbet and candied olives.

You can usually spot any newcomers – they're the ones walking up and down Bruton Street trying to find the very discreet entrance. Once in, you'll feel nicely cocooned from the outside world and transported somewhere infinitely more exotic. This branch may be a little more corporate in feel than the Hanway Place original, but it can still deliver a healthy dose of glamour. If you're here for some lunchtime dim sum, then the ground floor is perfectly fine; if you're coming for dinner, then ask for a table in the lower floor as it is markedly sexier, thanks to its flattering lighting and energising atmosphere. All the refined classics that have made the reputation of this group are here, like silver cod and jasmine tea smoked chicken, but there are also dishes specific to this branch worth exploring and these include the delicious wok-fried pork belly in lychee sauce, the Szechuan-style langoustine and, for dessert, the yuzu and sesame vacherin. The simplest and least expensive dishes can also be the best, like the salt and pepper tofu or the golden soft shell crab.

- 17 Bruton St ✉ W1J 6QB
  ✆ 020 7907 1888 – **www.**hakkasan.com
  ⊖ Green Park
- Menu £38 (lunch and early dinner)/128 – Carte £37/110
  Closed 24-25 December – booking essential

HAM YARD

Modern cuisine • Brasserie

MAP: 2-13

At Ham Yard's stylish and exuberantly decorated restaurant, you might not even make it past the pewter-topped bar: the bitters, syrups and even the tonic water are homemade, using herbs grown in the hotel's rooftop garden, and the cocktails are as good as the range of little nibbles they serve. The room comes with bright colours and bold patterns; there are kilim prints from India and silk-lined walls - and the tables are all immaculately laid. The menu moves with the seasons and the kitchen has the confidence to keep the cooking appealingly simple. If it's a nice day the smart money is outside on the courtyard terrace - it may be a thoroughfare but the mature trees and parasols bring a continental air rarely seen in this part of town.

- Ham Yard Hotel, 1 Ham Yard, W1D 7DT
  020 3642 1007 — **www**.firmdalehotels.com
  Piccadilly Circus
- Menu £20 (dinner) - Carte £28/46

HAOZHAN

Chinese • Design

MAP: 2-13

A plethora of Chinatown restaurants vie for your attention by offering special deals or just brightening their neon; Haozhan adopts the more worthy policy of serving food that's a cut above the norm. Inside the somewhat garish looking menu is not the usual vast list but rather an interesting collection of dishes that owe more to a fusion style, with mostly Cantonese but other Asian influences too; head straight for the specialities, such as jasmine ribs or wasabi prawns. You'll find there's a freshness to the ingredients that also marks this restaurant out - try the Tom Yum prawns in their pancake cones and leave room for the egg custard buns. Appropriately enough, the name Haozhan translates as 'a good place to eat'.

- 8 Gerrard St W1D 5PJ
  020 7434 3838 — **www**.haozhan.co.uk
  Leicester Square
- Menu £14 - Carte £15/43
  Closed 24-25 December

HAWKSMOOR

Meats and grills • Fashionable

MAP: 2-H3

For the fourth, and possibly the best Hawksmoor, they took over the old L'Odeon restaurant and gave it a great little art deco makeover; there are mirrors down one side and the famous arched windows have been frosted and stained. As with the other branches, the sourcing of British beef is top-notch – the 35-day aged Longhorn beef comes with a charred exterior and a juicy centre – but the difference is that here they also offer great seafood, with charcoal-grilled turbot, Dover sole and monkfish proving popular. The prices are 'Mayfair' but not extreme; there's an excellent Express Menu at lunch and very early evening, and staff are a delightful and well-organised lot. Soak up the boisterous atmosphere by first having a cocktail in the bar.

- 5a Air St W1J 0AD
  020 7406 3980 — **www**.thehawksmoor.com
  Piccadilly Circus
- Menu £28 (lunch and early dinner) - Carte £23/58
  Closed 24-26 December - booking advisable

HEDDON STREET KITCHEN

Modern cuisine • Brasserie

MAP: 2-H3

There was once a time when the only person you'd see in Heddon Street would be a David Bowie fan paying homage to the place where the Ziggy Stardust album cover was shot. These days the street looks far less shadowy and indeed plays host to a number of restaurants, including Gordon Ramsay's follow up to his Bread Street Kitchen. The place is spread over two floors but the ground floor is the more fun, helped along by – or perhaps entirely due to – the fact that this is where the cocktail bar is positioned. This is all-day dining at its best: breakfast covers all tastes, there's brunch at weekends, and the à la carte offers an appealing range of largely European dishes, all executed with a palpable degree of care and precision.

- 3-9 Heddon St W1B 4BE
  020 7592 1212 — **www**.gordonramsayrestaurants.com
  Oxford Circus
- Menu £23 (lunch and early dinner) - Carte £26/63
  Closed 25 December

HÉLÈNE DARROZE AT THE CONNAUGHT ✿✿

Modern cuisine • Luxury

XXXX A/C ⊡ ✿ **MAP:** 2-G3

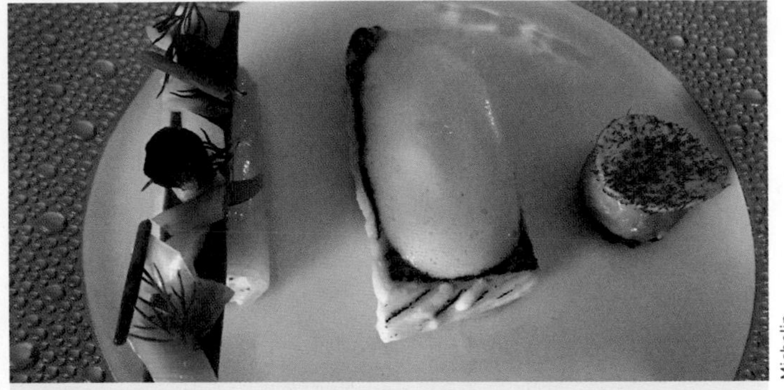

Michelin

FIRST COURSE: Norfolk lobster with almond, peach, mint and bottarga. • Red mullet with chorizo, razor clam and coco bean.

MAIN COURSE: Duck with beetroot, cherry and buckwheat. • Salmon with potato, seaweed and béarnaise reduction.

DESSERT: Strawberry, vanilla, thyme and olive oil. • Rhubarb, cashew nuts and ginger.

When it's time to choose what you're going to eat you'll be handed a Solitaire board featuring 13 marbles, each bearing the name of a single ingredient – you choose 5, 7 or 9 (courses). The board is accompanied by a menu showing the other components of the dishes in question, which are delivered in any order you wish. Some will love this game, others will hate it, but at least it highlights the fact that the dishes are built around a stunning main ingredient and it also allows Hélène Darroze to shine a light on her wonderful French and British suppliers. Her cooking is largely informed by her homeland but she's not averse to using the occasional unexpected flavour, be it Asian or Indian, if she feels it brings something to the dish; she is also aware of the modern diners' preference for a lighter, less elaborate style of cooking. The wood-panelled room is comfortable and elegant and considerable credit must go to the service team who keep the atmosphere light, relaxed and never overbearingly formal.

■ Connaught Hotel, Carlos Pl. ✉ W1K 2AL
✆ 020 7107 8880 — **www**.the-connaught.co.uk
⊖ Bond Street

■ Menu £52/95
Booking essential

HIX

Traditional British • Fashionable

MAP: 2-H3

Leaded, frosted windows similar to those of The Ivy hint at exclusivity within, as does the huge wooden door and the discreet name plaque. Once entry has been secured, one finds oneself in an enormous space with specially commissioned artwork from Damien Hirst, Sue Webster and Sarah Lucas, reflecting Mark Hix's close relationship with London's artists. Meanwhile, his menu reflects his passion for British recipes and ingredients, which translates as plenty of game in season, unusual cuts of meat, rediscovered classics and proper puddings. Portions aren't over-generous - side dishes are required which makes the bill rise quickly - and sometimes a dish may not quite deliver the promise of the menu, but it's a fun, inclusive place.

- 66-70 Brewer St. WIF 9UP
  020 7292 3518 — **www**.hixsoho.co.uk
  Piccadilly Circus
- Menu £20 (lunch and early dinner) - Carte £25/68
  Closed 25-26 December

HIX MAYFAIR

Traditional British • Traditional décor

MAP: 2-H3

Brown's is a thoroughly British hotel with a long history so it makes sense for its restaurant to celebrate Britain's own culinary traditions. Mark Hix - one of London's busier restaurateurs - was the man entrusted with the task and he has put together an appealing looking menu that's big on seasonality and provenance. Good use is made of ingredients from across the UK, such as Portland crab, Morecambe Bay shrimps and Aberdeenshire beef and there's also a daily roast for lunch, served from the trolley. The traditional feel of the wood-panelled dining room is enlivened by works from leading contemporary British artists, which ensure that the atmosphere never gets too solemn.

- Brown's Hotel, 33 Albemarle St W1S 4BP
  020 7518 4004 — **www**.hixmayfair.com
  Green Park
- Menu £35 (dinner) - Carte £29/110

HOPPERS

South Indian • Simple

MAP: 2-I3

Having made their name with Trishna and cemented their reputation with Gymkhana, the Sethi family then turned their attention to street food inspired by the flavours of Tamil Nadu, in the south of India, and Sri Lanka. This diminutive restaurant takes its name from the bowl-shaped pancakes made from fermented rice and coconut milk that are the perfect accompaniment to their creamy 'karis' such as lamb or guinea fowl. But this is far from a single-dish restaurant – there are plenty of other great dishes for sharing, from the delicious 'short eats' like bone marrow varuval, to the spit chicken served with Gotu Kola sambol. Add in some great cocktails and terrific prices and it's no wonder there are customers queuing outside.

49 Frith St ✉ W1D 4SG
020 3011 1021 — **www**.hopperslondon.com
Tottenham Court Road

Carte £15/25
Closed 25-27 December and 1-3 January. – bookings not accepted

HUSH

Modern cuisine • Fashionable

MAP: 2-H3

No one is more grateful for a bit of summer warmth than us Brits – and certainly no one could ever accuse us of not making the most of it – which is why the large courtyard terrace in front of Hush is often packed to the gunnels. The brasserie is hidden down a cobbled side street so when you find it you really feel like you know our secretive city. It also comes with a cocktail bar on the first floor and a smart private dining room above that. Give the menu a cursory glance and it would appear to be a fairly generic one of the brasserie kind, but the dishes, like crab with avocado or veal chop with truffled mash, are prepared with considerably more care than one expects. Service too is bright and enthusiastic.

8 Lancashire Ct., Brook St. ✉ W1S 1EY
020 7659 1500 — **www**.hush.co.uk
Bond Street

Carte £27/64
Closed 25 December and 1 January – booking essential

IMPERIAL CHINA

Chinese • Elegant

MAP: 2-I3

Heave open the heavy smoked-glass double doors, cross the bamboo bridge and you'll be transported to a calm oasis that seems a world away from the bustle outside. Sharp, well-organised service and comfortable surroundings are not the only things that set this restaurant apart: the Cantonese cooking exudes freshness and vitality, whether that's the steamed dumplings or the XO minced pork with fine beans. Indeed, they pride themselves on seafood and their 'lobster feasts' are very popular – the personable staff are also more than happy to offer recommendations. There are eight private rooms of various sizes available upstairs and these are often in full swing. The owners also run Beijing Dumpling a few doors down.

- White Bear Yard, 25a Lisle St ✉ WC2H 7BA
  020 7734 3388 — **www**.imperialchina-london.com
  Leicester Square
- Menu £20/46 - Carte £15/57
  Closed 25 December - booking advisable

JINJUU

Asian • Design

MAP: 2-H3

American-born TV chef Judy Joo's restaurant celebrates her Korean heritage; it's not only great fun but also the perfect spot for those who think Korean food just means barbecue. It has an industrial feel and is spread over two floors - the ground floor bar offers a great selection of cocktails, many of which use Korean's famous spirit, soju, as a base, but the heart of the operation is downstairs. Much of the menu is designed for sharing, especially the Ssam platters and the Tong Dak, their signature whole chicken dish. The Bibimbap bowls burst with flavour and there are some dishes, like the Sae-woo pops and the prawn cakes, that you won't want to give up without a fight. There's another branch in Mayfair.

- 15 Kingly St ✉ W1B 5PS
  020 8181 8887 — **www**.jinjuu.com
  Oxford Circus
- Menu £17 (weekday lunch) - Carte £29/41
  Closed 25 December

Ⓝ JAMAVAR ✿

Indian • Exotic décor

XX A/C MAP: 2-G3

Michelin

FIRST COURSE: Malabar prawns with turmeric, onion and curry leaves. • Kid goat shami kebab with black cardamom and mint chutney.

MAIN COURSE: Tulsi chicken tikka with sweet basil, pickled radish and raita. • Adraki lamb chops with cumin, crushed onion, fennel and ginger.

DESSERT: Port-poached pear with chocolate and pink peppercorn kulfi. • Rhubarb chuski falooda.

Thanks to the success of Jamavar, it's third time lucky for this site in Mount Street after its two previous occupants failed to tempt the city's dining community. Leela Palaces and Resorts are the brains behind it and they have a Jamavar restaurant in a number of their hotels – this is their first venture outside India and it didn't take long to establish itself in the premier league of London's Indian restaurants. The various menus on offer, which include vegetarian tasting menus, look to all parts of India for their influences, although there is a slight bias towards specialities from the north. The 'small plates' section includes plenty of jewels, like Malabar prawns and kid goat shami kebab; from the tandoor the stone bass tikka is a must; and the biryanis are also excellent, especially the Dum Nalli which uses Hampshire lamb. The smartly dressed, dark-hued restaurant is spread over two floors – the ground floor is the better choice. Service is quite formally organised but always attentive.

■ 8 Mount St ✉ W1K 3NF
✆ 020 7499 1800 — **www**.jamavarrestaurants.com
⊖ Bond Street

■ Menu £25 (lunch and early dinner) - Carte £34/54
Closed 25 December, 1 January and Sunday - booking essential at dinner

KAI ✿

Chinese • Intimate

XXX A/C MAP: 2-G3

Kai

FIRST COURSE: Pork belly open bao and char siew with BBQ glaze, crispy bao and pickled cucumber. • Soft shell crab with chilli, shallots and mango.

MAIN COURSE: Roasted Chilean sea bass with sweet lime, chilli and lemongrass sambal. • Soy and honey marinated roast lamb with shallots and garlic.

DESSERT: 'Chocolate does grow on trees'. • Pandan crème brûlée with Malaysian coffee ice cream.

Traditionalists will find a few familiar classics on the menu but Chef Alex Chow's strengths are his modern creations and re-workings of traditional Chinese recipes. There are Cantonese, Shanghainese, Hunanese and Sichuanese influences but he also uses the occasional flavour from other Asian countries. The resulting dishes have real depth, use superb ingredients and are wonderfully balanced. Vegetarians are well catered for and desserts are given a bigger billing than one usually sees. The lunch menu offers further proof that this isn't your typical Chinese restaurant: instead of dim sum, they call their smaller versions of the dinner specialities 'little plates of loveliness'. The service team in their silk jackets expertly anticipate their customers' needs, whether that's demonstrating how to construct a pork pancake, expertly filleting sea bass or offering jasmine tea to those awaiting a soufflé. The clientele is international and the interior unashamedly glitzy, with the only discordant note being the incongruously clubby music.

■ 65 South Audley St ✉ W1K 2QU
✆ 020 7493 8988 — **www**.kaimayfair.co.uk
⊖ Hyde Park Corner

■ Carte £44/199
Closed 25-26 December and 1 January - booking essential

KEEPER'S HOUSE

Modern British • Intimate

MAP: 2-H3

The Keeper's House, built in the 1860s and fully restored, sits in the corner of the courtyard of Burlington House and acts as a members' club for Royal Academicians and Friends of the RA. In the evenings, though, it's open to all of us – to find it, look for the Tracey Emin neon 'Keep me safe' above the door. The two intimate, interconnecting rooms come with low ceilings and walls lined with green baize and hung with architectural casts; there's also a modern bar which leads out into a hidden garden. The menu is appealingly concise and the emphasis is on seasonality, freshness and contrasts in textures and flavours. The kitchen strives for a certain amount of originality and, when the dishes work, they work very well.

- Royal Academy of Arts, Burlington House, Piccadilly ✉ W1J 0BD
  020 7300 5881 — **www**.keepershouse.org.uk
  Green Park
- Menu £21 (lunch) - Carte £28/39
  Closed 25-26 December and Sunday

KIKU

Japanese • Neighbourhood

MAP: 2-H4

It's not just the fact that it's family owned and has been here for over 35 years that makes Kiku unlike most Mayfair restaurants – this Japanese restaurant is also very sweet. There's an authentic simplicity to its decoration and a pleasing earnestness to the service; most evenings the majority of diners appear to be homesick Japanese. Virtually every style of Japanese cuisine is on offer, from shabu shabu to sukiyaki; yakitori to teriyaki and if you want to try something a little different, like sliced squid and guts or salmon zosui (rice soup), then here's your chance. The extensive à la carte menu is supplemented by a number of set menus and these are worth exploring if you want an all-round experience.

- 17 Half Moon St. ✉ W1J 7BE
  020 7499 4208 — **www**.kikurestaurant.co.uk
  Green Park
- Menu £26 (weekday lunch) - Carte £37/125
  Closed 25-27 December, 1 January and lunch Sunday and bank holidays

KILN

Thai • Simple

MAP: 2-H3

There are lots of open kitchens in London but few provide as much fire, heat and theatre as Kiln – sit at the stainless-steel counter to watch chefs prepare fiery and delicious Thai food using clay pots, woks and grills. The menu is nominally rural Thai but there are other influences that the chef-owner picked up on his travels in Laos, Myanmar and Yunnan. The ingredients, though, are largely British; along with daily fish deliveries, the kitchen buys in whole pigs and hogget – even the herbs are home-grown. Start with the aged lamb skewer, then have a curry and the baked glass noodles claypot – the commendable prices allow for unabashed ordering. The counter is for walk-ins only but parties of four can book a table in the downstairs room.

58 Brewer St ✉ W1F 9TL
www.kilnsoho.com
Piccadilly Circus

Carte £14/20
Bookings not accepted

KITTY FISHER'S

Modern cuisine • Bistro

MAP: 2-H4

Named after an 18C courtesan, presumably in honour of the profession for which Shepherd Market was once known, Kitty Fisher's is a small, intimate and refreshingly unpretentious restaurant. Its best seats are downstairs, in a room which has something of a Dickensian feel and from where you can see into the kitchen – be sure to ask for the 'Lord's Table', the best seat in the house. Service is relaxed and friendly, with the cheerful owner on hand to oversee things. The menu changes twice a day and is ingredient-led; the cooking is rustic, unfussy and all about flavour. The star of the show is undoubtedly the wood grill which gives the dishes depth and character – don't miss the chargrilled bread with burnt onion butter.

10 Shepherd Mkt ✉ W1J 7QF
020 3302 1661 — **www**.kittyfishers.com
Green Park

Carte £30/63
Closed Christmas, New Year, Easter, Sunday and bank holidays – booking essential

KOYA BAR

Japanese • Simple

MAP: 2-13

Those suffering udon noodle withdrawal symptoms by the closure of Koya will find Koya Bar a more than suitable replacement. Their udon noodles are made fresh each morning and cooked to order; choose hot or cold ones to go with your flavoursome broth which is finished with onions and includes a choice of beef, chicken or duck amongst others. Extra toppings allow you to create your own bespoke bowl, and there are small dishes also available such as tofu, pickles and tempura. It's a simple spot with counter seats looking into the kitchen – bookings aren't taken so there'll probably be a queue but it moves quite quickly. Service is sweet and polite and staff are happy to make recommendations to novice slurpers.

50 Frith St ✉ W1D 4SQ
020 7494 9075 — **www**.koyabar.co.uk
⊖ Tottenham Court Road

Carte £12/25
Closed 24-25 December and 1 January – bookings not accepted

Ⓝ KRICKET

Indian • Simple

MAP: 2-13

Such was the success of their pop-up in Brixton that opening a permanent restaurant for their Anglo-Indian cuisine was inevitable for the two young owners. An L-shaped counter, an open kitchen, sharing plates and cocktails may be unusual for an Indian restaurant but here in Soho they all add up to fun old time. The four dishes under each heading of 'Meat, 'Fish' and 'Veg' are made with home-grown ingredients, are appealingly priced and designed for sharing; standouts include the Keralan fried chicken, the butter garlic crab and the pumpkin with fresh paneer. Bookings aren't taken for the counter – you leave your number and they call you when seats are free – but tables of four or more can book space at the communal tables downstairs.

12 Denman St ✉ W1D 7HH
020 7734 5612 — **www**.kricket.co.uk
⊖ Piccadilly Circus

Carte £12/34
Bookings not accepted

LITTLE SOCIAL

French • Bistro

MAP: 2-H3

In contrast to his more formal Pollen Street Social sitting on the other side of the street, Jason Atherton's Little Social is a lively little French bistro with a clubby, masculine feel and an appealingly lived-in look. The best seats are undoubtedly the leather booths and the low ceiling adds to the sense of intimacy; if you arrive too early you could do a lot worse than have a cocktail at the little bar. Service is bright and confident and the French food is pretty classic, with the occasional modern twist. The menu constantly evolves and the choice is enhanced by daily specials; meats cooked on the Josper grill are a feature and the burger is good, but there are also some more interesting options like braised ox cheeks.

■ 5 Pollen St ✉ W1S 1NE
020 7870 3730 — **www.**littlesocial.co.uk
Oxford Circus

■ Menu £21 (weekday lunch) - Carte £37/56
Closed Sunday and bank holidays - booking essential

MASH

Meats and grills • Brasserie

MAP: 2-H3

It took a brave team to take on the daunting task of raising the old Titanic restaurant from the depths of Brewer Street but that is what a group of experienced Copenhagen restaurateurs did back in 2012. In restoring many of the original art deco features and combining them with contemporary fittings, they created a striking 350-seater restaurant. Instead of showcasing Danish cuisine, they went for a 'Modern American Steak House'. They offer mostly Danish prime and corn-fed Nebraskan and Uruguayan beef and it's clear the kitchen knows what it's doing. Starters are equally robust and include charcuterie and foie gras. Add in a great cocktail bar, slick service and an impressive wine list and you have a seriously grown up restaurant.

■ 77 Brewer St ✉ W1F 9ZN
020 7734 2608 — **www.**mashsteak.co.uk
Piccadilly Circus

■ Menu £30 (lunch) - Carte £30/96
Closed 24-26 December and Sunday lunch

MAYFAIR CHIPPY

Fish and chips • Vintage

MAP: 2-G3

Any roll call of classic British institutions would have to include the local chippy, as fish and chips rank alongside a full English breakfast and afternoon tea as our most celebrated contributions to world cuisine. When the local area is Mayfair, however, things start to look a little different – indeed, The Mayfair Chippy is unlike any other. For a start, it serves cocktails and wine, and also provides starters and desserts – it even has reserved seating. However, any fears that this isn't a real chippy are assuaged by the sight of the 'Mayfair Classic' – fried cod or haddock, with chips, tartar sauce, mushy peas and curry sauce. For those who like doing things in a more traditional way, there is a takeaway service available.

- 14 North Audley St ✉ W1K 6WE
  020 7741 2233 — **www**.eatbrit.com
  Marble Arch
- Carte £21/38
  Closed 25 December and 1 January

MAZE

Modern cuisine • Fashionable

MAP: 2-G3

This Gordon Ramsay restaurant still offers a glamorous night out, thanks to its great cocktails, effervescent atmosphere and easy-to-eat food. The lower level is best if you want to feel part of the action, while the upper level offers greater intimacy; if you're part of a group consider the 'Maze View' private dining room with views into the kitchen. The style of the menu, with its smaller plates and Asian influences, has changed little over the years; three or four dishes per person are about the going rate, especially as they're not really built for sharing, despite what the serving team may say. What has changed is that some of the precision has gone out of the cooking, caused perhaps by regular changes in kitchen personnel.

- London Marriott Hotel Grosvenor Square, 10-13 Grosvenor Sq ✉ W1K 6JP
  020 7107 0000 — **www**.gordonramsayrestaurants.com
  Bond Street
- Menu £30 - Carte £33/53

MAZE GRILL MAYFAIR

Meats and grills • *Fashionable*

MAP: 2-G3

Maze Grill is the more down-to-earth sibling to next door Maze and steak is its thing. Expect a good range of properly aged meat, including Aberdeen Angus (28 days), Dedham Vale (31), USDA Prime (36) and Wagyu 9th Grade (49). Cooked on the Josper grill and properly rested, the steaks are presented on wooden boards, which means they lose their temperature quite quickly but which at least ensures the Laguiole knives stay sharp. A choice of seven sauces is offered alongside assorted sides which can pump up the bill quite rapidly. There's also sushi available for less-committed carnivores. If you enter from the Marriott hotel the staff can seem taken by surprise, so you're better off using the main entrance on Grosvenor Square.

■ London Marriott Hotel Grosvenor Square, 10-13 Grosvenor Sq ✉ W1K 6JP
✆ 020 7495 2211 — **www**.gordonramsayrestaurants.com
⊖ Bond Street

■ Menu £23 - Carte £26/105

MELE E PERE

Italian • *Friendly*

MAP: 2-I3

Faced with a wall of Murano glass apples and pears as colourful as the street you're standing in, you'd be forgiven for thinking this is a gallery. But head downstairs – the 'apple and pears'? – and you'll find yourself in a vaulted room in the style of a homely Italian kitchen, and one that happens to have an appealing vermouth bar attached. The owner-chef worked in some decent London kitchens over a number of years but as he hails from Verona you can expect a selection of gutsy Italian dishes, like rabbit with olives, shoulder of lamb, and tripe with grated Parmigiano. Main courses come with a side dish that you get to choose and puds are excellent, especially the panna cotta.

■ 46 Brewer St ✉ W1F 9TF
✆ 020 7096 2096 — **www**.meleepere.co.uk
⊖ Piccadilly Circus

■ Menu £23 (lunch and early dinner) - Carte £23/44
Closed 25-26 December and 1 January

MILOS

Seafood • *Elegant*

MAP: 2-I3

London's branch of this international group of Greek seafood estiatorios takes full advantage of the grand listed building it occupies - this was originally British Columbia House. The ceiling's so high there's a mezzanine floor and a staggering amount of white marble has been used. The menu is almost more of a guideline - for the main event you wander over to the impressive display of fish flown in daily from Greek waters to choose what you fancy; it's then weighed to calculate the price while you discuss your preferred method of preparation. There's no denying it's expensive, but that doesn't seem to bother the clientele who give the impression that, when they venture down to the Greek Islands, they do so in their own vessel.

- 1 Regent St ✉ SW1Y 4NR
  020 7839 2080 — **www**.milos.ca
  Piccadilly Circus
- Menu £29/49 - Carte £58/131
  Closed 25 December and 1 January

MOMO

Moroccan • *Exotic décor*

MAP: 2-H3

Whether you're a couple looking to rekindle that Marrakech magic or just out with a group of friends, Momo and its Moroccan food should fit the bill. For one thing, there's depth and authenticity to the decoration here, with antiques, kilim rugs, Berber artwork, bright fabrics and lanterns; even the open kitchen adds to the feeling that you're dining close to the souk - shut your eyes and you can imagine Jemaa el Fna Square just outside the door. When it comes to the food, the classics are the highlights: zaalouk, briouats, pigeon pastilla and all manner of tagines accompanied by mountains of fluffy couscous; be sure to have the milk pastilla for dessert. If you want to experience a slightly more relaxed pace, then try the weekend brunches.

- 25 Heddon St. ✉ W1B 4BH
  020 7434 4040 — **www**.momoresto.com
  Oxford Circus
- Menu £19 (weekday lunch) - Carte £29/81
  Closed 25 December

MURANO ✿

Italian • Fashionable

XXX ♿ A/C MAP: 2-G4

Michelin

FIRST COURSE: Manzo di pozza with ricotta, broad beans, spring onion and hazelnuts. • Quail with baby turnip, figs, fennel, walnuts and pancetta.

MAIN COURSE: Hake, crab and ginger raviolo with savoy cabbage, baby leek and ginger veloute. • Barbary duck breast with hispi cabbage, raspberry, blackberry and hazelnut brittle.

DESSERT: Honey panna cotta with macadamia clusters and brown bread ice cream. • Chestnut Bakewell tart with marjoram ice cream and caramel.

For some chefs, attaining a certain level of success means they all but abandon their stoves for the more glitzy existence of TV and travel. Not so Angela Hartnett, who is very much in evidence at her restaurants and none more so than at her flagship, Murano: the elegant yet understated restaurant named after the famous Venetian glassware. Seasonal, Italian-inspired dishes – like baked potato gnocchi with homemade coppa and curly kale or Carnaroli risotto with Cornish crab – have their roots in the love of food and cooking engendered by her Italian grandparents, who came from Bardi in the heart of Emilia-Romagna. Angela's cooking exhibits an appealing lightness of touch, dishes are uncluttered and balanced, and flavours assured and defined. The menu is divided into 5 sections and diners can choose however many dishes they want, with 3 or 4 being the ideal number. This relaxed approach is reflected in both the décor and the service, with staff striking the right balance between friendliness and formality.

■ 20 Queen St ✉ W1J 5PP
☎ 020 7495 1127 — **www**.muranolondon.com
⊖ Green Park

■ Menu £33/70
Closed Christmas and Sunday

NEO BISTRO

Modern British • Rustic

MAP: 2-G3

A two-floored former pub is home to Neo Bistro: a collaboration between Mark Jarvis from Anglo and Alex Harper, formerly of the Harwood Arms – and named after the Paris-based movement that's seen classically trained chefs buying intimate, informal restaurants in which to serve ingredient-led menus with more scope for self-expression. An oasis of calm just off perpetually busy Oxford Street, it offers a tasting menu alongside a concise and ever-evolving à la carte. The easy-eating, vividly coloured dishes are aesthetically pleasing and packed with flavour: sourdough comes with a lovely seaweed-spiked butter; green strawberries add an interesting twist to Anjou pigeon with lentils; and the hay-baked new potatoes are a side worth getting excited about.

- 11 Woodstock St W1C 2AE
  020 7499 9427 — **www**.neobistro.co.uk
  Bond Street
- Menu £42 (dinner) - Carte £31/37
  Closed Christmas, Sunday, Monday and lunch Tuesday

NOBU

Japanese • Fashionable

MAP: 2-G4

These days there are Nobu restaurants stretching from Beijing to Budapest and Malibu to Moscow but back in 1997 when Europe's first branch opened here at The Metropolitan hotel it sent shockwaves through the city. Not only did it add serious sparkle and bags of glamour to the dining out scene but also its innovative cuisine - an intriguing mix of Japanese cooking and South American ingredients - was unlike anything else at the time. Nobu's heyday may have slipped past but the restaurant remains buzzy and fun, and if you need proof of the influence it has had then simply check out the menus of some of its competitors and imitators and you'll see plenty of evidence of some pretty shameless culinary plagiarism.

- Metropolitan by COMO Hotel, 19 Old Park Ln W1Y 1LB
  020 7447 4747 — **www**.noburestaurants.com
  Hyde Park Corner
- Menu £33 (lunch) - Carte £24/73
  Booking essential

NOBU BERKELEY ST

Japanese • Fashionable

MAP: 2-H3

The cries of "irasshaimase" may not be quite as heartfelt as they once were and the food may be lacking some of the lustre of previous years but this branch of the international chain can still provide a glamorous night out. That night out does not come cheap but you do get a huge menu of specialities blending Japanese cuisine with South American influences so everyone will find something they want. Be sure to get some dishes from the wood-fired oven – and you can't go too wrong if you order some of the classics. This branch has always been more of a party animal than its elder sibling at The Metropolitan so get in the mood with cocktails in the downstairs bar – or come at lunch for a less-frenzied experience.

- 15 Berkeley St. W1J 8DY
  020 7290 9222 — **www**.noburestaurants.com
  Green Park
- Menu £33 (lunch) - Carte £30/92
  Closed 25 December and Sunday lunch except December - booking essential

NOPI

Mediterranean cuisine • Design

MAP: 2-H3

There isn't an Aga in the country that doesn't share kitchen space with a few of his cookbooks and his terrific delis are now much copied – so it's no surprise that Yotam Ottolenghi's restaurant is a great success too. It's cleverly designed because you'd think those white walls would make it stark and cold but it actually feels warm and soothing – and the brass lamps and marble add a hint of the exotic. The flavours take in the Med, the Middle East and Asia and whether you share a few smaller dishes or plough your own furrow, you'll find the food refreshing and vibrant and will feel healthy just eating it. This is a relaxed, informal all-day restaurant that is genuinely well run – the staff really make an effort to ensure you enjoy yourself.

- 21-22 Warwick St. W1B 5NE
  020 7494 9584 — **www**.nopi-restaurant.com
  Piccadilly Circus
- Carte £21/50
  Closed bank holidays

OLIVER MAKI

Japanese • Minimalist

MAP: 2-13

This small restaurant group has branches in Bahrain and Kuwait so it's perhaps surprising that their first European outpost is a small corner restaurant in Soho and not somewhere big and shiny in Mayfair. What London is certainly used to is modern interpretations of Japanese food, but few restaurants have pushed the fusion element quite so much – even the soy dipping sauce is mixed with olive oil. Purists, however, will find themselves charmed and reassured by the eagerness of the staff and the obvious quality of the produce. Not every dish works but the kitchen has an undeniable confidence and clearly understands the importance of textures and temperatures. The upstairs room is the nicer of the two.

■ 33 Dean St ✉ W1D 4PW
020 7734 0408 — **www.**olivermaki.co.uk
Leicester Square

■ Menu £12/65 - Carte £22/56
Closed 23-30 December

100 WARDOUR ST

Modern cuisine • Contemporary décor

MAP: 2-13

Cocktails, food and live music usually equal a fun night out, so if you've got friends from out of town looking for a bit of glamour think about bringing them to the vast 100 Wardour St. This was the site of the original Marquee Club; some will remember the space as Mezzo restaurant; others as Cuban-influenced Floridita. At night you want to be downstairs, for music and a menu that's an amalgam of all that is contemporary - with its Japanese and South American influences, its use of the robata grill and its dishes designed for sharing. During daylight hours everything happens at ground level, with a simpler, all-day menu; here you'll also find a bar, a billiards table and a pop-in/ plug-in lounge popular with itinerant bloggers.

■ 100 Wardour St ✉ W1F 0TN
020 7314 4000 — **www.**100wardourst.com
Tottenham Court Road

■ Menu £15/35 - Carte £27/59
Closed 25-26 December and Sunday-Monday

ORMER MAYFAIR

Modern British • *Traditional décor*

MAP: 2-H4

Following a comprehensive refit, Flemings hotel was re-launched in 2016 and with it came the unveiling of its new restaurant – Ormer Mayfair. In partnership with Shaun Rankin, chef-owner of the original Ormer in Jersey, this London outpost follows the same principles of focusing on prime, seasonal ingredients – indeed, much of the produce used here is flown in from the Channel Islands. Fish and shellfish are very much a highlight and this emphasis on home-grown produce is also reflected in the wine list with its focus on English wines. The room may suffer slightly from its lower floor position but its subtle art deco styling gives it some personality – and it is run with genuine care, attention and enthusiasm.

- Flemings Hotel, 7-12 Half Moon St ✉ W1J 7BH
  ✆ 020 7016 5601 — **www**.flemings-mayfair.co.uk
  ⊖ Green Park
- Menu £30 (lunch) – Carte £50/70
  Closed Sunday and lunch Monday

PALOMAR

World cuisine • *Trendy*

MAP: 2-I3

Run by a brother and sister team who used to own a nightclub, Palomar brings a hip slice of modern-day Jerusalem to the heart of theatreland. Inside it's a bit of a squeeze, with a zinc kitchen counter running back to an intimate wood-panelled dining room, but the limited space, its propensity to get packed and the proximity to the animated chefs make for a high-energy buzz. Like the atmosphere, the food here is fresh and vibrant, with contemporary Middle Eastern cooking taking a tour round Southern Spain and Italy, through North Africa and to the Levant. Starters come from the raw bar, unless you choose the 'Daily 6' assorted meze, while main dishes come from the stove, the Josper or the plancha and are designed for sharing.

- 34 Rupert St ✉ W1D 6DN
  ✆ 020 7439 8777 — **www**.thepalomar.co.uk
  ⊖ Piccadilly Circus
- Carte £26/33
  Closed dinner 24-26 December – booking advisable

PARK CHINOIS

Chinese • Exotic décor

MAP: 2-H3

The inspiration for this opulent, exquisitely decorated destination restaurant comes from 1920s Shanghai – it's all about old fashioned glamour, good food and live music. The restaurant comes in two parts: the richly furnished ground floor exudes comfort and luxury, while downstairs has more of a nocturnal, mischievous feel. There's dim sum at lunchtime and afternoon tea at weekends, but the main event is dinner, when an army of white-jacketed waiters deliver the dishes course by course instead of all together. The menu traverses the length of China; two specialities of note being roast duck served with caviar, and carbonara with Inaniwa udon and sea urchin – and the atmosphere is electric, especially when the music kicks in.

- 17 Berkeley St W1J 8EA
  020 3327 8888 — **www.**parkchinois.com
  Green Park
- Menu £30 (lunch) - Carte £37/107
  Closed 25 December - booking essential

PEYOTE

Mexican • Trendy

MAP: 2-H3

This energetic and moodily lit Mexican restaurant comes from the same stable as Zuma and Roka, so expect it to be full of youthful, well-heeled diners who look good and know a decent Margarita when they taste one. It has the slight feel of a glamorous private members club and music thumps out from the DJ's decks at the end of the week. The kitchen offers a 'refined interpretation of Mexican cuisine' which means that the dishes, which are designed for sharing, are well-judged, use good ingredients and come with an exhilarating freshness. Start with the terrific guacamole and don't miss the cactus salad or the tostados nopales; the lime-driven ceviche is very refreshing; the quesadillas are satisfying; and you just have to end with churros.

- 13 Cork St W1S 3NS
  020 7409 1300 — **www.**peyoterestaurant.com
  Green Park
- Menu £25 (weekday lunch) - Carte £32/63
  Closed Saturday lunch and Sunday - booking essential

PLUM VALLEY

Chinese • Design

MAP: 2-13

Is Chinatown finally casting off its tourist-trap reputation? Plum Valley is the latest venture with genuine aspirations in Gerrard Street and its contemporary styling gives the street a much-needed boost. The striking black façade makes it easy to notice, while flattering lighting and layered walls give the interior a dash of sophistication. The chef is from Chiu Chow, a region near Guangdong, and his menu is largely based on Cantonese cooking, with occasional forays into Vietnam and Thailand, as well as the odd nod towards contemporary presentation. Dim sum is his kitchen's main strength which fits nicely with the all-day opening of the restaurant. If only those doing the service could muster the same levels of enthusiasm.

- 20 Gerrard St. W1D 6JQ
  020 7494 4366
  Leicester Square
- Menu £38 – Carte £19/37
  Closed 23-24 December

POLPETTO

Italian • Simple

MAP: 2-13

Following its short stint above the French House, restaurateur Russell Norman spent quite some time finding and decorating new premises for Polpetto – but the wait was worth it. It's almost three times the size of its former incarnation and set over two floors, and it manages the trick of being all new but looking lived-in. Waiting for a table is still an inevitability as bookings aren't accepted at dinner but your odds improve if you don't mind eating at the bar. The style of food chimes perfectly with the appealingly relaxed environment: the small, seasonally inspired Italian dishes are uncomplicated, appealingly priced and deliver great flavours; order a few and they arrive when ready but at an even pace.

- 11 Berwick St W1F 0PL
  020 7439 8627 — **www**.polpetto.co.uk
  Tottenham Court Road
- Carte £12/21
  (bookings not accepted at dinner)

POLLEN STREET SOCIAL ✿

Creative • Fashionable

XX A/C ⚙ ⓥ ✿ 🍸 **MAP:** 2-H3

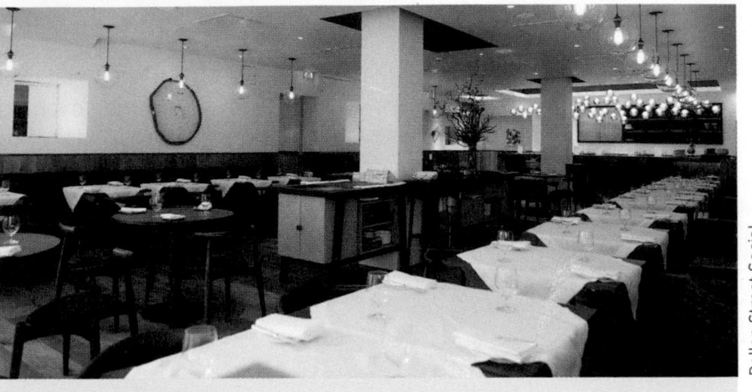

Pollen Street Social

FIRST COURSE: Pine-smoked quail, 'English breakfast'. • Lincolnshire smoked eel with buttermilk, beetroot reduction and 'jellied eel'.

MAIN COURSE: Loin & braised shoulder of lamb hotpot with spiced tomato and mint sauce. • Turbot with cauliflower & yoghurt purée, wild garlic and cockle dressing.

DESSERT: Bitter chocolate pavé, olive biscuit and olive oil ice cream. • Pistachio soufflé with chocolate & vanilla ice cream.

Pollen Street Social is where it all started for Jason Atherton when he went solo and, even though he now has an impressive international portfolio of restaurants to his name, it's clear it remains his flagship operation. Top quality British produce lies at the heart of a menu which offers a hugely appealing selection of modern dishes that are always very easy to eat; the cooking is clearly undertaken with great care and the confident kitchen brings out the best in those ingredients. There are moments of originality and innovation, even the occasional little playfulness, but never for its own sake. The à la carte prices can get a little dizzying but there's a decent value lunch menu. The wine list has impressive breadth and is rooted in the classic regions - and the care and consideration customers receive from the sommeliers is another of the restaurant's strengths. Think twice if you're offered a table in the bar area rather than in the main room, as you end up feeling a little detached from proceedings.

- 8-10 Pollen St ✉ W1S 1NQ
  ✆ 020 7290 7600 — **www**.pollenstreetsocial.com
  ⊖ Oxford Circus
- Menu £37 (lunch) - Carte £62/87
  Closed Sunday and bank holidays - booking essential

POLPO SOHO

Italian • Tapas bar

MAP: 2-H3

Opening a Venetian bacaro in an 18C townhouse where Canaletto once lodged does seem providential and Polpo has indeed been packing them in since day one. The stripped-down faux-industrial look is more New York's SoHo than London's Soho, as is the evening no-reservation policy which means you'll probably have to wait. But the fun atmosphere and the appealing prices of the small plates will assuage any impatience you feel in waiting your turn. Order a couple of cicchetti, like arancini or prosciutto; a plate of fritto misto, ham and pea risotto or Cotechino sausage; and a vegetable dish per person and you should leave satisfied – if you do over-order, it's not going to break the bank. Venetian wines, available by the carafe, complete the picture.

■ 41 Beak St ✉ W1F 9SB
020 7734 4479 — **www.**polpo.co.uk
Oxford Circus

■ Carte £14/28
(bookings not accepted at dinner)

PORTRAIT

Modern cuisine • Design

MAP: 2-I3

The rooftop view from Portrait – situated on the third floor of the National Portrait Gallery – is perfect for filling any awkward silences over lunch; Big Ben, the London Eye and Nelson's Column are among the more recognisable sights and identifying the others could keep you busy for hours. The restaurant is run by Company of Cooks and although it's also open for breakfast and afternoon tea, this is principally a lunchtime operation, with dinner limited to Thursday, Friday and Saturday – the nights of the gallery's extended opening hours. The à la carte menu keeps things relatively light and the influences mostly from Europe; the freshly prepared food is delivered with care and there are some good value pre-theatre and weekend set menus.

■ National Portrait Gallery (3rd floor), St Martin's Pl. ✉ WC2H 0HE
020 7312 2490 — **www.**npg.org.uk/portraitrestaurant
Charing Cross

■ Menu £32 – Carte £36/48
Closed 24-26 December – booking essential – (lunch only and dinner Thursday-Saturday)

QUAGLINO'S

Modern cuisine • Design

MAP: 2-H4

The old girl may have been around for a while now but she can still shake it like the best of them if you're looking for a fun night out. This colourful, glamorous restaurant manages to be cavernous and cosy at the same time, with live music and its late night bar adding a certain sultriness and energy to proceedings. The kitchen specialises in contemporary, brasserie-style food with an extensive à la carte menu that includes a grill section and dishes to share. There's a shellfish and crustacean section – the Quaglino's Cocktail with lobster, langoustine and crab is a popular choice – as well as oysters, caviar and several well-stocked cheese trolleys. Come at the weekend for brunch, which includes an appealing offer of bottomless fizz.

16 Bury St SW1Y 6AJ
020 7930 6767 — **www**.quaglinos-restaurant.co.uk
Green Park

Menu £23 (weekdays)/33 - Carte £37/68
Closed Easter Monday and Sunday dinner

QUO VADIS

Traditional British • Traditional décor

MAP: 2-I3

So who knew the home of Quo Vadis wasn't a 'listed' building? In 2016 half of this historic Soho institution was annexed to accommodate Barrafina when its lease ran out on Frith Street; upstairs was then turned into a private members' dining club, leaving just 6 or 7 tables of the original restaurant for the rest of us – at least they kept those famous neon signs and the very charming reception area. What hasn't changed is the cooking – chef Jeremy Lee's food is big on flavour and refreshingly free of ostentation. Who can resist a menu that offers 'today's pie' or runs a great value 'Soho Set' menu alongside the à la carte? You can grab a smoked eel sandwich or some oysters, or go the whole hog and opt for roast mutton or brill.

26-29 Dean St W1D 3LL
020 7437 9585 — **www**.quovadissoho.co.uk
Tottenham Court Road

Menu £23 - Carte £36/50
Closed 25-26 December, 1 January, Sunday and bank holidays

RED FORT

Indian • *Exotic décor*

MAP: 2-13

Soho now boasts one of London's most buoyant restaurant scenes but that wasn't the case back in 1983 when Red Fort opened its doors on Dean Street. Its longevity is down to the professionalism with which it is run, the fact that it keeps on top of its looks and, of course, the ability and ambition of the kitchen. Inside is bigger than you think and the smart, stylish and contemporary decoration pays homage to Lal Quila, Delhi's Red Fort. The cooking also takes its cue from the Mughal Court while making good use of produce from the UK like Welsh lamb and Scottish lobster. The tandoor oven is used to good effect, especially with the breads, and you can expect to see more unusual ingredients like rabbit. Zenna is its intimate basement bar.

- 77 Dean St. ✉ W1D 3SH
  020 7437 2525 — **www**.redfort.co.uk
  Tottenham Court Road
- Menu £15/49 - Carte £31/59
  Closed Sunday - bookings advisable at dinner

REFUEL

Modern British • *Fashionable*

MAP: 2-13

It comes as no surprise that a hotel as fashionable as The Soho has a restaurant as cool as Refuel. A large part of the room is given over to a slick cocktail bar and the lively atmosphere here tends to seep into the restaurant through osmosis. Service in the hotel is one of its great strengths and the serving team here are a bright and enthusiastic bunch who are always ready with a smile. The menu is all about ease of eating and includes a popular section of grilled dishes, which could range from burgers to Dover sole, as well as assorted pasta dishes and salads for the image-conscious. Side dishes are needed but can leave you with a sizeable bill so it's worth considering the better value set menu.

- Soho Hotel, 4 Richmond Mews ✉ W1D 3DH
  020 7559 3007 — **www**.firmdalehotels.com
  Tottenham Court Road
- Menu £23/30 - Carte £30/62

RITZ RESTAURANT ✿

Classic cuisine • Luxury

XXXXX 🏠 A/C 🍴 **MAP:** 2-H4

Michelin

FIRST COURSE: Norfolk crab with pickled cucumber, egg yolk and oscietra caviar. • Terrine of goose liver with mango, gingerbread and tonka bean.

MAIN COURSE: Fillet of veal with wild mushrooms and smoked bone marrow. • Sea bass with quinoa, sea vegetables and smoked eel.

DESSERT: Crêpes Suzette. • Coconut mousse with compressed pineapple and passion fruit sorbet.

The world may be considerably less formal these days but one of the reasons why London is such an exciting and dynamic city is its variety of restaurants. Thanks to the lavishness of its Louis XVI decoration, there is nowhere grander or more opulent than The Ritz – this is the place for the most special of special occasions, so it's hardly surprising they insist on a jacket and tie. To match the luxurious surroundings comes classic cuisine using the most extravagant of ingredients, but where the kitchen has been clever is in adopting subtle contemporary elements and techniques to lift those dishes to new heights, while still respecting their spirit and heritage. This new vitality is not just in the cooking – the service is also unrecognisable from what it was. There may be more ranks than your average ship's company but a younger breed of staff have brought greater enthusiasm and more personality to proceedings. The Ritz may have been here for over a century but it has probably never been better.

■ Ritz Hotel, 150 Piccadilly ✉ W1J 9BR
✆ 020 7300 2370 — **www**.theritzlondon.com
⊖ Green Park

■ Menu £52 (weekday lunch) – Carte £75/136

ROKA

Japanese • Elegant

MAP: 2-G3

Rainer Becker and Arjun Waney's empire now stretches to all parts of the globe but London was where it all began and is where they continue to open new restaurants. For the capital's third Roka they ventured into the rarefied surroundings of Mayfair and the restaurant's sultry, seductive looks prove a good fit. Tempting aromas fill the air as once again the robata grill takes centre stage – quite literally if you haven't booked and find yourself seated at the Indonesian elm counter that surrounds it. All the favourites from their modern Japanese repertoire are on show here; the tasting menu is often the best way of getting a good all-round experience and the dessert platter really is a sight. Even the doggy bags look good.

■ 30 North Audley St ✉ W1K 6HP
020 7305 5644 — **www.**rokarestaurant.com
Bond Street

■ Carte £24/99
Closed Christmas-New Year

ROSA'S SOHO

Thai • Simple

MAP: 2-I3

Those instinctively suspicious of anywhere too shiny and flashy will find Rosa's worn-in appearance suitably reassuring. The simple, pared-down look of this authentic Thai café also adds to its intimate feel; the waitresses, in bright red T-shirts to match the colour of the façade, provide swift and cheerful service. The menu is appealing and wide-ranging and the relative heat levels of each dish are indicated. The chef may be from Chiang Mai but his cooking is influenced by all parts of the country. Signature dishes include warm minced chicken salad, and a sweet pumpkin red curry; while squid, prawns, mussels and scallops all go into their seafood Pad Cha. The refreshing Tom Yam soup comes with a lovely balance of sweet, sour and spice.

■ 48 Dean St ✉ W1D 5BF
020 7494 1638 — **www.**rosasthaicafe.com
Leicester Square

■ Menu £20 - Carte £18/30
Closed 25-26 December - booking advisable

Ⓝ SAKAGURA

Japanese • *Exotic décor*

MAP: 2-H3

Not only does its name translate as 'sake cellar' but this contemporary styled Japanese restaurant is also part owned by Gekkeikan, one of Japan's oldest sake manufacturers, so unsurprisingly sake plays a big part here. The other owners are the Japan Centre Group so an equal spotlight is shone on the traditional Japanese cuisine or 'washoku' to accompany the impressive drinks list. The extensive menu covers a variety of styles - from sashimi and sushi to tempura and soba. Highlights are the skewers cooked on the robata charcoal-grill, and 'kamameshi' - flavoured rice dishes cooked to order and served in cast iron pots (they take about 30mins to prepare). The service staff are endearingly sweet and offer helpful advice.

■ 8 Heddon St ✉ W1B 4BS
020 3405 7230 — **www**.sakaguralondon.com
Oxford Circus

■ Menu £30/80 - Carte £27/55
Closed 25 December

SAKE NO HANA

Japanese • *Minimalist*

MAP: 2-H4

The Grade II listed former offices of The Economist play host to this modern Japanese restaurant and the '60s edifice needed an awful lot of cedar wood and bamboo to soften its appearance. The escalator remains, which doesn't really add a great deal to the experience, but you'll receive a warm welcome and feel well looked after. There's a huge number of dishes on offer and the food is certainly best shared with a group, although as prices fluctuate fairly wildly it may be worth appointing someone in your party the designated bill monitor before starting on their excellent cocktails. The sashimi is worthy of inclusion, as are the very good kamameshi or rice pot dishes, like black cod. There's a separate sushi bar on the ground floor.

■ 23 St James's ✉ SW1A 1HA
020 7925 8988 — **www**.sakenohana.com
Green Park

■ Menu £31 - Carte £24/121
Closed 25 December and Sunday

SARTORIA

Italian • Chic

MAP: 2-H3

Competition is hotting up in this little district west of Regent Street, so everyone's been busy raising their game. Sartoria has long been a well-dressed feature on Savile Row but is now looking considerably more dapper and a great deal sharper. That wasn't the only change: in 2015 Francesco Mazzei, formerly of L'Anima restaurant, hooked up with D&D to take the kitchen reins and the place feels more energised because of it. While there is evidence of Francesco's Calabrian roots with ingredients like 'nduja and liquorice, the menu covers all regions of Italy and keeps things fairly classic. The dishes for two prove very popular, whether that's risotto, salt-crusted sea bass, veal Milanese or a wonderfully rich zabaglione.

- 20 Savile Row W1S 3PR
  020 7534 7000 — **www**.sartoria-restaurant.co.uk
  Oxford Circus
- Menu £27 (weekday lunch) - Carte £38/61
  Closed 25-26 December, Saturday lunch, Sunday except lunch September-June and bank holidays

SCOTT'S

Seafood • Fashionable

MAP: 2-G3

When a restaurant is considered an 'institution', one usually assumes its best days are in the past. Scott's proves that a restaurant can have a long, proud history but can still be glamorous, relevant and fashionable. It is the clubby feel of the place that is particularly appealing: sit at the counter - which dominates the room and must surely be the most comfortable one in London - and you immediately feel part of a club, as you'll be surrounded by regulars on all sides. The seafood is of prime quality and there's enough choice for everyone, whether you just want oysters and simply grilled fish or something more adventurous with Asian influences. Prices may be high but you'll remember the experience - this is Scott's, after all.

- 20 Mount St W1K 2HE
  020 7495 7309 — **www**.scotts-restaurant.com
  Bond Street
- Carte £37/83
  Closed 25-26 December

SEVEN PARK PLACE ✿

Modern cuisine • Cosy

XXX A/C

MAP: 2-H4

Michelin

FIRST COURSE: Warm salad of poached native lobster tail with spring vegetables. • Seared foie gras with peach and golden raisin chutney.

MAIN COURSE: Saddle of Lune Valley lamb with garlic and rosemary. • Fillet of turbot with artichokes, chicken wings and sherry vinegar.

DESSERT: Passion fruit soufflé with dark chocolate sauce. • Tarte Tatin with vanilla ice cream and toffee apple sauce.

Not every chef chases TV fame or product endorsements – William Drabble is happiest when he's in his kitchen, here at St James's Hotel and Club. He describes his cooking as being "all about the ingredients" and his food provides an object lesson in the importance of using the best quality produce available. He eschews alchemy or elaborate experimentation and instead focuses on clarity and precision, which in turn allows the natural flavours of the ingredients to shine. He forged a close relationship with his butcher in the Lake District when he worked in that part of the world and their loyalty to each other clearly pays off – both know what each animal has been fed and where it has eaten it. Barbon Fell venison and Lune Valley lamb feature regularly and are a must but you can also expect supremely fresh seafood – the scallops are particularly good. The diminutive, secreted restaurant is in a curious spot as you have to slither past the bar stools in the hotel brasserie to reach it. It's divided into two areas; try to secure one of the three tables in the gilded back room.

■ St James's Hotel and Club, 7-8 Park Pl ✉ SW1A 1LS
☏ 020 7316 1615 — **www**.stjameshotelandclub.com
⊖ Green Park

■ Menu £33/71
Closed Sunday and Monday - booking essential

SEXY FISH

Seafood • Design

MAP: 2-H3

Everyone will have their own opinion about the name but what is indisputable is that this is a very good-looking restaurant. Works by Frank Gehry and Damien Hirst decorate the large, grand room which was, unsurprisingly, once a bank; the ceiling, designed by Michael Roberts, is a thing of beauty and the private dining room has two live coral reef tanks. The restaurant quickly became the glitterati's de facto HQ yet the pleasant staff exude none of that too-cool-for-school attitude which blights similar places. The large Asian-influenced menu is heavily weighted towards seafood; dishes are meant for sharing and those from the robata grill are often the highlight – but don't ignore the meat dishes like the beef rib skewers.

- Berkeley Sq. ✉ W1J 6BR
  020 3764 2000 — **www**.sexyfish.com
  Green Park
- Menu £36 (weekday lunch) - Carte £34/147
  Closed 25-26 December

SHORYU

Japanese • Simple

MAP: 2-I3

The restorative powers of ramen are so great it should be prescribed on the NHS. Shoryu is owned by the Japan Centre opposite and specialises in Hakata tonkotsu ramen, which originated in Kyushu in the south and is the most popular style of ramen in Japan. At Its base is a milky broth made from pork bones; to this is added springy hosomen noodles made in-house; nitamago (the boiled, marinated egg – an important element); sesame, and extra toppings of your choice; if you want a more robust flavour try a miso-based ramen. The surprisingly large menu includes other items with their roots in Chinese cooking, such as gyoza dumplings. If the queue is too long, try one of the two larger branches in Soho.

- 9 Regent St. ✉ SW1Y 4LR
  020 3405 1391 — **www**.shoryuramen.com
  Piccadilly Circus
- Carte £15/33
  Closed 25 December and 1 January – bookings not accepted

SKETCH (THE GALLERY) ꟷ

Modern cuisine • *Trendy*

MAP: 2-H3

It's been the HQ of RIBA, a safe house for the suffragette movement and an atelier of Christian Dior, but it's as a nesting place for London's art, fashion and culinary cognoscenti that this striking Georgian house really shines. Reinvention has always been key here and The Gallery's most recent look is from India Mahdavi and comes with artwork from Turner Prize nominated David Shrigley. At dinner the room transmogrifies from art gallery to restaurant when it suddenly reverberates to the rattle of the barman's cocktail shaker and the buzz of contented diners. The menu is a mix of the classic, the modern and the esoteric – beef burger with foie gras, fish and chips with a twist, sweet and sour snails – which suits the surroundings perfectly.

- 9 Conduit St ✉ W1S 2XG
  020 7659 4500 — **www**.sketch.london
  Oxford Circus
- Carte £38/79
  Closed 25 December and 1 January – booking essential – (dinner only)

SPUNTINO

North American • *Rustic*

MAP: 2-I3

Despite its Italian name – meaning 'snack'– Spuntino draws its influences from Downtown New York and is so convincing you feel you could be on Clinton Street. It has the so-discreet-you-walk-straight-past-it entrance, a no-reservations policy (not even a phone number) and an interior that more than hints at a former industrial life – this was once a dairy. Just grab, or wait for, a space at the counter and, from the brown paper menu, go for the more American dishes such as mac 'n' cheese, soft-shell crab, farmhouse cheddar grits or 'sliders'. The peanut butter and jelly sandwiches for dessert will be always on your mind. The staff, who look like they could also fix your car, really add to the fun.

- 61 Rupert St. ✉ W1D 7PW
  www.spuntino.co.uk
  Piccadilly Circus
- Carte £12/30
  Closed dinner 24 December, 25-26, 31 December and 1 January – bookings not accepted

SKETCH (THE LECTURE ROOM & LIBRARY) ✿✿

French • Luxury

XXXX A/C 🍷 ✿ **MAP:** 2-H3

Michelin

FIRST COURSE: Perfume of the Earth. • Black truffle with leek, onion, ham and chicken.

MAIN COURSE: Wild turbot on the bone with plankton butter and broccoli. • Rack of veal with oregano and lemon thyme.

DESSERT: Pierre Gagnaire's 'grand dessert'. • Millefeuille with vanilla cream and wild strawberries.

We all need a little luxury in our lives from time to time – so praise be for Mourad Mazouz and Pierre Gagnaire's 18C funhouse. As you're whisked past the braided rope and up the stairs to the Lecture Room & Library, you'll feel your expectations rise with every step. The room is lavishly decorated in a kaleidoscope of colours and the impeccably set tables are so far apart they're virtually in different postcodes. The staff are unfailingly polite and professional and it appears that nothing is too much trouble. The French cooking bears all the Pierre Gagnaire hallmarks. The main 'plate' comes surrounded by a number of complementary dishes and at first you don't quite know what to focus on – now is the time to relax into that comfortable armchair and just enjoy the variety of textures and tastes, the complexity and depth of flavours and the quality of the ingredients. The wine list is a tome of epic proportions; take the sommeliers' advice; they know what they're talking about. And do make sure you order the array of treats that make up the 'grand dessert' – pudding it ain't.

■ 9 Conduit St (1st floor) ✉ W1S 2XG
✆ 020 7659 4500 — **www**.sketch.london
⊖ Oxford Circus

■ Carte £110/143
Closed 25 December, 1 January, 2 weeks late August-early September, Sunday, Monday and lunch Tuesday to Thursday. – booking essential

SOCIAL EATING HOUSE ✿

Modern cuisine • Fashionable

MAP: 2-H3

Michelin

FIRST COURSE: Scorched mackerel and tartare with pickled walnuts, apple and chicory. • Saddleback pork belly with black pudding, maple glaze and golden raisins.

MAIN COURSE: Roast rack of lamb, braised neck, baby gem, cured lamb and rocket. • Cornish hake with hispi cabbage gratin, Salcombe crab, Tokyo turnip and saffron.

DESSERT: Caramelised milk and brown sugar tart with ginger wine and fromage frais sorbet. • Raspberry cheesecake with cream cheese, lemon sorbet and meringue.

If you're looking for somewhere with terrific food that represents all that is great about this dynamic part of town then this Jason Atherton restaurant is it – it's huge fun, noisy and gloriously unstuffy. The low-ceilinged speakeasy-style bar upstairs is a great place to have in your address book, while the restaurant, with its bare bricks and raw plastered walls has something of Brooklyn about it. They've certainly made the best use of the available room as virtually every space is set for dining, including the counter of the bar and in the kitchen where the 'pass' would be. The menu makes an eminently good read but while you do so be sure to order a cocktail – those in the know ask for the more comprehensive list from upstairs. Kick things off on the food front by sharing one or two of their 'jars' – something like ham hock terrine or smoked hummus, before ordering robustly flavoured dishes like the ever-popular wild mushrooms on toast with cep purée, or hake with smoked celeriac mousseline.

■ 58 Poland St ✉ W1F 7NR
☎ 020 7993 3251 — **www**.socialeatinghouse.com
⊖ Oxford Circus

■ Menu £27 (lunch and early dinner) – Carte £39/56
Closed Christmas, Sunday and bank holidays – booking advisable

THE SQUARE ✿

Creative French • Elegant

XXXX A/C ⊡ Ⅰ♡ ✿ **MAP:** 2-H3

Michelin

FIRST COURSE: Marinated langoustine sandwich with mushroom, apple and coral mayonnaise. • Quail terrine with truffle, foie gras and Dijon mustard.

MAIN COURSE: Pyrenean milk-fed lamb, Roscoff onion, Tokyo turnip and tarragon. • Pan-fried Dover sole with red cabbage jus and beurre noisette.

DESSERT: Jura whisky chestnut cake with buckwheat praline and toasted malt ice cream. • Almenara clementines with mascarpone and clove.

When chef Philip Howard left The Square in 2016 it felt very much like the end of an era, as the two had been inexorably linked for nearly 25 years. Not only was there going to be a new chef but new owners too – and many gave a sigh of relief when Marlon Abela stepped up and added it to his international portfolio of restaurants. His first task was finding a new chef – Yu Sugimoto arrived with an impressive CV which included some illustrious names like Le Meurice and L'Espérance in Paris. His cooking is certainly different from his predecessor; while dishes display a classical base, there is greater originality and dishes feature more unusual flavour combinations, whether that's the rosemary syrup and smoked anchovy cream that accompany the crispy sweetbreads, or the peanut and coriander that go with the roasted pineapple dessert. Service remains as well organised and as keen as ever and the wine list is now even bigger and better than before, with a particularly impressive selection of burgundies.

- 6-10 Bruton St. ✉ W1J 6PU
  ✆ 020 7495 7100 — **www**.squarerestaurant.com
  ⊖ Green Park
- Menu £40/105
  Closed 24-26 December and Sunday

Ⓝ STREETXO ℩O

Creative • Trendy

XX 🍸 MAP: 2-H3

The menu at celebrated Madrid chef David Muñoz's London outpost is inspired by European, Asian and even South American cuisines. Many of the dishes - which are designed for sharing and, refreshingly, are big enough for that purpose - involve explosions of colour and a riot of different flavours, techniques and textures. If your palate is feeling jaded, this is certainly the place to come. A seat at the counter is far better than a table, as you get to watch the rock 'n' roll kitchen in action. The quasi-industrial style of the room, with its exposed piping, neon and concrete, works well in creating a moody, noisy and exciting atmosphere. Equal thought has gone into creating a fun and original cocktail list.

■ 15 Old Burlington St ✉ W1S 2JL
020 3096 7555 — **www**.streetxo.com
Oxford Circus
■ Menu £25/90 - Carte £38/54
Closed 22-26 December

Ⓝ TAMARIND KITCHEN ℩O

Indian • Exotic décor

XX A/C MAP: 2-I2

Imli occupied this space for a few years before the Tamarind Collection revamped and relaunched it in 2017. As its name suggests, it's now more aligned to their flagship restaurant Tamarind in Mayfair and, although things here in Soho are more relaxed and the noise levels are higher, they are presumably hoping for a little cross-pollination. That being said, it more than stands on its own two feet and comes with service that's endearingly earnest. There's a nominal Northern Indian emphasis to the fairly priced menu, with Awadhi kababs a speciality, but there are also plenty of curries and fish dishes. The kitchen displays a light yet assured touch and, while presentation is contemporary, the flavour combinations are more traditional.

■ 167-169 Wardour St ✉ W1F 8WR
020 7287 4243 — **www**.tamarindkitchen.co.uk
Tottenham Court Road
■ Carte £21/36
Closed 25-26 December, 1 January

TAMARIND ✿

Indian • Chic

XXX A/C ⓥ **MAP:** 2-G4

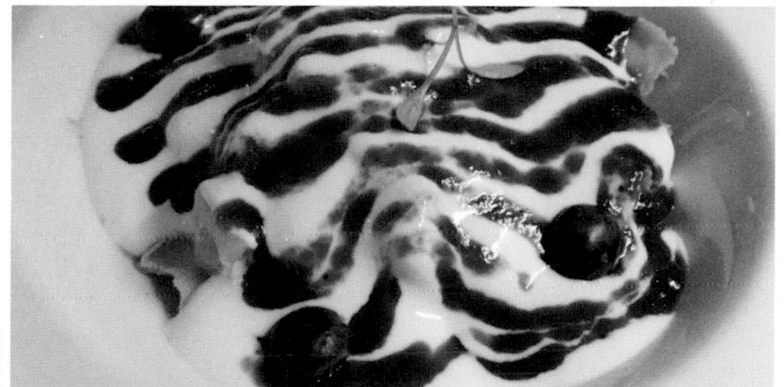

Michelin

FIRST COURSE: Pudhina chops with dried mint and tomato & coriander chutney. • Steamed shrimps, halibut and squid with black olives and fennel & ginger dressing.

MAIN COURSE: Murgh tikka masala with dried fenugreek leaves. • Monkfish marinated in mint with coriander, pine nuts and pickled golden beets.

DESSERT: Mango kulfi. • Chocolate and coconut ganache with chocolate silk and blackberry sorbet.

Tamarind is a perpetually busy restaurant so you need to book; when you do so, ask for a table around the edge of the room as it can feel a little like Piccadilly Circus in the middle section with the army of staff all buzzing around. The reason for this restaurant's enduring popularity is less to do with its looks - although the gilded pillars and smoked mirrors do make the most of the basement location - and everything to do with the assured Indian cuisine. Despite the chef being from the south, the menu remains largely influenced by the traditional Moghul cuisine of Northern India, so don't expect showy or elaborate dishes but do think delicate spicing and balanced flavours. The kebabs are a favourite and the tandoor oven - a definite influence from the Northwest - is used to good effect. The Hyderabadi lamb shank is another highlight, as are the well-judged vegetable dishes such as saag aloo and bhindi do pyaza. The 6 course tasting menu is a good way to try a cross-section of dishes in smaller portions.

- 20 Queen St. ✉ W1J 5PR
  ✆ 020 7629 3561 — **www.**tamarindrestaurant.com
  ⊖ Green Park
- Menu £25 (weekday lunch)/75 - Carte £37/66
  Closed 25-26 December and 1 January

Ⓝ TEMPER ℩O

Barbecue • Contemporary décor

MAP: 2-H/13

As you descend the stairs from the small, ground floor reception area, you slowly become aware of the action, the noise, and the enticing aromas of this large basement restaurant, which is all about barbecue and meats, available by the 100g, and served on baked flatbread. The beasts are cooked whole, some are also smoked in-house and there's a distinct South African flavour to the salsas that accompany them. Kick off with some tacos - they make around 1200 of them every day and the toppings could include crab or duck fat. You'll certainly leave feeling sated and, as mezcal is also a big thing here, feeling pretty pleased with life. Although there are plenty of tables, the large square counter is where you'll want to perch if you're a couple.

- 25 Broadwick St ✉ W1F 0DF
  ✆ 020 3879 3834 — **www**.temperrestaurant.com
  ⊖ Oxford Circus
- Carte £16/37
  Closed 25-26 December and 1 January

THEO RANDALL ℩O

Italian • Classic décor

MAP: 2-G4

A lighter, fresher and less formal look to the room was unveiled in 2016 to celebrate Theo's 10 years of residency here at the InterContinental hotel. The lack of windows and the corporate nature of the hotel have never done the room any favours but at least there is now greater synergy between its look and the type of food being served - and from some tables you get tantalising glimpses into the kitchen. That food is rustic Italian, with the appealing dishes featuring top quality ingredients sourced from Italy or the British Isles or sometimes both, like Devon Crab with Sardinian bottarga, or Hereford beef with fritto misto. The pasta dishes are always a highlight and for dessert look no further than the Amalfi lemon tart.

- InterContinental London Park Lane Hotel, 1 Hamilton Pl, Park Ln ✉ W1J 7QY
  ✆ 020 7318 8747 — **www**.theorandall.com
  ⊖ Hyde Park Corner
- Menu £29 (weekdays) - Carte £34/65

34

Meats and grills • *Brasserie*

MAP: 2-G3

Caprice Holdings' restaurants are all about glamour and exclusivity and 34 is no exception. Both its main culinary influences and intended customer base are announced by the flying of the Union Flag and the Stars and Stripes above the door. Inside is a wonderful mix of art deco styling and Edwardian warmth – it feels like a classic brasserie that's been around for years, but in a good way. The star is the parrilla, an Argentinian charcoal grill used for the cooking of the Dover sole, brochettes and beef – choose from Scottish dry-aged, US prime, organic Argentinian and Australian Wagyu; good quality game also features and they do a decent weekend brunch. It may not come cheap but then glitz never does.

- 34 Grosvenor Sq (entrance on South Audley St) W1K 2HD
  020 3350 3434 — **www**.34-restaurant.co.uk
  Marble Arch
- Menu £28 (weekdays) - Carte £34/60
  Closed 25-26 December, dinner 24 December and lunch 1 January

TOKIMEITĒ

Japanese • *Chic*

MAP: 2-H3

Yoshihiro Murata is one of Japan's most celebrated chefs but Chrysan, his first London restaurant, never bedded in. For his second attempt he teamed up with the Zen-Noh group, an arm of Japan's largest agricultural cooperative. Their aim is to promote Wagyu beef in the UK and Europe so, naturally enough, it features heavily on the menu – in everything from tartare to sukiyaki and teriyaki – with the kitchen using A4 quality. It's certainly worth ordering and proves more successful than other choices like the sushi and tempura. The handsome restaurant is spread over two floors, with sparkling golden lights and lots of wood that you find you want to occasionally stroke. It's worth coming at lunch for a well-priced bento or donburi.

- 23 Conduit St W1S 2XS
  020 3826 4411 — **www**.tokimeite.com
  Oxford Circus
- Carte £28/143
  Closed 25 December, 1-3 January and Sunday

TONKOTSU

Japanese • Rustic

MAP: 2-I3

If you want to see why ramen is all the rage in various cities around the world then stand in line and wait for a table at this simple Soho stop. Good ramen is all about the base stock and here 18 hours goes into its preparation to ensure the bowls of soup and homemade wheat-based noodles reach a depth of flavour that seems to nourish one's very soul. Tonkotsu is named after the pork bone broth favoured in southern Japan; you can also try the soy based Tokyo ramen or go for a little northern Japanese influence with the miso base ramen - and when it arrives, with its seasoned egg and assorted toppings like pork belly and bamboo shoots, don't forget to slurp. While you wait for your ramen, share some of the gyoza - handmade Japanese dumplings.

63 Dean St ✉ W1D 4QG
020 7437 0071 — **www**.tonkotsu.co.uk
Tottenham Court Road

Carte £17/26
Bookings not accepted

VASCO AND PIERO'S PAVILION

Italian • Friendly

MAP: 2-H2/3

Not only does Vasco still oversee the kitchen - he keeps a particularly keen eye on the pasta making - but he also likes to help out in the restaurant so he can keep in touch with his regulars, for it is they who have ensured that this institution is still going strong after 40 years. The simply decorated room, closely set tables and matter-of-fact service blend nicely together and there's usually a good mix of customer, including a few tourists, who, by luck or judgement, have stumbled into the right place. The twice daily changing menu is made up of comforting Italian classics but its heart and soul is firmly in Umbria. The presence of Vasco's son will hopefully ensure the future looks bright for another 40 years.

15 Poland St ✉ W1F 8QE
020 7437 8774 — **www**.vascosfood.com
Oxford Circus

Carte £27/49
Closed Saturday lunch, Sunday and bank holidays - booking essential at lunch

UMU ✿✿

Japanese • Fashionable

XXX A/C 🍇 MAP: 2-H3

Umu

FIRST COURSE: Sake-steamed abalone sunomono. • Cornish lobster tempura with asparagus, mushrooms and courgette.

MAIN COURSE: Charcoal-grilled quail with sake kasu egg and sansho pepper. • Crispy Dover sole with bonito flakes.

DESSERT: Gariguette strawberry, sakura mousse and yomogi. • Mugicha peach with wild flowers.

The kaiseki menu is the best way to truly experience chef Yoshinori Ishii's cuisine – he trained at Kitcho in Kyoto, a bastion of tradition where the central tenets and philosophy of kaiseki are preserved and celebrated. Here at Umu he has steadily been shifting the food away from a Western idea of Japanese food to a more authentic base, which means that flavours are more delicate and subtle than many expect. It hasn't always been easy: to get hold of fish in the right condition he went out with Cornish fishermen himself to teach them the ikejime method of killing fish – and you'll see the benefit in the firmer texture of the tsukuri. But that's not to say he's trying to replicate what happens in Kyoto – he wisely acknowledges that this is a London restaurant by incorporating the best of the UK's larder as well as dropping in an occasional playfulness – how many Japanese are familiar with a scotch egg? Instead of tatami rooms there's a neatly laid out restaurant which makes good use of warm woods and natural materials.

■ 14-16 Bruton Pl. ✉ W1J 6LX
☎ 020 7499 8881 — **www.**umurestaurant.com
⊖ Bond Street

■ Menu £45/155 - Carte £46/151
Closed Christmas, New Year, Easter, Sunday and bank holidays

VEERASWAMY ✿

Indian • Design

XX A/C ⊕ ⓥ

MAP: 2-H3

Veeraswamy

FIRST COURSE: Tandoori green prawns. • Venison mutta kebab with tamarind glaze.

MAIN COURSE: Hyderabadi lamb biryani. • Banana leaf wrapped fillets of cumin & mint marinated sea bass.

DESSERT: Coconut and palm sugar crème brûlée. • Almond and pineapple halwa tart.

If anyone needs an example of somewhere that has never rested on its laurels, they need look no further than Veeraswamy. London's oldest surviving Indian restaurant opened in 1926 yet it continues to go from strength to strength, even after 90 years. It's not unreasonable to expect that a restaurant with this sort of heritage might be a little old-fashioned but it's actually awash with colour and full of life – as soon as you get out of the lift, you're aware of the bustle and the vitality. It is also run with enormous charm by a committed and enthusiastic team – even when there's a mass exodus in the early evening by those heading to the theatres they display a reassuring calmness and control. The really significant improvements, however, have been in the food. The menu's main focus is on updated classic dishes from across the country and the genuine care taken by the kitchen is palpable, whether that's in the freshly made crab cakes, the succulent lamb chops with a pistachio and almond crust, or the rich Keralan prawn curry.

■ Victory House, 99 Regent St (Entrance on Swallow St.) ✉ W1B 4RS
☎ 020 7734 1401 — **www**.veeraswamy.com
⊖ Piccadilly Circus

■ Menu £34/45 - Carte £33/75

Ⓝ VENETA

Italian • Brasserie

MAP: 2-I3

For their restaurant in the new development of St James's Market, the Salt Yard Group kept to its successful formula of serving small plates but was more specific when it came to the provenance of the food. The menu here is largely Italian and there's a particular emphasis on specialities from Venice, so expect dishes like sardines in saor, bigoli pasta and a generous use of polenta. There is much to enjoy and the accompanying wine list has been thoughtfully put together. The place itself is also a little more comfortable than the other branches in the group – it has the feel and look of a bright, modern brasserie, with double-height doors and a mezzanine floor – but it doesn't always quite match them for fun and atmosphere.

- 3 Norris St., St James's Market ✉ SW1Y 4RJ
  020 3874 9100 — **www**.saltyardgroup.co.uk
  ⊖ Piccadilly Circus
- Carte £17/36

WILD HONEY

Modern cuisine • Design

MAP: 2-H3

Elegant wood panelling, immaculately kept leather seating, ornate plasterwork and a handsome hand-blown chandelier all tell you this is a classic Mayfair institution. There is nothing crusty or old-fashioned about it however, because the customers and the personable service team combine to keep the atmosphere enjoyably light and easy-going. The style of food remains the same: the kitchen uses good quality British ingredients and a French base but is not afraid of adding the occasional international flavour; what has become more elusive is the precision with which those dishes are prepared. There are a number of menus available, including a weekend tasting menu – the set menu offered represents very good value.

- 12 St George St. ✉ W1S 2FB
  020 7758 9160 — **www**.wildhoneyrestaurant.co.uk
  ⊖ Oxford Circus
- Menu £35 (lunch and early dinner) – Carte £33/55
  Closed 25-26 December, 1 January, Sunday and bank holidays except Good Friday

THE WOLSEY

Modern cuisine • Fashionable

MAP: 2-H4

The Wolseley didn't take long to earn iconic status, thanks to its stylish décor and celebrity following. Its owners, Chris Corbin and Jeremy King, created a restaurant in the style of a grand European café: all pillars, arches and marble. It's open from breakfast until late, and the flexible menu offers everything from Austrian and French classics to British staples, so the daily special could be coq au vin or Lancashire hotpot. Pastries come from the Viennoiserie and lunch merges into afternoon tea - so one table could be tucking into Beluga caviar or a dozen oysters while their neighbours enjoy a salt beef sandwich or eggs Benedict. The large clock and swift service are reminders that there are probably people waiting for your table.

■ 160 Piccadilly ✉ W1J 9EB
020 7499 6996 — **www**.thewolseley.com
⊖ Green Park

■ Carte £23/69
Booking essential

ZELMAN MEATS

Meats and grills • Rustic

MAP: 2-I2

You don't build up a couple of successful restaurant chains without recognising an opportunity when you see it. Those clever people behind Goodman and Burger & Lobster noticed a lack of fun, affordable steakhouses and so created Zelman Meats, named after the company boss. It serves three cuts of beef, priced per 100g: picanha (from the rump) and Chateaubriand - which are cooked in the open kitchen over charcoal and served sliced - and a wonderfully smoky short rib. Start with oysters or a lovely red prawn ceviche and bear in mind that the side dishes are big enough to share. The prices are certainly reasonable and there are plenty of booths to be had in the dimly lit, semi-industrial space. Two traditional roasts are offered on Sundays.

■ 2 St Anne's Ct ✉ W1F 0AZ
020 7437 0566 — **www**.zelmanmeats.com
⊖ Tottenham Court Rd

■ Carte £18/49
Closed Monday lunch and bank holidays

YAUATCHA SOHO ✿

Chinese • Design

MAP: 2-13

Yauatcha Soho

FIRST COURSE: Venison puff. • Spicy soft shell crab with almond.

MAIN COURSE: Stir-fried rib-eye beef. • Steamed wild prawns with chilli sauce.

DESSERT: Raspberry délice. • Chocolate pebble with caramelised white chocolate.

One of Soho's grandees, the original Yauatcha may have been here nearly fifteen years, but thanks to subtle changes it still manages to feel fresh and contemporary. The bright ground floor is home to well-spaced tables, a bar and a patisserie offering chocolates and macaroons to take home, while downstairs offers a moody basement with low banquettes, an aquarium bar and a sparkly star-lit ceiling. The extensive à la carte means there's something for everyone, from seafood to excellent ribs, and over-ordering is easy to do. Cooking is undertaken with care and consistency and dishes are colourful and attractive with strong flavours and excellent texture contrasts. Stand-outs include the scallop shui mai, the duck roll and the wonderfully light venison puff. Dishes arrive at a good pace and prices are pretty good when you consider how much food you get for your money. Tea is the natural choice when it comes to what to drink – but the cocktails are definitely worth exploring too.

■ 15 Broadwick St ✉ W1F 0DL
✆ 020 7494 8888 — **www.**yauatcha.com
⊖ Tottenham Court Road

■ Menu £30 (lunch) - Carte £29/67
Closed 25 December

STRAND · COVENT GARDEN

It's fitting that Manet's world famous painting 'Bar at the Folies Bergère' should hang in the **Strand** within a champagne cork's throw of theatreland and Covent Garden. This is the area perhaps more than any other which draws in the ticket-buying tourist, eager to grab a good deal on one of the many shows on offer, or eat and drink at fabled landmarks like J.Sheekey or Rules. It's here the names already up in lights shine down on their potential usurpers: celeb wannabes heading for The Ivy, West Street's perennially fashionable restaurant. It's here, too, that Nell Gwyn set up home under the patronage of Charles II, while Oscar Wilde revelled in his success by taking rooms at the Savoy.

The hub of the whole area is the piazza at **Covent Garden,** created by Inigo Jones four hundred years ago. It was given a brash new lease of life in the 1980s after its famed fruit and veg market was pulled up by the roots and re-sown in Battersea. Council bigwigs realised then that 'what we have we hold', and any further redevelopment of the area is banned. Where everyone heads is the impressive covered market, within which a colourful jumble of arts and crafts shops gels with al fresco cafés and classical performers proffering Paganini with your cappuccino. Outside, under the portico of St Paul's church, every type of street performer does a turn for the tourist trade. The best shops in Covent Garden, though, are a few streets north of the market melee, emanating out like bicycle spokes from Seven Dials.

For those after a more highbrow experience, one of London's best attractions is a hop, skip and *grand jeté* from the market. Around the corner in **Bow Street** is the city's famed home for opera and ballet, where fire – as well as show-stopping performances – has been known to bring the house down. The **Royal Opera House** is now in its third incarnation, and it gets more impressive with each rebuild. The handsome, glass-roofed Paul Hamlyn Hall is a must-see, so enjoy a drink in the Champagne Bar before curtain up or during the interval. At the other end of the Strand the **London Coliseum** offers more opera, this time all performed in English. Down by Waterloo Bridge, art lovers are strongly advised to stop at **Somerset House** and take in one of London's most sublime collections of art at the Courtauld Gallery. This is where you can get up close and personal to Manet's barmaid, as well as an astonishing array of Impressionist masters and twentieth century greats. The icing on the cake is the compact and accessible eighteenth century building that houses the collection: real icing on a real cake can be found in a super little hidden-away café downstairs.

Of a different order altogether is the huge **National Gallery** at Trafalgar Square which houses more than two thousand Western European pieces (it started off with 38). A visit to the modern Sainsbury Wing is rewarded with some unmissable works from the Renaissance. It can get just as crowded in the capital's largest Gallery as in the square outside, so a good idea is to wander down **Villiers Street** next to Charing Cross station and breathe the Thames air along the Victoria Embankment. Behind you is the grand Savoy Hotel; for a better view of it, you can head even further away from the crowds on a boat trip from the **Embankment,** complete with on-board entertainment. And if the glory of travel in the capital, albeit on the water, has whetted your appetite for more, then pop into the impressively renovated Transport Museum in Covent Garden piazza, where gloriously preserved tubes, buses and trains from the past put you in a positive frame of mind for the real live working version you'll very probably be tackling later in the day.

coldsnowstorm/iStock

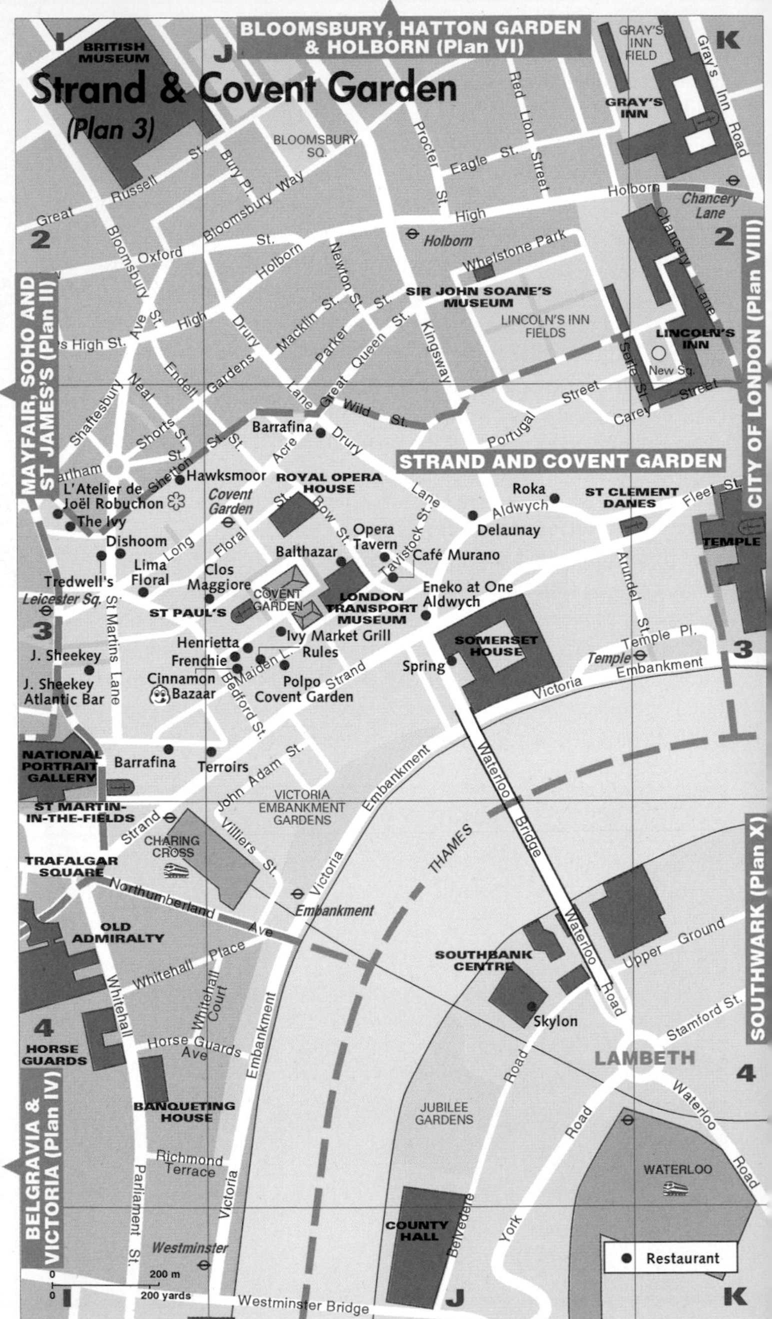
Strand & Covent Garden
(Plan 3)
BLOOMSBURY, HATTON GARDEN & HOLBORN (Plan VI)
MAYFAIR, SOHO AND ST JAMES'S (Plan II)
CITY OF LONDON (Plan VIII)
SOUTHWARK (Plan X)
BELGRAVIA & VICTORIA (Plan IV)
STRAND AND COVENT GARDEN
BRITISH MUSEUM
BLOOMSBURY SQ.
GRAY'S INN FIELD
GRAY'S INN
SIR JOHN SOANE'S MUSEUM
LINCOLN'S INN FIELDS
LINCOLN'S INN
New Sq.
Holborn
Chancery Lane
Covent Garden
Leicester Sq.
Temple
Embankment
Westminster
Barrafina
Hawksmoor
L'Atelier de Joël Robuchon
The Ivy
Dishoom
Lima Floral
Tredwell's
Clos Maggiore
Balthazar
Opera Tavern
Café Murano
Roka
Delaunay
Eneko at One Aldwych
Ivy Market Grill
Rules
Henrietta
Frenchie
Cinnamon Bazaar
Polpo Covent Garden
J. Sheekey
J. Sheekey Atlantic Bar
Spring
Terroirs
Skylon
ROYAL OPERA HOUSE
ST PAUL'S
COVENT GARDEN
LONDON TRANSPORT MUSEUM
SOMERSET HOUSE
ST CLEMENT DANES
TEMPLE
NATIONAL PORTRAIT GALLERY
ST MARTIN-IN-THE-FIELDS
TRAFALGAR SQUARE
CHARING CROSS
VICTORIA EMBANKMENT GARDENS
OLD ADMIRALTY
HORSE GUARDS
BANQUETING HOUSE
SOUTHBANK CENTRE
JUBILEE GARDENS
COUNTY HALL
WATERLOO
LAMBETH
THAMES
Restaurant
200 m
200 yards

L'ATELIER DE JOËL ROBUCHON ✿

French • Elegant

MAP: 3-13

Michelin

FIRST COURSE: Langoustine and truffle ravioli with savoy cabbage. • Quail with foie gras and truffle mashed potato.

MAIN COURSE: Fillet of beef with Malabar pepper and spring vegetables. • Halibut with young vegetables and butter & lemon thyme sauce.

DESSERT: Passion fruit soufflé with exotic fruit sorbet. • Praline with vanilla mousseline and chocolate sorbet.

For a special night out in the West End, this restaurant should be on everyone's list; it's sexy and lively, with intensely flavoured cooking, confident, capable staff and an atmospheric top floor bar. It differs from many of the Ateliers around the world as it features two dining experiences under one roof: on the ground floor is the moody red and black L'Atelier, with its counter dining and open kitchen, while upstairs monochrome La Cuisine offers table dining in an intimate setting just a few nights a week. Apart from a few wood-fired dishes upstairs, the menus are largely similar; those here to celebrate should go all out with the 8-course menu découverte, but you can also have the more competitively priced lunch or pre-theatre menus. Cooking is assured and accomplished with an emphasis on the Mediterranean; dishes are creative and well-balanced, and there's a pleasing simplicity to their presentation - despite the fact that there are over thirty chefs in the building. The tasting plates are a good option and perhaps the best way to fully appreciate Robuchon's craft and vision.

- 13-15 West St. ✉ WC2H 9NE
  ✆ 020 7010 8600 — **www**.joelrobuchon.co.uk
  ⊖ Leicester Square
- Menu £45 (lunch and early dinner) - Carte £64/119

BALTHAZAR

French • Brasserie

MAP: 3-J3

It's not just musicals and plays that transfer between London and New York – the world's two greatest cities now trade in restaurants as well. Balthazar has long been a landmark in Manhattan's SoHo district but now there's a London version occupying the old Theatre Museum in Covent Garden which, thanks to its red leather seats, mosaic floor, mirrors and flattering lighting, will seem uncannily familiar to anyone who knows the original. This being a London copy of a New York copy of a classic Parisian brasserie means that the Franglais menu plays it safe and focuses on reassuringly familiar dishes like moules frites, coq au vin and duck confit. It's open from breakfast onwards, the cocktails are great, and the atmosphere is lively and excitable.

- 4-6 Russell St. ✉ WC2B 5HZ
  ✆ 020 3301 1155 — **www**.balthazarlondon.com
  ⊖ Covent Garden
- Menu £20 (lunch and early dinner) - Carte £31/62
  Closed 25 December - booking essential

BARRAFINA

Spanish • Tapas bar

MAP: 3-I3

The second Barrafina is not only brighter than the Frith Street original, it's also bigger and, although that doesn't mean the queues are shorter, it does mean you can wait inside with a drink for a couple of the 29 counter seats to become available. Once safely ensconced, order a glass of Manzanilla and some plump olives and set about choosing your tapas. Don't fill up with pan con tomate, good though it is; instead, go for the wonderful crab on toast and try more unusual offerings like ortiguillas, crispy sea anemone, or succulent meats like suckling pig or herb-crusted rabbit shoulder. The kitchen's deft touch is also much in evidence with specialities like frit Mallorquin and crisp monkfish cheeks.

- 10 Adelaide St ✉ WC2N 4HZ
  ✆ 020 7440 1456 — **www**.barrafina.co.uk
  ⊖ Charing Cross
- Carte £15/41
  Closed Christmas, New Year and bank holidays - bookings not accepted

BARRAFINA

Spanish · Tapas bar

MAP: 3-J3

The third of the Barrafinas is tucked away at the far end of Covent Garden; as at its sisters, there are no bookings taken, so arrive early or enjoy a drink while you wait for one of the burnished red leather stools to become vacant. This is a busy, buzzy place where you can admire your neighbour's food at close quarters; service is friendly and well-paced - and the theatre of watching the chefs at work adds to the appeal. A seat just inside the door affords a view of the seafood counter - fresh, vibrantly flavoured fish and shellfish dishes like octopus with paprika and capers or lemon sole cooked on the chargrill are a real highlight here. The menu covers all bases but the tortillas y huevos are another special feature.

- 43 Drury Ln ✉ WC2B 5AJ
  020 7440 1456 — **www**.barrafina.co.uk
  Covent Garden
- Carte £28/41
  Closed bank holidays - bookings not accepted

CAFE MURANO

Italian · Neighbourhood

MAP: 3-J3

The second Cafe Murano is in the heart of Covent Garden, in a space much larger than the St James's original; avoid the front tables and head for the smart marble-topped counter at the back. Upstairs are more tables under a glass roof, while the pastificio shop next door means you can take freshly made pasta home with you too. This might be a café in name but it's much smarter and more comfortable than one in reality, although the menu of Northern Italian dishes is rather café-like in terms of its flexibility and appeal. Nibble on a few cicchetti or have four courses including one of the delicious pasta dishes - and leave room for the Muscavado tart! Everything sounds tempting and it'll only be your purse or your appetite that holds you back.

- 36 Tavistock St ✉ WC2E 7PB
  020 7240 3654 — **www**.cafemurano.co.uk
  Charing Cross
- Menu £17 (weekdays) - Carte £19/38
  Closed Sunday dinner

CINNAMON BAZAAR

Indian • *Exotic décor*

MAP: 3-J3

Vivek Singh's latest venture provides relaxed, all-day contemporary Indian dining in the heart of Covent Garden, with a bright, colourful interior evoking a marketplace; all orange silk drapes, hanging planters and vibrantly coloured walls. Appealing, inventive menus are influenced by the trade routes of the subcontinent, with twists that encompass Afghanistan, the Punjab and even the Middle East. There's all manner of snacks – perfect with one of their quirky cocktails – as well as an impressive range of chaats, while the 'Bazaar Plates' are ideal for sharing and come in mouthwatering combinations. Sides are obligatory, the set menus offer excellent value for money and dishes are original, well-executed and very tasty.

28 Maiden Ln ✉ WC2E 7JS
020 7395 1400 – **www**.cinnamon-bazaar.com
Leicester Square

Menu £16/24 - Carte £20/31

CLOS MAGGIORE

French • *Classic décor*

MAP: 3-J3

Any West End restaurateurs still half-hearted about pre and post theatre dining should come to Clos Maggiore to see how it can be done: the menu represents excellent value, the kitchen is well-organised and the staff get on with the serving, which means the theatregoer doesn't have to keep checking the time. Clos Maggiore is also one of the most romantic restaurants around – just be sure to ask for the table in the enchanting conservatory at the back, with its retractable roof. The chef is from Provence and you can almost smell the lavender when reading his menu. The French dishes are sophisticated in their make-up while the ingredients come mostly from the British Isles. The wine list has great depth and reflects the owner's passion.

33 King St ✉ WC2E 8JD
020 7379 9696 – **www**.closmaggiore.com
Leicester Square

Menu £28 (weekday lunch) - Carte £39/81
Closed 24-25 December

DELAUNAY

Modern cuisine • Elegant

MAP: 3-J3

Just like The Wolseley, its hugely successful older sibling, The Delaunay was inspired by the grand cafés of Europe and boasts a similar celebrity clientele, yet this is more than a mere replica. It may have opened in 2011, but the 150-seater dining room manages to evoke the 1920s with all its wood panelling, brass and leather. The menu is also more mittel-European, with great schnitzels and wieners featuring prominently. Daily specials could include daube of beef or fish stew, or you could just come for some eggs or a salad – it's that sort of place. There's a nostalgic element too; you'll find Black Forest gateau, banana split, and even a cover charge. The staff are engaging and swift but never make you feel rushed.

55 Aldwych WC2B 4BB
020 7499 8558 — **www**.thedelaunay.com
Temple

Carte £27/70
Closed 25 December - booking essential

DISHOOM

Indian • Trendy

MAP: 3-I3

Dishoom is a facsimile of the sort of café that populated Bombay in the early 20th century. They were opened by Persian immigrants and served snacks and specialities that merged the two countries, along with other dishes displaying some colonial influences; and, because they were classless and casteless, they appealed to everyone. That same inclusiveness is evident here in Covent Garden: the place is full of everyone from couples to business-types enjoying a table of shared dishes. It's all about ordering as little or as much as you want, whether that's a full breakfast; some baked roti rolls with chai; vada pav – Bombay's version of the chip butty; a curry; or meats cooked on the grill in the open kitchen.

12 Upper St Martin's Ln WC2H 9FB
020 7420 9320 — **www**.dishoom.com
Leicester Square

Carte £12/26
Closed 24 December dinner, 25-26 December and 1-2 January - booking advisable

Ⓝ ENEKO AT ONE ALDWYCH ℩O

Basque • Design

XX ♿ A/C 🎭 **MAP:** 3-J3

Bringing a modern taste of the Basque country to the heart of London is the eponymous Eneko Atxa, known for restaurant Azurmendi near Bilbao. It is set in the One Aldwych Hotel, occupying what was once the headquarters of the Morning Post, and its stylish, ultra-modern design includes a gleaming copper-edged staircase, curved semi-private booths and a bar which seems to float above the restaurant like a spaceship. Menus offer a refined reinterpretation of classic Basque dishes from the sea (Itsasotik), land (Lurretik) and garden (Hortutik). The concise, all-Spanish wine list features a number from Eneko's own vineyards, and service hits the right note between friendliness and formality. Come at the weekend for a brunch of Basque street food.

- One Aldwych Hotel, 1 Aldwych ✉ WC2B 4BZ
  ✆ 020 7300 0300 — **www**.eneko.london
  ⊖ Temple
- Menu £25 (lunch and early dinner) - Carte £30/39
  Closed 2 weeks January

FRENCHIE ℩O

Modern cuisine • Bistro

X ♿ A/C 🍸 **MAP:** 3-J3

The eponymous Frenchie is chef-owner Greg Marchand – the nickname was given to him by Jamie Oliver when he was head chef at Fifteen and is also the name of his original restaurant in Paris' 2nd arrondissement. This time round, the modern-day bistro is in the heart of Covent Garden and split over two levels: the basement, home to the open kitchen, is the more intimate space, but the ground floor, which is dominated by a handsome white marble bar counter, is the better place to sit. Marchand's cooking is informed by his extensive travels, so expect to see ingredients like yuzu, Madras spices and preserved lemons featuring alongside Yorkshire rhubarb and Cornish clotted cream in the adventurous, ambitious dishes.

- 16 Henrietta St ✉ WC2E 8QH
  ✆ 020 7836 4422 — **www**.frenchiecoventgarden.com
  ⊖ Covent Garden
- Menu £26 (weekday lunch) - Carte £43/58
  Closed 25-26 December and 1 January - booking advisable

HAWKSMOOR

Meats and grills • Rustic

MAP: 3-I3

Impressive renovation work from those clever Hawksmoor people turned this former brewery cellar into a very atmospheric restaurant whose primary function is the serving and eating of red meat - a suitably apt activity as one of the brewery's 18C owners used to host a steak club. You'll get a friendly greeting at the bottom of the stairs and can either eat in the bar or in the large, bustling dining room with its ersatz-industrial look. Steaks from Longhorn cattle lovingly reared in North Yorkshire and dry-aged for at least 35 days are the stars of the show. A blackboard shows availability and meat is priced per 100g - but beware, as side orders and competitive over-ordering on the size of the cut can push up the final bill.

- 11 Langley St ✉ WC2H 9JG
  020 7420 9390 — **www**.thehawksmoor.com
  Covent Garden
- Menu £25 (weekdays) - Carte £25/75
  Closed 24-26 December

N HENRIETTA

Modern cuisine • Fashionable

MAP: 3-J3

Here at the boutique Henrietta hotel - two 17C townhouses in the heart of Covent Garden - is a hotel restaurant worth spending your money in. Ollie Dabbous is the consultant and he's installed his former head chef to lead the team, so it's no surprise that the cooking shows all the Dabbous hallmarks: colourful, well-balanced dishes with an appealing modern style and well-defined yet delicate flavours. The ingredient-led menu follows the seasons: grilled flatbreads from the Josper oven are a good place to start, and the freshly-baked madeleines an excellent way to finish. With a cocktail bar at one end and an open kitchen at the other, the informal, lounge-style room can feel a little like a thoroughfare, so ask to sit on the mezzanine instead.

- Henrietta Hotel, 14-15 Henrietta St ✉ WC2E 8QH
  020 3794 5314 — **www**.henriettahotel.com
  Covent Garden
- Carte £29/47
  Booking advisable

THE IVY

Traditional British • Fashionable

MAP: 3-I3

The Ivy once had a virtual monopoly as a celebrity hangout but competition is a lot fiercer these days. Add in the fact that the owners had started rolling out Ivy Grills and it was clear something needed to be done with 'head office'. So it closed, everything from its signs to its front doors was sold off as a clever PR stunt, and it re-emerged with a new look in time for its centenary in 2017. The biggest difference is that there's now an oval bar in the centre of the room – and gone are the 'Siberia' tables. The menu has also evolved: you can still find the old classics, but now they're accompanied by a few more international choices. The service, from a bevy of personable staff, is as on-the-button as ever.

- 9 West St ✉ WC2H 9NE
  020 7836 4751 — **www**.the-ivy.co.uk
  Leicester Square
- Menu £24 (weekday lunch) - Carte £31/70
  Closed 25 December

IVY MARKET GRILL

Traditional British • Design

MAP: 3-J3

Its heyday may have been in the 1990s but, for us mere mortals, The Ivy is still one of the hardest restaurants at which to get a table. Thanks to the largesse or, more likely, the business acumen of Caprice Holdings, far more people can now share in that Ivy experience by eating here at Ivy Market Grill. The look is smart brasserie deluxe, with a few decorative touches that pay homage to the original. The menu keeps things mostly British with a roll-call of classics; there's also a large Grill section. Breakfast and a roaring trade in afternoon tea keep it busy all day - and as well as a decently priced pre-theatre menu, they also offer shepherd's pie and champagne when the show finishes. There's another even busier branch in Chelsea.

- 1 Henrietta St ✉ WC2E 8PS
  020 3301 0200 — **www**.theivymarketgrill.com
  Covent Garden
- Menu £21 (early dinner) - Carte £27/61

J.SHEEKEY

Seafood • *Fashionable*

MAP: 3-13

Named after the restaurant's first chef, who cooked for its then owner Lord Salisbury, J. Sheekey proves that longevity and tradition need not mean old and crusty. It is as fashionable now as it was in 1896 and remains one of the first choices for the theatrical world and those whose business is show. The wood panelling and silver on the tables add to the timeless British feel and service is as charming and efficient as ever. Seafood is handled deftly: the Arbroath smokie and potted shrimps are permanent fixtures and the fish pie and lemon sole are rightly renowned. Avoiding pre and post-theatre times will shorten the odds of your getting a table; ask for 'Dining Room 4' which is the largest of the five rooms.

■ 28-32 St Martin's Ct ✉ WC2N 4AL
☏ 020 7240 2565 — **www**.j-sheekey.co.uk
⊖ Leicester Square

■ Carte £36/58
Closed 25-26 December - booking essential

J.SHEEKEY ATLANTIC BAR

Seafood • *Intimate*

MAP: 3-13

When the opportunity arose a few years back for J. Sheekey to expand next door, the obvious decision would have been to extend the restaurant which has, after all, been working well since 1896. Instead, they decided to create this terrific oyster bar - and for that we should all be grateful. There are four or five tables but you're much better off sitting at the bar as you can chat with the chaps behind it and, if you're on the far side, watch the chefs in action. The menu offers the same high quality seafood as next door but at slightly lower prices; along with favourites like oysters and the fish pie, come dishes designed for sharing such as the fruits de mer. The staff know what they're doing, the atmosphere is lively and you're in for a fun night.

■ 33-34 St Martin's Ct. ✉ WC2 4AL
☏ 020 7240 2565 — **www**.j-sheekey.co.uk
⊖ Leicester Square

■ Carte £25/38
Closed 25-26 December - booking advisable

LIMA FLORAL

Peruvian • Fashionable

MAP: 3-I3

When your second branch is located this close to the original it needs to do something a little different - and that's what Lima Floral does. For a start, it has a terrific basement Pisco Bar which serves piqueos, or Peruvian tapas, along with an impressive array of cocktails and infusions to get your heart pumping. The colourful restaurant is a little smaller than the original but manages to feel light and airy at lunch and cosy and intimate at dinner. The cooking is also a little different - dishes are a little less refined but more substantial in size, bringing in more regional Peruvian flavours and vibrancy. Don't ignore the side dishes - the cusco corn cake is worth the price of admission alone - or the desserts, which are rich and comforting.

- 14 Garrick St ✉ WC2E 9BJ
  020 7240 5778 — **www**.limalondongroup.com/floral
  Leicester Square
- Menu £20 (early dinner) - Carte £33/52
  Closed 25-27 December, 1-2 January and bank holiday Mondays

OPERA TAVERN

Mediterranean cuisine • Tapas bar

MAP: 3-J3

Another in the Salt Yard stable, this former pub is located in the heart of theatreland, with a lively ground floor perfect for walk-ins; if you're booking ahead, you may prefer the quieter first floor dining room instead. The Spanish-Italian menus follow the seasons, with a selection of small plates designed for sharing headed Fish, Meat and Vegetables. Three per person is about right (plus a dessert), and dishes have an appealing Mediterranean style and plenty of flavour, whether you go for the chargrilled octopus, the Venetian-style mackerel or the roast pigeon with morcilla. The wine list offers a good selection of rarely seen Italian and Spanish wines, arranged by style - look out for the fine wines at the back of the list.

- 23 Catherine St. ✉ WC2B 5JS
  020 7836 3680 — **www**.operatavern.co.uk
  Covent Garden
- Menu £21 (lunch) - Carte £14/29
  Closed 25 December and 1 January

POLPO COVENT GARDEN 𝇗

Italian • Simple

MAP: 3-J3

After sewing up Soho with their first three restaurants, this clever little group then turned its attention to neighbouring Covent Garden to open this Venetian bacaro. Behind the delicately embroidered linen screens is another shrewdly designed spot, with a tin ceiling imported from New York and church pews contrasting with the ersatz-industrial look. It covers two floors – the ground floor is best. Over-ordering is easy, as the small plates are surprisingly filling, with delights such as the wonderfully fresh flavours of white anchovy pizzette vying with fennel and almond salad; fritto misto competing with spaghettini and meatballs. A no-bookings policy after 5.30pm means that there will be queues but turnover is naturally quick.

- 6 Maiden Ln. ✉ WC2E 7NA
  020 7836 8448 — **www**.polpo.co.uk
  Leicester Square
- Carte £13/21
  Closed 25-26 December - (bookings not accepted at dinner)

ROKA

Japanese • Fashionable

MAP: 3-J3

The 10th anniversary of the original Roka in Charlotte Street was marked with the opening of this fourth branch, the largest in the group, which sits in the strip of town that separates the West End from The City. The smart interior features a sleek black marble counter running around the robata grill, stained grey timbers on the walls and soft leather seating. All the signature dishes are here, along with a few that are unique to this branch, such as the langoustine and cod cheek skewers, the Wagyu beef tartare and the Hokkaido-style cheesecake. Service is unfailingly attentive – to such a degree that you may have to ask them to slow down the delivery of dishes. Consider the better value tasting menu as it gives you a good all-round experience.

- 71 Aldwych ✉ WC2B 4HN
  020 7294 7636 — **www**.rokarestaurant.com
  Temple
- Menu £31 (weekday lunch) - Carte £32/85
  Closed 25 December

RULES

Traditional British • Traditional décor

MAP: 3-J3

Some restaurants don't even last 1,798 days but Rules opened in 1798, at a time when the French were still revolting, and it has been a bastion of Britishness ever since. Virtually every inch of wall is covered with a cartoon or painting and everyone from Charles Dickens to Buster Keaton has passed through its doors. The first floor is now a bar; time it right and you'll spot some modern-day theatrical luminaries who use it as a Green Room. The hardest decision is whether to choose the game, which comes from their own estate in the Pennines, or one of their celebrated homemade pies. Be sure to leave room for their proper puddings, which come with lashings of custard – no wonder John Bull was such a stout fellow. It makes you proud.

- 35 Maiden Ln ✉ WC2E 7LB
  ✆ 020 7836 5314 — **www**.rules.co.uk
  ⊖ Leicester Square
- Carte £36/64
  Closed 25-26 December – booking essential

SPRING

Italian • Fashionable

MAP: 3-J3

Spring occupies the 'new wing' of Somerset House which for many years was inhabited by the Inland Revenue – it's hard to believe that this is where taxes were once calculated. The bright room, with its Doric columns, ornate cornicing and arched windows looking towards Waterloo Bridge, comes with an appealingly feminine feel which is appropriate as the whole operation is under the aegis of Australian-born chef Skye Gyngell, previously of Petersham Nurseries. Her cooking is Italian-influenced and led by the ingredients, albeit largely luxury ingredients that come at a price; her menu is written daily and the dishes are without fuss and adornment, which allows the flavours to be the focus.

- New Wing, Somerset House, Strand (Entrance on Lancaster Pl) ✉ WC2R 1LA
  ✆ 020 3011 0115 — **www**.springrestaurant.co.uk
  ⊖ Temple
- Menu £32 (lunch) – Carte £39/67
  Closed Sunday – booking advisable

TERROIRS

Mediterranean cuisine • Wine bar

MAP: 3-J3

Eat in the lively ground floor bistro/wine bar or head down to the more intimate cellar with its bare brick walls and counter; it's the same menu throughout although they also have a blackboard menu downstairs offering sharing dishes like rib of beef for two. Tables down here are a little bigger which makes sharing easier and, despite being two floors down, it is more atmospheric. The flavoursome and satisfying French cooking has added Italian and Spanish influences and the wine list is thoughtfully compiled, varied and well-priced, with many organic and biodynamic choices from artisan producers. Service remains a mixed bag and can be of the headless chicken variety, but the slightly chaotic feel adds to the charm.

- 5 William IV St ✉ WC2N 4DW
  020 7036 0660 — **www**.terroirswinebar.com
  Charing Cross
- Carte £26/72
  Closed 25-26 December, 1 January, Sunday and bank holidays

TREDWELL'S

Modern British • Brasserie

MAP: 3-I3

Considering its central location, it's a surprise that Seven Dials hasn't been awash with good restaurants for years - but at least it has Tredwell's, a modern brasserie courtesy of Marcus Wareing. It's named after the butler in Agatha Christie's 'The Seven Dials Mystery' and one could argue that the dark, sleek look of the place does evoke the art deco period during which the book was written. Cooking is best described as modern English, although the robata grill gets a good workout with steaks from the Lake District and Wales and there is an occasional Mediterranean note too. As you would expect from this stable, dishes show a degree of refinement and a commendable amount of thought has gone into addressing allergen issues.

- 4a Upper St Martin's Ln ✉ WC2H 9EF
  020 3764 0840 — **www**.tredwells.com
  Leicester Square
- Menu £30 (lunch and early dinner) - Carte £27/56
  Closed 24-26 December and 1 January

BELGRAVIA · VICTORIA

The well-worn cliché 'an area of contrasts' certainly applies to these ill-matched neighbours. To the west, Belgravia equates to fashionable status and elegant, residential calm; to the east, Victoria is a chaotic jumble of backpackers, milling commuters and cheap-and-not-always-so-cheerful hotels. At first sight, you might think there's little to no common ground, but the umbilical cord that unites them is, strange to say, diplomacy and politics. Belgravia's embassies are dotted all around the environs of **Belgrave Square,** while at the furthest end of bustling Victoria Street stands **Parliament Square.**

Belgravia – named after 'beautiful grove' in French - was developed during the nineteenth century by Richard Grosvenor, the second Marquess of Westminster, who employed top architect Thomas Cubitt to come up with something rather fetching for the upper echelons of society. The grandeur of the classical designs has survived for the best part of two centuries, evident in the broad streets and elegant squares, where the rich rub shoulders with the uber-rich beneath the stylish balconies of a consulate or outside a high-end antiques emporium. You can still sample an atmosphere of the village it once was, as long as your idea of a village includes exclusive designer boutiques and even more exclusive mews cottages.

By any stretch of the imagination you'd have trouble thinking of **Victoria** as a village. Its local railway station is one of London's major hubs and its Coach station brings in visitors from not only all corners of Britain, but Europe too. Its main 'church', concealed behind office blocks, could hardly be described as humble, either: **Westminster Cathedral** is a grand concoction based on Istanbul's Hagia Sophia, with a view from the top of the bell tower which is breathtaking. From there you can pick out other hidden charms of the area: the dramatic headquarters of Channel 4 TV, the revolving sign famously leading into New Scotland Yard, and the neat little Christchurch Gardens, burial site of Colonel Blood, last man to try and steal the Crown Jewels. Slightly easier for the eye to locate are the grand designs of **Westminster Abbey,** crowning glory and resting place of most of England's kings and queens, and the neo-gothic pile of the **Houses of Parliament.** Victoria may be an eclectic mix of people and architectural styles, but its handy position as a kind of epicentre of the Westminster Village makes it a great place for political chit-chat. And the place to go for that is The Speaker, a pub in Great Peter Street, named after the Commons' centuries-old peacekeeper and 'referee'. It's a backstreet gem, where it's not unknown for a big cheese from the House to be filmed over a pint.

Winston Churchill is someone who would have been quite at home holding forth at The Speaker, and half a mile away in King Charles Street, based within the **Cabinet War Rooms** – the secret underground HQ of the war effort - is the Churchill Museum, stuffed full of all things Churchillian. However, if your passion is more the easel and the brush, then head down to the river where another great institution of the area, **Tate Britain,** gazes out over the Thames. Standing where the grizzly Millbank Penitentiary once festered, it offers, after the National Gallery, the best collection of historical art in London. There's loads of space for the likes of Turner and Constable, while Hogarth, Gainsborough and Blake are well represented, too. Artists from the modern era are also here, with Freud and Hockney on show, and there are regular installations showcasing upwardly mobile British talent. All of which may give you the taste for a trip east along the river to Tate Modern; this can be done every forty minutes courtesy of the Tate to Tate boat service.

I. Dimitrov/age fotostock

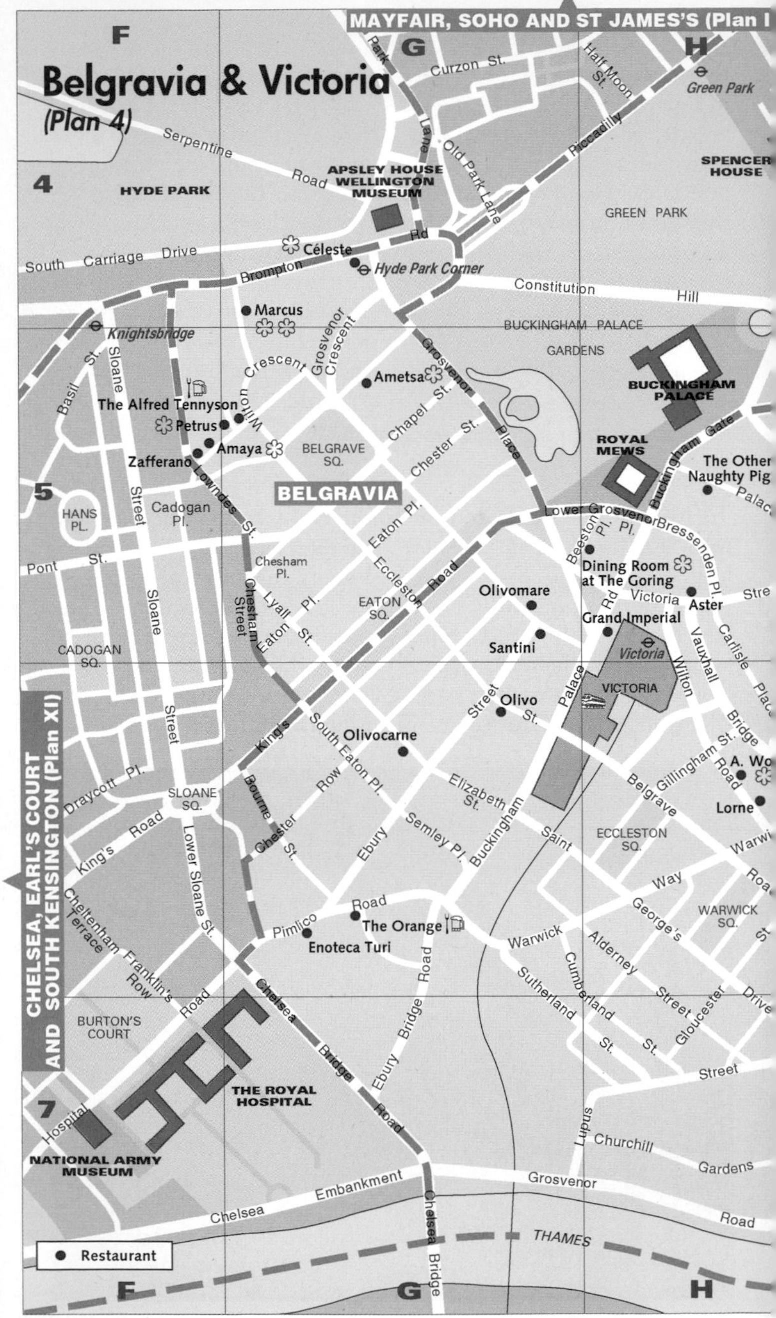

Belgravia & Victoria
(Plan 4)
MAYFAIR, SOHO AND ST JAMES'S (Plan I
CHELSEA, EARL'S COURT AND SOUTH KENSINGTON (Plan XI)
HYDE PARK
APSLEY HOUSE WELLINGTON MUSEUM
GREEN PARK
SPENCER HOUSE
Green Park
Hyde Park Corner
Knightsbridge
Victoria
BUCKINGHAM PALACE GARDENS
BUCKINGHAM PALACE
ROYAL MEWS
BELGRAVIA
BELGRAVE SQ.
EATON SQ.
CADOGAN SQ.
HANS PL.
SLOANE SQ.
ECCLESTON SQ.
WARWICK SQ.
VICTORIA
BURTON'S COURT
THE ROYAL HOSPITAL
NATIONAL ARMY MUSEUM
THAMES
Céleste
Marcus
Ametsa
The Alfred Tennyson
Petrus
Amaya
Zafferano
The Other Naughty Pig
Dining Room at The Goring
Aster
Olivomare
Grand Imperial
Santini
Olivo
Olivocarne
A. Wo
Lorne
The Orange
Enoteca Turi
Restaurant

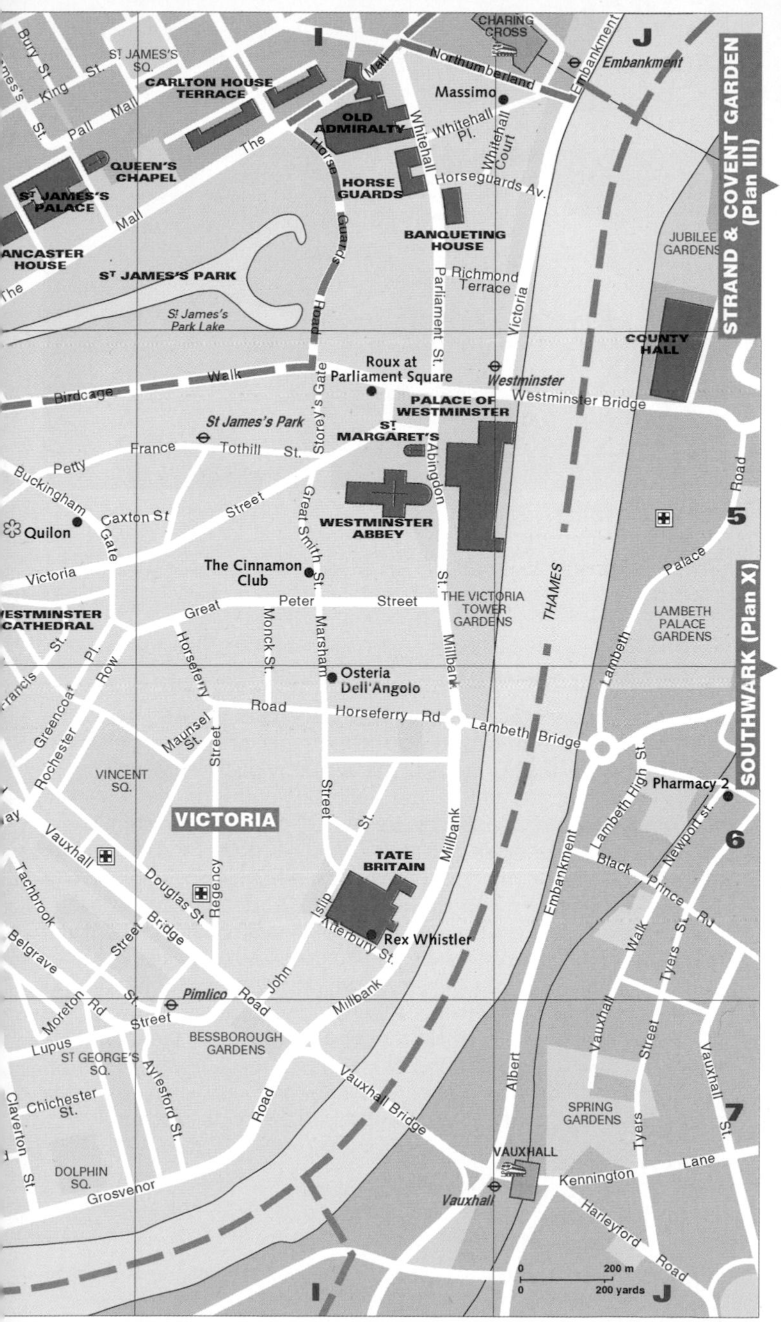

CHARING CROSS
Embankment
Northumberland
Massimo
ST JAMES'S SQ.
CARLTON HOUSE TERRACE
OLD ADMIRALTY
Whitehall
Whitehall Pl.
Whitehall Court
QUEEN'S CHAPEL
HORSE GUARDS
Horseguards Av.
ST JAMES'S PALACE
BANQUETING HOUSE
LANCASTER HOUSE
ST JAMES'S PARK
St James's Park Lake
Richmond Terrace
Parliament St.
Victoria
JUBILEE GARDENS
STRAND & COVENT GARDEN (Plan III)
COUNTY HALL
Roux at Parliament Square
Westminster
Westminster Bridge
Birdcage Walk
PALACE OF WESTMINSTER
St James's Park
ST MARGARET'S
Tothill St.
Storey's Gate
Abingdon
WESTMINSTER ABBEY
Quilon
Caxton St
The Cinnamon Club
Great Smith St.
Great Peter Street
THE VICTORIA TOWER GARDENS
THAMES
LAMBETH PALACE GARDENS
SOUTHWARK (Plan X)
WESTMINSTER CATHEDRAL
Osteria Dell'Angolo
Horseferry Road
Lambeth Bridge
VINCENT SQ.
Pharmacy 2
VICTORIA
TATE BRITAIN
Rex Whistler
Pimlico
BESSBOROUGH GARDENS
ST GEORGE'S SQ.
Vauxhall Bridge
SPRING GARDENS
VAUXHALL
Kennington Lane
Harleyford Road
DOLPHIN SQ.
Grosvenor Road
200 m
200 yards

A. WONG ✿

Chinese • Neighbourhood

MAP: 4-H6

Michelin

FIRST COURSE: Hong Kong egg waffle with marinated scallop salad. • Rabbit and carrot puff.

MAIN COURSE: 'Gold Fish' dumpling with foie gras, dried pork and chive flower oil. • Sweet & sour corn-fed chicken with smoked meat and marinated pineapple.

DESSERT: Poached meringue with lychee granité, mango purée, orange sorbet and lotus root. • Coconut water ice with blackberries.

Before taking over the family business, the talented Andrew Wong spent many months travelling through the provinces of China, garnering ideas for his menus. This was obviously time well spent as the restaurant has a huge local following and is regularly packed with people wanting to taste his fresh, well-balanced and stimulating cooking. His skill lies in taking classic Cantonese dishes and reinventing them using creative, modern techniques; retaining the essence of a dish whilst adding an impressive lightness and intensity of flavour. Lunchtime dim sum is very popular, but the main menu is where you really see the chef's skill, in dishes like 'Moo shu' pancake wraps or crispy chilli, caramelised beef and pickled carrots, as well as fun choices like the disconcertingly lifelike 'gold fish' dumplings. If you want the full-on experience then opt for the modern 10 course Taste of China menu; a 3 hour journey around China, with a focus on the 14 border regions. The atmosphere's buzzing and the service is keen, as are the prices. Sit at the counter if you want to see the chefs in action.

■ 70 Wilton Rd ✉ SW1V 1DE
☏ 020 7828 8931 — **www**.awong.co.uk
⊖ Victoria

■ Carte £18/42
Closed 23 December-4 January, Sunday and lunch Monday – booking essential

THE ALFRED TENNYSON

Modern British • Pub

MAP: 4-G5

What used to be The Pantechnicon is now The Alfred Tennyson; the esteemed Victorian poet who wrote 'The Charge of the Light Brigade' used to live nearby and you feel he would have approved of the parquet floor and leather armchairs that give this cosy pub its clubby feel - although it's a moot point whether he'd enjoy seeing quotations from his work on the backs of the toilet doors! The ground floor is crammed with tables and works on a first-come-first-served basis; upstairs you'll find a more formal, Georgian-style dining room and, above that, there's even a cocktail bar - this is Belgravia after all. Classic dishes have light, modern touches, so expect potted smoked mackerel to come with rhubarb purée, or Scottish scallops with chorizo dressing.

- 10 Motcomb St ✉ SW1X 8LA
  020 7730 6074 — **www**.thealfredtennyson.co.uk
  Knightsbridge.
- Carte £30/43
  Closed 26 December-4 January - booking advisable

ASTER

Modern cuisine • Contemporary décor

MAP: 4-H5

The flagship eatery of the Nova SW1 development, set over the road from Victoria Station, covers all bases with a deli, a café, a bar and a terrace, as well as the restaurant itself; a stylish, airy space with full-length windows situated on the first floor. Finnish chef Helena Puolakka brings a Nordic slant to proceedings with the likes of cinnamon buns and open sandwiches in the deli, and a smörgåsbord and Nordic classics alongside more modern European favourites in the café. Scandinavian ingredients also feature in the restaurant upstairs, but Puolakka's background is in French cuisine and it is this that forms the basis of the modern menu. Dishes are light, refined and full of flavour; try the hot-smoked Arctic char with aubergine and dill.

- 150 Victoria St ✉ SW1E 5LB
  020 3875 5555 — **www**.aster-restaurant.com
  Victoria
- Carte £29/58
  Closed Sunday

AMAYA ꕤ

Indian • Design

XXX A/C MAP: 4-F5

Amaya

FIRST COURSE: Black pepper chicken tikka. • Tandoori wild prawns with tomato and ginger.

MAIN COURSE: Smoked chilli lamb chops. • Wild venison seekh kebab.

DESSERT: Almond and saffron crème brûlée. • Gulab jamun.

A decade and a half on and Amaya is still as bright and lively as ever, thanks to the buzz of excited diners and the theatre of its open kitchen, where shooting flames and enticing aromas from the tawa, tandoor and sigri grills do a fabulous job of whetting the appetite. Amaya loosely translates as 'without boundaries' and this is reflected in the restaurant's open layout as well as its desire to attract all types of diner, from families and friends to businesspeople and couples. It's run with passion and professionalism, both in the kitchen and front of house; this keeps it feeling fresh and current – as does the menu, which evolves with the seasons, enabling the experienced chef to try out original combinations of ingredients alongside permanent fixtures like grilled lamb chops, tandoori-cooked wild prawns and wild venison seekh kebab. Bring an appetite with you and order a couple of small plates from the first two sections of the menu, then a curry or a biryani and some naan; and don't ignore the excellent vegetable dishes like spinach and fig tikka or char-grilled aubergine.

■ Halkin Arcade, 19 Motcomb St ✉ SW1X 8JT
✆ 020 7823 1166 — **www**.amaya.biz
⊖ Knightsbridge

■ Menu £26 (weekday lunch) - Carte £34/78

AMETSA ✿

Creative • Elegant

XXX A/C MAP: 4-G5

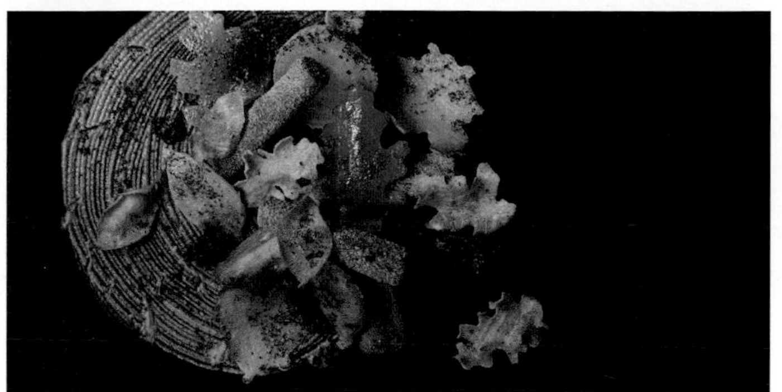

Ametsa

FIRST COURSE: Scallops with hemp seeds. • Morels, rice and chilli.

MAIN COURSE: Sea bass 'Tamal'. • Venison with longan.

DESSERT: Chocolate emeralds and strata. • Mango and orange flan.

Ametsa has matured considerably since opening on the ground floor of the Halkin hotel in 2013. Service not only comes with warmth and personality but the staff also display a willingness to engage with their customers, which is especially important considering the menu descriptions vary from the economical to the nebulous. The restaurant's confidence is reflected in the cooking, with the kitchen secure in its own identity. Juan Mari and Elena Arzak are behind the restaurant and whilst they come over regularly to advise and assist, they have always been keen for Ametsa to find its own feet and not be a facsimile or a clone of their iconic San Sebastián restaurant. Apart from items like the Ibérico hams, most of the ingredients used are sourced from within the British Isles but the flavours, combinations and colours are typically Basque. There is a wonderful vitality to the cooking and, whilst the techniques are clever and the presentation striking, the dishes are very easy to eat and always manage to satisfy.

- COMO The Halkin Hotel, 5 Halkin St ✉ SW1X 7DJ
  ✆ 020 7333 1234 — **www**.comohotels.com/thehalkin
  ⊖ Hyde Park Corner
- Menu £29/110 - Carte £60/85
  Closed 24-26 December, lunch 31 December, Sunday and lunch Monday

CÉLESTE ✿

Creative French • Elegant

XXXX ♿ A/C 🍽V 🚗 **MAP:** 4-G4

Michelin

FIRST COURSE: Pressed foie gras terrine, corn-fed chicken, mustard vinaigrette and brioche. • Blue lobster with smashed avocado and spicy tomato juice.

MAIN COURSE: Stone bass with globe artichoke, mussels and seaweed butter. • Roast breast of quail with confit legs, pea purée and pommes soufflés.

DESSERT: Fudge ice cream with roast almonds, caramel and fudge sauce. • Strawberry 'Charlotte'.

While most restaurants have been paring back their interior decoration, the multi-million pound refurbishment of the Lanesborough Hotel gave its light-filled, glass-roofed restaurant a luxurious Regency look, with mirrors, portraits, vast chandeliers, Wedgwood blue friezes and fluted columns. Well-spaced tables are dressed with thick linen; deep armchairs cosset diners; and an army of staff deliver formal, attentive service of the kind you'd expect in a hotel of this stature. Chef Florian Favario is a protégé of Eric Fréchon - head chef of Le Bristol in Paris - who oversees the restaurant. His classic French cuisine is delivered in an original, modern style and the richness of dishes like venison smoked on juniper wood with a civet sauce or chocolate soufflé with pistachio ice cream reflect the opulence of the décor. Ingredients are top-class, cooking well-executed and flavours nicely pronounced. The à la carte and tasting menus offer plenty of choice, and vegetarians are well catered for too.

■ The Lanesborough Hotel, Hyde Park Corner ✉ SW1X 7TA
✆ 020 7259 5599 — **www**.lanesborough.com
⊖ Hyde Park Corner

■ Menu £38 (lunch) - Carte £77/107

THE CINNAMON CLUB

Indian • Historic

MAP: 4-I5

Locals and tourists, business people and politicians, The Cinnamon Club attracts them all, which explains why you'll be greeted by that appealing wall of noise. It's set within the listed former Westminster library and it certainly makes good use of its surroundings. You'll be faced with quite a few menus, so grab the drinks one first as you'll need time to decide what to eat. The style here is quite different from most Indian restaurants, with the somewhat elaborately constructed dishes arriving fully garnished and a separate section of the menu dedicated to sharing plates; maybe Old Delhi style butter chicken on the bone. Spicing is quite subtle – in fact, any watering of eyes is more likely to be caused by some of the prices.

- 30-32 Great Smith St ✉ SW1P 3BU
  020 7222 2555 — **www**.cinnamonclub.com
  St James's Park
- Menu £26 (weekday lunch) - Carte £35/69
  Closed 2 April, 27 August and bank holidays

ENOTECA TURI

Italian • Neighbourhood

MAP: 4-G6

In 2016 Putney's loss was Pimlico's gain when, after 25 years, Giuseppe and Pamela Turi were forced to find a new home for their Italian restaurant. They took over the site previously home to Tinello, also an Italian restaurant, made it a little lighter and wisely brought their manager Cesare with them – he does an admirable job of looking after all diners, both old and new. The chef introduced a broader range of influences – with each dish signalling the particular region from which it originates – but what didn't change was the classic style of preparation in accord with the principles of the Italian kitchen. The other thing that everyone should be delighted they brought with them is their superb wine list.

- 87 Pimlico Rd ✉ SW1W 8PU
  020 7730 3663 — **www**.enotecaturi.com
  Sloane Square
- Menu £25 (lunch) - Carte £31/61
  Closed 25-26 December, 1 January, Sunday and bank holiday lunch

DINING ROOM AT THE GORING ✿

Traditional British • Elegant

XXX 🌳 A/C ✿ **MAP:** 4-H5

The Goring

FIRST COURSE: Cured sea bream with pickled lemon, iced celery and cucumber. • Watercress & horseradish soup with Cornish mackerel and cured trout roe.

MAIN COURSE: Roast squab with Tokyo turnip, crispy leg parcel and cider vinegar sauce. • Cotswold White chicken with calçot onions, artichoke, ratte potatoes and riesling sabayon.

DESSERT: Gianduja chocolate with Williams pear, caramelised hazelnut and sweet cream cheese. • Vanilla rice pudding with blood oranges and caramelised puff pastry.

If you've ever wondered what the difference is between a restaurant and a dining room then book a table here. The Goring hotel is a model of British style and understatement and its ground floor dining room the epitome of grace and decorum. Designed by Viscount Linley, it appeals to those who 'like things done properly' and is one of the few places in London for which everyone appears to dress up – but don't come thinking it's going to be stuffy in any way. It is supremely well run; even those who decry tradition will be charmed by the well-choreographed service team and the earnestness with which they undertake their duties. Chef Shay Cooper's menu shows respect for the hotel's reputation for classic British food while also acknowledging that tastes and techniques move on, so there are more modern, lighter options available alongside recognisable old favourites. All the dishes are prepared with equal care and equally superb ingredients, and the skilful kitchen displays an impressive understanding of balance, flavour and texture.

- Goring Hotel, 15 Beeston Pl ✉ SW1W 0JW
  ✆ 020 7396 9000 — **www**.thegoring.com
  ⊖ Victoria
- Menu £35/60
  Closed Saturday lunch

GRAND IMPERIAL

Chinese • Elegant

MAP: 4-H5

Grand it most certainly is, as this elegant Chinese restaurant is to be found in the impressive surroundings of The Grosvenor Hotel's former ballroom. In fact, in between the pillars and the ornate ceiling, the only indication that this is a Chinese restaurant is the calligraphy on the walls. The Grand Imperial is a collaboration between the hotel owners and a Malaysian restaurant company and specialises in Cantonese cuisine, particularly the version found in Hong Kong. Techniques of steaming and frying are used to great effect with such signature dishes as diced beef steak with black pepper sauce and steamed lobster with Chinese wine and egg white. There is no fusion food here; just authentic flavours and quality ingredients.

- Grosvenor Hotel, 101 Buckingham Palace Rd ✉ SW1W OSJ
  020 7821 8898 — **www**.grandimperiallondon.com
  Victoria
- Menu £16/26 - Carte £24/78
  Closed 25-26 December

LORNE

Modern cuisine • Simple

MAP: 4-H6

Small, simply furnished and fresh, with plenty of plants and natural light, Lorne's look is perfectly suited to the fiercely seasonal style of cooking it champions. With the likes of Brawn, Chez Bruce and The Square under his belt, Peter Hall is a mature and experienced chef who understands that less is more, and the modern menu is an enticing list of unfussy, well-balanced British and European dishes which rely on a handful of accurately cooked, high quality ingredients. Co-Partner Katie Exton is equally experienced and uses her knowledge to great effect; not only in overseeing Lorne's friendly young team but also in delivering an interesting wine list, with a diverse, good value range of bottles from some excellent producers.

- 76 Wilton Rd ✉ SW1V 1DE
  020 3327 0210 — **www**.lornerestaurant.co.uk
  Victoria
- Menu £22 (lunch) - Carte £35/43
  Closed 1 week Christmas, Sunday, Monday lunch and bank holiday Mondays - booking essential

MARCUS ✿✿

Modern cuisine • Elegant

XXXX A/C MAP: 4-G4

Marcus

FIRST COURSE: Tropea onion with truffle, Old Winchester cheese and wild garlic. • Portland crab with cucumber, potato, caviar and finger lime.

MAIN COURSE: Goosnargh duck with chickweed, cauliflower and cumin. • Cornish brill with pickled egg, clams and rock samphire.

DESSERT: Yorkshire rhubarb, vanilla, mascarpone and pistachio. • Toffee, peanut and milk chocolate nougat.

Anticipation builds as you approach the glamorous Berkeley Hotel, the setting of Marcus Wareing's eponymous flagship. Once inside those expectations are met, if not surpassed, as the restaurant is elegant, stylish and eminently comfortable, with a relaxed feel and professional yet engaging staff – who, refreshingly, seem to be hired as much for their personality as their experience and know-how. Without any fanfare, Wareing has handed over the day-to-day running of the restaurant to two long-serving protégés: a husband and wife team who share his philosophy and are now joint chef-patrons. There remains a Britishness to the menu and dishes like 'salmon, langoustine, buttermilk and quince' and 'Herdwick lamb, onion and anchovy' are sophisticated and interesting yet come with a refreshing lack of complication; relying on excellent quality ingredients and accurate techniques to deliver intense, well-defined flavours. While the 5 or 8 course tasting menu showcases the kitchen's talents, the à la carte menu comes with in-built flexibility allowing you to choose 2, 3 or 4 courses.

- Berkeley Hotel, Wilton Pl ✉ SW1X 7RL
  ☏ 020 7235 1200 — **www**.marcusrestaurant.com
  ⊖ Knightsbridge
- Menu £55/120
  Closed Sunday

MASSIMO

Italian • Elegant

MAP: 4-J4

Few dining rooms are as impressive as this opulent, David Collins designed restaurant in the Corinthia Hotel; a huge space fittingly dominated by vast, striped Corinthian columns, with plenty of marble to augment the feeling of luxury and leather booths to add warmth and comfort to proceedings. The all-Italian kitchen team taking up the challenge provided by these surroundings bring their own regional influences to the seasonal menu and dishes are rustic, authentic and full of flavour. There's a wonderful selection of pasta – try the linguine with clams – as well as plenty of dishes to share; perhaps a whole sea bass or a roasted lobster. The three course Menu Di Stagione, which comes with a glass of fizz, is a great value option.

Corinthia Hotel, 10 Northumberland Ave. WC2N 5AE
020 7321 3156 — **www**.corinthia.com/london
Embankment

Menu £30 (dinner) - Carte £37/71
Closed Sunday

OLIVO

Italian • Neighbourhood

MAP: 4-G6

The first of Mauro Sanna's 'Olivo' restaurants – sister to Olivocarne and Olivomare – is this long-standing neighbourhood Italian: popular, pleasant and relaxed, with modern décor, rough wooden floorboards and intimate lighting. Sit in the brighter front room with its street view to enjoy authentic, highly capable and reassuringly reliable cooking. The menu showcases the robust flavours of Sardinia and changes fortnightly, although some dishes, such as the spaghetti bottarga and linguine with crab, remain permanent features. There are normally a few daily specials – designed with the regulars in mind – and dishes are clearly prepared with care. Desserts continue the regional theme; try the sebada, a traditional Sardinian cheese fritter.

21 Eccleston St SW1W 9LX
020 7730 2505 — **www**.olivorestaurants.com
Victoria

Menu £27 (weekday lunch) - Carte £38/50
Closed lunch Saturday-Sunday and bank holidays – booking essential

OLIVOCARNE

Italian • Fashionable

MAP: 4-G6

Mauro Sanna seems to have this part of town sewn up - and, as suggested by its name, here the focus is on meat dishes. This place is smarter, chicer and larger than his others; head up the steps to the brighter section which has a striking mural themed around Sardinian folklore. Regulars at his other establishments will be familiar with the range of tasty, rustic dishes, but here meat is the principle ingredient, from suckling pig to oxtail, and there's a whole section of the menu dedicated to beef. The dishes are delicious and satisfying; none more so than the roast bone marrow with Mirto salt and crostini. Classic Sardinian pasta dishes like lorighittas with duck sauce are also much in demand. Head upstairs first, for a cocktail in Joe's Bar.

- 61 Elizabeth St ✉ SW1W 9PP
  020 7730 7997 — **www**.olivorestaurants.com
  Sloane Square
- Menu £27 (weekday lunch) - Carte £39/53

OLIVOMARE

Seafood • Design

MAP: 4-G5

Italian seafood, particularly Sardinian seafood, is celebrated here at Olivomare, a bright and lively restaurant whose design owes as much to Barbarella as it does M.C. Escher. Bottarga naturally features and not just with spaghetti - it also comes with Sardinian artichokes and even burrata. The stews are terrific as are the couscous soups; the octopus, whether in a salad, a stew or just roasted, is always worth ordering. For pud the 'gelato allo yoghurt' is good and is just one of the items that can also be bought from their well-stocked deli next door. The wine list is a little limited by the glass but otherwise this is a very warmly run and understandably popular local, where freshness and simplicity combine to great effect.

- 10 Lower Belgrave St ✉ SW1W 0LJ
  020 7730 9022 — **www**.olivorestaurants.com
  Victoria
- Carte £36/49
  Closed bank holidays

THE ORANGE

Modern cuisine • Friendly

MAP: 4-G6

The former home of the Orange Brewery is a handsome pub that's as charming as its stucco-fronted façade suggests. The locals will no doubt have filled the bar, where the wood-burning oven is quite a feature, but it's still worth trying your luck to get one of the tables here or in the adjacent room; if you book ahead you'll be upstairs which is just as pleasantly decorated but a little more sedate. There's a clear Mediterranean bias to the menu which also includes plenty of salads along with spelt or wheat-based pizzas with some original toppings; there are also roasts on a Sunday and pies for the traditionalists. Unusually for a London pub, there are bedrooms upstairs: these are stylish and comfortable.

- 37 Pimlico Rd ✉ SW1W 8NE
  020 7881 9844 — **www**.theorange.co.uk
  Sloane Square.
- Carte £31/41

OSTERIA DELL' ANGOLO

Italian • Neighbourhood

XX A/C

MAP: 4-I6

The name may suggest a simple little neighbourhood trattoria but this is, in fact, a rather smart, conscientiously run restaurant offering some authentic, carefully prepared Italian food. As it's opposite the Home Office, lunch is quite a busy time and regulars, who include the odd MP, tend to get the tables on the raised section at the back rather than the less comfortable area by the bar where the Johnny-come-latelys get seated. The kitchen team, visible behind the glass, offer a fairly comprehensive culinary tour of the country's regions and their dishes deliver reassuringly emphatic flavours. There's also a decent selection of wines by the glass for anyone who fears the ignominy of having their expense claims examined.

- 47 Marsham St ✉ SW1P 3DR
  020 3268 1077 — **www**.osteriadellangolo.co.uk
  St James's Park
- Menu £23 (lunch) - Carte £26/47
  Closed 1-4 January, 24-28 December, Easter, Saturday lunch, Sunday and bank holidays - booking essential at lunch

Ⓝ THE OTHER NAUGHTY PIGLET

Modern cuisine • *Simple*

MAP: 4-H5

Pre-theatre dining is an altogether less stressful experience when the dining is actually done in the theatre, so this open-plan restaurant on the first floor of The Other Palace, owned by Andrew Lloyd Webber, fits the bill perfectly. Head up the marble staircase from the foyer and you find yourself on a light, spacious mezzanine with a lived-in look and a long open kitchen; the denim-clad staff are friendly and the atmosphere, relaxed. Small plates for sharing are what's on the menu; these are eclectic in their influences and modern in their interpretation; the results being interesting, original and mighty tasty. Just as intriguing is their list of natural wines, which includes some bottles from Lloyd Webber's private cellar.

- The Other Palace, 12 Palace St ✉ SW1E 5JA
  020 7592 0322 — **www**.theothernaughtypiglet.co.uk
  Victoria
- Carte £25/32
  Closed Christmas, Sunday and lunch Monday - booking essential

REX WHISTLER

Modern cuisine • *Classic décor*

MAP: 4-I6

Tucked away on the lower ground floor of the magnificent Tate Britain art gallery, this hidden gem is well worth seeking out. Its most striking element is Whistler's restored mural, 'The Expedition in Pursuit of Rare Meats', which envelops the room; all the more impressive when you learn that it was finished in 1927, when the artist was 23. As befits a gallery which celebrates the best of British art, the bi-monthly menus pay homage to our indigenous cuisine, with dishes such as grilled pork chop with apple and spinach, or crispy ham hock with caramelised pineapple, quails egg and kale. It is the terrific wine list that really leaves an impression, however: some of the prices are remarkable and the 'half bottle' selection is unrivalled.

- Tate Britain, Millbank ✉ SW1P 4RG
  020 7887 8825 — **www**.tate.org.uk
  Pimlico
- Menu £35
  Closed 24-26 December - (lunch only)

PÉTRUS ✿

French • Elegant

MAP: 4-G5

Michelin

FIRST COURSE: Curried Orkney scallop with egg sabayon, braised kombu and bacon. • Roast veal sweetbreads with polenta and oyster mushroom ragu.

MAIN COURSE: Poulet de Bresse with pancetta, foie gras, morels and leeks. • Fillet of turbot with razor clams, asparagus, peas, seaweed and lemongrass.

DESSERT: 'Black Forest', Kirsch mousse and Morello cherry sorbet. • Coconut parfait with dark chocolate, lime and coconut sorbet.

The experienced kitchen at Gordon Ramsay's sophisticated Belgravia restaurant has a clear passion for classic French cuisine but isn't afraid of adding its own touches of creativity alongside some unexpected flavours, particularly when it comes to desserts. They also know that customers in these parts like having plenty of choice so provide an extensive main menu along with tasting and vegetarian options. For anyone who wants to see how it is all done, there's a Chef's Table downstairs in the kitchen facing the 'pass'. For the rest of us, there's a smart, sophisticated and well-dressed room, at the centre of which is a striking circular wine store. Its contents are highly prized as the wine list is quite staggering and includes, appropriately enough, Château Pétrus going back to 1928. Meanwhile, the service is undertaken by a courteous and highly professional team who make everyone feel at ease as soon as they step through the door.

1 Kinnerton St ✉ SW1X 8EA
✆ 020 7592 1609 — **www.**gordonramsayrestaurants.com/petrus
⊖ Knightsbridge

Menu £38/85
Closed 21-27 December, 1 January and Sunday

QUILON ✿

Indian • Design

XXX A/C ⌂ I♡ **MAP:** 4-H5

Michelin

FIRST COURSE: Chargrilled scallops with pawpaw, poppy seeds and chilli relish. • Mango ginger chicken with ground spices.

MAIN COURSE: Pan-fried duck breast with coconut cream sauce. • Spiced baked black cod.

DESSERT: Hot vermicelli kheer with rose ice cream. • Pistachio cake with black sesame fondant and pistachio ice cream.

Anyone jaded by the generic fare found in many a local Indian restaurant could do with a visit to Quilon – the experience will remind them how fresh, vibrant, colourful and indeed healthy, Indian food can be. This restaurant's great strength is that it focuses largely on just one region of the country, namely the southwest coast. That means lots of fish and a cooking style that eschews oil and butter – a style which, in turn, makes the dishes lighter and easier to eat. That's not to say they don't pack a punch as Chef Sriram Aylur and his team understand how to get the best out of their prime produce and they add their own modern and original touches. They also put equal care into the vegetable dishes: the baby aubergines are excellent and okra, that most maligned of vegetables, is served wonderfully crisp. The set menu, rather than the à la carte, will give you the best and most rounded experience; pescatarians can go for the wholly seafood set menu. The restaurant itself is stylish and comfortable and the service team are bright and enthusiastic.

- St James' Court Hotel, 41 Buckingham Gate ✉ SW1E 6AF
  ✆ 020 7821 1899 — **www**.quilon.co.uk
  ⊖ St James's Park
- Menu £31/60 - Carte £42/57
  Closed 25 December

ROUX AT PARLIAMENT SQUARE 🍴

Modern cuisine • Elegant

XXX ♿ A/C ⌂ **MAP:** 4-I5

The offices of the Royal Institute of Chartered Surveyors play host to this attractive Westminster restaurant. It's really a Compass-run operation, in conjunction with Michel Roux of Le Gavroche fame. However, instead of the classical French cuisine for which M. Roux is known, here the food is more contemporary in style and adopts some modern techniques. Dishes are still carefully crafted but occasionally you can find some interesting combinations of flavours. The decoration is cool and comfortable, with plenty of natural light flooding through the Georgian windows. Service, from a well-trained team, comes with personality and there is a particularly attractive private dining room in the library.

- Royal Institution of Chartered Surveyors, Parliament Sq. ✉ SW1P 3AD
  ✆ 020 7334 3737 — **www**.rouxatparliamentsquare.co.uk
  ⊖ Westminster
- Menu £42/59
  Closed Christmas, Saturday, Sunday and bank holidays - bookings advisable at lunch

SANTINI 🍴

Italian • Fashionable

XXX 🏠 A/C 🎭 **MAP:** 4-G5

This elegant restaurant was set up by Gino Santin in 1984 and quickly established itself as a proper Italian, true to its roots. Over thirty years later, it's still pulling in the crowds, thanks to its tasty, filling food and impeccable service, with loyal regulars welcomed as the old friends that they have become over the years. The extensive menu of classic Italian dishes is broadly Venetian in style, and supplemented with daily specials; cooking is reliable and confident and the homemade pasta, the star of the show. Main courses cover all bases, from lamp chops and fritto misto to an excellent veal cutlet Milanese; desserts might include a traditional zabaione or tiramisu. Come summer, book a table on the charming terrace.

- 29 Ebury St ✉ SW1W 0NZ
  ✆ 020 7730 4094 — **www**.santinirestaurant.com
  ⊖ Victoria
- Carte £33/81
  Closed 25-26 December, 1 January dinner

ZAFFERANO

Italian • Fashionable

MAP: 4-F5

It's hard to believe that Zafferano once felt like an intimate little Italian restaurant - over the years it has steadily been expanded and extended and now it's something of a colossus. Fortunately, it all seems to work, proof being in the high number of impeccably dressed regulars that continue to support it. Large tables are easily absorbed without dominating the space; the atmosphere positively hums along; and an army of staff is on hand to ensure no one has to wait too long for their food. The menu concentrates on recognisable, easy-to-eat classics from all parts of Italy and the portions are quite generous, which is just as well because the prices can be pretty steep - even for Belgravia.

- 15 Lowndes St ✉ SW1X 9EY
  020 7235 5800 — **www**.zafferanorestaurant.com
  Knightsbridge
- Carte £37/84
  Closed 25 December - booking essential

L. Worcester / Getty Images

REGENT'S PARK · MARYLEBONE

The neighbourhood north of chaotic Oxford Street is actually a rather refined place where shoppers like to venture for the smart boutiques, and where idlers like to saunter for the graceful parkland acres full of rose gardens and quiet corners. In fact, Marylebone and Regent's Park go rather well together, a moneyed village with a wonderful park for its back garden.

Marylebone may now exude a fashionable status, but its history tells a very different tale. Thousands used to come here to watch executions at Tyburn gallows, a six hundred year spectacle that stopped in the late eighteenth century. Tyburn stream was covered over, and the area's modern name came into being as a contraction of St Mary by the Bourne, the parish church. Nowadays the people who flock here come to gaze at less ghoulish sights, though some of the inhabitants of the eternally popular Madame Tussauds deserved no better fate than the gallows. South across the busy Marylebone Road, the preponderance of swish restaurants and snazzy specialist shops announces your arrival at **Marylebone High Street.** There are patisseries, chocolatiers, cheese shops and butchers at every turn, nestling alongside smart places to eat and drink. At St Marylebone Church, each Saturday heralds a posh market called Cabbages & Frocks, where artisan food meets designer clothing in a charming garden. Further down, the century old Daunt Books has been described as London's most beautiful bookshop: it has long oak galleries beneath graceful conservatory skylights. Close by, the quaintly winding Marylebone Lane boasts some truly unique shops like tiny emporium The Button Queen, which sells original Art Deco, Victorian and Edwardian buttons. In complete contrast, just down the road from here is the mighty **Wigmore Hall,** an art nouveau gem with great acoustics and an unerringly top-notch classical agenda that can be appreciated at rock-bottom prices. Meanwhile, art lovers can indulge an eclectic fix at the **Wallace Collection** in **Manchester Square,** where paintings by the likes of Titian and Velazquez rub shoulders with Sevres porcelain and grand Louis XIV furniture.

Regent's Park – an idyllic Georgian oasis stretching off into

London's northern suburbs - celebrated its two hundredth birthday in 2011. Before architect John Nash and his sponsor The Prince Regent gave it its much-loved geometric makeover, it had been farming land, and prior to that, one of Henry VIII's hunting grounds. His spirit lives on, in the sense that various activities are catered for, from tennis courts to a running track. And there are animals too, albeit not roaming free, at **London Zoo,** in the park's northerly section. Most people, though, come here to while away an hour or two around the boating lake or amble the Inner Circle which contains **Queen Mary's Gardens** and their enchanting bowers of fragrant roses. Others come for a summer sojourn to the Open Air Theatre where taking in a performance of 'A Midsummer Night's Dream' is very much *de rigueur*. The Regent's Canal provides another fascinating element to the park. You can follow its peaceful waters along a splendid walk from the **Little Venice** houseboats in the west, past the golden dome of the **London Central Mosque,** and on into the north-west confines of Regent's Park as it snakes through London Zoo, before it heads off towards Camden Lock. On the other side of Prince Albert Road, across from the zoo, the scenic glory takes on another dimension with a climb up Primrose Hill. Named after the grassy promontory that sets it apart from its surrounds, to visitors this is a hill with one of the best panoramas in the whole of London; to locals (ie, actors, pop stars, media darlings and the city set) it's an ultra fashionable place to live with pretty Victorian terraces and accordingly sky-high prices. Either way you look at it (or from it), it's a great place to be on a sunny day with the breeze in your hair.

O. Krüger/imageBROKER/age fotostock

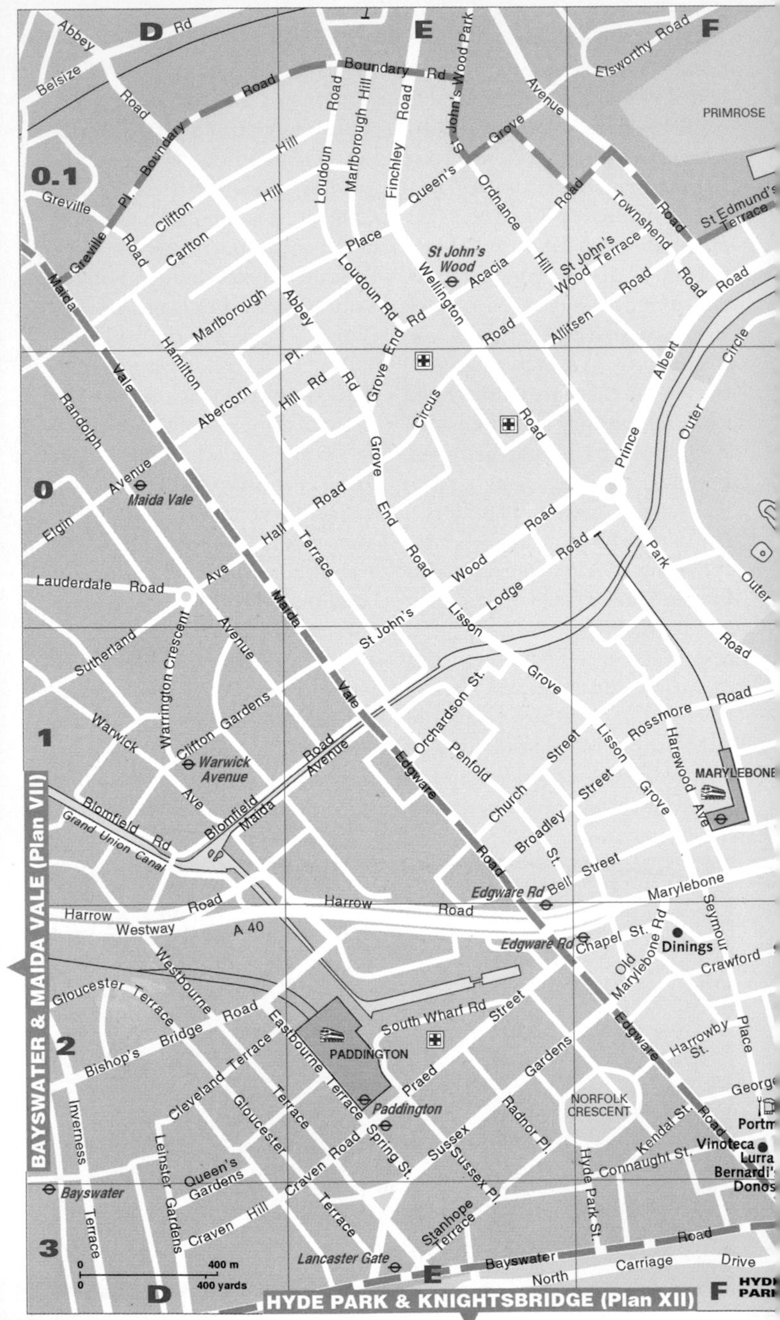
D
E
F
0.1
0
1
2
3
PRIMROSE
St John's Wood
Maida Vale
Warwick Avenue
MARYLEBONE
PADDINGTON
Paddington
Edgware Rd
Dinings
NORFOLK CRESCENT
Vinoteca
Lurra
Bernardi's
Donos
Bayswater
Lancaster Gate
Grand Union Canal
BAYSWATER & MAIDA VALE (Plan VIII)
HYDE PARK & KNIGHTSBRIDGE (Plan XII)
0 400 m
0 400 yards

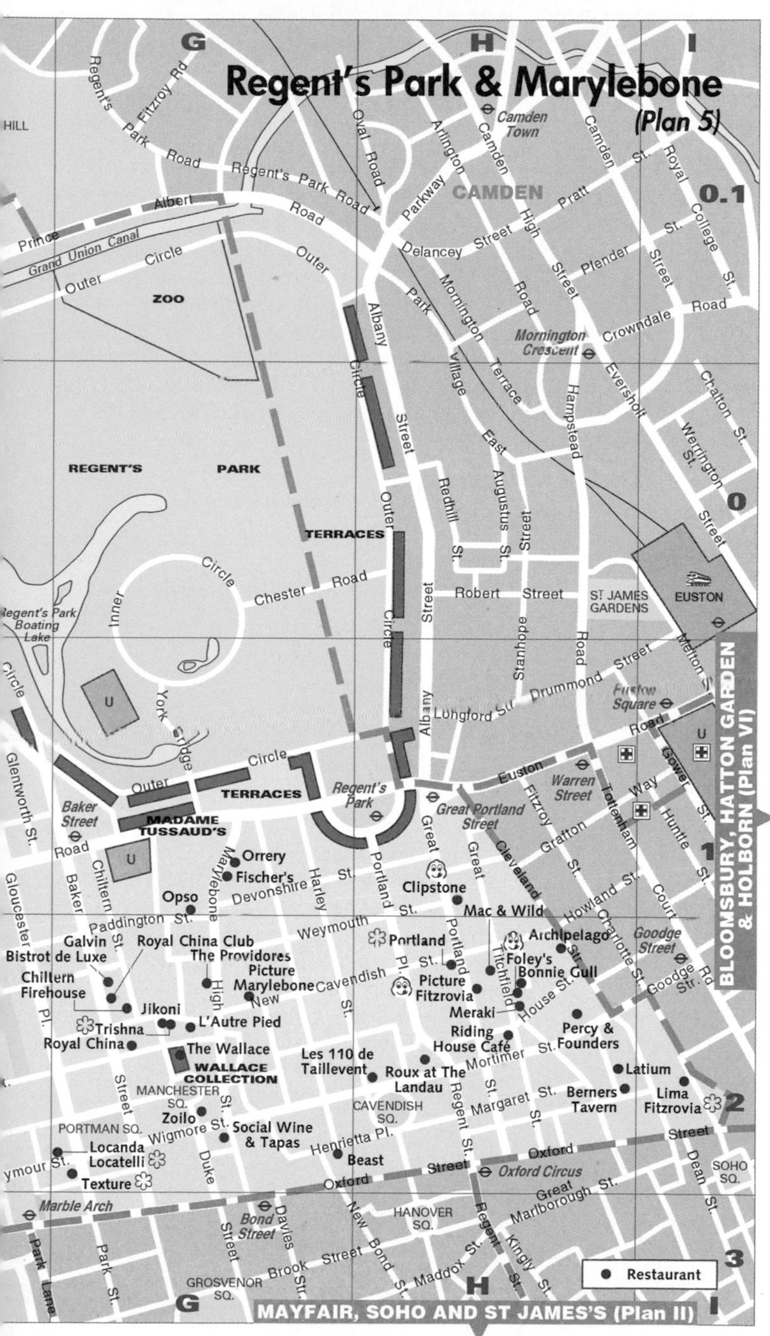
Regent's Park & Marylebone
(Plan 5)
CAMDEN
ZOO
REGENT'S
PARK
TERRACES
EUSTON
ST JAMES GARDENS
MADAME TUSSAUD'S
WALLACE COLLECTION
Camden Town
Mornington Crescent
Euston Square
Warren Street
Great Portland Street
Regent's Park
Baker Street
Goodge Street
Oxford Circus
Bond Street
Marble Arch
Regent's Park Boating Lake
Orrery
Fischer's
Opso
Clipstone
Mac & Wild
Portland
Archipelago
Foley's
Bonnie Gull
Picture Fitzrovia
Meraki
Riding House Café
Percy & Founders
Galvin Bistrot de Luxe
Royal China Club
The Providores
Picture Marylebone
Chiltern Firehouse
Jikoni
Trishna
L'Autre Pied
Royal China
The Wallace
Les 110 de Taillevent
Roux at The Landau
Latium
Berners Tavern
Lima Fitzrovia
Zoilo
Social Wine & Tapas
Beast
Locanda Locatelli
Texture
MANCHESTER SQ.
PORTMAN SQ.
CAVENDISH SQ.
HANOVER SQ.
GROSVENOR SQ.
SOHO SQ.
Restaurant
BLOOMSBURY, HATTON GARDEN & HOLBORN (Plan VI)
MAYFAIR, SOHO AND ST JAMES'S (Plan II)

ARCHIPELAGO

Creative • Exotic décor

MAP: 5-H2

The gloriously oddball Archipelago is unlike any other restaurant in London – its exuberant decoration makes you feel as if you're eating in an eccentric Oriental bazaar which is running out of space and, foodwise, it pushes boundaries to the point where tales of your meal could be used to frighten small children. 'Exploring the exotic' is their slogan, although 'eating the exotic' would be more exact: with choices like crocodile wrapped in vine leaves, crispy zebra 'jerky' and sweet chilli smoked python carpaccio, the menu reads like an inventory at a safari park. Several dishes are given an Asian twist and side dishes include the 'love-bug salad' made with locusts and crickets – which makes for a memorable experience.

- 53 Cleveland St ✉ W1T 4JJ
  020 7637 9611 — **www**.archipelago-restaurant.co.uk
  Goodge Street
- Carte £30/46
  Closed 23-26 December, Saturday lunch, Sunday and bank holidays

L'AUTRE PIED

Modern cuisine • Design

MAP: 5-G2

It's been a quick 10 years since David Moore opened this more relaxed sibling to his Pied à Terre restaurant, and back in 2007 it was one of the restaurants that helped establish this part of town as a destination for those looking for a night out. This sense of neighbourhood has always been one of its most appealing features, coupled with the easy going atmosphere – ask for one of the window tables around the corner if you want to enjoy this local feel. The European-influenced cooking has always managed to feel contemporary yet without becoming too innovative and unfamiliar. There are a number of menus on offer, including some good value choices at lunch.

- 5-7 Blandford St. ✉ W1U 3DB
  020 7486 9696 — **www**.lautrepied.co.uk
  Bond Street
- Menu £24/50
  Closed 4 days Christmas, 1 January and Sunday dinner

BEAST

Meats and grills • Elegant

MAP: 5-G2

Owned by the Goodman people, who also brought us 'Burger and Lobster', this unique destination restaurant is 'Steak and Crab' – otherwise known as Beast. A full-sized bear welcomes you in; you then head down to an underground banquet hall furnished with three exceedingly long tables set for communal dining. There's a chiller full of USDA imported beef, hung for 30 days, and numerous tanks teeming with live male Norwegian king crabs. Get stuck into starters like Mersea oysters, shrimp tempura or Volzhenka sturgeon caviar before enjoying mains like a perfectly cooked rib-eye steak or a large platter of succulent, warm king crab – besides which sides and puddings seem superfluous. Bring a big appetite and a fat wallet.

- 3 Chapel Pl W1G 0BG
  020 7495 1816 — **www**.beastrestaurant.co.uk
  Bond Street
- Carte £49/110
  Closed Sunday, lunch Monday-Wednesday and bank holidays

BERNARDI'S

Italian • Neighbourhood

MAP: 5-F2

This modern Italian offers all you might ask of a neighbourhood restaurant: it's chic yet relaxed, with a friendly atmosphere and a firm belief that tables should always be held back for locals; food is fresh and unfussy, and is served all day and all week, so you can pop in for pizzette and prosecco at the sparkly cocktail bar, catch up with a friend over breakfast, or linger over a three course dinner. Brothers Gabriel and Marcello Bernardi are the brains behind the operation and have hired a twice Roux scholarship finalist to run the kitchen. Everything is homemade, using the best quality ingredients possible and dishes like pappardelle with veal and fennel sausage are vibrantly flavoured, with a lightness of touch.

- 62 Seymour St W1H 5BN
  020 3826 7940 — **www**.bernardis.co.uk
  Marble Arch
- Menu £18 (weekday lunch) - Carte £31/56

BERNERS TAVERN

Modern British • Brasserie

MAP: 5-H2

There's nothing like a bit of glamour to see off the monochrome days of austerity and Berners Tavern is certainly one of the most beautiful rooms in London – just don't turn up thinking it's a pub. It's like a grand salon and was the original ballroom of the Berners hotel which has been transformed by Ian Schrager in conjunction with Marriott into the London Edition. Every inch of wall is filled with gilt-framed prints, oils and photographs while the vast ceiling, ornate plasterwork and opulent chandeliers keep many pairs of eyes raised towards the heavens. Jason Atherton, whose empire is expanding faster than a trencherman's waistline, has put together an appealing and accessible menu and the cooking is satisfying and assured.

- The London Edition Hotel, 10 Berners St ✉ WIT 3NP
  020 7908 7979 — **www**.bernerstavern.com
  Tottenham Court Road
- Menu £25 (lunch) – Carte £34/76

BONNIE GULL

Seafood • Simple

MAP: 5-H2

Bonnie Gull calls itself a 'seafood shack' – a reference perhaps to its modest beginnings as a pop-up before it docked permanently here in the West End. It's kitted out in a pretty fishing village kind of way and the tables are packed into the small room in an appropriately sardine-like manner. There's a decent raw bar to kick things off, offering oysters and cockles, winkles and whelks. The main menu is a mix of traditional favourites and more ambitious dishes, although the kitchen appears to be more adept at the former. Many go for the fish and chips but you can also get a decent Cullen skink and a huge Devon cock crab; it's also worth getting a side order of chunky chips cooked in beef dripping. There's another branch in Soho.

- 21a Foley St ✉ W1W 6DS
  020 7436 0921 — **www**.bonniegull.com
  Goodge Street
- Carte £27/45
  Closed 25 December-3 January – booking essential

CHILTERN FIREHOUSE

World cuisine • Fashionable

MAP: 5-G2

What could be more appropriate than one of the hottest tickets in town being a converted fire station? Everyone from Prime Ministers to pop stars have been papped on their way into this New York style brasserie, their smiles revealing the relief they feel in having secured a reservation. A wall of sound hits you as you enter and the room positively bursts with energy, but what makes this celebrity hangout unusual is that the food is good. The kitchen is overseen by Nuno Mendes and he has used all his experience working in North and South America to create a clever menu full of vibrant and flavoursome dishes. If you're more interested in checking out the cooking rather than your fellow diners, ask to sit at the kitchen counter.

- Chiltern Firehouse Hotel, 1 Chiltern St ✉ WIU 7PA
  ✆ 020 7073 7676 – **www**.chilternfirehouse.com
  ⊖ Baker Street
- Carte £37/74

N CLIPSTONE

Modern cuisine • Fashionable

MAP: 5-H1

Hot on the heels of the success of Portland comes another wonderful neighbourhood spot just around the corner, from restaurateurs Will Lander and Daniel Morgenthau. They've installed the former sous chef of Portland at the stoves and have devised a great value sharing menu bursting with flavour and originality. Three to four dishes should suffice, with one from the charcuterie, one from the seasonal vegetable-based section of small plates and one main course; desserts like the traditional Paris-Brest or the chocolate Pithivier are not to be missed, so make sure you leave room. Add a cleverly conceived wine list which includes rarely seen keg wines 'on-tap', along with a couple of cocktails, and you've a recipe for all-round contentment.

- 5 Clipstone St ✉ W1W 6BB
  ✆ 020 7637 0871 – **www**.clipstonerestaurant.co.uk
  ⊖ Great Portland Street
- Carte £24/38
  Closed Sunday dinner - booking advisable

DININGS

Japanese • Cosy

MAP: 5-F2

In Tokyo the sign hanging outside would be considered positively flamboyant but in London it's the very definition of discretion, making this sweet little place easy to miss. There are half a dozen seats at the counter on the ground floor and a few tables downstairs in the somewhat claustrophobic basement; but wherever you sit, it's hard not to be charmed by it all. The menu is a very extensive document, supplemented by some interesting specials, and takes many of its influences from the style of Japanese food found at Nobu, the owner's alma mater: accordingly, highlights are the more creative dishes like the 'sashimi four ways'. The temptation is to order plenty to share but beware because the prices can make this an expensive activity.

- 22 Harcourt St. ✉ W1H 4HH
  020 7723 0666 – **www**.dinings.co.uk
  Edgware Road
- Carte £21/65
  Closed Christmas – booking essential

DONOSTIA

Basque • Tapas bar

MAP: 5-F2

As London's love affair with tapas continues, many diners are now keen on learning more about Spain's regional specialities. The bright and lively Donostia, which is the Basque name for San Sebastián, was opened by two young owners inspired by this coastal municipality. Anyone who has visited the area, known for the quality of its restaurants and its terrific pintxos, will recognise classic Basque dishes like cod with pil-pil sauce, chorizo from the native Kintoa pig and tender, slow-cooked pig's cheeks. Add in a thoughtful wine list along with the traditional drinks of cider and Txakoli and you have a winning recipe. You can book a table but it's worth trying for one of the 10 seats at the marble counter in front of the kitchen.

- 10 Seymour Pl ✉ W1H 7ND
  020 3620 1845 – **www**.donostia.co.uk
  Marble Arch
- Carte £20/43
  Closed Christmas, New Year and Monday lunch

FISCHER'S

Austrian • Brasserie

MAP: 5-G1

This stylish Austrian café and konditorei that summons up the spirit of old Vienna has made a great success of a site which many of its previous occupants struggled to make work. It stays open from 8 until late, with breakfast possibly being the best time to visit - the Viennoiserie are made in-house and are as good as they look. The main menu is a comprehensive document, supplemented by a mittel-European wine list with an impressive choice available by the glass. The schnitzels are first rate - do upgrade to a Holstein - and save room for desserts like the poppy seed parfait. As you'd expect for a restaurant from the Chris Corbin and Jeremy King stable, service from the international aproned-staff is fluent and well-choreographed.

- 50 Marylebone High St ✉ W1U 5HN
  020 7466 5501 — **www**.fischers.co.uk
  Baker Street
- Carte £23/59
  Closed 25 December

FOLEY'S

World cuisine • Neighbourhood

MAP: 5-H2

Mitz Vora, former sous chef at Palomar, has brought his vibrant, original cooking to foodie Fitzrovia. Cosy up in one of the intimate ground floor booths or head downstairs to the engine room of this lively restaurant, with its busy open kitchen and counter seating, and its barrel-vaulted caves for six. The fresh, flavourful small plates reflect the international spice trail so your sweet potato fritters come with grilled pineapple, jalapeño yoghurt and saffron coconut sauce and your pork belly with tamarind, apple, green papaya, red onions and cashews. Although you will want to order more, 3 or 4 dishes will suffice - but hold back, because desserts include baklava cheesecake, and homemade spiced milk chocolate with banana doughnuts.

- 23 Foley St ✉ W1W 6DU
  020 3137 1302 — **www**.foleysrestaurant.co.uk
  Goodge Street
- Carte £17/28
  Closed Christmas-New Year, Easter and Sunday - booking advisable

GALVIN BISTROT DE LUXE

French • Bistro

MAP: 5-G2

Despite the great success of Galvin La Chapelle in The City, brothers Chris and Jeff Galvin have never taken their eyes off the ball here at their eponymous Bistrot de Luxe. Regulars still flock here for the clubby, relaxed atmosphere and the traditional French food, which may look simple on the plate but is carefully constructed behind the scenes. The emphasis is very much on flavour; the kitchen's understanding and appreciation of ingredients, and the classic combinations in which they are used, really come through. The menu has enough variety to satisfy those happy to indulge but those with one eye on the cost should come for lunch or before 7pm to take advantage of the fixed price menu. An elegant basement cocktail bar adds to the comfy feel.

- 66 Baker St. W1U 7DJ
  020 7935 4007 – **www**.galvinrestaurants.com
  Baker Street
- Menu £20/22 - Carte £30/68
  Closed dinner 24, 25-26 December and 1 January

JIKONI

Indian • Elegant

MAP: 5-G2

It takes a brave person to open their first restaurant next to Trishna but Ravinder Bhogal, the chef Gordon Ramsay christened 'the new Fanny Cradock', has risen to the challenge admirably. Born in Kenya of Indian parents and brought up in London, Bhogal takes culinary inspiration from these sources and more, so you might find delicate snacks like cauliflower popcorn, small plates like prawn toast Scotch eggs, and filling mains like mutton keema Sloppy Joe or saffron prawn and fish pie. Bhogal's background is in fashion journalism and, just like the food, the restaurant itself has an idiosyncratic, deliciously different style, with brightly patterned Indian tablecloths, mismatched lamps and colourful cushions creating a cosy, homely feel.

- 19-21 Blandford St W1U 3DH
  020 7034 1988 – **www**.jikonilondon.com
  Baker Street
- Menu £20 (weekday lunch) - Carte £26/45
  Closed Saturday lunch and Sunday dinner

LATIUM 🍴O

Italian • Neighbourhood

XX A/C **MAP:** 5-H2

This Italian stalwart is tucked away discreetly in foodie Fitzrovia; still with a loyal following, but lighter and less formal than in previous years - and all the better for it. Tables by the entrance are given away first but it's worth asking to be seated further in; you'll almost certainly be accommodated as staff are a friendly and considerate bunch. The menu focuses on Lazio but travels the length of Italy for inspiration. A generous welcome comes in the form of freshly baked focaccia, carta di musica, cheese and olives; 'fatto a casa' is their motto and fresh pasta, their speciality. There's a window into the kitchen for those who like to know where their food comes from, and a chef's table for those who want to watch them at it.

- 21 Berners St. ✉ W1T 3LP
  ✆ 020 7323 9123 — **www**.latiumrestaurant.com
  ⊖ Oxford Circus
- Menu £18 (weekdays) - Carte £29/50
  Closed 25-26 December, 1 January and Sunday lunch

LURRA 🍴O

Basque • Design

XX A/C **MAP:** 5-F2

Sister to Donostia just over the road, is Lurra - again inspired by its owners' love of the Basque Country; its name meaning 'land' to reflect their use of the freshest produce, cooked over the sort of charcoal grill that's common in the region. There's an open kitchen with counter dining; an über-cool, Scandic-style room which opens onto a courtyard - and a buzz of contentment throughout. They have gained a reputation for the quality of their beef - 14 year old Galician cow aged for at least 45 days - and sell it by weight, as they do their whole grilled turbot. Slow-cooked shoulder of lamb completes the triumvirate of large sharing plates; the rest of the dishes are mostly 'picoteo' or nibbles, with the fries with paprika and aioli a must-try.

- 9 Seymour Pl ✉ W1H 5BA
  ✆ 020 7724 4545 — **www**.lurra.co.uk
  ⊖ Marble Arch
- Menu £20 (weekday lunch) - Carte £31/70
  Closed Monday lunch and Sunday dinner

LIMA FITZROVIA ✿

Peruvian • Neighbourhood

MAP: 5-12

Michelin

FIRST COURSE: Black bream ceviche with avocado, sweet potato and chilli. • King crab causa with Ají Amarillo and green quinoa.

MAIN COURSE: Suckling pig, chicharrón, sesame and celeriac. • Hot scallop ceviche with avocado, parsley, clam juice and fennel leaves.

DESSERT: Elderberry with avocado mousse, 75% chocolate and rocoto pepper. • Chirimoya parfait with Amazonian chocolate and blue potato crisps.

Lima Fitzrovia is one of those restaurants that just makes you feel good about life - and that's even without the pisco sours which, to be honest, will get you in the mood for anything. Peruvian food is the ideal antidote to times of austerity: it's full of punchy, invigorating flavours and fantastically vivid colours. Virgilio Martinez, who runs the acclaimed 'Central' restaurant in Lima, has created somewhere intimate, informal and fun in which to enjoy his refreshing and exciting cuisine. The menu may be awash with unfamiliar ingredients like tiger's milk and sacha inchi oil but the staff are more than willing to offer help. Most ingredients are from the UK but some are from small suppliers in Peru such as the 'potatoes 4,000 metres' (a reference to the altitude rather than the depth at which these tubers are grown). Tiradito and its cousin ceviche are popular starters (the former being a slightly punchier version) and there is plenty of originality throughout the menu along with some playfulness - but also great skill.

■ 31 Rathbone Pl ✉ W1T 1JH
020 3002 2640 — **www**.limalondongroup.com/fitzrovia
⊖ Goodge Street

■ Carte £41/57
Closed 24-26 December, 1 January, Monday lunch and bank holidays

LOCANDA LOCATELLI ✿

Italian • Fashionable

XXX ♿ A/C ⊕ ✿ **MAP:** 5-G2

Michelin

FIRST COURSE: Scallops with saffron. • Calf's foot salad with fruit mustard, mizuna and lemon zest.

MAIN COURSE: Linguine with Cornish lobster, tomato, garlic and sweet chilli. • Braised veal cheek with crushed potatoes, baby gem lettuce and black truffle.

DESSERT: Warm apple with sultanas, Grand Marnier and yoghurt. • Chocolate fondant with toffee sauce, popcorn and peanut butter ice cream.

A few minutes in the company of Giorgio Locatelli, whether face to face or through the medium of television, reveals a man who is passionate about Italian food and it is that very passion that has kept Locanda Locatelli at the top for so long. The restaurant may be into its second decade but still looks as dapper as ever and remains in the premier league of London's most fashionable addresses. The layout and style of the room were clearly designed with conviviality in mind and this is further helped along by service that is smooth but never intrusive. The other reason for its enduring popularity is the great food and the consistency that the kitchen maintains. The hugely appealing menu covers many of the regions of Italy and provides plenty of choice for everyone including coeliacs, as the terrific pasta dishes available include gluten-free options. Unfussy presentation and superlative ingredients allow natural flavours to shine through.

- 8 Seymour St. ✉ W1H 7JZ
  ☎ 020 7935 9088 — **www**.locandalocatelli.com
  ⊖ Marble Arch
- Carte £38/69
  Closed 24-26 December and 1 January

MAC & WILD

Scottish • Friendly

MAP: 5-H2

The warm welcome, the upbeat soundtrack and the rustic-looking interior make this one of those restaurants where you instantly feel that you're in for a good time. The owner is the son of a Highland butcher and after selling his family's produce in London, had a few 'pop-ups' before setting up home here. He's called it a 'Highland restaurant' which makes complete sense when you see the menu – it is all about their wild venison and top quality game and seafood from Scotland, with the provenance of all produce listed, including the names of the fishermen's boats! Don't miss the 'wee plates' like the deliriously addictive haggis pops. There's also a choice of over 100 whiskies, along with suggested whisky pairings for each dish.

65 Great Tichfield St ✉ W1W 7PS
020 7637 0510 — **www**.macandwild.com
Oxford Circus

Carte £23/50
Closed Sunday dinner

MERAKI

Greek • Fashionable

MAP: 5-H2

Its name reflects the modern Greek approach to life with its emphasis on putting one's body and soul into everything, including work; a philosophy discernible here at this lively Greek restaurant from the owners of Roka and Zuma. Menus offer a contemporary take on classic dishes, with a selection of meze, raw dishes, salads and pasta; a section called 'From the land' offering dishes like slow-cooked beef cheeks; and a section called 'From the sea' listing choices such as monkfish souvlaki. Much of the produce is imported from Greece, including the fish and the wines. Enter from Foley Street and you'll find yourself in the vibrant bar; the entrance on Great Titchfield Street leads to the bright restaurant with its open kitchen. Service is slick.

80-82 Great Titchfield St ✉ W1W 7QT
020 7305 7686 — **www**.meraki-restaurant.com
Goodge Street

Carte £25/60
Closed Sunday dinner and Christmas

LES 110 DE TAILLEVENT

French • Elegant

MAP: 5-H2

Les 110 de Taillevent brings a slice of Paris to London; the original, named after the 14C chef believed by many to have written the first cookbook, is somewhat of an institution. 110 refers to the number of wines they offer by the glass; that is, 4 different wine pairings for each dish on the menu, in 4 different price brackets. With choices like pâté en croûte, turbot meunière or rib of beef with béarnaise sauce, dishes are firmly in the French vein; they don't serve bread unless you ask for it and mains come unadorned so you will need to buy a side dish or two. Bottle green furnishings reflect the brasserie's raison d'être, and ornate high ceilings combine with deep green banquettes to create a stylish, elegant space.

- 16 Cavendish Sq W1G 9DD
  020 3141 6016 — **www**.les-110-taillevent-london.com
  Oxford Circus
- Menu £20 - Carte £31/64
  Closed 25 December and 1 January

OPSO

Greek • Neighbourhood

MAP: 5-G1

Andreas, a Greek national, created this modern Greek restaurant with a little help from the team behind Athens' Funky Gourmet restaurant. It has proved a good fit for the neighbourhood - and not just because it's around the corner from the Hellenic Centre. Come at the weekend for brunch or any night of the week for what they describe as 'social style dining': small sharing plates that mix the modern with the traditional. Many of the ingredients are imported from Greece and the vibrant, vividly coloured dishes are satisfying and easy to eat. The narrow room is bright and intimate, and a young friendly team keep the atmosphere animated; if you're coming in a larger group ask for one of the semi-private booths downstairs.

- 10 Paddington St W1U 5QL
  020 7487 5088 — **www**.opso.co.uk
  Baker Street
- Carte £17/53
  Closed 23 December-3 January

ORRERY

Modern cuisine • Neighbourhood

XXX **MAP:** 5-G1

Enthusiastic post-prandial shopping can be a perilously expensive pastime – the danger is doubled here as Orrery is perched temptingly above a Conran shop. These are actually converted stables from the 19C but, such is the elegance and style of the building, you'd never know. What is sure is the long, narrow restaurant looks its best when the daylight floods in; on warm days make time to have a drink on the terrific rooftop terrace. To complement these charming surroundings you'll be offered a bewildering array of menus, all of which feature quite elaborate, modern European cooking. Dishes are strong on presentation and there is the occasional twist but it's usually done with some meaning rather than merely straining for effect.

■ 55 Marylebone High St ✉ W1U 5RB
020 7616 8000 — **www**.orrery-restaurant.co.uk
Regent's Park

■ Menu £28/60 - Carte lunch £34/73
Booking essential

PERCY & FOUNDERS

Modern cuisine • Brasserie

XX **MAP:** 5-H2

Where Middlesex hospital once stood is now a residential development that includes this all-day operation which is regarded by its owners as the prototype for a new breed of pub. Named after Hugh Percy, the architect of the former teaching hospital, it is a distinctly smart affair but in looks it's perhaps more akin to a modern brasserie, with a comfortable cocktail lounge attached. The menu is kept quite short and seasonal and the kitchen brings quite a refined touch, although it also likes to inject a little playfulness now and then. It all kicks off first thing with breakfast, and bar snacks are served in the lounge during the day. As the neighbourhood develops this could become a useful local dining spot.

■ 1 Pearson Sq, (off Mortimer St) ✉ W1T 3BF
020 3761 0200 — **www**.percyandfounders.co.uk
Goodge Street

■ Carte £26/49

PICTURE FITZROVIA

Modern British • Simple

MAP: 5-H2

Alumnae of Wild Honey and Arbutus chose an area of Central London undersubscribed with restaurants when they opened their own place a few years ago. Such was their success,that there is now another Picture a short walk away in New Cavendish Street. The look here may be a little stark – there's a large counter at the front fashioned out of recycled flooring and tables at the back beneath a skylight – but the service team add enormous warmth to the place and their enthusiasm is contagious. What funds were saved on the decoration were clearly spent on the shiny kitchen downstairs, and it's paid dividends for the skilful chefs. Their small plates are vibrant, fresh and colourful, flavours are assured and the contrasting textures a delight.

- 110 Great Portland St. ✉ W1W 6PQ
  ✆ 020 7637 7892 — **www**.picturerestaurant.co.uk
  ⊖ Oxford Circus
- Menu £22 (lunch) - Carte £27/33
  Closed Sunday and bank holidays

PICTURE MARYLEBONE

Modern British • Design

MAP: 5-G2

Three years after launching their first restaurant, this young trio decided it was time to create a second. The two places might only be five minutes apart but following the success of their first venture, this smaller sister hit the ground running. The great value lunch menu changes daily and offers a choice of 3 or 4 courses, and there's a cleverly created à la carte of small plates which are divided into 3 vegetable, 3 fish and 3 meat choices, followed by 3 desserts - choose one from each section. Dishes are full of flavour and may include ravioli of caramelised onions with peas, broad beans and lettuce, cod with corn, chorizo and Paris brown mushrooms or warm almond cake with apricot and frozen lemon and thyme yoghurt.

- 19 New Cavendish St ✉ W1G 9TZ
  ✆ 020 7935 0058 — **www**.picturerestaurant.co.uk
  ⊖ Bond Street
- Menu £22 (lunch) - Carte £27/33
  Closed Sunday and bank holidays

PORTLAND ✿

Modern cuisine • Intimate

MAP: 5-H2

Portland

FIRST COURSE: Isle of Mull scallop, carrots, macadamia nuts and ramson. • Risotto of celeriac with pecorino, wild mushrooms and truffle.

MAIN COURSE: Denham Estate venison with brassica tops, burnt bread and black garlic jam. • Wiltshire chicken with grilled corn, pickled cherries and garlic.

DESSERT: Gariguette strawberries with yoghurt sorbet, lemon curd and tarragon. • Peach and almond tart with burnt honey ice cream.

Two friends, Will Lander - co-owner of Quality Chop House - and Daniel Morgenthau of 10 Greek Street fame, have created one of those restaurants that you warm to immediately because its exudes honesty. The look of the room may be somewhere between pared-down and austere but the open kitchen adds some colour and the atmosphere is welcoming and intimate. Their young chef, who came from In De Wulf restaurant in Belgium, proves to be the perfect fit. One glance at his daily menu and you know you're in for a good meal - the combinations of ingredients just sound right together. Start with snacks like wonderfully crisp pig's head croquette, before diving into perfectly cooked venison with pearl barley or turbot with white asparagus. The food is unfussy yet there is depth and real understanding here - quite an achievement for such a young team; the concise wine list and its 'single bottle' list contains some real gems. The economics of running such a relatively small restaurant mean that you're not encouraged to linger too long at your table, but you'll want to return soon anyway.

- 113 Great Portland St ✉ W1W 6QQ
  ✆ 020 7436 3261 — **www**.portlandrestaurant.co.uk
  ⊖ Great Portland Street
- Menu £39/65 - Carte dinner £43/55
  Closed 23 December-3 January and Sunday - booking essential

PORTMAN

Modern cuisine • Pub

MAP: 5-F2

When it went by the name of The Masons Arms this pub was widely known for its gruesome history. It was here that the condemned, on their way to Tyburn Tree gallows, would take their last drink, which purportedly led to the phrase "one for the road". Reincarnated as the Portman, the pub these days boasts a less disreputable clientele who are more attracted by the quality of the cooking. Food is served all day and you can choose to eat in the busy ground floor bar or in the unexpectedly formal upstairs dining room, all thick-pile carpet and starched tablecloths. Fortunately, the style of food remains thoroughly down-to-earth and satisfying and is accompanied by a well-organised wine list and an interesting selection of cocktails.

- 51 Upper Berkeley St ✉ W1H 7QW
  ✆ 020 7723 8996 — **www**.theportmanmarylebone.com
  ⊖ Marble Arch.
- Carte £26/46

THE PROVIDORES

Creative • Trendy

XX A/C

MAP: 5-G2

Still championing fusion cooking after more than a decade and a half is this stalwart of the vibrant Marylebone Village scene. The warmth of the staff and the general buzz hit you immediately in the ground floor Tapa Room, where tables and tapas are shared. Head upstairs and you'll find an elegant, slightly more sedate room where the staff are equally charming. While the interesting wine list showcases bottles from New Zealand, the menu offers choices like seared salmon with nori sauce, crispy buckwheat, gomasio and avocado. Dishes are assured, original and made with good quality ingredients, although there can sometimes be a flavour or two too many on the plate. Bookings are needed upstairs whereas downstairs, it's first-come-first-served.

- 109 Marylebone High St. ✉ W1U 4RX
  ✆ 020 7935 6175 — **www**.theprovidores.co.uk
  ⊖ Bond Street
- Carte £25/54
  Closed Easter, dinner 24 and 31 December and 25-26 December

RIDING HOUSE CAFÉ

Modern cuisine • *Rustic*

MAP: 5-H2

Riding House café is actually less a café and more an all-day Manhattan-style brasserie and cocktail bar, with some charming touches of quirky design – and it feels like a fun place to be as soon as you enter. Turn left to go into the restaurant or right for the more lively main section where booking's not an option – instead you sit either at a counter facing the kitchen or on a large refectory table where you rub shoulders with strangers. It's the same menu throughout, starting with breakfast and followed by a choice of small plates, along with more straightforward main courses like steaks or burgers. Stick with the small plates, which have a bit more zing to them, but be careful not to over-order.

- 43-51 Great Titchfield St W1W 7PQ
  020 7927 0840 — **www**.ridinghousecafe.co.uk
  Oxford Circus
- Carte £25/46
  Closed 25-26 December

ROUX AT THE LANDAU

French • *Elegant*

MAP: 5-H2

It does have its own street entrance but it's best to enter this grand, oval-shaped restaurant from the hotel, as you don't often get the chance to walk through a 'wine corridor'. The hotel brought in the considerable experience of the Roux organisation – which means Albert and Michel Jr – to add vigour and ambition to the operation. Classical, French-influenced cooking is the order of the day but one can detect the emergence of a lighter style of cuisine with the odd twist. The restaurant is also sensible enough to keep its more traditionally minded regulars happy by ensuring that their favourites, like grilled Dover Sole, remain constants. The daily special from the trolley goes down well with the busy lunchtime corporates.

- Langham Hotel, 1c Portland Pl., Regent St. W1B 1JA
  020 7636 1000 — **www**.rouxatthelandau.com
  Oxford Circus
- Menu £39 - Carte £41/95
  Closed Saturday lunch

ROYAL CHINA

Chinese • Exotic décor

XX A/C

MAP: 5-G2

It could be just as at home in Hong Kong's Wanchai or Central districts but, as it is, Royal China sits very comfortably in Baker Street. The large kitchen is staffed exclusively by Chinese chefs, including the early rising dim sum chef, who is responsible for the specialities served between midday and 5pm each day. The Cantonese dishes are strong on aroma and colour and, while the restaurant does not sell a great deal of seafood due to a lack of tank space, the lobster dishes remain some of the more popular choices. However, it is the barbecued meats, assorted soups, stir-fries and the choice of over 40 different types of dim sum that draw the large groups and ensure that this branch of the Royal China group remains as bustling as ever.

- 24-26 Baker St W1U 7AB
  020 7487 4688 — **www**.royalchinagroup.co.uk
  Baker Street
- Menu £34/38 - Carte £25/100
  Closed 23-25 December

ROYAL CHINA CLUB

Chinese • Elegant

XX A/C

MAP: 5-G2

'The Club' is the glittering bauble in the Royal China chain but along with the luxurious feel of the room comes an appealing sense of intimacy and calm. The service helps in this regard, as the staff are personable, offer sound advice and seem able to anticipate their customers' needs. At first glance the menu appears similar to the other branches but it soon becomes apparent that the ingredients here are from the luxurious end of the spectrum, especially when it comes to seafood – just check out the large tanks, holding everything from crabs and lobsters to eels and sea bass. The best time to come is at lunch, for their very good dim sum. At dinner, look out for the Cantonese dishes and the chef's seasonal specials.

- 40-42 Baker St W1U 7AJ
  020 7486 3898 — **www**.royalchinagroup.co.uk
  Baker Street
- Carte £35/80
  Closed 25-27 December

SOCIAL WINE & TAPAS

Mediterranean cuisine • Neighbourhood

MAP: 5-G2

The word 'social' lets you know that this lively venue is a Jason Atherton venture; the rest of the name tells you what it does. There's wine – lots of it – stored on-view over the two floors, with tuned-in sommeliers on hand to guide your choices. And then there's tapas to accompany your wine: a mix of Spanish and Mediterranean dishes with some Atherton classics for good measure; sent out by the chefs behind the counter, as and when they're ready. Head for the cosy, moodily lit basement and check out the menu; 3 or 4 dishes per person, plus a ham or cheese platter is about the right amount; and ordering a few at a time works well – just make sure you save room for a dessert, like their rather tasty version of a crema Catalana.

- 39 James St ✉ W1U 1DL
  020 7993 3257 — **www**.socialwineandtapas.com
  Bond Street
- Menu £16 (lunch) – Carte £15/34
  Closed bank holidays – bookings not accepted

VINOTECA

Modern cuisine • Wine bar

MAP: 5-F2

This was the second of the successful group and followed the winning formula of their Clerkenwell original: a great selection of wines, fresh, flavourful cooking and eager young staff. One side of the rustic room is given over to shelves of wine; not only is the selection immeasurably appealing but the staff display both a keen knowledge and, more importantly, enormous enthusiasm when giving advice. The daily changing menu takes its cue from the sunnier parts of Europe and includes some tasty bar snacks and good charcuterie, as well as a few firmly British dishes such as roast Ryeland lamb leg with mash and chard. There's a great value midweek lunch menu – and do try the themed monthly wine flight; a snip at £10 for three glasses.

- 15 Seymour Pl. ✉ W1H 5BD
  020 7724 7288 — **www**.vinoteca.co.uk
  Marble Arch
- Menu £16 (weekday lunch) – Carte £22/36
  Closed Christmas, bank holidays and Sunday dinner – booking advisable

TEXTURE ✿

Creative • Design

XX A/C ⊡ ✿ **MAP:** 5-G2

Michelin

FIRST COURSE: Chargrilled Anjou pigeon with sweetcorn, shallots, bacon popcorn and red wine essence. • Yellowfin tuna with ginger, soy, fennel and coriander.

MAIN COURSE: Salted cod with Jersey Royals, avocado and romanesco. • Organic Icelandic lamb with onions and heritage carrots.

DESSERT: Icelandic skyr with rye bread and Yorkshire rhubarb. • Coconut with dark chocolate.

Chef-owner Agnar Sverrisson has steadily gone about creating an exceedingly good restaurant. The Champagne Bar at the front has become a destination in itself and is separated from the restaurant by a large cabinet so you never feel too detached from it. The high ceilings add a little grandeur to the place and the service is very pleasant, with staff all willing and ready with a smile. Agnar's cooking is a little less showy than when Texture opened in 2007 and is all the better for that; you feel he's now cooking the food he wants to cook rather than the food he thought he should be cooking. Iceland is his country of birth so it is no surprise to find lamb, cod (whose crisp skin is served with drinks), langoustine and skyr, the dairy product that nourished the Vikings; the bread, and the olive oils are very good too. There's considerable technical skill and depth to the cooking but dishes still appear light and refreshing and, since the use of cream and butter is largely restricted to the desserts, you even feel they're doing you good.

■ 34 Portman St ✉ W1H 7BY
☎ 020 7224 0028 — **www**.texture-restaurant.co.uk
⊖ Marble Arch

■ Menu £34/95 - Carte £60/92
Closed first 2 weeks August, 1 week Easter, Christmas-New Year, Sunday, Monday and lunch Tuesday

TRISHNA ✿

Indian • Neighbourhood

MAP: 5-G2

Trishna

FIRST COURSE: Aloo tokri chaat. • Telicherry pepper fried shrimps with garlic and coconut & mango chutney.

MAIN COURSE: Seafood pilau with pink peppercorn raita. • Duck seekh kebab with Kashmiri chilli, shallots and pineapple chutney.

DESSERT: Chocolate mousse chikki. • Strawberry and rose falooda.

Trishna is dressed in an elegant, understated style and its charming staff exude a sense of calm. The coast of southwest India provides the kitchen with most of its influences and the interesting menu is full of vibrant, exciting dishes, ranging from the playful – try their own mini version of 'fish and chips' as a starter – to the original: the succulent guinea fowl comes with lentils, fennel seed and star anise. However, the undoubted star of the show is a version of the dish made famous by the original Trishna in Mumbai: brown crab, in this case from Dorset, comes with lots of butter and a little kick of wild garlic; it is so wondrously rich no man alone can finish a bowl, and you'll be licking your lips for days afterwards. The various tasting menus often provide the most rounded experience but all the dishes are as fresh tasting and beautifully spiced as they are colourful. Wine is taken seriously too, and much thought has gone into matching wines with specific dishes.

■ 15-17 Blandford St. ✉ W1U 3DG
✆ 020 7935 5624 — **www.**trishnalondon.com
⊖ Baker Street

■ Menu £35/70 - Carte £38/53
Closed 25-27 December and 1-3 January

THE WALLACE

Modern British • Friendly

MAP: 5-G2

The Wallace Collection of 18 and 19C decorative art is one of London's finest, if lesser known museums and is found within Sir Richard and Lady Wallace's former home, Hertford House. Go through the French windows in what was once the dining room of this imposing mansion and you'll find yourself in a vast, glass-roofed courtyard. Turn left into the café for healthy salads and home-baked cakes; head right into the restaurant for a menu of modern British dishes like pan-fried lemon sole with shrimps and caper butter or roasted rump of lamb with celery, feta and onion. With its indoor trees and comfy sofas, there's a sedate, restful feel to the restaurant, and service remains smooth and unruffled, even when the crowds descend.

- Hertford House, Manchester Sq ✉ W1U 3BN
  ✆ 020 7563 9505 — **www**.peytonandbyrne.co.uk
  ⊖ Bond Street
- Carte £32/49
  Closed 24-26 December and Easter Sunday - (lunch only and dinner Friday-Saturday)

ZOILO

Argentinian • Friendly

MAP: 5-G2

Argentina's regional specialities take centre stage at lively and fun Zoilo; it's also about sharing, so plonk yourself down at the counter and order away - prices are pretty decent for this postcode so overdoing it won't break the bank. Typical dishes include braised pig head croquettes with apricot jam or grilled scallops with sweet potato, caramelised pork belly and chorizo. The beef is predictably good but why not try the grilled sweetbreads with lemon instead? The ground floor is the livelier of the two but if you want to know how it's all done then sit downstairs in front of the open kitchen. Throw in an appealing all-Argentinian wine list and it's easy to see why London is in the grip of a South American love affair.

- 9 Duke St. ✉ W1U 3EG
  ✆ 020 7486 9699 — **www**.zoilo.co.uk
  ⊖ Bond Street
- Menu £15 (weekday lunch) - Carte £25/53

BLOOMSBURY · HATTON GARDEN · HOLBORN

A real sense of history pervades this central chunk of London. From the great collection of antiquities in the British Museum to the barristers who swarm around the Royal Courts of Justice and Lincoln's Inn; from the haunts of Charles Dickens to the oldest Catholic church in Britain, the streets here are dotted with rich reminders of the past. Hatton Garden's fame as the city's diamond and jewellery centre goes back to Elizabethan times while, of a more recent vintage, Bloomsbury was home to the notorious Group (or Set) who, championed by Virginia Woolf, took on the world of art and literature in the 1920s.

A full-on encounter with **Holborn** is, initially, a shock to the system. Coming up from the tube, you'll find this is where main traffic arteries collide and a rugby scrum regularly ensues. Fear not, though; the relative calm of London's largest square, part-flanked by two quirky and intriguing museums, is just round the corner. The square is **Lincoln's Inn Fields,** which boasts a canopy of characterful oak trees and a set of tennis courts. On its north side is **Sir John Soane's Museum,** a gloriously eccentric place with over forty thousand exhibits where the walls open out like cabinets to reveal paintings by Turner and Canaletto. On its south side, the Hunterian Museum, is a fascinating repository of medical bits and pieces. Visitors with a Damien Hirst take on life will revel in the likes of animal digestive systems in formaldehyde, or perhaps the sight of half of mathematician Charles Babbage's brain. Others not so fascinated by the gory might flee to the haunting silence of **St Etheldreda's church** in Ely Place, the only surviving example of thirteenth-century Gothic architecture in London. It survived the Great Fire of 1666, and Latin is still the language of choice.

Contemplation of a different kind takes centre stage in the adjacent **Hatton Garden.** This involves eager-eyed couples gazing at the glittering displays of rings and jewellery that have been lighting up the shop fronts here for many generations, ever since the leafy lane and its smart garden environs took the fancy of Sir Christopher Hatton, a favourite of Elizabeth I.

After gawping at the baubles, there's liquid refreshment on hand at one of London's most atmospheric old pubs, the tiny Ye Old Mitre hidden down a narrow passageway. The preserved trunk of a cherry tree stands in the front bar, and, by all accounts, Elizabeth I danced the maypole round it (a legend that always seems more believable after the second pint).

Bloomsbury has intellectual connotations, and not just because of the writers and artists who frequented its townhouses in the twenties. This is where the University of London has its headquarters, and it's also home to the **British Museum,** the vast treasure trove of international artefacts that attracts visitors in even vaster numbers. As if the exhibits themselves weren't lure enough, there's also the fantastic glass-roofed Great Court, opened to much fanfare at the start of the Millennium, which lays claim to being the largest covered public square in Europe. To the north of here by the Euston Road is the **British Library,** a rather stark red brick building that holds over 150 million items and is one of the greatest centres of knowledge in the world. Meanwhile, Dickens fans should make for the north east corner of Bloomsbury for the great man's museum in **Doughty Street:** this is one of many London houses in which he lived, but it's the only one still standing. He lived here for three years, and it proved a fruitful base, resulting in Nicholas Nickleby and Oliver Twist. The museum holds manuscripts, letters and Dickens' writing desk. If your appetite for the written word has been truly whetted, then a good tip is to head back west half a mile to immerse yourself in the bookshops of Great Russell Street.

P. Libera/Corbis Documentary/Getty Images

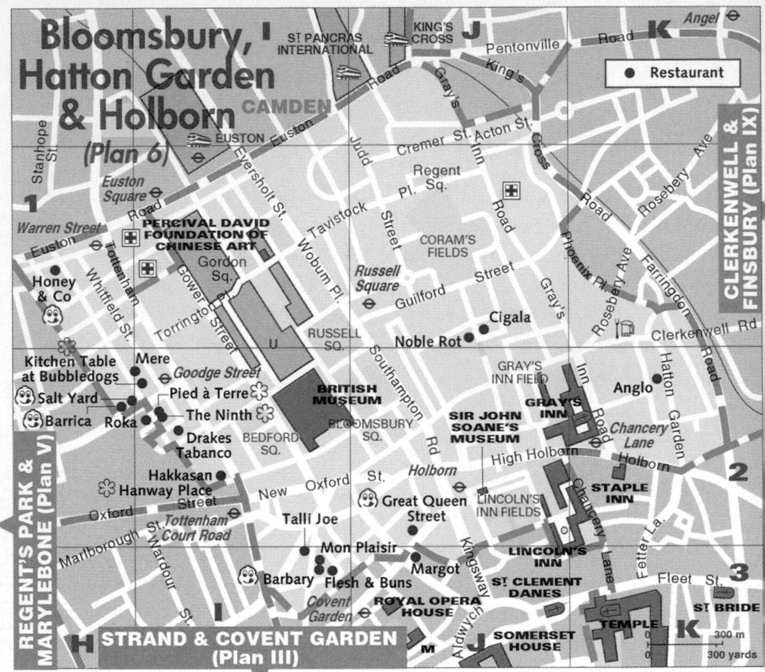
Bloomsbury, Hatton Garden & Holborn (Plan 6)
Restaurant
CLERKENWELL & FINSBURY (Plan IX)
REGENT'S PARK & MARYLEBONE (Plan V)
STRAND & COVENT GARDEN (Plan III)
ST PANCRAS INTERNATIONAL
KING'S CROSS
CAMDEN
EUSTON
Angel
PERCIVAL DAVID FOUNDATION OF CHINESE ART
BRITISH MUSEUM
CORAM'S FIELDS
SIR JOHN SOANE'S MUSEUM
GRAY'S INN
STAPLE INN
LINCOLN'S INN
ST CLEMENT DANES
ROYAL OPERA HOUSE
SOMERSET HOUSE
TEMPLE
ST BRIDE
Honey & Co
Kitchen Table at Bubbledogs
Mere
Salt Yard
Pied à Terre
Barrica
Roka
The Ninth
Drakes Tabanco
Hakkasan
Hanway Place
Talli Joe
Mon Plaisir
Barbary
Flesh & Buns
Margot
Great Queen Street
Noble Rot
Cigala
Anglo
300 m
300 yards

ANGLO

Creative British • *Rustic*

MAP: 6-K2

As its name suggests, British produce is the mainstay of the menu at this pared-down, personally run restaurant, and these 'home-grown' ingredients are often served in creative rather than conventional ways. Lunch offers a concise à la carte alongside a five course tasting menu, while the well-paced seven course tasting menu served in the evening delivers colourful dishes whose appearance is as vibrant as their taste. Cooking is confidently executed, and flavours are assured. Dishes might include cod with smoked potato and sea fennel or Swaledale lamb with lettuce and spruce, while desserts take recognisable ingredients and serve them in fresh new ways. The chefs bring dishes to the table and are happy to stop and chat.

- 30 St Cross St ✉ ECIN 8UH
  020 7430 1503 — **www**.anglorestaurant.com
  Farringdon
- Menu £39/45 - Carte lunch £34/53
  Closed 22 December-4 January, Sunday and Monday lunch

BARBARY

World cuisine • *Tapas bar*

MAP: 6-I3

The team behind Palomar have opened this sultry, atmospheric restaurant at the entrance to Neal's Yard. It's a tiny place with 24 non-bookable seats squeezed around a horseshoe-shaped, zinc-topped counter – all the cooking takes place here and the chefs are happy to chat as they work. The menu of small sharing plates takes in dishes from the former Barbary Coast. Start with freshly baked naan, Jerusalem bagel and dips before moving onto wholesome, richly flavoured dishes from Land, Sea and Earth. There is grilling over the coals, baking in the clay oven and some raw dishes too, with tahini, harissa and ras el hanout adding depth. Service is keen, as are the prices; impressive given that they don't impose a service charge and water is free.

- 16 Neal's Yard ✉ WC2H 9DP
  www.thebarbary.co.uk
  Covent Garden
- Carte £16/32
  Closed dinner 24-26 December - bookings not accepted

BARRICA

Spanish • Tapas bar

MAP: 6-H2

Staff at this lively little tapas bar all appear to be Spanish so perhaps it's national pride that makes them run it with a passion lacking in many of their competitors. They make a concerted effort to look after their diners, of whom there are always many, so it's worth booking ahead unless you're okay squeezing onto a seat at the counter. When it comes to the food, authenticity is high on the agenda and it's hard to avoid temptation. A couple of standouts are lamb chop with romesco sauce, and smoked duck breast with cherry butter; it's worth ordering another savoury dish or one of their Spanish cheeses in place of dessert. They also offer an interesting selection of around 20 sherries and assorted Spanish wines – try one from the blackboard.

62 Goodge St ✉ W1T 4NE
020 7436 9448 — **www**.barrica.co.uk
Goodge Street

Carte £17/36
Closed 25-31 December, 1 January, Easter, Sunday and bank holidays – booking essential

CIGALA

Spanish • Neighbourhood

MAP: 6-J1

Cigala may be more restaurant than bar but it was serving authentic Spanish food when all those fashionable little tapas bars were still in short pantalones. The reason for its longevity is that it gives the punters exactly what they want: an extensive menu that regularly changes but also recognises that some dishes must remain perennials, and a lively and convivial atmosphere. The owner personally seeks out producers in Spain and this care is particularly evident in the dried hams, which are a must. Chicken livers in sherry and salt cod fritters are always winners and it's well worth waiting the 30 minutes for a paella. Staff are approachable and it's wise to heed their counsel on what and how much to order.

54 Lamb's Conduit St. ✉ WC1N 3LW
020 7405 1717 — **www**.cigala.co.uk
Russell Square

Menu £25 (weekdays) - Carte £29/43
Closed 25-26 December, 1 January, Easter Sunday and Monday – booking essential

DRAKES TABANCO

Spanish • Simple

MAP: 6-12

Taking advantage of London's newfound fondness for fino is this simple tabanco, courtesy of the people behind nearby Barrica and Copita and named after Sir Francis in honour of the booty of butts he returned home with. Typical of Jerez, these taverns' unique feature is that they serve sherry straight from the barrel using a venencia; order a glass of Rare Old India or Oloroso and you'll wonder why you haven't been drinking sherry for years. The small, Andalusian-inspired tapas menu uses imported produce from Spain alongside British ingredients. Truffled goat's cheese and the pork and oxtail meatballs are musts, as is the board of charcuterie. They even do a tasting menu with a different sherry matched to each course.

- 3 Windmill St ✉ W1T 2HY
  020 7637 9388 – **www.**drakestabanco.com
  Goodge Street
- Carte £16/37
  Closed Sunday and bank holidays

FLESH & BUNS

Asian • Trendy

MAP: 6-13

If it's a fun night out with friends you're looking for, then this basement spot next to The Donmar could well be the place for you. It's loud, frenetic and packed with young Londoners; many sat at the huge communal table down the middle; others in smaller booths around the side. You can expect sashimi, rolls, teriyaki, tempura and steak, but star billing, as the slightly unappetising name of the place suggests, quite rightly goes to the gua bao bun - soft, steamed pillows of delight that sandwich your choice of meat or fish filling and come with a dipping sauce. Dishes are fresh, fairly priced and full of flavour; add to this cocktails, beers and an easy to navigate wine and sake list and you have all the makings of a night to remember.

- 41 Earlham St ✉ WC2H 9LX
  020 7632 9500 – **www.**bonedaddies.com
  Covent Garden
- Menu £22/40 - Carte £16/46
  Closed 24-25 December - booking advisable

GREAT QUEEN STREET

Modern British • Rustic

MAP: 6-J2

This is a great restaurant to choose on a cold winter's night, thanks to its friendly welcome, its bustling atmosphere and its heartwarming food. Its popularity does mean that service can sometimes need a prompt but there is no doubting the staff's enthusiasm for the food they serve. The menu descriptions are unapologetically concise but then dishes come equally unembellished. There's little difference between what constitutes a starter or main course and there's always a daily special or two. Highlights are the shared dishes such as the suet-crusted chicken pie or the seven hour shoulder of lamb, but offal is also done very well. The wine list is thoughtfully put together – and the 'Worker's Lunch' is a steal.

- 32 Great Queen St ✉ WC2B 5AA
  ✆ 020 7242 0622 — **www**.greatqueenstreetrestaurant.co.uk
  ⊖ Holborn
- Menu £18 (weekday lunch) - Carte £19/42
  Closed Christmas-New Year, Sunday dinner and bank holidays – booking essential

HONEY & CO

World cuisine • Simple

MAP: 6-H1

When Itamar and Sarit decided to open their own place they did so knowing that they didn't have to worry too much about the kitchen – they'd both been head chefs at Ottolenghi restaurants. The philosophy at their sweet little café is to offer the same sort of food and hospitality you'd get if you were guests in their home. The friendly girls certainly provide charming, chatty and tactile service and the cooking is full of freshness and colour. The influences stretch beyond Israel to the wider Middle East; start by sharing some mezze, and follow it with roasted baby chicken or delicious lamb shawarma. Breads are great, cakes are hard to resist and the prices are commendable – which is another reason why the place is packed most evenings.

- 25a Warren St ✉ W1T 5LZ
  ✆ 020 7388 6175 — **www**.honeyandco.co.uk
  ⊖ Warren Street
- Menu £33 - Carte £25/31
  Closed 24-26, 31 December, 1 January and Sunday – booking essential

HAKKASAN HANWAY PLACE ✿

Chinese • *Trendy*

MAP: 6-12

Hakkasan Hanway Place

FIRST COURSE: Dim sum platter. • Smoked beef rib with Jasmine tea.

MAIN COURSE: Grilled Chilean sea bass in honey. • Sweet and sour Duke of Berkshire pork with pomegranate.

DESSERT: Chocolate and olive oil ganache. • Lemon cream cheese mousse with caramelised hazelnuts.

Over recent years Hakkasans have opened in many cities around the world but it all started here in 2001 in this unexceptional alleyway just off Tottenham Court Road. Thanks to its sensual looks, air of exclusivity and glamorous atmosphere – characteristics now synonymous with the brand – the original Hakkasan wowed London back then and, judging by the crowds, continues to do so today. The restaurant has always managed the art of coping equally well with all types of customers, from large parties out to celebrate to couples on a date, and the well-organised and helpful staff are a fundamental part of that success. Lunchtime dim sum here is a memorable and more relaxed experience; at dinner try the Signature menus which represent better value than the à la carte. Thanks to the brigade of about twenty chefs in the kitchen, the Cantonese specialities are prepared with care and consistency; dishes are exquisitely presented and while there are moments of inventiveness, they never come at the expense of flavour.

8 Hanway Pl. ✉ W1T 1HD
✆ 020 7927 7000 — **www.**hakkasan.com
⊖ Tottenham Court Road

Menu £38/128 - Carte £29/98
Closed 24-25 December

KITCHEN TABLE AT BUBBLEDOGS ✿

Modern cuisine • Fashionable

XX A/C

MAP: 6-H2

Michelin

FIRST COURSE: Lobster and tomatoes with lemon verbena. • Mackerel with oyster leaves and green strawberries.

MAIN COURSE: Duck, cherry and turnips. • Dexter beef with broad bean and pea ragout.

DESSERT: Strawberries, black pepper meringue, tarragon and milk. • Chocolate cookie crumbs with white chocolate ice cream.

Fight your way past the throngs enjoying the curious combination of hotdogs with champagne and head for the curtain – for behind it is where you'll find a horseshoe counter and a look of expectation on the faces of your fellow diners. This is Kitchen Table where chef-owner James Knappett and his small team prepare a no-choice menu of around 12 dishes. Each one is described on the blackboard in a single noun so you have to put your trust in the kitchen. The produce is some of the best you can find and, while the cooking has a classical base, the small dishes come with a clever creative edge; they aren't made up of lots of ingredients – instead it is the combinations of flavours and textures that give them depth. With seating for just 19, the atmosphere is very convivial, especially if you're a fully paid up member of the foodie community. The chefs interact with their customers over the counter and offer more comprehensive explanations of each dish; they are helped out by James' wife Sandia, who is charm personified.

■ 70 Charlotte St ✉ W1T 4QG
✆ 020 7637 7770 — **www**.kitchentablelondon.co.uk
⊖ Goodge Street

■ Menu £98
Closed 1-14 January, 17 August-2 September, 23-27 December and Sunday-Tuesday - booking essential - (dinner only) - (tasting menu only)

MARGOT

Italian • Elegant

MAP: 6-J3

The trend over recent years may have been towards simpler, more casual restaurants but, luckily for London, the owners of Margot decided there is still a call for a place that oozes glamour and elegance. A bowler-hatted doorman greets you, staff sport tuxedos, the surroundings are sleek and stylish and, with cosy booths and a counter as well as a clubby basement, there isn't a bad seat in the house. The menu showcases seasonal, regional Italian cooking with bags of flavour and a rustic edge. It's accessible too, meaning you can come for charcuterie, cheese and cocktails or push the boat out with seven or eight courses and a bottle of 1985 Tignanello. Service is a strength of the ever-present owners, who have a knack of almost pre-empting your wishes.

- 45 Great Queen St WC2 5AA
  020 3409 4777 — **www**.margotrestaurant.com
  Holborn
- Menu £25 (lunch and early dinner) - Carte £30/53
  Closed 25 December

MERE

Modern cuisine • Fashionable

MAP: 6-H2

Despite her rather steely MasterChef persona, Monica Galetti is a natural hostess and at Mere, her first collaboration with her husband, David, she has focused on creating a feeling of home, warmth and hospitality. Monica is originally from Samoa and its influence is never too far away; the restaurant is named after her mother and its cooking has a nod to the South Pacific. Monica learnt her craft at Le Gavroche so French influences also come as no surprise; there is also an elegance and femininity to the ingredient-led cooking, with layers of texture and flavour bringing a subtle modernity to the plate. The understatedly stylish basement restaurant gets plenty of natural light and there's a plush cocktail bar on the ground floor.

- 74 Charlotte St W1T 4QH
  020 7268 6565 — **www**.mere-restaurant.com
  Goodge Street
- Menu £35 (weekday lunch) - Carte £44/67
  Closed Sunday and bank holidays

MON PLAISIR

French • Family

MAP: 6-I3

Mon Plaisir couldn't be more French if it wore a beret and whistled La Marseillaise; but because this institution has been around since the 1940s, and under the current ownership since the '70s, it can also give one an unexpected but palpable sense of old London. It's divided into four rooms, all of which have slightly different personalities but share the Gallic theme; even the bar was reportedly salvaged from a Lyonnais brothel. Service may lack some of the exuberance of the past but the serving team do get the job done. All the classics are on offer, from snails to terrines, duck to coq; the set menu represents good value while the à la carte can be a little pricey.

- 19-21 Monmouth St. ✉ WC2H 9DD
  ✆ 020 7836 7243 — **www**.monplaisir.co.uk
  ⊖ Covent Garden
- Menu £16 (weekdays)/28 - Carte £26/55
  Closed 25-26 December, Easter and bank holidays

NOBLE ROT

Traditional British • Rustic

MAP: 6-J1

In 2013 Mark Andrew and Dan Keeling launched a quarterly wine and food magazine for the 21st century oenophile; a couple of years later, this Bloomsbury restaurant and wine bar followed, inheriting the same name. Inside, it's a simple set up with a rustic, somewhat masculine feel; staff are friendly and attentive and customers an interesting mix. Wholesome, unfussy cooking comes with bold, gutsy flavours; Stephen Harris of The Sportsman is a consultant, so expect fish from the Kent coast as well as classics like terrines, rillettes and home-cured meats. The wine list is well-chosen, with strong leanings to France and Spain. Wine and food pairings are a feature; the Rock Oyster Raveneau has quickly established itself as a favourite.

- 51 Lamb's Conduit St ✉ WC1N 3NB
  ✆ 020 7242 8963 — **www**.noblerot.co.uk
  ⊖ Russell Square
- Carte £30/43
  Closed 25-26 December and Sunday - booking advisable

THE NINTH ✿

Mediterranean cuisine • Brasserie

MAP: 6-12

Michelin

FIRST COURSE: Sea bass carpaccio with salsa verde and pickled kohlrabi. • Salted beef cheek with wasabi and pickled radish.

MAIN COURSE: Chargrilled sea bream with lemon confit, miso and fennel salad. • Lamb en croûte with pea purée.

DESSERT: Pain perdu with vanilla ice cream. • Chocolate crémeux with strawberry sorbet.

Jun Tanaka's career began in the early '90s and this – the ninth restaurant in which he has worked – is also the first he has actually owned. Although situated on foodie Charlotte Street, it's very much a neighbourhood spot, and both the lively downstairs with its counter for walk-ins and the more intimate first floor have a great feel to them. The on-trend menu has sections including 'snacks', 'salads' and 'raw and cured', as well as 'meat' and 'fish'; staff suggest 3 starters, 2 mains and 2 vegetable dishes for two, although their flexible approach means you're equally welcome to come in for a couple of plates and a glass of wine. Skilful cooking uses classical French techniques with a spotlight on the Mediterranean; dishes arrive at a good pace and certainly look the part – but the focus here is firmly on flavour. Vegetables are much more than just an accompaniment, with dishes such as Savoy cabbage with hazelnut pesto or charcoal-roasted celeriac with smoked almonds and wild garlic a real highlight.

- 22 Charlotte St ✉ W1T 2NB
  ✆ 020 3019 0880 — **www**.theninthlondon.com
  ⊖ Goodge Street
- Menu £25 (weekday lunch) - Carte £32/57
  Closed Christmas-New Year, Sunday and bank holidays

PIED À TERRE ✿

Creative • Elegant

MAP: 6-12

Michelin

FIRST COURSE: Scallop ceviche with hazelnut, black radish and truffle. • Veal sweetbread with girolles, anchovy, parsley and garlic.

MAIN COURSE: Suckling pig with parsnip and cider. • Monkfish with artichoke, spinach and mussels.

DESSERT: Coconut rice pudding, sweet cheese, sake and yoghurt. • Pineapple, kaffir lime, cucumber and coriander.

Not only has Charlotte Street provided a good illustration of how restaurants have changed the landscape over recent years but it has also witnessed the breakneck speed at which the industry operates. Restaurants have come and gone but for over 25 years David Moore's Pied à Terre has stood apart from the fray, confident in its own abilities and the loyalty of its regulars. One of the reasons for its success has been its subtle reinventions: nothing ever too grandiose – just a little freshening up with some new art or clever lighting to keep the place looking relevant and vibrant. Of course, its longevity is also due to the consistent standard of the cooking. The kitchen offers a plethora of menus that include tasting and vegetarian choices; the food is elegant and refined and doesn't let the modern techniques or more technical components distract or detract from the true flavours. The wine list is divided into two weighty tomes and shows considerable depth and range, including a good selection of bottles for under £30.

■ 34 Charlotte St ✉ W1T 2NH
020 7636 1178 — **www**.pied-a-terre.co.uk
⊖ Goodge Street

■ Menu £30/80
Closed last week December-5 January, Saturday lunch, Sunday and bank holidays – booking essential

ROKA

Japanese • Fashionable

MAP: 6-I2

With its sleek, modern exterior, the original Roka still stands out from the crowd on trendy Charlotte Street, and its well-groomed clientele seem to come for the lively atmosphere as much as the cooking. Start with a cocktail in the basement bar; a relatively relaxed space compared to the hectic restaurant above, where the on-view chefs working the Robata grill set the pace. The kitchen takes the flavours, delicacy and strong presentation standards of Japanese food and adds its own contemporary touches. The menu can appear bewildering but there are numerous staff only too willing to help you make sense of it and, if you ask, they'll also ensure that dishes arrive at an even pace. Make sure you have one of the specialities from the grill.

- 37 Charlotte St ✉ W1T 1RR
  020 7636 5228 — **www**.rokarestaurant.com
  Goodge Street
- Carte £42/75
  Closed 25 December

SALT YARD

Mediterranean cuisine • Tapas bar

MAP: 6-H2

The ground floor is the more boisterous and you'll feel like you're in the middle of a fun party; downstairs is better if you don't know your dining companion that well, although it too is full of life. This is all about tapas, although not just Spanish tapas. One side of the menu has bar snacks, charcuterie and cheese but after ordering some olives or boquerones, turn over and you'll find three headings: 'Fish', 'Meat' and 'Vegetable' – one plate of each per person should do it. Unusual dishes like braised gurnard with smoked Jersey Royals sit alongside more traditional pairings like duck breast with parsnip purée. Prices are excellent, sharing is encouraged and service, young and sincere. Spain and Italy dominate the wine list.

- 54 Goodge St. ✉ W1T 4NA
  020 7637 0657 — **www**.saltyard.co.uk
  Goodge Street
- Carte £18/28
  Closed dinner 24 and 25, 31 December and 1 January

TALLI JOE

Indian • Fashionable

MAP: 6-13

Talli means 'tipsy' in Hindi – a fitting name given that this lively place was inspired by India's dive bars. When you enter, it certainly feels more like a bar than a restaurant; cocktails are the thing, so start with a 'Day in Delhi' or a 'Jaipur Fizz' before ordering several of the vibrant, tapas-style small plates. The 'Joe' of its title refers to a fictitious traveller; his journey around India highlighting the regionality of the various dishes, so you'll find creamy curries from the south alongside gutsier offerings from the north. Some dishes like Aunty Sucorina's Goan pork and offal pickle are old family favourites of the chef; others, like the devilled quail egg and the Lucknow-style nihari on veal bone marrow, have a Western edge.

- 152-156 Shaftesbury Ave ✉ WC2H 8HL
  020 7836 5400 — **www**.tallijoe.com
  Covent Garden
- Menu £10 (weekday lunch)/35 - Carte £16/26
  Closed 1-15 January, 25-26 December, bank holidays and Sunday

J. Arnold / Agency Jon Arnold Images/age fotostock

BAYSWATER · MAIDA VALE

There may not appear to be an obvious link between Maida Vale and Italy, but the name of this smart area to the west of central London is derived from a battle fought over two hundred years ago in Southern Italy, and the most appealing visitor attraction in the neighbourhood is the charming canalside **Little Venice.** To stroll around here on a summer's day brings to mind promenading in a more distant European clime; it's hard to believe that the ear-shattering roar of the Westway is just a short walk away. South of this iconic elevated roadway – a snaking route out from Marylebone to the western suburbs – is Bayswater, a busy area of imposing nineteenth century buildings that's the epicentre of London's Middle Eastern community.

During its Victorian heyday, **Bayswater** was a grand and glamorous address for affluent and elegant types who wanted a giant green space (Hyde Park) on their doorstep. The whole area had been laid out in the mid 1800s, when grand squares and cream stuccoed terraces started to fill the acres between Brunel's curvy Paddington station and the park. But during the twentieth century Bayswater's cachet nose-dived, stigmatised as 'the wrong side of the park' by the arrivistes of Knightsbridge and Kensington. Today it's still a backpacker's paradise: home to a bewildering number of tourist hotels, flatshares and B&Bs, converted from the grand houses. But this tells only a fraction of the modern story, because the area has undergone a massive facelift. The hub of this makeover was the **Paddington Basin,** a gigantic reclamation of the old Grand Union Canal basin in the shadow of the rail terminus. From a ramshackle wasteground, it's now a shimmering zone of metal, steel and glass, a phantasmagoria of blue chip HQs, homes, shops and leisure facilities. Even the barges have been turned into permanently moored 'business barges'. Tree-lined towpaths along the perimeter complete the picture of a totally modern waterscape.

Lovers of the old Bayswater can still relish what made it famous in the first place: radiating out from **Lancaster Gate,** away from Hyde Park, is a web of streets with handsome squares and tucked-away mews, and it still retains pockets of close-knit communities, such as Porchester Square, west of Paddington station. Meanwhile, the 'cathedral' of the area, Whiteleys shopping centre in **Queensway**, remains a pivotal landmark, as it has been for more than a century. Just beyond Whiteleys heading away from central London, **Westbourne Grove** is still reassuringly expensive, or at least the bit that heads determinedly towards Notting Hill. But the wind of change has rustled other parts of the neighbourhood: Connaught Street has evolved into a villagey quarter of boutiques, galleries and restaurants, while, further west, Craven Hill Gardens is the height of chic.

Little Venice pretty much acts as a dividing line between Bayswater and Maida Vale. Technically, it's the point where the Paddington arm of the Grand Union Canal meets the **Regent's Canal,** but the name, coined by poet Robert Browning who lived close by, has come to encompass the whole area just to the north of the soaring Westway. Narrow boat moorings vie for attention alongside the cafés and pubs that mercifully lack the frantic high street buzz so typical of their kind away from the water's edge. The permanently moored boats were here a long time before those upstarts at Paddington Basin. This is where you can find old-time favourites including a floating art gallery and a puppet theatre barge. A wander round the residential streets of Maida Vale is also very pleasant, dominated by the impressive Edwardian blocks of flats that conjure up a distinctive well-to-do scene.

TPX/Prisma/age fotostock

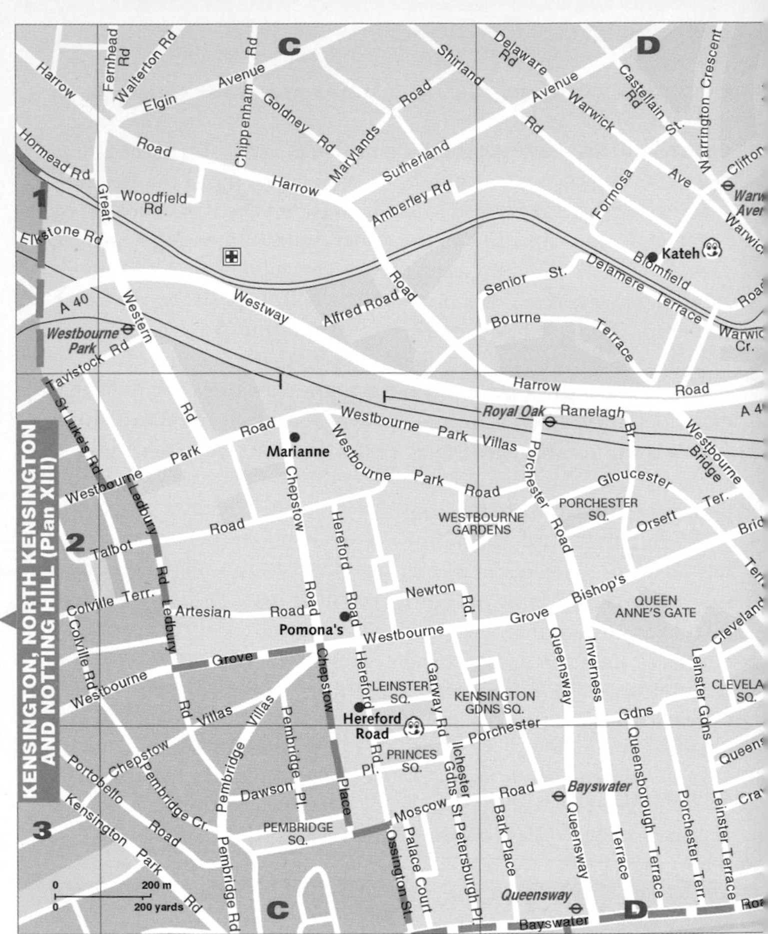
KENSINGTON, NORTH KENSINGTON AND NOTTING HILL (Plan XIII)
C
D
1
2
3
Harrow
Fernhead Rd
Walterton Rd
Elgin Avenue
Chippenham Rd
Goldney Rd
Shirland Road
Delaware Rd
Castellain Rd
Warrington Crescent
Clifton
Warwick Avenue
Warwick Avenue
Hormead Rd
Road
Harrow
Marylands
Sutherland Avenue
Warwick Rd
St.
Formosa
Ave
Great
Woodfield Rd.
Amberley Rd
Elkstone Rd
Kateh
Blomfield
Delamere Terrace
Road
Senior St.
Westway
Alfred Road
Road
A 40
Westbourne Park
Tavistock Rd
Western
Bourne
Terrace
Warwick Cr.
Harrow
Road
Royal Oak
Ranelagh
Br.
A 40
St Luke's Rd
Rd
Westbourne Park Villas
Westbourne Bridge
Road
Marianne
Westbourne Park Road
Porchester Road
Gloucester
Westbourne Park
Ledbury
Chepstow
PORCHESTER SQ.
Ter.
WESTBOURNE GARDENS
Orsett
Bridge
Talbot
Road
Hereford Road
Terr.
Newton Rd.
Bishop's
QUEEN ANNE'S GATE
Colville Terr.
Artesian
Road
Grove
Cleveland
Ledbury Rd
Pomona's
Westbourne
Colville Rd
Grove
Chepstow
Hereford
Queensway
Inverness
Leinster Gdns
Westbourne
LEINSTER SQ.
Garway Rd
KENSINGTON GDNS SQ.
CLEVELAND SQ.
Rd
Villas
Villas
Pembridge
Hereford Road
Gdns
Portobello
Chepstow
Pembridge Cr.
Pembridge
Pembridge Pl.
Rd
Porchester
Queensborough Terrace
Queens
Pl.
PRINCES SQ.
Ilchester Gdns
Dawson Pl.
Place
Road
Bayswater
Kensington
Road
Moscow
Porchester Terr.
Leinster Terrace
Craven
PEMBRIDGE SQ.
Palace Court
Bark Place
Queensway
Terrace
Pembridge Rd
Ossington St.
St Petersburgh Pl.
Park
0 200 m
0 200 yards
Rd
Queensway
Bayswater
Road

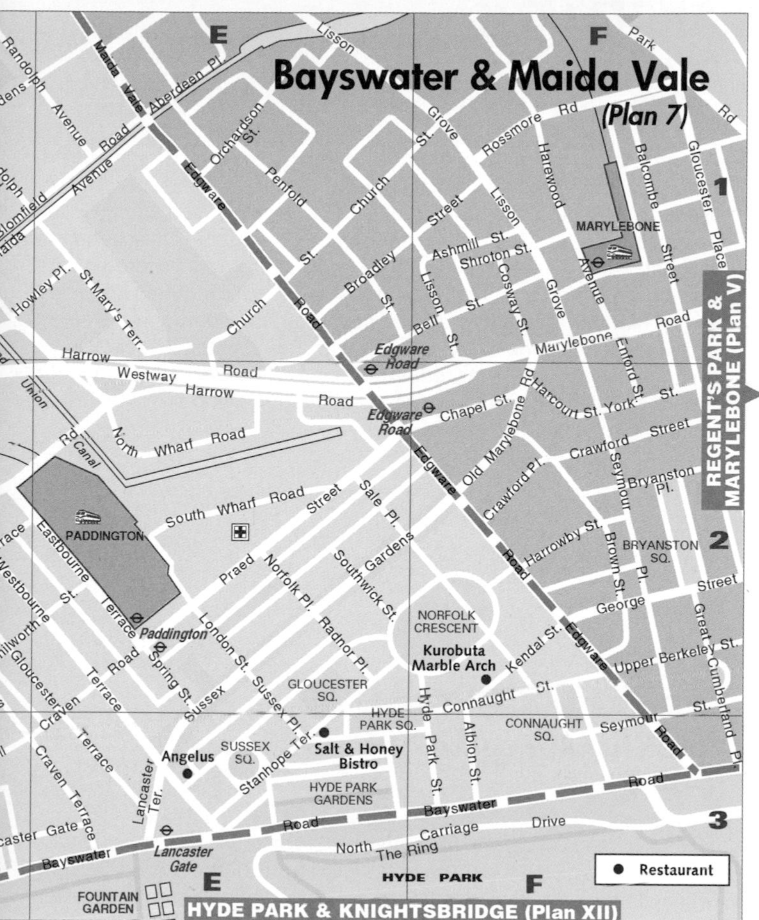
Bayswater & Maida Vale
(Plan 7)
MARYLEBONE
PADDINGTON
Edgware Road
Paddington
Lancaster Gate
NORFOLK CRESCENT
Kurobuta Marble Arch
GLOUCESTER SQ.
HYDE PARK SQ.
CONNAUGHT SQ.
SUSSEX SQ.
Angelus
Salt & Honey Bistro
HYDE PARK GARDENS
BRYANSTON SQ.
HYDE PARK
FOUNTAIN GARDEN
Restaurant
REGENT'S PARK & MARYLEBONE (Plan V)
HYDE PARK & KNIGHTSBRIDGE (Plan XII)

ANGELUS

French • Brasserie

MAP: 7-E3

Angelus has a delightfully warm and inclusive feel and much of the credit for that goes to its amiable and truly hospitable owner, Thierry Tomasin – if you're not already one of his regulars, you soon will be. The restaurant occupies what was formerly the Archer Tavern and the building dates from the 1850s. It has been charmingly decorated with art nouveau mirrors and prints and the bell that his mother would ring to call him in for meals when he was a boy growing up in the south of France takes pride of place in the bar. The cooking is French in its base but English in its ingredients; game will always be a highlight here but the kitchen is equally adept at lightly grilling some halibut or whipping up a soufflé.

- 4 Bathurst St ✉ W2 2SD
  020 7402 0083 — **www**.angelusrestaurant.co.uk
  ⊖ Lancaster Gate
- Menu £23/41 - Carte £39/70
  Closed 24-25 December and 1 January

HEREFORD ROAD

Traditional cuisine • Neighbourhood

MAP: 7-C2

Hereford Road is, first and foremost, a local restaurant. Lunch is usually a relaxed affair, with the room brightened by the large domed skylight, while dinner is the livelier feast, where everyone gives the impression that they live near enough to have walked here. The delightful owner-chef Tom Pemberton is often the first person you see, as the open kitchen is by the entrance – this was once a butcher's shop. He is an acolyte of St John and his cooking shares the same principles but not the same prices, so expect seasonal, British ingredients in very tasty dishes devoid of frippery. Offal is handled with aplomb and dishes designed for two, such as the shoulder of lamb or the whole oxtail, are so good you won't actually want to share them.

- 3 Hereford Rd ✉ W2 4AB
  020 7727 1144 — **www**.herefordroad.org
  ⊖ Bayswater
- Menu £16 (weekday lunch) - Carte £24/32
  Closed 24 December-3 January and August bank holiday – booking essential

KATEH

Mediterranean cuisine • Neighbourhood

MAP: 7-D1

If you want to join those locals who have already discovered what a little jewel they have here in the form of this buzzy, busy Persian restaurant then you will need to book ahead. Their multinational kitchen produces an appealingly priced menu that offers lots of choice, from small plates to stews and dishes expertly grilled over charcoal. The octopus is delicious; warm sesame-coated flatbreads are moreish; and be sure to finish with an authentic dessert like baklava or 'kolouche' (date and walnut pastries) along with tea made with cardamom. The atmosphere is great and the place is run with spirit, although when it's busy it can suffer from its own success. There's a delightful conservatory at the back.

- 5 Warwick Pl ✉ W9 2PX
  020 7289 3393 — **www**.katehrestaurant.co.uk
  Warwick Avenue
- Carte £21/35
  Closed 25-26 December - booking essential - (dinner only and lunch Friday-Sunday)

KUROBUTA MARBLE ARCH

Japanese • Neighbourhood

MAP: 7-F2

Having practiced with a pop-up in Chelsea, the Australian chef-owner hit the ground running when he opened his flagship Japanese restaurant - which was just as well because the crowds soon piled in. It's modelled somewhat on a Japanese izakaya, although it's bigger than anything usually seen in Tokyo. The bar is the best place to sit - start with a cocktail or a beer with a frozen head and then get ordering. The robata grill provides the stickiest BBQ pork belly, which is served in steamed buns; the lamb chops are lip-tinglingly good; the black pepper soft shell crabs fly out of the kitchen; and the yuzu tart is the star of the desserts. The place is a lot of fun and the staff are knowledgeable and helpful.

- 17-20 Kendal St ✉ W2 2AW
  020 3475 4158 — **www**.kurobuta-london.com
  Marble Arch
- Carte £17/32
  Closed 25 December

MARIANNE

French • Cosy

MAP: 7-C2

Marianne Lumb spent several years travelling the world as a private chef to a host of names from the sunny side of Celebrity Street. She then entered BBC's 'MasterChef: The Professionals' and reached the final. The next step was to open her own restaurant and it's a delightful little place – a panelled corner room that holds just six tables. She has more help in the kitchen now than when she started so, alongside the concise daily lunch menu with a choice of two dishes per course, you'll find a seasonal six course tasting menu. In essence, her food is classically based using sound French principles and, while flavours are pronounced, it also comes with a pleasing lightness of touch; the presentation is impeccable and the desserts stand out.

■ 104a Chepstow Rd ✉ W2 5QS
020 3675 7750 — **www.**mariannerestaurant.com
⊖ Westbourne Park

■ Menu £35/95
Closed 22 December-4 January , August bank holiday and Monday – booking essential – (dinner only and lunch Friday-Sunday) – (tasting menu only)

Ⓝ POMONA'S

World cuisine • Neighbourhood

MAP: 7-C2

This large neighbourhood restaurant has a laid-back Californian vibe, with music, friends and fun a vital part of the agenda. Fresh modern décor sets the scene, with bright colours and an airy, open feel; light streams in the windows and cocktails go flying out of the bar. All-day menus start with breakfast dishes ranging from French toast with cinnamon cream to buttermilk chicken and waffle, with smoothies and salads to please the health-conscious, house specials like the Ginger Pig hanger steak and small plates like tuna poke. This is soulful, colourful cooking which kicks things up a gear at dinner, where the fish tacos and the crispy pork belly are fast becoming firm favourites. Dining here is like diving into a pool on a sunny day.

■ 47 Hereford Rd ✉ W2 5AH
020 7229 1503 — **www.**pomonas.co.uk
⊖ Bayswater

■ Carte £23/51
Closed 25 December

SALT & HONEY BISTRO

Modern cuisine • Bistro

MAP: 7-E3

A residential area just north of Hyde Park is the location of the second venture from the owners of Fulham's Manuka Kitchen: this is a cosy spot with a real neighbourhood feel – run with enthusiasm by its hands-on owner. The kitchen creates well-priced, colourful, boldly flavoured dishes using the best British ingredients. You'll find Mediterranean and Middle Eastern flavours on the appealing menu, as well as influences from the chef's homeland, New Zealand – Manuka honey is used in dishes like lemongrass and Manuka honey cured salmon and their famous saffron and Manuka honey crème brûlée. The wine list is short but sweet, with each available by the glass, pichet and bottle. Ask to sit in one of the booths by the entrance.

- 28 Sussex Pl ✉ W2 2TH
  020 7706 7900 — **www**.saltandhoneybistro.com
  Lancaster Gate
- Menu £15 (weekday lunch) - Carte £26/39
  Closed 25-26 December, 1 January and Monday - bookings advisable at dinner

CITY OF LONDON · CLERKENWELL FINSBURY · SOUTHWARK

Say what you like about London, **The City** is the place where it all started. The Romans developed this small area – this square mile – nearly two thousand years ago, and today it stands as the economic heartbeat of not only the capital, but the country as a whole. Each morning it's besieged with an army of bankers, lawyers and traders, and each evening it's abandoned to an eerie ghost-like fate. Of course, this mass exodus is offset by the two perennial crowd-pullers, **St Paul's** and the **Tower of London**, but these are both on the periphery of the area, away from the frenetic commercial zone within. The casual visitor tends to steer clear of the City, but for those willing to mix it with the daytime swarm of office workers, there are many historical nuggets hidden away, waiting to be mined. You can find here, amongst the skyscrapers, a tempting array of Roman ruins, medieval landmarks and brooding churches designed by Wren and Hawksmoor. One of the best ways of encapsulating everything that's happened here down the centuries is to visit the Museum of London, on London Wall, which tells the story of the city from the very start, and the very start means 300,000 BC.

For those seeking the hip corners of this part of London, the best advice is to head slightly northwest, using the brutalist space of the **Barbican Arts Centre** as your marker. You're now entering **Clerkenwell**. Sliding north/south through here - and ending up at the historic Smithfield Meat Market - is the bustling and buzzy St John Street, home to the original St John restaurant, pioneer of nose-to-tail eating. Further West, Exmouth Market teems with trendy bars and restaurants, popular with those on their way to the perennially excellent dance concerts at Sadler's Wells Theatre. Clerkenwell's revivalist vibe has seen the steady reclamation of old warehouse space: during the Industrial Revolution, the area boomed with the introduction of breweries, print works and the manufacture of clocks and watches. After World War II, decline set in, but these days city professionals and loft-dwellers are drawn to the area's zeitgeist-leading galleries and clubs, not to mention the wonderful floor-to-ceiling delicatessens.

The area was once a religious centre, frequented by monks and nuns; its name derives from the parish clerks who performed Biblical mystery plays around the Clerk's Well set in a nunnery wall. This can be found in **Farringdon Lane** complete with an exhibition explaining all. Close by in St John's Lane is the 16C gatehouse which is home to the Museum of the Order of St John (famous today for its ambulance services), and chock full of fascinating objects related to the Order's medieval history.

Not too long ago, a trip over London Bridge to **Southwark** was for locals only, its trademark grimness ensuring it was well off the tourist map. These days, visitors treat it as a place of pilgrimage as three of London's modern success stories reside here in the shadow of The Shard. **Tate Modern** has become the city's most visited attraction, a huge former power station that generates a blistering show of modern art from 1900 to the present day, its massive turbine hall a must-see feature in itself. Practically next door but a million miles away architecturally is Shakespeare's **Globe,** a wonderful evocation of medieval showtime. Half a mile east is tourists' favourite, **Borough Market.** Foodies can't resist the organic, feel-good nature of the place, with, its mind-boggling number of stalls selling produce ranging from every kind of fruit and veg to rare-breed meats, oils, preserves, chocolates and breads. And that's just for hors-d'œuvres…

I. Dimitrov/age fotostock

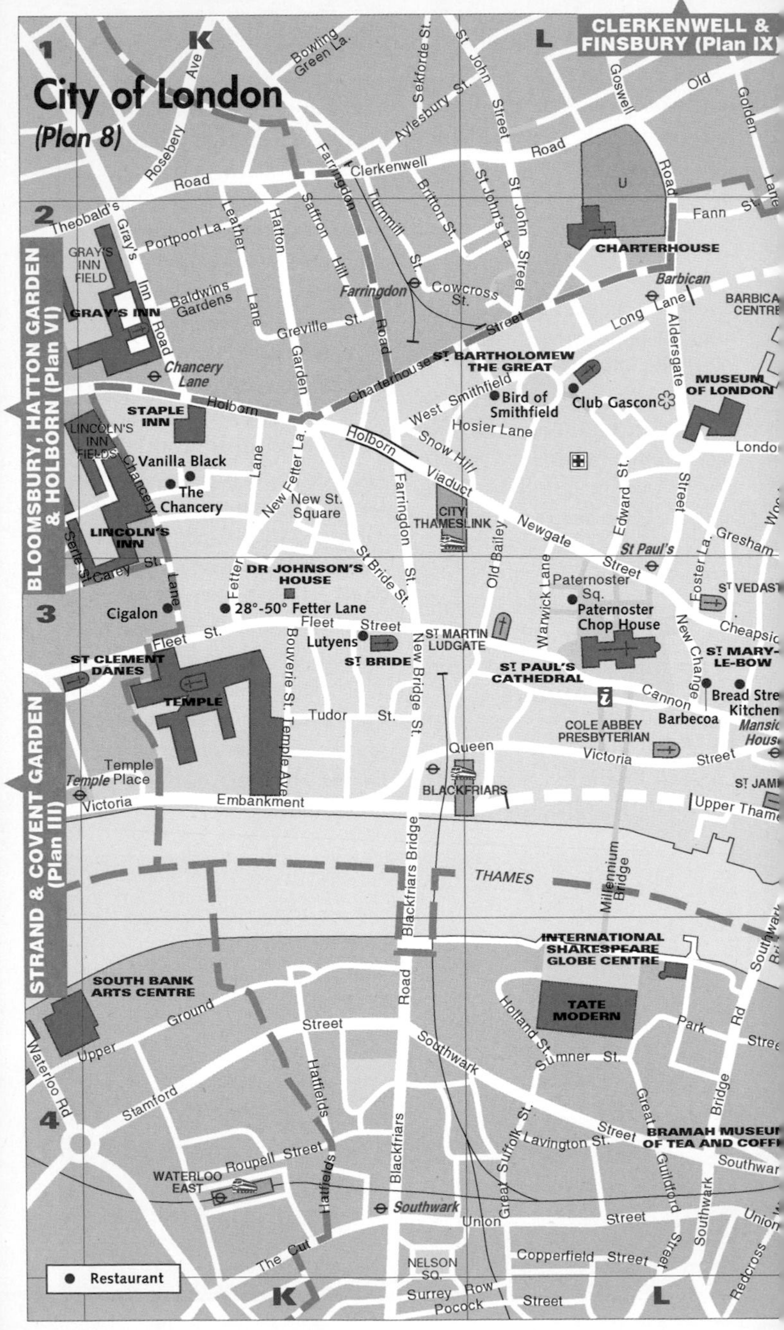
City of London
(Plan 8)
CLERKENWELL & FINSBURY (Plan IX)
BLOOMSBURY, HATTON GARDEN & HOLBORN (Plan VI)
STRAND & COVENT GARDEN (Plan III)
GRAY'S INN FIELD
GRAY'S INN
Chancery Lane
STAPLE INN
LINCOLN'S INN FIELDS
Vanilla Black
The Chancery
LINCOLN'S INN
Cigalon
ST CLEMENT DANES
TEMPLE
Temple Place
DR JOHNSON'S HOUSE
28°-50° Fetter Lane
Lutyens
ST BRIDE
ST MARTIN LUDGATE
CITY THAMESLINK
Farringdon
ST BARTHOLOMEW THE GREAT
Bird of Smithfield
Club Gascon
CHARTERHOUSE
Barbican
BARBICAN CENTRE
MUSEUM OF LONDON
St Paul's
Paternoster Sq.
Paternoster Chop House
ST PAUL'S CATHEDRAL
ST VEDAST
ST MARY-LE-BOW
Bread Street Kitchen
Barbecoa
COLE ABBEY PRESBYTERIAN
BLACKFRIARS
Mansion House
THAMES
Millennium Bridge
Blackfriars Bridge
INTERNATIONAL SHAKESPEARE GLOBE CENTRE
TATE MODERN
SOUTH BANK ARTS CENTRE
BRAMAH MUSEUM OF TEA AND COFFEE
WATERLOO EAST
Southwark
NELSON SQ.
Restaurant
K
L
1
2
3
4

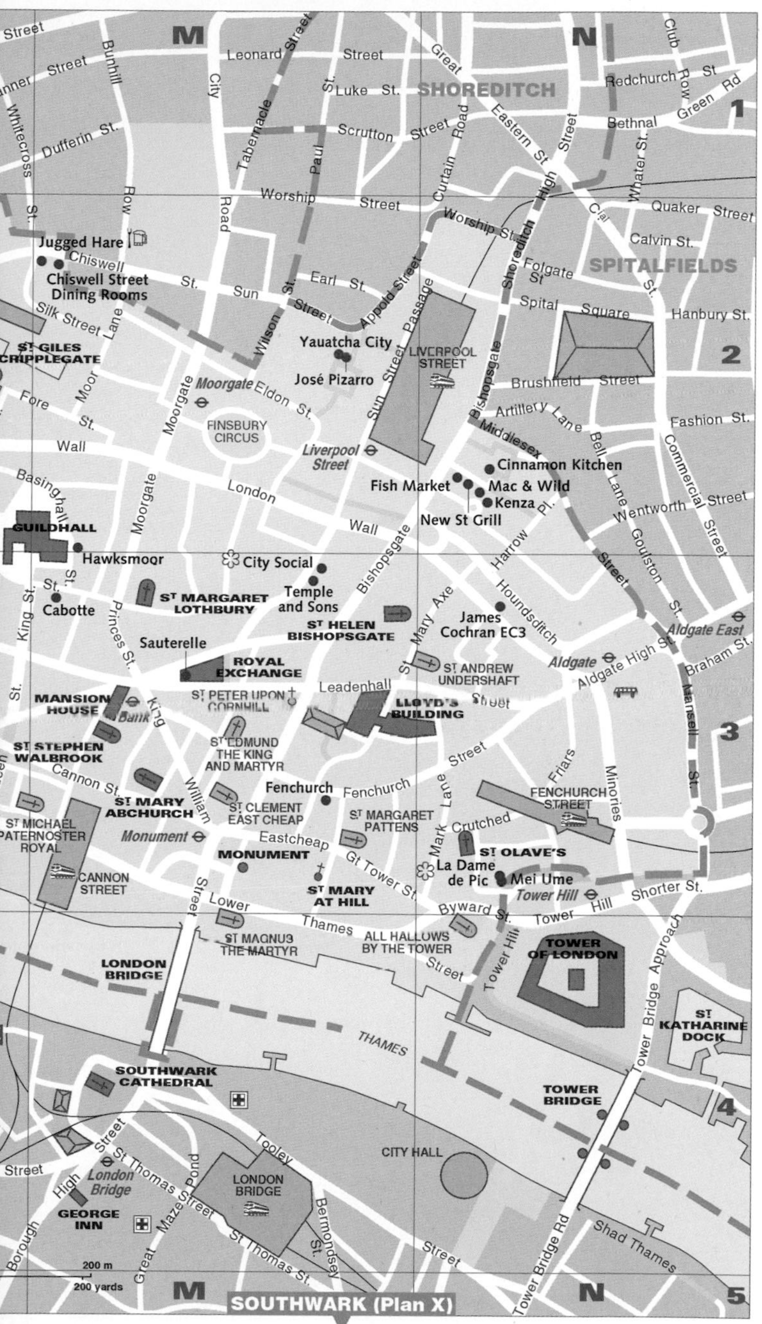
SHOREDITCH
SPITALFIELDS
Jugged Hare
Chiswell Street Dining Rooms
Yauatcha City
José Pizarro
LIVERPOOL STREET
FINSBURY CIRCUS
Cinnamon Kitchen
Fish Market
Mac & Wild
Kenza
New St Grill
GUILDHALL
Hawksmoor
City Social
Temple and Sons
Cabotte
ST MARGARET LOTHBURY
ST HELEN BISHOPSGATE
James Cochran EC3
Sauterelle
ROYAL EXCHANGE
ST ANDREW UNDERSHAFT
MANSION HOUSE
ST PETER UPON CORNHILL
LLOYD'S BUILDING
ST STEPHEN WALBROOK
ST EDMUND THE KING AND MARTYR
Fenchurch
ST MARY ABCHURCH
ST CLEMENT EAST CHEAP
ST MARGARET PATTENS
FENCHURCH STREET
ST MICHAEL PATERNOSTER ROYAL
MONUMENT
ST OLAVE'S
La Dame de Pic
Mei Ume
CANNON STREET
ST MARY AT HILL
ST MAGNUS THE MARTYR
ALL HALLOWS BY THE TOWER
TOWER OF LONDON
LONDON BRIDGE
THAMES
ST KATHARINE DOCK
SOUTHWARK CATHEDRAL
TOWER BRIDGE
CITY HALL
LONDON BRIDGE
GEORGE INN
200 m
200 yards
M
N
1
2
3
4
5
SOUTHWARK (Plan X)

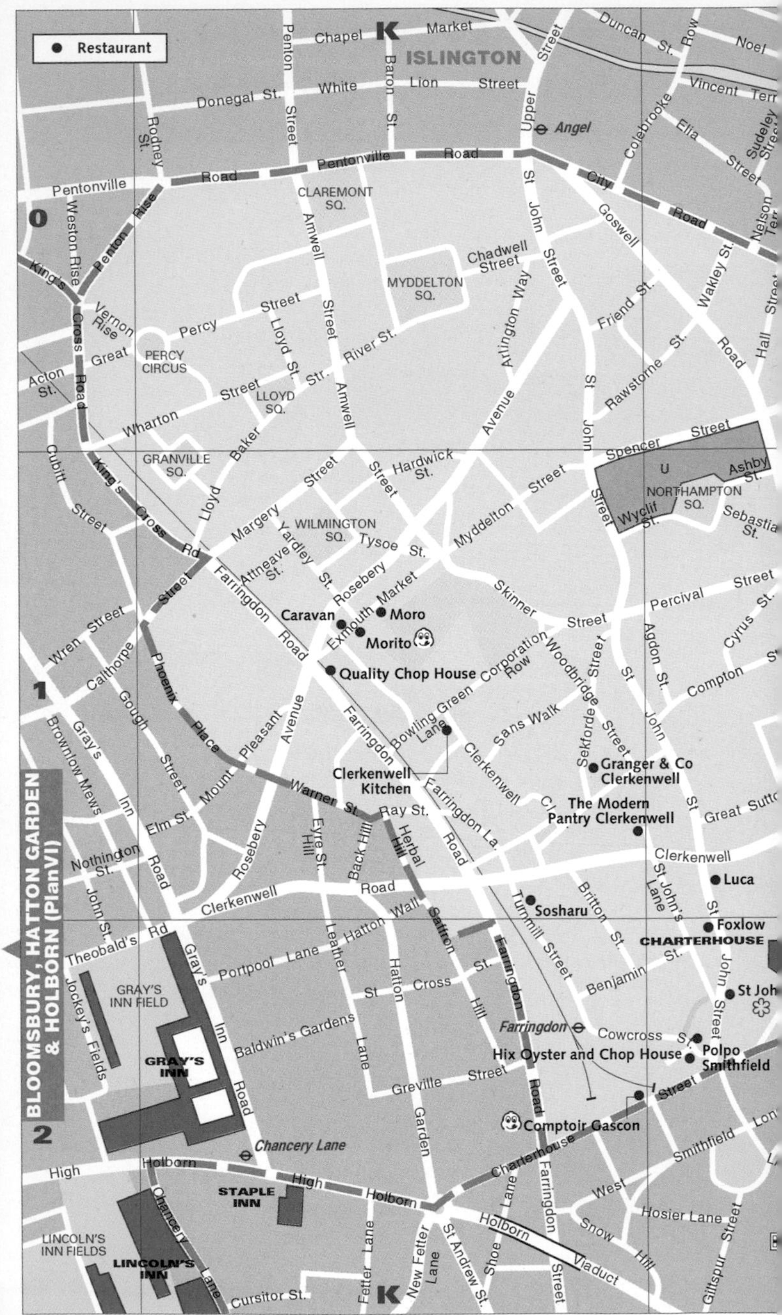

Restaurant
ISLINGTON
Angel
Caravan
Moro
Morito
Quality Chop House
Clerkenwell Kitchen
Granger & Co Clerkenwell
The Modern Pantry Clerkenwell
Luca
Sosharu
Foxlow
CHARTERHOUSE
St John
Hix Oyster and Chop House
Polpo Smithfield
Comptoir Gascon
Farringdon
Chancery Lane
CLAREMONT SQ.
MYDDELTON SQ.
PERCY CIRCUS
LLOYD SQ.
GRANVILLE SQ.
WILMINGTON SQ.
NORTHAMPTON SQ.
GRAY'S INN FIELD
GRAY'S INN
STAPLE INN
LINCOLN'S INN FIELDS
LINCOLN'S INN
Pentonville Road
City Road
Goswell Road
St John Street
Farringdon Road
Clerkenwell Road
Gray's Inn Road
King's Cross Road
Rosebery Avenue
Amwell Street
Charterhouse Street
Holborn Viaduct
High Holborn
Theobald's Rd
Hatton Garden
Leather Lane
Saffron Hill
Cowcross St.
Exmouth Market
BLOOMSBURY, HATTON GARDEN & HOLBORN (Plan VI)
K
0
1
2

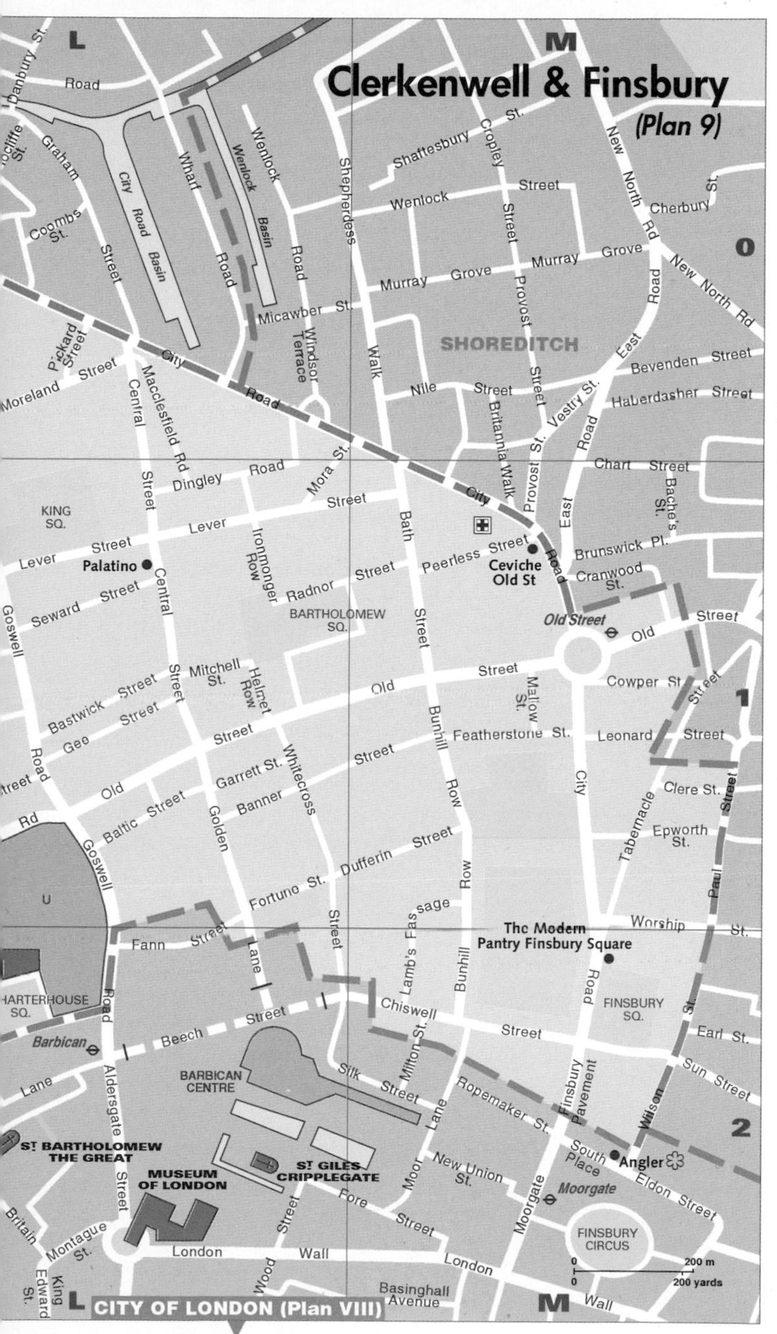

Clerkenwell & Finsbury
(Plan 9)
SHOREDITCH
KING SQ.
BARTHOLOMEW SQ.
FINSBURY SQ.
BARBICAN CENTRE
ST BARTHOLOMEW THE GREAT
MUSEUM OF LONDON
ST GILES CRIPPLEGATE
FINSBURY CIRCUS
Palatino
Ceviche Old St
The Modern Pantry Finsbury Square
Angler
Old Street
Barbican
Moorgate
CITY OF LONDON (Plan VIII)
200 m
200 yards

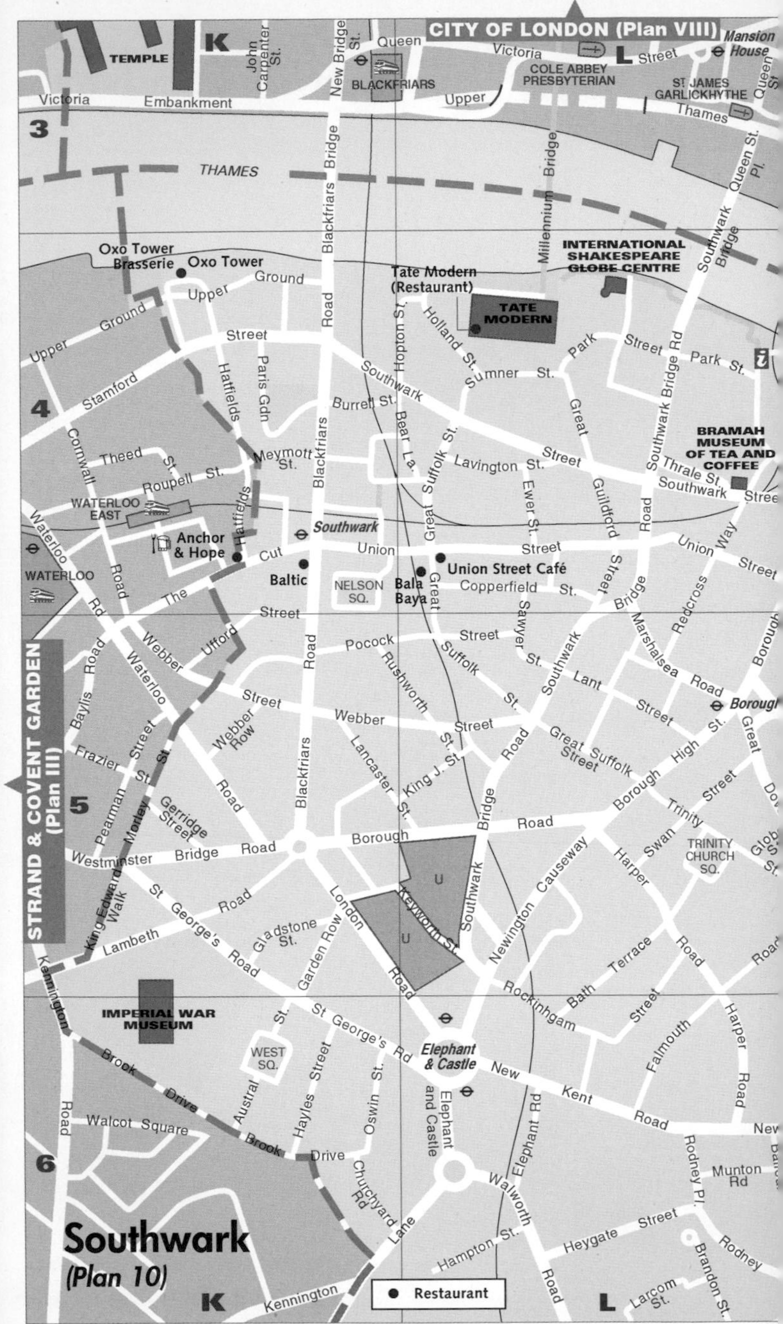
CITY OF LONDON (Plan VIII)
STRAND & COVENT GARDEN (Plan III)
Southwark
(Plan 10)
Restaurant
THAMES
TEMPLE
BLACKFRIARS
COLE ABBEY PRESBYTERIAN
ST JAMES GARLICKHYTHE
Mansion House
Oxo Tower Brasserie
Oxo Tower
Tate Modern (Restaurant)
TATE MODERN
INTERNATIONAL SHAKESPEARE GLOBE CENTRE
BRAMAH MUSEUM OF TEA AND COFFEE
WATERLOO EAST
WATERLOO
Anchor & Hope
Southwark
Baltic
NELSON SQ.
Bala Baya
Union Street Café
Borough
TRINITY CHURCH SQ.
IMPERIAL WAR MUSEUM
WEST SQ.
Elephant & Castle

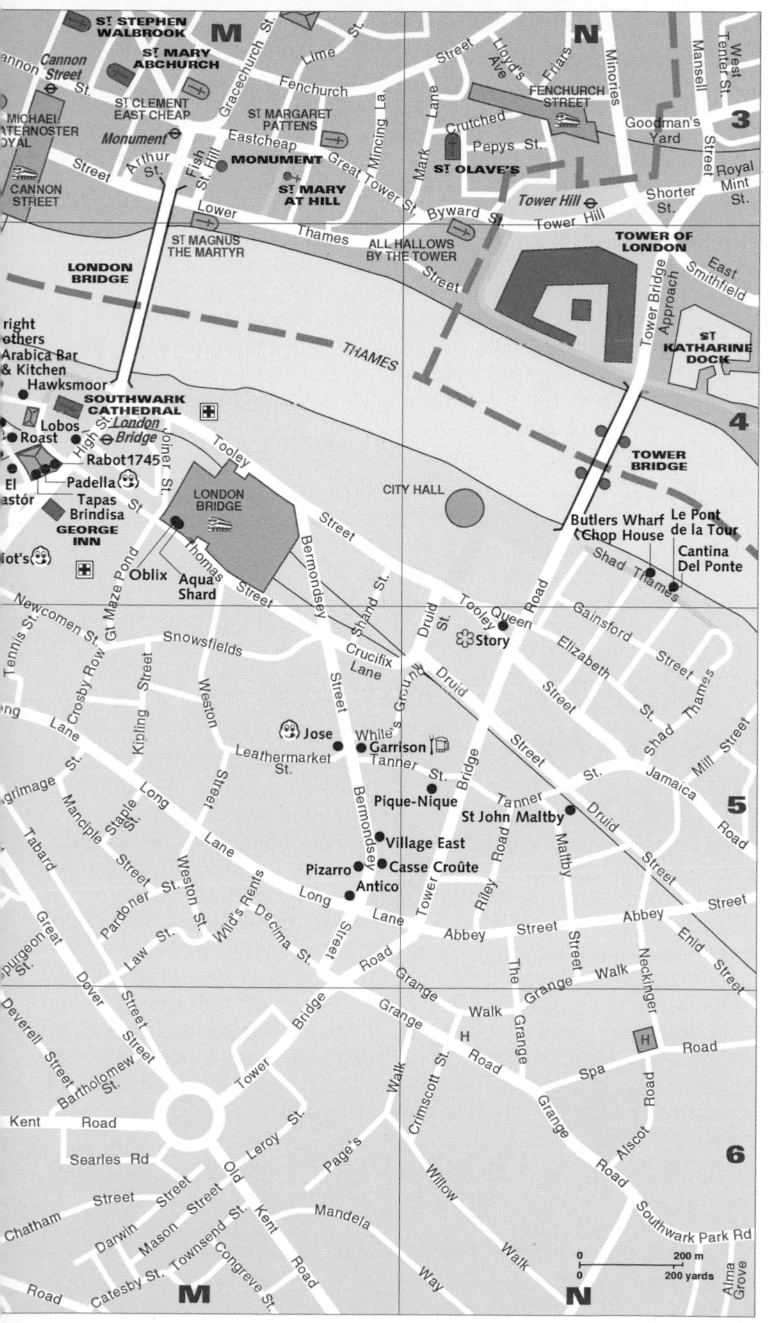
M
N
ST STEPHEN WALBROOK
ST MARY ABCHURCH
ST CLEMENT EAST CHEAP
ST MARGARET PATTENS
MONUMENT
ST MARY AT HILL
ST OLAVE'S
FENCHURCH STREET
CANNON STREET
ST MAGNUS THE MARTYR
ALL HALLOWS BY THE TOWER
TOWER OF LONDON
LONDON BRIDGE
ST KATHARINE DOCK
THAMES
SOUTHWARK CATHEDRAL
TOWER BRIDGE
CITY HALL
GEORGE INN
Hawksmoor
Lobos
Roast
Rabot1745
Padella
Tapas Brindisa
Oblix
Aqua Shard
Butlers Wharf Chop House
Le Pont de la Tour
Cantina Del Ponte
Story
Jose
Garrison
Pique-Nique
St John Maltby
Village East
Pizarro
Casse Croûte
Antico
3
4
5
6
200 m
200 yards

ANCHOR & HOPE

Modern British · *Pub*

MAP: 10-K4

The Anchor & Hope is still running at full steam and its popularity shows no sign of abating. It's not hard to see why: combine a menu that changes with each service and is a paragon of seasonality, with cooking that is gutsy, bold and wholesome, and you end up with immeasurably rewarding dishes like suckling kid chops with wild garlic, succulent roast pigeon with lentils or buttermilk pudding with poached rhubarb. The place has a contagiously congenial feel and the friendly staff all pull in the same direction; you may spot a waiter trimming vegetables or a chef delivering dishes to the tables. The no-reservation policy remains, so either get here early or be prepared to wait a while; you can, however, book for Sunday lunch.

- 36 The Cut ✉ SE1 8LP
  ✆ 020 7928 9898 — **www**.anchorandhopepub.co.uk
  ⊖ Southwark.
- Menu £17 (weekday lunch) - Carte £19/45
  Closed Christmas-New Year, Sunday dinner, Monday lunch and bank holidays - bookings not accepted

ANTICO

Italian · *Neighbourhood*

MAP: 10-M5

At the top end of busy Bermondsey Street – home to numerous pubs, bars and restaurants as well as art galleries, boutiques and markets – is this former antiques warehouse; its exposed brickwork and counter seating typical of the street's rustic-meets-hipster style. Downstairs, cocktail bar 214 Bermondsey offers over 80 gins as well as their own bottled brand of tonic water; back upstairs they serve honest Italian food with the focus firmly on comfort. Start with fluffy focaccia and some plump green olives; homemade pasta dishes like slow-roasted pork shoulder tortelloni are a highlight and desserts like lemon tart, very tasty. The atmosphere is fun, the staff full of smiles and the clientele pleasingly mixed in age and circumstance.

- 214 Bermondsey St ✉ SE1 3TQ
  ✆ 020 7407 4682 — **www**.antico-london.co.uk
  ⊖ London Bridge
- Menu £18 (lunch and early dinner) - Carte £23/39
  Closed 24-26 December, 1 January and Monday

ANGLER ✿

Seafood • Elegant

XX hTT ♿ A/C ✿ 🍸 **MAP:** 9-M2

Angler

FIRST COURSE: Tartare of yellowfin tuna with avocado, wasabi and shiso. • Veal sweetbread with garlic, girolles and broad beans.

MAIN COURSE: Cornish turbot with crab and Jersey Royals. • Roast Goosnargh chicken with Scottish langoustines, sweetcorn and almonds.

DESSERT: Seville orange soufflé with toasted brioche ice cream and marmalade. • Gariguette strawberries with clotted cream, buckwheat waffle and cream cheese.

It may be built into the eaves of D&D's South Place hotel, but this 7th floor room with its skyline views feels very much like a separate, stand-alone entity. It's a bright and comfortable space and one that feels intimate and elegant; it also comes with its own terrace where, on a warm evening, you'll see the cocktails go flying out. As the restaurant's name suggests, fish remains the mainstay of the menu - the majority of it comes from Cornwall and it's immediately clear that its quality is supreme. Head chef Gary Foulkes brought many of his team from The Square with him when he arrived back in 2016 and the kitchen's skill is clear to see. Cooking displays a light and delicate touch but there's no compromising on flavour, and colour plays an important role in the visual appeal of the dishes. There's a good value lunch menu available, while dinner is a little more elaborate, with the offer of both an à la carte and a very popular 5 course set menu, which comes with suggested wine pairings.

■ South Place Hotel, 3 South Pl ✉ EC2M 2AF
📞 020 3215 1260 — **www**.anglerrestaurant.com
⊖ Moorgate

■ Menu £38 (weekday lunch) - Carte £61/72
Closed 26-30 December, Saturday lunch and Sunday - booking advisable

AQUA SHARD

Modern cuisine • Fashionable

MAP: 10-M4

The Shard's most accessible restaurant covers all bases by serving breakfast, brunch, lunch, afternoon tea and dinner. You can even come here just for a drink and a gander which is surely preferable to paying for the viewing platform, but be warned – at weekends the queue is at street level and can be dispiritingly long. If you have booked to eat then the express lift will whisk you straight up here to the 31st floor where you should ask to sit on the west side for the better views. The contemporary cooking makes good use of British ingredients and comes with a degree of finesse in both flavour and presentation. The à la carte prices can be a little steep though, so your best bet is to come for lunch and go for the Market Menu.

- Level 31, The Shard, 31 St Thomas St, ✉ SE1 9RY
  020 3011 1256 — **www**.aquashard.co.uk
  London Bridge
- Menu £32 (weekday lunch) - Carte £49/82
  Closed 25 December - booking advisable

ARABICA BAR & KITCHEN

World cuisine • Rustic

MAP: 10-M4

Self-taught chef-owner James Walters started selling mezze from a trestle table at Borough Market around 14 years ago, so it's no surprise he chose to open his Levantine-inspired restaurant under a railway arch at the side of the market. It's a fun, lively and cavernous place with tightly packed tables and a map on the wall which highlights the countries on which the kitchen's attention is focused: Egypt, Syria, Iraq, Jordan and Lebanon. Order some dips and flatbread from the clay oven while you look at the menu. What stands out is the sheer freshness of the produce and the vivid colours on the plate. This is food to be celebrated and shared, with the charcoal dishes proving particularly succulent and salads pleasingly vibrant.

- 3 Rochester Wk. Borough Market ✉ SE1 9AF
  020 3011 5151 — **www**.arabicabarandkitchen.com
  London Bridge
- Carte £21/36
  Closed 25-27 December and 1 January - bookings advisable at dinner

Ⓝ BALA BAYA

Middle Eastern • Design

MAP: 10-L4

Tucked under a huge Victorian railway arch, its thumping soundtrack interspersed with the rumble of trains overhead, is this lively, super-friendly restaurant which celebrates the Middle Eastern heritage of its passionate chef-owner, Eran Tibi. Its bright, modern interior is inspired by the Bauhaus architecture of Tel Aviv, with a buzzing ground floor home to the open kitchen, a bar counter and a scattering of tables – and an atmospheric mezzanine high above. Dishes are fresh, vibrant and designed for sharing; don't miss the crispy, sticky, crunchy chicken or the aubergine with tea milk. If you're here for lunch go for one of the deliciously plump pitta breads, cooked in Tibi's father's oven, which has been brought over specially from Israel.

- Arch 25, Old Union Yard Arches, 229 Union St ✉ SE1 0LR
  ✆ 020 8001 7015 — **www**.balabaya.co.uk
  ⊖ Southwark
- Menu £20 (lunch) - Carte £22/41
  Closed 25-26 December and Sunday dinner - bookings advisable at dinner

BALTIC

World cuisine • Brasserie

MAP: 10-K4

With an entrance akin to that of a small bar, this restaurant comes as something of a surprise; carry on past the long cocktail bar and you emerge in a bright, buzzing space with wooden trussed ceilings, skylights and sleek styling. The daily menu is an appealing read and specialises in dishes from various countries out east - Poland, Russia, Bulgaria, and even Siberia. Expect a selection of blinis, assorted dumplings including pierogi and spaetzle, lots of meat dishes such as pork schnitzel and lamb shashlik - and over 70 varieties of vodka, available by the glass or carafe. The cooking is executed with more subtlety than you expect and the largely Polish staff are clearly proud and pleased to be serving food with which they are familiar.

- 74 Blackfriars Rd ✉ SE1 8HA
  ✆ 020 7928 1111 — **www**.balticrestaurant.co.uk
  ⊖ Southwark
- Menu £22 (lunch and early dinner) - Carte £26/38
  Closed 24-27 December and Monday lunch - bookings advisable at dinner

BARBECOA ꟷ

Meats and grills • Design

MAP: 8-L3

Good barbecue is about using prime ingredients and choosing the appropriate cooking method. At Jamie Oliver's Barbecoa the kitchen uses fire pits, smokers, tandoors, grills and ovens to ensure maximum flavour on your plate, whether you've chosen prawns, ribs, pulled pork shoulder or dry-aged British steak. Another thing BBQ needs is a good appetite: ideally you'd have spent the morning chopping down trees although, judging by the clientele and the suit jackets hanging off the backs of the chairs, it seems that working in finance does just as well. Don't ignore the starters, like pig's cheek or beetroot salad, as they're more than a run-up to the main course – and if you manage dessert too then you won't need to eat again for days.

- 20 New Change Passage ✉ EC4M 9AG
  020 3005 8555 — **www**.barbecoa.com
  St Paul's
- Menu £27 (weekday lunch) - Carte £32/64
  Closed 25-26 December and 1 January - booking essential

BIRD OF SMITHFIELD

Modern cuisine • Contemporary décor

MAP: 8-L2

This attractive Victorian townhouse offers a relaxed look and the atmosphere of a private members' club but without the smugness. Five floors of fun include a basement club, a ground-floor lounge with a menu of light dishes, a private dining room and an appealing rooftop terrace where you can enjoy a cocktail with views over Smithfield Market. The intimate restaurant has a contemporary look, with art from the owner's collection on the walls. There's an obvious classic French base to the cooking but it's delivered in a gentle, modern manner and dishes like roasted quail with sweetcorn and girolles or steamed loin of cod with seaweed butter and prawns are carefully crafted and full of flavour.

- 26 Smithfield St ✉ EC1A 9LB
  020 7559 5100 — **www**.birdofsmithfield.com
  Farringdon
- Menu £18 (lunch and early dinner) - Carte £28/53
  Closed Christmas, New Year, Sunday and bank holidays - booking essential

BREAD STREET KITCHEN

Modern cuisine • Trendy

MAP: 8-L3

Influenced perhaps by the time he has spent in the US in recent years, Bread Street Kitchen is Gordon Ramsay's take on New York loft-style dining. With floor to ceiling windows, a large bar, thumping music, an open kitchen running down one side and enough zinc ducting on the ceiling to kit out a small industrial estate, the space is big, butch and full of buzz. In a further departure from his usual style of operation, the food is quite simple and rustic – think modern bistro dishes with the odd touch of refinement – and there is enough choice to provide something for everyone. The short rib burger is a best seller; the wood oven is used to good effect with dishes like braised pork collar; and the desserts are particularly well done.

- 10 Bread St ✉ EC4M 9AJ
  020 3030 4050 — **www**.breadviewkitchen.com
  St Paul's
- Carte £31/63
  Booking advisable

BUTLERS WHARF CHOP HOUSE

Traditional British • Brasserie

MAP: 10-N4

A chophouse means meat and, where there is meat, there are usually men. You'll see plenty of them here, their suit jackets slung over their seats as they get stuck into a charcoal-grilled rib-eye or prepare to wrestle with a game bird. The menu is a paean to all things British so other choices such as steak and kidney pudding or lamb with haggis are equally sturdy; finish off with a sticky toffee pudding and you'll wonder if you'll ever be hungry again. The large room comes with light wood panelling that'll prompt cricketers to think of linseed oil, and the bar at the entrance offers a simpler and cheaper menu. Come in the summer for a table on the fantastic terrace – few restaurants can match the stunning views.

- 36e Shad Thames, Butlers Wharf ✉ SE1 2YE
  020 7403 3403 — **www**.chophouse-restaurant.co.uk
  London Bridge
- Menu £29 - Carte £28/69
  Closed 1 January

Ⓝ CABOTTE

French • Wine bar

MAP: 8-M3

A cabotte is a type of small hut, built to shelter wine growers in the Burgundy region of France, and a well-chosen name for this Burgundy-obsessed restaurant. It is owned by two master sommeliers who share a passion for wine and, in particular, the wines of Burgundy – and is backed by twelve of the region's most influential producers. The wine list is quite simply stunning – staff also share the owners' knowledge and are happy to make recommendations, and if the full list proves too bewildering, there is also a more manageable 'short' list. Cooking from the talented kitchen comes with the same regional bias; accomplished Burgundian classics like oeuf en meurette and beef cheek bourguignon en cocotte being simple in style and rich in flavour.

■ 48 Gresham St ✉ EC2V 7AY
020 7600 1616 — **www.**cabotte.co.uk
⊖ Bank

■ Carte £30/44
Closed Saturday and Sunday – booking essential

CANTINA DEL PONTE

Italian • Rustic

MAP: 10-N4

A refurbishment a few years back revitalised this Italian stalwart. They kept the large mural on one wall and created a pleasantly relaxing, faux-rustic environment. The menu was also tweaked: it was out with the pizzas and in with a greater degree of authenticity. The focus is on appealing and flavoursome dishes and the set menu represents decent value. There's a good selection on offer, with the focus very much on recognisable standards and old favourites; flavours are well-defined and portions are bigger than expected. The wine list covers all of Italy and there's ample choice by the glass. The first tables to go on a summer's day are naturally those on the riverside terrace under the awning.

■ 36c Shad Thames, Butlers Wharf ✉ SE1 2YE
020 7403 5403 — **www.**cantina.co.uk
⊖ London Bridge

■ Menu £20 (weekday lunch) – Carte £31/42
Closed 26-27 December

CARAVAN

World cuisine • Trendy

MAP: 9-K1

A discernible Antipodean vibe pervades this casual eatery, from the laid-back, easy-going charm of the serving team to the kitchen's confident combining of unusual flavours; even in the excellent flat-whites served by the barista. There's an ersatz industrial feel to the room and a randomness to the decorative touches that belies the seriousness of the ambition. The 100% Arabica beans are roasted daily in the basement, the wine list features an unusual selection of producers and plenty of organic wines, and the owners' travels (hence the name) inform the innovative and inventive cooking. There's something for everyone, from breakfast to small plates to share, or even main courses for two – this really is a caravan of love.

- 11-13 Exmouth Market ✉ EC1R 4QD
  020 7833 8115 — **www.**caravanrestaurants.co.uk
  Farringdon
- Carte £18/35
  Closed 25-26, 31 December and 1 January - booking advisable

CASSE CROÛTE

French • Bistro

MAP: 10-M5

The joys of Bermondsey Street are legion and the variety of restaurants on offer is considerable but if you'd still prefer to feel you're somewhere else then squeeze into this tiny bistro and you'll be instantly transported to rural France. From the fleur de lys decoration and the tiled flooring to the red leather seating and the gingham table cloths, this place is so French that if a film studio had created it they would be accused of perpetuating cultural clichés. The blackboard menu offers just three choices for each course but does evolve during the day, with new dishes added as others run out. The cooking is rustic and authentic and the flavours heartening and wholesome; go the whole way and have the cheese course too.

- 109 Bermondsey St ✉ SE1 3XB
  020 7407 2140 — **www.**cassecroute.co.uk
  London Bridge
- Carte £30/36
  Closed Sunday dinner - booking essential

CEVICHE OLD ST ℩O

Peruvian • Brasserie

MAP: 9-M1

This younger sister to the original Ceviche in Soho is housed on the ground floor of the Grade II listed former Alexandra Trust Dining Rooms, built in 1898 by tea magnate Sir Thomas Lipton for the people of East London, who could enjoy a three course meal for the princely sum of tuppence. These days, the place has a buzzy brasserie feel and the food is designed for sharing. A pisco sour is the best way to start proceedings, followed by star of the show, ceviche. Three small plates per person plus a side dish is ideal; dishes arrive quickly and are easy to eat, vibrant and full of flavour. Keep your eyes peeled when nature calls – there is a constantly changing collection of Peruvian art in the corridor, all of it for sale.

- 2 Baldwin St ✉ EC1V 9NU
  020 3327 9463 — **www.**cevicheuk.com
  ⊖ Old Street
- Menu £20/50 - Carte £15/37

THE CHANCERY ℩O

Modern cuisine • Chic

MAP: 8-K2

The Chancery is an elegant, discreet restaurant that's so close to the law courts you'll assume your fellow diners are all barristers, jurors or the recently acquitted. The ground floor, with its contemporary artwork and smartly laid tables, is slightly more comfortable than the basement and, despite having to deal with all those formal types, the service team remain bright and friendly. The menu is appealingly concise and understated and most of the dishes have a reassuringly classical backbone, whether that's the mackerel escabeche or the saddle of rabbit. The kitchen clearly knows what it is doing – flavours are bold and sauces are a particular highlight.

- 9 Cursitor St ✉ EC4A 1LL
  020 7831 4000 — **www.**thechancery.co.uk
  ⊖ Chancery Lane
- Menu £40 (weekdays)/65
  Closed 23 December-4 January, Saturday lunch, Sunday and bank holidays

CHISWELL STREET DINING ROOMS

Modern British • Brasserie

MAP: 8-M2

In a corner spot of the former Whitbread brewery is this Martin brothers' restaurant and, although it may double as a dining room for the Montcalm Hotel, the place really comes alive in the evening, thanks in no small part to its lively bar. Wood-panelled walls, lithographs and lime green chairs give the place an appealingly clubby style and there's a pleasing Britishness to the menu, with classics like roast fillet of golden bream with samphire or Mrs Kirkham's twice-baked cheddar soufflé. Those who prefer more muscular cooking should go for the Herdwick lamb rump or one of the Cumbrian rare breed steaks; dishes are satisfying, carefully cooked and full of flavour. The smartly kitted-out staff cope well and help with the buzzy atmosphere.

- Montcalm London City Hotel, 56 Chiswell St ✉ EC1Y 4SA
  020 7614 0177 – **www**.chiswellstreetdining.com
  Barbican
- Menu £38 - Carte £31/57
  Closed 25-26 December, 1 January, Saturday and Sunday

CIGALON

French • Elegant

MAP: 8-K3

Its name might refer to a 1935 Marcel Pagnol film about a haughty chef, but it's also the French word for the summer cicada and, sitting in this stylish, high-ceilinged dining room with its huge skylight and trailing foliage, you are indeed reminded of sunny Mediterranean days. The kitchen pays homage to the food of Provence with occasional hints of Corsica and the menu is a good value affair; expect flavoursome French classics like salade Niçoise, bouillabaisse and ratatouille alongside popular grilled meat and fish specials. Start with an aperitif in the atmospheric downstairs bar; if it's privacy you're after, sit in one of the central booths – ask for no. 9 if you want to watch the chefs in action.

- 115 Chancery Ln ✉ WC2A 1PP
  020 7242 8373 – **www**.cigalon.co.uk
  Chancery Lane
- Menu £22/37 - Carte lunch £29/39
  Closed Christmas, New Year, Saturday, Sunday and bank holidays

CINNAMON KITCHEN

Indian • *Trendy*

MAP: 8-N2

A wall of sound hits you as you enter this contemporary Indian restaurant; a sure sign of its continued popularity. This was the second of the Cinnamons and it's massive, modern and minimalistic, with a terrace, a trendy bar and zinc ducting to lend an industrial edge. The cooking is creative and original, with dishes that bear little resemblance to the usual Indian fare and include ingredients like quinoa, red deer and squid. Meat dishes are a highlight and the arresting presentation doesn't come at the expense of punchy flavours. A tasting menu is offered in the evening with well-chosen wine matches, service is keen and sprightly, and enthusiastic amateur cooks should position themselves at the Grill Bar to watch all the action.

- 9 Devonshire Sq ✉ EC2M 4YL
  ✆ 020 7626 5000 – **www**.cinnamon-kitchen.com
  ⊖ Liverpool Street
- Menu £21 (lunch) - Carte £27/52
  Closed Saturday lunch, Sunday and bank holidays

CLERKENWELL KITCHEN

Modern cuisine • *Friendly*

MAP: 9-K1

Time spent working in Dorset with Hugh Fearnley-Whittingstall has clearly influenced Emma, the owner of this busy, tucked away eatery: she sources her ingredients from small producers who use traditional methods and is committed to sustainability, recycling and the reduction of food miles. But this is more than just a worthy enterprise - the food is rather good too. Local office workers flock in for breakfast and takeaway sandwiches but it is well worth booking for the appealing daily changing lunch menu. Two of the six main courses will be vegetarian and offer, along with dishes like venison and pancetta pie, plenty of freshness and flavour. Even the juices are seasonal and the tarts, pies and cakes are all made daily.

- 27-31 Clerkenwell Cl ✉ EC1R 0AT
  ✆ 020 7101 9959 – **www**.theclerkenwellkitchen.co.uk
  ⊖ Farringdon
- Carte £15/28
  Closed Christmas-New Year, Saturday, Sunday and bank holidays - booking advisable - (lunch only)

CITY SOCIAL ✿

Modern cuisine • Elegant

XXX ⋞ ♿ A/C ⊡ ✿ 🍸 **MAP:** 8-M3

Michelin

FIRST COURSE: Yellowfin tuna tataki with cucumber salad and radish with ponzu dressing. • Orkney scallops with truffled mash and cured ham.

MAIN COURSE: Cornish sea bass with deep-fried oyster, cucumber, cauliflower and oyster velouté. • Duck breast with confit leg & heart, carrot reduction and leeks.

DESSERT: Hazelnut plaisir sucré with chocolate syrup, biscuit and milk ice cream. • Banana parfait with honeycomb and salted caramel ice cream.

The buzz from the bar is the first thing you notice when you come up in the lift to Jason Atherton's handsome, well-run restaurant on the 24th floor of Tower 42. Dark and moody with a subtle art deco twist, it boasts impressive views of the City's ever-changing skyline – especially if you're sitting at one of the coveted window tables. Large parties should request one of the comfortable circular booths; those wanting to bag themselves a husband or a wife should ask for table 10, the proposal table. The menu is the same at lunch and dinner, but has some flexibility built in. Influences are largely European and dishes like côte de boeuf for two, lobster and chips and black olive potato gnocchi are not only incredibly tasty but also very good value. The kitchen has a deft touch but wisely acknowledges its customer base by making dishes quite robust in flavour and generous in size – this is elegant, refined but satisfying cooking, without the frills and fripperies. The wine list is also noteworthy, with a good mix of styles and prices.

- Tower 42 (24th floor), 25 Old Broad St ✉ EC2N 1HQ
  ✆ 020 7877 7703 — **www**.citysociallondon.com
  ⊖ Liverpool Street
- Carte £43/68
  Closed Sunday and bank holidays

CLUB GASCON ✿

French • Intimate

XX A/C ✿ **MAP:** 8-L2

Club Gascon

FIRST COURSE: Flamed duck and smoked pine with aromatic razor clams. • Elderflower and sake scallop with strawberries and frosted watermelon.

MAIN COURSE: Barbecued 'white gold' fish with maize, truffle and bacon sauce. • Pastrami beef rib with artichoke, samphire and broad beans.

DESSERT: 'Millionaire' 72% Colombian chocolate with black olive, lemon gel and thyme ice cream. • Cherries with lavender, almonds and iced tarragon.

Those living in Gascony enjoy a diet with the highest fat content in France yet they tend to live longer than their compatriots. Leaving aside the magical powers of Armagnac, this 'Gascony paradox' is surely reason enough to explore further this most indulgent of cuisines. Chef-owner Pascal Aussignac is passionate about all things south-western: get him started on the quality of the produce and he'll talk the hind legs off an âne. Whilst familiar ingredients appear on the menu, the cooking is surprisingly contemporary and often quite original; the ambition may not always be matched by the execution but the dishes will certainly grab your attention. Lunch is a slightly pared-down version of the evening menu but the tasting menu remains the benchmark and comes with some intelligent and well-considered wine matches. Service is appropriately and unapologetically Gallic, while marble pillars, panelling and huge floral displays add grandeur to the high-ceilinged room, which was once a Lyons Corner House.

- 57 West Smithfield ✉ EC1A 9DS
  ✆ 020 7600 6144 — **www**.clubgascon.com
  ⊖ Barbican
- Menu £45/80 - Carte £50/70
  Closed August, Christmas-New Year, Saturday lunch, Sunday-Monday and bank holidays - booking essential

COMPTOIR GASCON

French • Bistro

MAP: 9-K2

This buzzy restaurant should be subsidised by the French Tourist Board as it does more to illustrate one component of Gascony's famed 'douceur de vivre' - sweetness of life - than any glossy brochure. The wines, breads, foie gras, duck and cheeses all celebrate SW France's reputation for earthy, proper man-food. The menu starts with 'humble beginnings', followed by 'surf and turf'; be sure to order something from the 'best of duck' section, whether as rillettes, confit or in a burger. After these big flavours, it'll come as a relief to see that the desserts are delicate little things. Prices are commendable; even the region's wine comes direct from the producers to avoid the extra mark-up. There's further booty on the surrounding shelves.

- 61-63 Charterhouse St. ✉ EC1M 6HJ
  020 7608 0851 — **www**.comptoirgascon.com
  Farringdon
- Carte £18/34
  Closed Christmas-New Year, Sunday, Monday and bank holidays - booking essential

EL PASTÓR

Mexican • Trendy

MAP: 10-M4

The Hart brothers of Barrafina fame are the masterminds behind El Pastór; putting Mexican food on the map with this lively, informal spot under the railway arches at London Bridge. Arrive early if you want the pick of the seats, as there's a no-booking policy; the best place is opposite the two-storey open kitchen, where corn tortillas are made from scratch twice-daily. Order a few carafes of mescal and get acquainted with the menu - if you don't know your tostados from your tacos, then the cool staff will happily guide you through proceedings. Flavours are beautifully fresh, fragrant and spicy; don't miss the Taco Al Pastór after which the restaurant is named; an explosive mix of marinated pork shoulder, caramelised pineapple and guacamole.

- 7a Stoney St, Borough Market ✉ SE1 9AA
  www.tacoselpastor.co.uk
  London Bridge
- Carte £12/20
  Closed 25-26 December, 1-2 January and Sunday - bookings not accepted

Ⓝ LA DAME DE PIC ✿

Modern French • Design

MAP: 8-N3

La Dame de Pic

FIRST COURSE: Berlingots with smoked Pélardon cheese, wild mushrooms and Voatsiperifery pepper. • Langoustines in shellfish butter with herb-infused carrot bouillon.

MAIN COURSE: Wild turbot with beetroot, lovage sabayon and saffron. • Sake-marinated chicken with hispi cabbage, razor clams, lemon and sauce suprême.

DESSERT: The white millefeuille. • Kalingo chocolate with aromatic herb ice cream and cocoa nibs Chantilly.

You'd expect a famous chef bringing her brand from Paris to London to seek out a grand space for her restaurant. And while this high-ceilinged, columned room, situated in the impressive Beaux-Arts style Four Seasons Hotel, is certainly striking; the restaurant is not so much a formal temple of gastronomy as a charming brasserie deluxe – stylish, spacious and contemporary, with lots of white, plenty of light and some attractive modern art. Pic's cuisine is refined, feminine and original: firmly rooted in classic French techniques yet delivered in a modern manner; relying on exciting flavour combinations of top quality ingredients to deliver impact. Signature dishes include Berlingots (pasta parcels of smoked Pélardon cheese), wild sea bass with caviar and champagne sauce, and the arresting 'white millefeuille' for dessert. The well-structured wine list highlights wines from the Rhône Valley – home of restaurant Maison Pic, the Valence institution owned by the Pic family and where it all began for la Dame herself.

■ Four Seasons Hotel London at Ten Trinity Square, 10 Trinity Sq ✉ EC3N 4AJ
✆ 020 3297 3790 — **www**.ladamedepiclondon.co.uk
⊖ Tower Hill

■ Menu £39 (weekday lunch) - Carte £65/102
Closed Sunday dinner

ELLIOT'S

Modern cuisine • Rustic

X **MAP:** 10-M4

This lively, unpretentious café provides a masterclass in keeping things simple. They take top quality ingredients - sourced directly from Borough Market in which the café stands - and marry several of them together to create earthy, uncomplicated dishes that are full of flavour and will leave anyone feeling sated and satisfied. The menu is concise, regularly changing and instantly appealing; try one of their sharing dishes like the slow-cooked lamb shoulder or the 40-day dry-aged Dexter beef; this has become quite a feature, as has the fish from the Sussex day boats. If you're not sharing, then around four plates per person will suffice; staff are more than happy to guide your choices. Ask for a table at the far end under the skylight.

- 12 Stoney St, Borough Market ✉ SE1 9AD
  ☎ 020 7403 7436 — **www**.elliotscafe.com
  ⊖ London Bridge
- Carte £25/33
  Closed Sunday and bank holidays - booking advisable

FENCHURCH

Modern cuisine • Design

XX **MAP:** 8-M3

It's wise to arrive here at the 'Walkie Talkie' early, not only because you have to go through the faff of airport-style security on the ground floor but also because you'll want to have a wander around the Sky Garden - a vast atrium with greenery at the top of the building. This is also the time to take in the vista because the restaurant is housed in a glass box within it and actually the views from here aren't great. At least the restaurant understands it has to offer more than a great location, so the welcome is warm, the room is smartly kitted out and the food is prepared with care. The dishes are seasonal and largely British and the accomplished cooking uses excellent ingredients and modern techniques.

- Level 37, 20 Fenchurch St ✉ EC3M 3BY
  ☎ 0333 772 0020 — **www**.skygarden.london
  ⊖ Monument
- Menu £35 (weekday lunch) - Carte £49/69
  Closed 25-26 December - booking advisable

FISH MARKET ꟾO

Seafood · Friendly

MAP: 8-N2

An antidote to the plethora of steakhouses comes in the form of this traditional seafood restaurant, courtesy of the D&D group. Housed within a former warehouse of the East India Company, it has an appealing ersatz industrial look, with cast-iron pillars, rough-hewn walls and limed oak; the chef shucking oysters behind the full-length marble-topped bar adds to the feeling that you've stepped from Liverpool Street straight into St Ives. From its lengthy, well-priced menu of classics, the kitchen concentrates on delivering familiar flavours – and by using Cornish crab, oysters from Colchester and West Mersea, day boat plaice, line-caught cod and farmed bass from Greece, it demonstrates it has the appropriate sustainability credentials.

- 16b New St ✉ EC2M 4TR
  ✆ 020 3503 0790 — **www**.fishmarket-restaurant.com
  ⊖ Liverpool Street
- Menu £20 - Carte £29/50
  Closed 25-26 December, 1 January, Sunday dinner and bank holidays - booking advisable

FOXLOW ꟾO

Meats and grills · Neighbourhood

MAP: 9-L2

When those clever people behind the Hawksmoor chain took over the site of the former North Road restaurant, they decided it would make the ideal spot in which to serve something a little different to the usual offerings found in their various steakhouses. Granted, there are steaks on offer but there are plenty of other choices whose influences come from Italy, Asia and the Middle East – highlights include the 8-hour bacon rib, which is smoked overnight, assorted fresh salads, and ice cream sundaes in a myriad of flavours. The vibe is fun and lively, especially on the ground floor and the place has a funky look too, with a reclaimed oak floor and glazed bricks from a London Underground station on display.

- 69-73 St John St ✉ EC1M 4AN
  ✆ 020 7680 2702 — **www**.foxlow.co.uk
  ⊖ Farringdon
- Menu £18 - Carte £22/39
  Closed 24 December-1 January and bank holidays

GARRISON

Mediterranean cuisine • Pub

MAP: 10-M5

You'd be hard pressed to find a more charming pub than The Garrison. With its appealing vintage look, warm atmosphere and delightful staff, it's the perfect antidote to those hard-edged boozers that we've all accidentally found ourselves in at some point. Open from 8am for smoothies and breakfast, it gets busier as the day goes on – and don't bother coming for dinner if you haven't booked. Booth numbers 4 and 5, opposite the open kitchen, are the most popular while number 2 at the back is the cosiest. Daily specials on the blackboard supplement the nicely balanced menu and the cooking is perky and bright, with a subtle Mediterranean slant. Salads are done well and there's a daily steak, while puds are of a more traditional bent.

- 99-101 Bermondsey St ✉ SE1 3XB
  ✆ 020 7089 9355 — **www**.thegarrison.co.uk
  ⊖ London Bridge.
- Carte £26/39
  Closed 25 December - booking essential at dinner

GRANGER & CO. CLERKENWELL

Modern cuisine • Family

MAP: 9-K1

By turning to Clerkenwell for his second London restaurant, Aussie food writer and restaurateur Bill Granger showed his knack for picking the right location. This bright and stylish environment proves the ideal backdrop for a menu inspired by his peregrinations around the world. There's something for everyone, with small and big plates, BBQ dishes, pizzas, salads, bowls of rice and grains, and, of course, his celebrated breakfasts which include his deliriously creamy scrambled eggs. His best dishes are often those enlivened with the flavours of southeast Asia and are especially appealing after you've spent time exploring the cocktail list. The chummy service contributes considerably to the appealingly laid back atmosphere.

- 50 Sekforde St ✉ EC1R 0HA
  ✆ 020 7251 9032 — **www**.grangerandco.com
  ⊖ Farringdon
- Carte £13/39
  Closed 24-26 December and Sunday dinner

HAWKSMOOR

Meats and grills • Traditional décor

MAP: 8-M2

Fast and furious, busy and boisterous, Hawksmoor provides another testosterone filled celebration of the serious business of beef eating – this is about red meat, red wine and red-faced City types in duels to see who can order the biggest steak. It's a handsome room, with its low ceiling, leather seating and wood panelling which was once used in specimen cupboards at the Natural History Museum. The place comes with a great cocktail list and an impressive wine list offering plenty of Mouton Rothschild for the big earners. The Longhorn steaks are nicely aged, particularly the D-Rump, and well-rested before coming to the table. With notice you can order 'meat feasts' which take you on a 7 course 'tour of a cow'.

- 10-12 Basinghall St ✉ EC2V 5BQ
  020 7397 8120 — **www**.thehawksmoor.com
  Bank
- Menu £28 (lunch and early dinner) - Carte £23/63
  Closed 24 December-2 January, Saturday, Sunday and bank holidays - booking essential

N HAWKSMOOR

Meats and grills • Brasserie

MAP: 10-M4

As restaurant chains expand, it's often the case that the standard of their offering suffers; not so Hawksmoor, whose lively 7th branch is situated a stone's throw from Borough Market, with a daily changing Market Specials menu that makes good use of its produce. As with most of their restaurants, the building has a history: formerly a hop warehouse, and then an auction house for fruit specialists J.O. Sims, it comes with characterful features like weathered beams, a parquet floor and warm oak panelling. Foodwise, the focus is on chargrilled, grass-fed, 35-day dry-aged British steaks - properly cooked and rested and very, very tasty. Desserts are creative and worth saving room for; killer cocktails and a well-chosen wine list complete the picture.

- 16 Winchester Walk ✉ SE1 9AQ
  020 7234 9940 — **www**.thehawksmoor.com
  London Bridge
- Menu £25 (lunch and early dinner) - Carte £23/68
  Closed 24-26 December and 1 January

HIX OYSTER AND CHOP HOUSE

Traditional British • Bistro

MAP: 9-L2

Utilitarian surroundings, seasonal British ingredients, plenty of offal and prissy-free cooking: this may sound like a description of St John but was in fact Mark Hix's first solo venture and the start of his rapidly expanding restaurant empire. Smithfield Market seems an appropriate location for a restaurant that not only celebrates Britain's culinary heritage with old classics like rabbit brawn, nettle soup and beef and oyster pie but also reminds us of our own natural bounty, from sand eels to asparagus, whiting to laver bread. It's also called an Oyster and Chop House for a reason, with four types of oyster on offer as well as plenty of meat, including Aberdeen beef aged for 28 days and served on the bone.

- 36-37 Greenhill Rents ✉ EC1M 6BN
  020 7017 1930 — **www**.hixoysterandchophouse.co.uk
  Farringdon
- Menu £15 (lunch) - Carte £15/48
  Closed 25-29 December and bank holidays

N JAMES COCHRAN EC3

Modern cuisine • Simple

MAP: 8-N3

After stints at the Harwood Arms and The Ledbury, the eponymous James embarked on a series of pop-ups, allowing him to cut his teeth in the business of running a restaurant. With its spacious, simply furnished room, his first permanent site keeps the basic feel of a pop-up - but people are here for the food, not the furnishings, and the menu more than measures up. James' cooking is very much his own, with original combinations of interesting ingredients making up the array of gutsy, good value small plates; try the signature Jamaican jerk buttermilk chicken with Scotch bonnet jam or the treacle-cured smoked salmon with cod's roe, whiskey and apple jelly, radish and rye. The 6 course evening tasting menu is available with matching wines.

- 19 Bevis Marks ✉ EC3A 7JA
  020 3302 0310 — **www**.jcochran.restaurant
  Liverpool Street
- Carte £26/46
  Closed Christmas, Saturday lunch, Sunday and bank holidays - booking essential at lunch

JOSÉ

Spanish • Minimalist

MAP: 10-M5

You may be in Bermondsey but, standing inside this tapas bar, you feel you could well be in Barcelona. Standing is what you'll most likely be doing, as it's rather snug, they don't take bookings and they like to pack people in – but you won't mind one bit because the atmosphere is so great. Start with a sherry and some of the acorn-fed Iberico ham that hangs above the counter; the food is dictated by the markets but all the classics are here and Pluma Iberica (pork shoulder) is the house speciality. The vibrant dishes are intensely flavoured; five plates per person should be more than enough but it's hard to stop ordering when you see what the person next to you has got. There's a great list of sherries and all wines are available by the glass.

- 104 Bermondsey St ✉ SE1 3UB
  020 7403 4902 — **www**.josepizarro.com
  London Bridge
- Carte £14/28
  Closed 24-26 December and Sunday dinner – bookings not accepted

JOSÉ PIZARRO

Spanish • Tapas bar

MAP: 8-M2

In amongst all the chains that flocked to the Broadgate Circle development when it was unveiled in 2015 was this restaurant from José Pizarro who, having called his first 'José' and his second 'Pizarro', decided in this instance to go with his full name. Open from breakfast, the place is a good fit for the City, as it's flexible and efficiently run. There are tables both inside and out but the counter in front of the open kitchen is the best place to sit. The Spanish menu is an appealing mix of familiar favourites and updated classics; the seafood dishes tend to be the standouts, especially the octopus which is excellent. The exclusively Spanish wine list is well-priced, with many wines served by the carafe.

- 36 Broadgate Circle ✉ EC2M 1QS
  020 7256 5333 — **www**.josepizarro.com
  Liverpool Street
- Menu £25/35 - Carte £15/40
  Closed Sunday

JUGGED HARE

Traditional British • Pub

MAP: 8-M2

The famous 18C recipe created by Hannah Glasse, the UK's first domestic goddess, provided the inspiration for the renaming of this Grade II listed pub, previously known as The King's Head. It's an apt name because committed vegetarians may feel ill at ease – and not just because of the collection of glass cabinets in the bar which showcase the art of taxidermy. The atmospheric and appealingly noisy dining room, which has a large open kitchen running down one side, specialises in stout British dishes, with Denham Estate venison, Yorkshire guinea fowl and Cumbrian Longhorn steaks from the rotisserie and grill being the highlights. If the main course doesn't fill you, puddings like treacle tart or bread and butter pudding will.

- 42 Chiswell St ✉ EC1Y 4SA
  020 7614 0134 — **www**.thejuggedhare.com
  Barbican.
- Menu £25 (early dinner) - Carte £27/58
  Closed 25-26 December - booking essential

KENZA

Lebanese • Exotic décor

MAP: 8-N2

Proving that a party atmosphere and good food are not mutually exclusive, Kenza's Middle Eastern exotica instantly transports you away from the city institutions above. It's not easy to find which adds a frisson of expectation, as does descending the staircase into a room full of Moroccan tiles, beaded lamps, lanterns, silk cushions, mosharabi screens and thumping lounge music. Most of the menu is Lebanese but with Moroccan influences; meze is varied and satisfying and the best main courses are slow-cooked lamb shoulder, chargrilled chicken and marinated swordfish; all meat is Halal. Larger parties need not waste time choosing and can order the 'feasting' menus thus allowing more time to appreciate the skills of the belly dancers.

- 10 Devonshire Sq. ✉ EC2M 4YP
  020 7929 5533 — **www**.kenza-restaurant.com
  Liverpool Street
- Carte £31/38
  Closed 24-25 December, Saturday lunch and bank holidays

LOBOS ℩O

Spanish • Tapas bar

MAP: 10-M4

Dimly lit and decidedly compact, this tapas bar is tucked away under the railway arches near the entrance to Borough Market and has a feel not unlike that of an air raid shelter - complete with Edison light bulbs. Downstairs is for walk-ins and upstairs for bookings; sit here to enjoy the theatre of the open kitchen, with the shouts of the chefs and the sizzle of la plancha. The concise menu offers a range of appetisers alongside traditional tapas like tortilla and croquetas; head for the meat dishes, which are the speciality here, and you can't go wrong - try the leg of slow-roasted Castilian milk-fed lamb or the Iberico pork selection to share. Service comes with a smile, and the wine list covers a good many of the Spanish regions.

- 14 Borough High St ✉ SE1 9QG
  ✆ 020 7407 5361 — **www**.lobostapas.co.uk
  ⊖ London Bridge
- Carte £18/45
  Closed 25-26 December and 1 January

N LUCA ℩O

Italian • Design

MAP: 9-L1

Owned by the people behind The Clove Club, Luca is less a little sister; more a distant cousin - and an Italian one at that. Art deco meets modern bistro inside: there's a front bar for small plates and snacks - try the legendary parmesan fries - but the best place to sit is in the elegant rear dining room. Best described as Italian dishes made with British ingredients, the frequently changing à la carte menu - from which a traditional four courses are encouraged - covers all regions of Italy, with ingredient-led dishes ranging from the authentic to the more unusual. As with all good Italian restaurants, service is a strength and the genuine welcome and cheery atmosphere bring some of the warmth of the Med to a cold British evening.

- 88 St. John St ✉ EC1M 4EH
  ✆ 020 3859 3000 — **www**.luca.restaurant
  ⊖ Farringdon
- Menu £55 - Carte £32/52
  Closed Sunday - booking essential

LUTYENS 🍴

Modern cuisine • *Elegant*

XXX A/C MAP: 8-K3

In the shadow of St Bride's Church on Fleet Street stands this impressive building, designed by Sir Edwin Lutyens, and previously Reuters' HQ. It's the ideal backdrop to Sir Terence Conran's elegant and understated restaurant, which comes with a wine bar and a basement members' club lounge as well as a number of intimate private dining rooms. The menu follows the seasons and is an appealing blend of the classic and the more contemporary; ingredients are top-class, cooking is crisp and confident and the accompanying wine list, wide-ranging and well-chosen. This is a smoothly run operation, and the professional staff deal as efficiently with the lunchtime full house as they do the more relaxed evening crowd.

- 85 Fleet St. ✉ EC4Y 1AE
  ✆ 020 7583 8385 — **www**.lutyens-restaurant.com
  ⊖ Blackfriars
- Menu £33 (weekday lunch) - Carte £31/61
  Closed Christmas, Saturday, Sunday and bank holidays

THE MODERN PANTRY CLERKENWELL 🍴

World cuisine • *Design*

X A/C MAP: 9-K1

This Georgian building has been everything from a foundry to a carpentry workshop but these days plays host to New Zealander Anna Hansen's fusion restaurant. The smart glass doors lead into a simple, crisp space; there's an upstairs too, split between two rooms, which offers a little more intimacy but lacks the buzz of downstairs. The kitchen's travels are reflected in a menu that has few boundaries. You'll probably need to ask for an explanation of at least one ingredient but the staff are clued up, which is no mean feat since menus change daily as ingredients come in. Despite all that's happening on the plate, flavours are well-judged and complementary. Most dishes also come with thoughtfully suggested wine matches.

- 47-48 St John's Sq. ✉ EC1V 4JJ
  ✆ 020 7553 9210 — **www**.themodernpantry.co.uk
  ⊖ Farringdon
- Menu £26 (weekday lunch) - Carte £25/38
  Closed August bank holiday and 25-26 December - booking advisable

THE MODERN PANTRY FINSBURY SQUARE

World cuisine • *Brasserie*

MAP: 9-M2

Anna Hansen's second Modern Pantry is on the ground floor of the imposing, Grade II listed Alphabeta Building. The lively bar counter is the place to come for 'global tapas' like salted liquorice macadamias or pickled garlic, Iranian lime and herb-marinated olives; best when accompanied by a sherry livener. The main part of the operation is the elegant, spacious dining room; there are no prizes for guessing that this was formerly a bank. The extensive menu takes a while to read and digest – Google may have to be your friend when it comes to ingredients like ajowan or wattleseed, or alternatively ask one of the cheery staff. Some of the ingredients may be unusual but every one of them is on the plate for good reason. Puddings are a highlight.

■ 14 Finsbury Sq ✉ EC2A 1AH
020 3696 6565 — **www**.themodernpantry.co.uk
Moorgate

■ Carte £26/37
Closed 25 December and Sunday dinner

N MAC & WILD

Scottish • *Trendy*

MAP: 8-N2

It could easily just have been another fun burger joint for city workers to relax in after a hard day's trading but happily Mac & Wild is so much more, offering not only good service and good value but also prime Scottish ingredients, with a focus on wild game, seafood and whisky. The menu lists the likes of venison tartare, Inverawe smoked salmon and the must-try side of 'dirty buttery mash'; these might be simple dishes but their freshness and flavour elevate them to something more. Sister to the Fitzrovia original, this branch is located in the impressive surroundings of Devonshire Square, and its tree trunk tables, loud soundtrack and rough-and-ready feel are a good fit for the food – much like the whisky pairings.

■ 9a Devonshire Sq ✉ EC2M 4YN
020 7637 0510 — **www**.macandwild.com
Liverpool Street

■ Carte £22/31
Closed Sunday

Ⓝ MEI UME

Asian • Elegant

MAP: 8-N3

'Plum Blossom' is set within the impressive surroundings of the Four Seasons Hotel; an elegant, high ceilinged room with striking columns - much like sister La Dame de Pic across the hall - but with subtle Asian touches, like the beautiful themed friezes which decorate the walls. There's a chic bar for cocktails and sushi, or you can take a seat at one of the tables to enjoy formal service from the professional staff. While the menu focuses on Chinese dishes, it also incorporates some Japanese elements, so expect a selection of sushi and sashimi alongside the steamed dim sum. Confidently executed Chinese classics like the signature whole Peking duck mix with more modern dishes; all come with a pleasing refinement and a lightness of touch.

- Four Seasons Hotel London at Ten Trinity Square, 10 Trinity Sq ✉ EC3N 4AJ
  020 3297 3799 — **www**.meiume.com
  Tower Hill
- Menu £29 (lunch) - Carte £42/75
  Closed Sunday

MORITO

Spanish • Tapas bar

MAP: 9-K1

Morito may not seduce you with its looks but once you start eating you'll find it hard to tear yourself away. This authentic tapas bar comes courtesy of the owners of next door Moro and shares their passion for Moorish cuisine. It's modestly kitted out but endearingly so, with a two-tone formica counter and half a dozen small tables; just turn up and if they haven't got space they'll take your number and you can have a drink in Exmouth Market while you wait. Seven or eight dishes between two should be enough but at these prices you can never overspend. Highlights of the immensely appealing menu include jamon and chicken croquetas and succulent lamb chops with cumin and paprika, all served in authentic earthenware dishes.

- 32 Exmouth Mkt ✉ EC1R 4QE
  020 7278 7007 — **www**.morito.co.uk
  Farringdon
- Carte £14/29
  Closed 24 December-2 January, Sunday dinner and bank holidays - (bookings not accepted at dinner)

MORO

Mediterranean cuisine • Friendly

MAP: 9-K1

It's the stuff of youthful dreams - pack up your worldly goods in a camper van, drive through Spain, Portugal, Morocco and the Sahara and then, once back in Blighty, open a restaurant, share your love of Moorish cuisine and never look back. Sam and Sam Clark created something back then that has since been much copied and their peregrinations continue to inform their cooking. The utilitarian look adds a continental feel to the room while the wood-fired oven and chargrill fill the air with wonderful aromas. Freshness is key - don't be surprised to see fish being delivered during service; spicing is subtle and the concise menu changes every three weeks. The wine list is dominated by Spain and has plenty of gems from lesser known regions.

- 34-36 Exmouth Mkt ✉ EC1R 4QE
  020 7833 8336 — **www**.moro.co.uk
  Farringdon
- Carte £32/42
  Closed dinner 24 December-2 January, Sunday dinner and bank holidays - booking essential

NEW ST GRILL

Meats and grills • Friendly

MAP: 8-N2

Once used by the East India Company to store spices, this 18th Century warehouse was converted into an intimate and atmospheric space by the people at D&D, in order to satisfy London's ever increasing appetite for red meat. The kitchen has a sure hand when it comes to classics like lobster cocktail, Cornish dressed crab and rack of lamb, but beef is the main event here, with steaks cooked on a Josper grill. They use Black Angus and the choice is between grass-fed British beef, aged for 28 days, or corn-fed American beef, aged for 40 days. Prices can be high so, unless you've just received your bonus, it's probably wise to stick to the set menu. The wine list is strong on older red Bordeaux and mixes the classic with the more esoteric.

- 16a New St ✉ EC2M 4TR
  020 3503 0785 — **www**.newstreetgrill.com
  Liverpool Street
- Menu £29 (weekdays) - Carte £30/85
  Closed 25 December-3 January except dinner 31 December

OBLIX

Meats and grills • Trendy

MAP: 10-M4

Inspired by the bar in Tokyo's Park Hyatt, but with infinitely better views, Oblix occupies the 32nd floor of The Shard and comes from the same stable as Zuma and Roka. Instead of another Japanese restaurant, however, Rainer Becker choose to create a New York grill style operation, where meats and fish from the rotisserie, grill and Josper oven are the stars of the show. Starters are light and easy, from salads to sliced yellowtail, and a NY cheesecake is the only way to end. The designer wisely decided against competing with the far-reaching views; window tables (which are mostly tables for two) are highly prized. An abbreviated version of the menu is available in the adjacent lounge bar – where they also serve brunch at weekends.

- Level 32, The Shard, 31 St Thomas St. SE1 9RY
  020 7268 6700 — **www**.oblixrestaurant.com
  London Bridge
- Menu £55 (weekday lunch) - Carte £30/164

OXO TOWER

Modern cuisine • Fashionable

MAP: 10-K4

There can be few brighter restaurants than this one on the 8th floor of the Oxo Tower, thanks to its huge windows and enthusiastic application of white paint. The menu provides a fairly promising read, with dishes made up of ingredients from the luxury end of the spectrum, although the kitchen doesn't always quite deliver the goods. Meanwhile, service is a little more ceremonial than the brasserie next door and all this is reflected in the prices – the final bill can dazzle as much as the surroundings, so at least try to get a table by the window to make it memorable. Lunchtimes are largely invaded by city types from across the river, while at night the restaurant becomes a popular setting for those celebrating special occasions.

- Oxo Tower Wharf (8th floor), Barge House St SE1 9PH
  020 7803 3888 — **www**.oxotower.co.uk
  Southwark
- Menu £35 (lunch) - Carte £38/81
  Closed 25 December

OXO TOWER BRASSERIE

Modern cuisine • Design

MAP: 10-K4

The light-filled, glass-encased brasserie on the eighth floor of the iconic Oxo Tower makes much of its riverside location but that's not to say that this is just a spot for a summer's day as the bold, zingy Mediterranean flavours ensure that the cooking is bright and sunny even when it's dull outside. They've moved the bar to the front so that everyone gets a better view these days. Even so, if you've never asked for a window table before, then now is the time to start. Better still, ask for the terrace and face east towards St Paul's for the best views. Staff do their bit by being a responsive bunch and the place really rocks in the evenings. It's much more fun than their restaurant and the prices are friendlier too.

- Oxo Tower Wharf (8th floor), Barge House St ✉ SE1 9PH
  020 7803 3888 — **www**.oxotower.co.uk
  Southwark
- Menu £30 (lunch) - Carte £27/49
  Closed 25 December

PADELLA

Italian • Bistro

MAP: 10-M4

This lively little sister to Trullo isn't difficult to find: just look for the queue. Padella means 'pan' in Italian and the idea behind it is brilliant in its simplicity. This is a restaurant dedicated to pasta, which is hand-rolled in house; sauces and fillings are inspired by the owners' trips to Italy and prices are extremely pleasing to the pocket. Grab a seat at the ground floor counter overlooking the open kitchen; there are a handful of starters on the short, seasonal menu but it's dishes like tagliatelle with smoked eel, cream and Amalfi lemon or papardelle with 8-hour Dexter beef shin ragu that take centre stage. There's a concise but eminently drinkable wine list - and it's hard not to warm to a place that offers free filtered water.

- 6 Southwark St, Borough Market ✉ SE1 1TQ
  www.padella.co
  London Bridge
- Carte £12/22
  Closed 25-26 December, Sunday dinner and bank holidays - bookings not accepted

PALATINO

Italian • Design

MAP: 9-L1

Clerkenwell is a fitting setting for the latest restaurant in Stevie Parle's burgeoning portfolio; it was previously known as 'Little Italy', due to its large numbers of Italian immigrants. An open kitchen and a communal table act as focal points in the airy, canteen-like dining room, while exposed ceiling ducting adds an industrial feel; if it's intimacy you're after, ask to sit in one of the bright yellow booths. Breakfast offers everything from bucatini carbonara to buttermilk pancakes with ricotta, and the seasonal Italian menu has a strong emphasis on Rome, with dishes like fried courgette flowers with honey vinegar, or rigatoni with veal pajata. You will need at least one side dish – the pillowy polenta is a great choice.

- 71 Central St ✉ EC1V 8AB
  020 3481 5300 — **www**.palatino.london
  Old Street
- Carte £18/38
  Closed Sunday

PATERNOSTER CHOP HOUSE

Traditional British • Brasserie

MAP: 8-L3

If you could make just one restaurant legally obliged to serve British food then it would probably be the one that lies in the shadow of St Paul's Cathedral, one of Britain's most symbolic landmarks. Fortunately, Paternoster Chop House negates the need for a bye-law by offering classics from all parts of these isles. The first thing you see on the neatly laid-out menu is the comfortingly patriotic sight of a 'Beer of the Day'. Their livestock comes from small farms, their fish from day boats in the southwest and all the old favourites are present and correct: native oysters, cottage pie, potted hough, liver and bacon, and apple crumble. The dining room is large and open; you might have to fight your way through the busy bar.

- Warwick Ct., Paternoster Sq. ✉ EC4M 7DX
  020 7029 9400 — **www**.paternosterchophouse.co.uk
  St Paul's
- Menu £24 (lunch and early dinner) – Carte £25/63
  Closed 26-30 December, 1 January, lunch Saturday and dinner Sunday

Ⓝ PIQUE-NIQUE

French • Bistro

MAP: 10-N5

Sister to bijoux bistro Casse Croute just around the corner and situated, somewhat unusually, in a converted 1920s park shelter overlooking the tennis courts of Tanner Street Park, is this fun French restaurant with a focus on rotisserie-cooked Bresse chicken. The concise but interesting menu of French classics might include vol au vent, quenelle de volaille or entrecôte with pommes paille – but plump instead for the 'Menu autour du poulet de Bresse': 6 courses based around the king of chickens. It uses every part of the bird – from liver for the pâté to the cockscomb and gizzard for the consommé – and reminds you just how good chicken can taste. They also offer le petit dejeuner – best enjoyed on the sun terrace with a steaming café au lait.

■ Tanner St. Pk ✉ SE1 3LD
020 7403 9549 — **www**.pique-nique.co.uk
London Bridge

■ Menu £38 - Carte £32/39
Booking essential

PIZARRO

Mediterranean cuisine • Neighbourhood

MAP: 10-M5

José Pizarro has a refreshingly simple way of naming his establishments: first came José, a bustling little tapas bar, and then Pizarro, a larger, more structured restaurant a few doors down. The good news is that Pizarro now takes bookings so you no longer need to hang around waiting for a window seat or a place at the large communal table; in fact, when you do book it's worth asking for one of the prized semi-circular booths. The atmosphere in the restaurant is great and the food equally enjoyable. The menu offers a selection of small and large plates; dishes such as prawns with piquillo peppers and jamón are as tasty as they are easy on the eye. Larger plates could include hake with artichoke, and pork fillet with almonds.

■ 194 Bermondsey St ✉ SE1 3UW
020 7378 9455 — **www**.josepizarro.com
London Bridge

■ Carte £28/42
Closed 24-28 December

LE PONT DE LA TOUR

French • Elegant

MAP: 10-N4

Few London restaurants can boast a more glorious setting than Pont de la Tour, especially on a summer's day when you're sitting on the terrace taking in the breathtaking views of Tower Bridge. To celebrate its 25th anniversary, a sympathetic, top-to-toe refurbishment gave the interior a warmer, more sumptuous feel, while still respecting the style and elegance of the original look. Enhancing the restaurant's credentials as a special-occasion destination is a team of smartly dressed staff who flutter and fuss over every guest. You wouldn't want to encounter the prices on the à la carte every day of the week so the better value Prix Fixe menu is the way to go to experience the French-influenced and appealingly presented dishes.

- 36d Shad Thames, Butlers Wharf ✉ SE1 2YE
  020 7403 8403 — **www**.lepontdelatour.co.uk
  London Bridge
- Menu £24/55 - Carte £33/62
  Closed 1 January

POLPO SMITHFIELD

Italian • Friendly

MAP: 9-L2

If you've been to a Polpo, or even if you've just bought the cookbook, then you'll know what to expect here – refreshingly straightforward and familiar dishes designed for sharing. For his third Venetian-style bacaro, Russell Norman converted a former meat market storage facility and the place has a charming, elegantly battered feel. Head first to the Negroni bar downstairs, with its appealingly relaxed atmosphere, and order the eponymous cocktail. Afterwards, you'll find yourself eagerly over-ordering dishes such as crisp pizzette or hearty meatballs – and don't ignore the salads. The Venetian and Northern Italian wines come by the glass, carafe and bottle. Arrive early as bookings are only taken up to 5.30pm and service can get a little frantic.

- 3 Cowcross St ✉ EC1M 6DR
  020 7250 0034 — **www**.polpo.co.uk
  Farringdon.
- Menu £28 - Carte £20/30
  Closed Christmas, New Year and Sunday dinner

QUALITY CHOP HOUSE

Traditional British • Cosy

MAP: 9-K1

This Grade II listed room has been an eating house since 1869 and has an almost Orwellian feel; its etched windows proclaim 'Progressive working class caterer' and 'London's noted cup of tea'. It's in the hands of owners who respect its history and it does a fine job championing gutsy British grub: ox tongue, brown crab, Middle White pork, Ayrshire veal and Cornish pollock – they're all here, in refreshingly unadorned dishes. Game is a highlight, as are the steaks from the butcher next door. You're also unlikely to find a better example of a concise wine list – there are gems aplenty, prices are generous and, for something special, check out the Collector's list at the back. The adjoining 'wine bar' has an all-day menu.

- 92-94 Farringdon Rd ✉ EC1R 3EA
  020 7278 1452 — **www**.thequalitychophouse.com
  Farringdon
- Carte £24/49
  Closed 24-31 December, Sunday dinner and bank holidays – booking advisable

RABOT 1745

Modern cuisine • Design

MAP: 10-M4

Bored by the ordinary? Looking for something different? Then try Rabot 1745, from the owners of Hotel Chocolat, which celebrates the cocoa bean in all its infinite majesty. Named after their estate in St Lucia and its founding year, the restaurant uses wood from the island to add to the plantation feel of the upstairs room. A light-hearted yet knowledgeable introduction is given at the start of the meal explaining how, in its natural state, the flavour of the bean is bitter with a little spice. These flavours are then used in the classically based cooking, with crushed nibs playing a key role, and the resulting dishes have genuine substance. Naturally enough, the desserts are a highlight – don't miss the trio of chocolate mousses.

- 2-4 Bedal St, Borough Market ✉ SE1 9AL
  020 7378 8226 — **www**.rabot1745.com
  London Bridge
- Carte £25/43
  Closed 25-30 December, Sunday and Monday

ROAST

Modern British · Friendly

MAP: 10-M4

These days every restaurant seemingly name-checks its suppliers – but Roast was one of the first and has always been known for promoting British producers, whether they rear pigs or make cider. Mind you, could they do anything else considering their location – bang in the heart of Borough Market? The kitchen show obvious care in the preparation of their dishes, with the highlight often being the 'dish of the day'; perhaps rare breed suckling pig with apple sauce or fillet of beef Wellington with roasties in dripping. Prices can be a little high though, as most main courses need side dishes. Service is personable and the bar, which hosts live music at night, is a destination in its own right. Ask for a window table on the market side.

- The Floral Hall, Borough Market ✉ SE1 1TL
  020 3006 6111 — **www**.roast-restaurant.com
  London Bridge
- Menu £30 (weekdays) - Carte £31/63
  Closed 25-26 December, 1 January and Sunday dinner - booking essential

ST JOHN MALTBY

Traditional British · Bistro

MAP: 10-N5

Those living south of the river no longer have to cross the water to witness just how good British cooking can be, thanks to Fergus Henderson and Trevor Gulliver's place, tucked under a railway arch in deepest Bermondsey. With its austere, industrial-style décor, its scratched chequered floor and its church pews, the utilitarian dining space is far from pretty – and a trip to the bathroom will see you going for a wander down the street. But it's the food that you come for and the food that impresses – tasty, satisfying and as British as John Bull. Start with smoked sprats followed by pigeon; add in some sides and finish off with an Eccles cake or Lancashire cheeses. The earthy, original selection of wines are also available to take away.

- 41 Ropewalk, Maltby St ✉ SE1 3PA
  020 7553 9844 — **www**.stjohngroup.uk.com
  London Bridge
- Carte £31/35
  Closed Christmas, New Year and Sunday dinner-Tuesday - booking advisable - (dinner only and lunch Friday-Sunday)

ST JOHN ✿

Traditional British • Simple

MAP: 9-L2

St John

FIRST COURSE: Roast bone marrow with parsley salad. • Cuttlefish with leeks and laverbread.

MAIN COURSE: Pigeon and trotter pie. • Braised rabbit with turnips.

DESSERT: Dr Henderson ice cream. • Chocolate and prune trifle.

There's no standing on ceremony here at St John; indeed, very little ceremony at all, and that makes eating here such a joyful experience as one's focus is directed entirely at the food. There's little distraction from the surroundings either, which come in a shade of detention centre white. You can play it safe and go for some crab and then roast beef but this is the place to try new flavours, whether that's cuttlefish or ox tongue. Game is a real favourite and the only gravy will be the blood of the bird – this is natural, 'proper' food. Seasonality is at its core – the menu is rewritten for each service – and nothing sums up the philosophy more than the potatoes and greens: they are always on the menu but the varieties and types change regularly. The waiters wear chef's jackets and spend time in the kitchen so they know what they're talking about and are worth listening to. There are dishes for two as well as magnums of wine for real trenchermen – and be sure to order a dozen warm madeleines to take home.

■ 26 St John St ✉ EC1M 4AY
✆ 020 7251 0848 — **www.**stjohnrestaurant.com
⊖ Farringdon

■ Carte £27/61
Closed Christmas-New Year, Saturday lunch, Sunday dinner and bank holidays – booking essential

SAUTERELLE

Modern cuisine • Historic

MAP: 8-M3

This D&D restaurant is in the somewhat unenviable position of having to compete with the grandeur of its own setting. Along with a bar/lounge and brasserie, it occupies the mezzanine floor of the Royal Exchange, and overlooks what was once the trading floor and is now a Grand Café by day and a cocktail bar by night. This City landmark was twice destroyed by fire and was rebuilt in 1844, but its layout remains largely true to Sir Thomas Gresham's 1566 original. In this most British of scenes one finds a menu of a largely European persuasion, with a particular fondness for all things Italian; dishes like Lenticchie di Castelluccio soup and cod alla Livornese sit on the menu next to Denham Estate venison with chestnuts, smoked speck and rosemary jus.

- The Royal Exchange, Threadneedle St ✉ EC3V 3LR
  020 7618 2480 — **www**.royalexchange-grandcafe.co.uk
  Bank
- Menu £25 (weekdays) - Carte £36/52
  Closed Christmas, Easter, Saturday, Sunday and bank holidays

SKYLON

Modern cuisine • Design

MAP: 3-J4

The original Skylon was a steel structure built for the Festival of Britain in 1951 to promote better quality design. Its name now lives on as the restaurant within the Royal Festival Hall, which was built just yards from where this 'vertical feature' once stood. The South Bank is now a much appreciated area of London and the restaurant offers wonderful river views. It's a large space, with a busy central cocktail bar, a formally laid out restaurant on one side and a simpler grill-style operation on the other. The latter serves fishcakes, burgers, steaks and the like; the restaurant uses more expensive ingredients and puts a modern spin on classic combinations. Be sure to ask for a window table.

- 1 Southbank Centre, Belvedere Rd ✉ SE1 8XX
  020 7654 7800 — **www**.skylon-restaurant.co.uk
  Waterloo
- Menu £30/35 - Carte £39/58
  Closed 25 December

SOSHARU

Japanese • Fashionable

MAP: 9-K1

This is the seventh London restaurant from Jason Atherton and the first serving Japanese food; his right hand man here is chef Alex Craciun, previously of Pollen Street Social, who spent a year in Kyoto in preparation. It's a bustling operation with a long sushi counter; the furniture has been imported from Japan and the style is chic and understated. The menu is extensive but staff will happily guide you through; six small plates with a large rice pot or a 'classic' between two will do nicely - and although prices can be steep, dishes are meant for sharing. Special occasions call for Kisetsu - a private dining room where a set omakase-style menu is served - and special occasion or not, a cocktail in the downstairs bar is a must.

■ 64 Turnmill St ✉ EC1M 5RR
✆ 020 3805 2304 — **www**.sosharulondon.com
⊖ Farringdon

■ Menu £30 (lunch and early dinner) - Carte £28/50
Closed Sunday and bank holidays except Good Friday

TAPAS BRINDISA

Spanish • Tapas bar

MAP: 10-M4

The owners spent years importing Spanish produce so it was no surprise that their restaurant on the edge of Borough Market took off immediately. It not only provided the blueprint for many of the tapas bars that subsequently sprung up over London but was also one of the first restaurants not to take bookings - a less welcome but wholly understandable policy that has become more widespread. The place has an infectious energy and vitality and the young staff are as efficient as they are unflappable. Start with a glass of Fino and crisp parcels of morcilla, then share a selection of hand-carved Ibérico hams and robust, generously sized dishes such as Galician-style octopus, black rice with squid and beef and pork meatballs.

■ 18-20 Southwark St, Borough Market ✉ SE1 1TJ
✆ 020 7357 8880 — **www**.brindisatapaskitchens.com
⊖ London Bridge

■ Carte £25/32
Bookings not accepted

STORY ✿

Modern cuisine • Design

XX ♿ A/C **MAP:** 10-N5

Michelin

FIRST COURSE: Crab with avocado and sea vegetables. • Snail ravioli.

MAIN COURSE: Herdwick lamb with sheep's curd. • Pollock with oats and sea buckthorn.

DESSERT: Almond and dill. • Sour milk, apple and mint.

As a teenager, Tom Sellers dreamed of owning his own restaurant – and by the time he was twenty-six, he had achieved his fairytale ending in the shape of Story. What was once a public toilet now resembles a sort of Nordic eco-lodge – all wood, glass and grass; the huge picture window allows light to flood in by day, while by night it's a surprisingly intimate space, with the glassed-in kitchen providing a muted buzz. The Nordic touch is evident not only in the design but also in the food, which comes in a set 6 or 10 course lunch and a 12 course dinner menu; modern techniques and a pleasingly light touch result in food with a back-to-nature feel and strong earthy flavours. A range of imaginative snacks kicks things off thick and fast; idiosyncratic touches like the menu arriving on a Charles Dickens book add to the experience and there's an impressive originality to dishes like the signature bread and dripping. With only 12 tables to serve, staff are refreshingly enthusiastic; getting a seat at one of those tables is another story.

■ 199 Tooley St ✉ SE1 2JX
☎ 020 7183 2117 — **www**.restaurantstory.co.uk
⊖ London Bridge

■ Menu £45 (weekday lunch)/120
Closed 2 weeks Christmas-New Year, Sunday dinner and Monday lunch – booking essential – (tasting menu only)

TATE MODERN (RESTAURANT)

Modern British • Design

MAP: 10-L4

The Tate Modern's striking Herzog and de Meuron designed Switch House extension, which opened in 2016, is the location of this contemporary restaurant. Fight your way through the gallery-goers up to the ninth floor and you'll find yourself in a light-filled, wood and concrete furnished, faux-industrial space. Being this high up, you might expect a meal with a view but, unless you're particularly tall, you won't be able to see much out of the windows. Focus on the food instead: the seasonal modern menu champions British ingredients and the kitchen keeps things relatively light, so lunch need never impinge on plans for post-prandial art appreciation. Desserts are a highlight and the wine list interesting and well-priced.

Switch House (9th floor), Tate Modern, Bankside ✉ SE1 9TG
020 7401 5621 — **www**.tate.org.uk
Southwark

Carte £27/56
Closed 24-26 December - (lunch only and dinner Friday-Saturday)

TEMPLE AND SONS

Traditional British • Bistro

MAP: 8-M3

Squeezed in between - and dwarfed by - Tower 42 and its neighbouring office block, is the glass cube containing Temple and Sons; a relaxed restaurant styled on a Victorian grocer's shop. The bar serves - among other things - cocktails in tin cans and milk cartons; head upstairs past a display of British essentials like Colman's Mustard and Atora Suet, to where staff in grocers' coats serve classic dishes to a backdrop of British pop. While essentially a grill menu, there's more to it than simply steaks, with dishes like pig's head and trotter fritters alongside salads, pasta and market fish. Desserts are headed 'If I must': just one of the things that shows this 'Purveyors of Fine English Food' doesn't take itself too seriously.

22 Old Broad St ✉ EC2N 1HQ
020 7877 7710 — **www**.templeandsons.co.uk
Liverpool Street

Carte £19/62
Closed Sunday

28°-50° FETTER LANE

Modern cuisine • *Wine bar*

MAP: 8-K3

All things vinous are celebrated at this cellar restaurant and wine bar, which is named after the latitudes between which most wine-making grapes are grown. Owned by Agnar Sverrisson from Texture restaurant, it offers a good choice of grilled meats, charcuterie, cheese and assorted European dishes – and all the dishes come with a pleasing underlying simplicity which allows the wine star billing. Oenophiles will appreciate the carefully compiled wine list which consists of 15 reds and 15 whites, all available by the glass, carafe and bottle; sherries and dessert wines are not forgotten either. The Collector's List offers some real gems, the cross section of regions is spot on and the wines are served at their perfect temperatures.

- 140 Fetter Ln ✉ EC4A 1BT
  020 7242 8877 — **www**.2850.co.uk
  Temple
- Menu £25 (weekday lunch) - Carte £32/53
  Closed Saturday, Sunday and bank holidays

UNION STREET CAFÉ

Italian • *Trendy*

MAP: 10-L4

Even the news that David Beckham wasn't actually involved in this Gordon Ramsay restaurant didn't seem to deter all those promiscuous restaurant twitchers from booking tables long before it had even opened his doors. But what began as a Mediterranean restaurant quickly morphed into a fully-fledged Italian one – albeit one that has seemingly spent quite a lot of time in New York. A former warehouse, it ticks all the boxes for that faux industrial look and comes with a basement cocktail bar and excitable diners. The menu, written in a curious lingua franca, stays pretty true to the classics and keeps things simple. Portions are not overly generous though, which means that you may need all four courses to leave feeling satisfied.

- 47-51 Great Suffolk St ✉ SE1 0BS
  020 7592 7977 — **www**.gordonramsayrestaurants.com
  London Bridge
- Menu £26 (lunch) - Carte £31/55

VANILLA BLACK

Vegetarian • Intimate

MAP: 8-K2

One of the stubbornly lingering myths about restaurants in the City is that they mostly cater for red-faced, red-meat eaters in a rush – Vanilla Black proves there's room for every type of restaurant and that includes vegetarian ones. The seriousness with which they run this restaurant is palpable and it's obvious that real thought has gone into the creation of the menu – to such an extent that choosing dishes can be hard as they all sound so appealing. Dishes are light and easy to eat and deliver an array of interesting texture and flavour contrasts. Modern techniques are subtly incorporated and while there are some original combinations they are well-judged. The restaurant is warm and comfortable and the service sweet and sincere.

- 17-18 Tooks Ct. ✉ EC4A 1LB
  ✆ 020 7242 2622 — **www**.vanillablack.co.uk
  ⊖ Chancery Lane
- Menu £27 (weekday lunch)/55
  Closed 2 weeks Christmas and bank holidays – booking essential

VILLAGE EAST

Modern cuisine • Trendy

MAP: 10-M5

Village East was one of the first restaurants to open on this trend-setting street. It's sandwiched between two Georgian houses and the bright blue awning and illuminated signs proudly point it out. Counter dining is the focus in the main room, with the tables opposite the kitchen affectionately nicknamed the 'ringside' seats; those celebrating can tuck themselves away in a separate elevated bar. The cocktail list is worth exploring, with names such as 'Nettle Fizz' and 'Orient Express' making an appearance – take some friends along and really get into the party spirit. Cooking mixes contemporary dishes with Mediterranean-inspired plates; the confit turkey leg is a speciality and you'll have to go a long way to find a better burger.

- 171-173 Bermondsey St ✉ SE1 3UW
  ✆ 020 7357 6082 — **www**.villageeast.co.uk
  ⊖ London Bridge
- Carte £22/50
  Closed 24-26 December

WRIGHT BROTHERS

Seafood • Cosy

MAP: 10-M4

If you want to take a breather from the crowds at Borough Market then nip into Wright Brothers, but do it early as it quickly fills. Their motto is 'not just oysters' but then they do excel in them – hardly surprising when you consider that this small place started as an oyster wholesaler. Grab a table and enjoy them raw or cooked, by candlelight, along with the perfect accompaniment – a glass of porter – or else share a bench or the counter and opt for a platter of fruits de mer and a bottle of chilled Muscadet. If the bivalve is not your thing, then there are daily specials such as skate knobs, as well as pies and, for dessert, either chocolate truffles or crème brûlée. An air of contentment reigns.

- 11 Stoney St, Borough Market ✉ SE1 9AD
  020 7403 9554 — **www**.thewrightbrothers.co.uk
  London Bridge
- Carte £28/38
  Closed bank holidays – booking advisable

YAUATCHA CITY

Chinese • Fashionable

MAP: 8-M2

For 10 years the only Yauatcha in London was the Soho original but now, after opening branches across India, the Hakkasan Group have created the capital's second. It's a huge operation with seating for around 180 and it takes up half of the newly developed Broadgate Circle. It has a more corporate feel than the original and the circular shape means that some tables leave you feeling you're eating in a corridor, but it does have something Broadwick Street doesn't – a terrace at both ends. You'll find all their dim sum greatest hits on the menu, from venison puffs to scallop shui mai, with desserts from the patisserie downstairs, but the chefs have some work to do to match the high standard, care and precision of the cooking found in Soho.

- Broadgate Circle ✉ EC2M 2QS
  020 3817 9880 — **www**.yauatcha.com
  Liverpool Street
- Carte £26/67
  Closed 24 December-3 January and bank holidays

CHELSEA · EARL'S COURT · HYDE PARK · KNIGHTSBRIDGE · SOUTH KENSINGTON

Though its days of unbridled hedonism are long gone - and its 'alternative' tag is more closely aligned to property prices than counter-culture - there's still a hip feel to **Chelsea.** The place that put the Swinging into London has grown grey, distinguished and rather placid over the years, but tourists still throng to the **King's Road,** albeit to shop at the chain stores which have steadily muscled out SW3's chi-chi boutiques. It's not so easy now to imagine the heady mix of clans that used to sashay along here, from Sixties mods and models to Seventies punks, but for practically a quarter of a century, from the moment in 1955 when Mary Quant opened her trend-setting Bazaar, this was the pavement to parade down.

Chelsea's most cutting-edge destination these days is probably the gallery of modern art that bears the name of Margaret Thatcher's former favourite, Charles Saatchi. Which isn't the only irony, as Saatchi's outlandishly modish exhibits are housed in a one-time military barracks, the Duke of York's headquarters. Nearby, the traffic careers round **Sloane Square,** but it's almost possible to distance yourself from the fumes by sitting amongst the shady bowers in the centre of the square, or watching the world go by from a prime position in one of many cafés. Having said that, *the* place to get away from it all, and yet still be within striking distance of the King's Road, is the delightful **Physic Garden,** down by the river. Famous for its healing herbs for over 300 years, it's England's second oldest botanic garden.

Mind you, if the size of a green space is more important to you than its medicinal qualities, then you need to head up to **Hyde Park,** the city's biggest. Expansive enough to accommodate trotting horses on Rotten Row, swimmers and rowers in the Serpentine, up-to-the-minute art exhibitions at the Serpentine Gallery, and ranting individualists at Speakers' Corner, the park has also held within its borders thousands of rock fans for concerts by the likes of the Rolling

Stones, Simon and Garfunkel and Pink Floyd.

Just across from its southern border stands one of London's most imperious sights, The **Royal Albert Hall,** gateway to the cultural hotspot that is South Kensington. Given its wings after the 1851 Great Exhibition, the area round **Cromwell Road** invested heavily in culture and learning, in the shape of three world famous museums and three heavyweight colleges. But one of its most intriguing museums is little known to visitors, even though it's only a few metres east of the Albert Hall: the Sikorski is, by turns, a moving and spectacular showpiece for all things Polish.

No one would claim to be moved by the exhibits on show in nearby **Knightsbridge,** but there are certainly spectacular credit card transactions made here. The twin retail shrines of Harvey Nichols and Harrods are the proverbial honey-pots to the tourist bee, where a 'credit crunch' means you've accidentally trodden on your visa. Between them, in **Sloane Street,** the world's most famous retail names line up like an A-lister's who's who. At the western end of Knightsbridge is the rich person's Catholic church of choice, the Brompton Oratory, an unerringly lavish concoction in a baroque Italianate style. Behind it is the enchanting Ennismore Gardens Mews, a lovely thoroughfare that dovetails rather well with the Oratory.

Further west along Old Brompton Road is **Earl's Court,** an area of grand old houses turned into bedsits and spartan hotels. An oddly bewitching contrast sits side by side here, the old resting alongside the new. The old in this case is Brompton Cemetery, an enchanting wilderness of monuments wherein lie the likes of Samuel Cunard and Emmeline Pankhurst. At its southwest corner, incongruously, sits the new, insomuch as it's the home of a regular influx of newcomers from abroad, who are young, gifted and possessed of vast incomes: the players of Chelsea FC.

xeipe/iStock

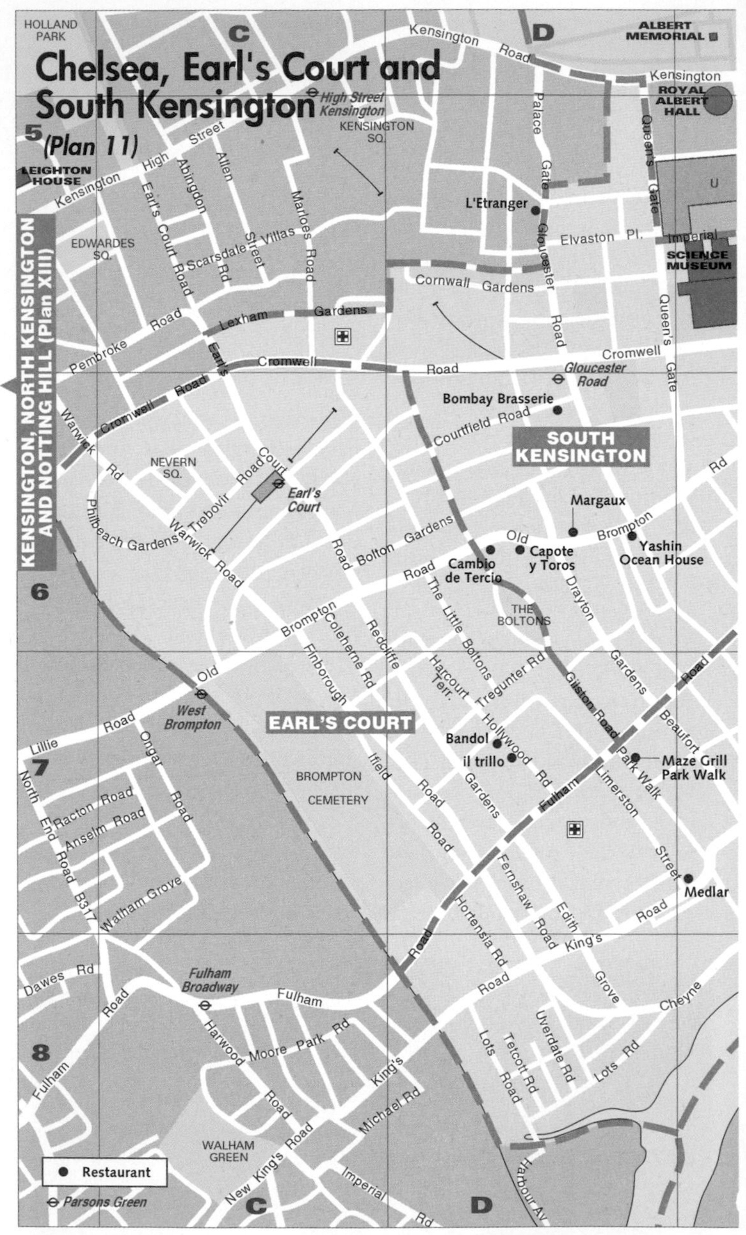
Chelsea, Earl's Court and South Kensington
(Plan 11)
HOLLAND PARK
ALBERT MEMORIAL
ROYAL ALBERT HALL
LEIGHTON HOUSE
KENSINGTON, NORTH KENSINGTON AND NOTTING HILL (Plan XIII)
High Street Kensington
KENSINGTON SQ.
EDWARDES SQ.
SCIENCE MUSEUM
L'Etranger
Bombay Brasserie
SOUTH KENSINGTON
Gloucester Road
NEVERN SQ.
Earl's Court
Margaux
Yashin Ocean House
Capote y Toros
Cambio de Tercio
THE BOLTONS
West Brompton
EARL'S COURT
Bandol
il trillo
Maze Grill Park Walk
BROMPTON CEMETERY
Medlar
Fulham Broadway
WALHAM GREEN
Restaurant
Parsons Green
Kensington Road
Kensington High Street
Earl's Court Road
Abingdon
Allen Street
Marloes Road
Scarsdale Villas
Lexham Gardens
Cornwall Gardens
Palace Gate
Gloucester Road
Queen's Gate
Elvaston Pl.
Imperial
Cromwell Road
Pembroke Road
Warwick Rd
Courtfield Road
Philbeach Gardens
Trebovir Road
Warwick Road
Bolton Gardens
Old Brompton Road
Drayton Gardens
The Little Boltons
Coleherne Rd
Redcliffe
Finborough
Harcourt Terr.
Tregunter Rd
Gilston Road
Beaufort
Park Walk
Hollywood Rd
Limerston Street
Fulham Road
Lillie Road
Ongar Road
North End Road B317
Racton Road
Anselm Road
Walham Grove
Ifield Road
Gardens
Fernshaw Road
Hortensia Rd
Edith Grove
King's Road
Cheyne
Dawes Rd
Harwood Road
Moore Park Rd
Lots Road
Tetcott Rd
Uverdate Rd
Lots Rd
Michael Rd
New King's Road
Imperial Rd
Harbour Av
C
D
5
6
7
8

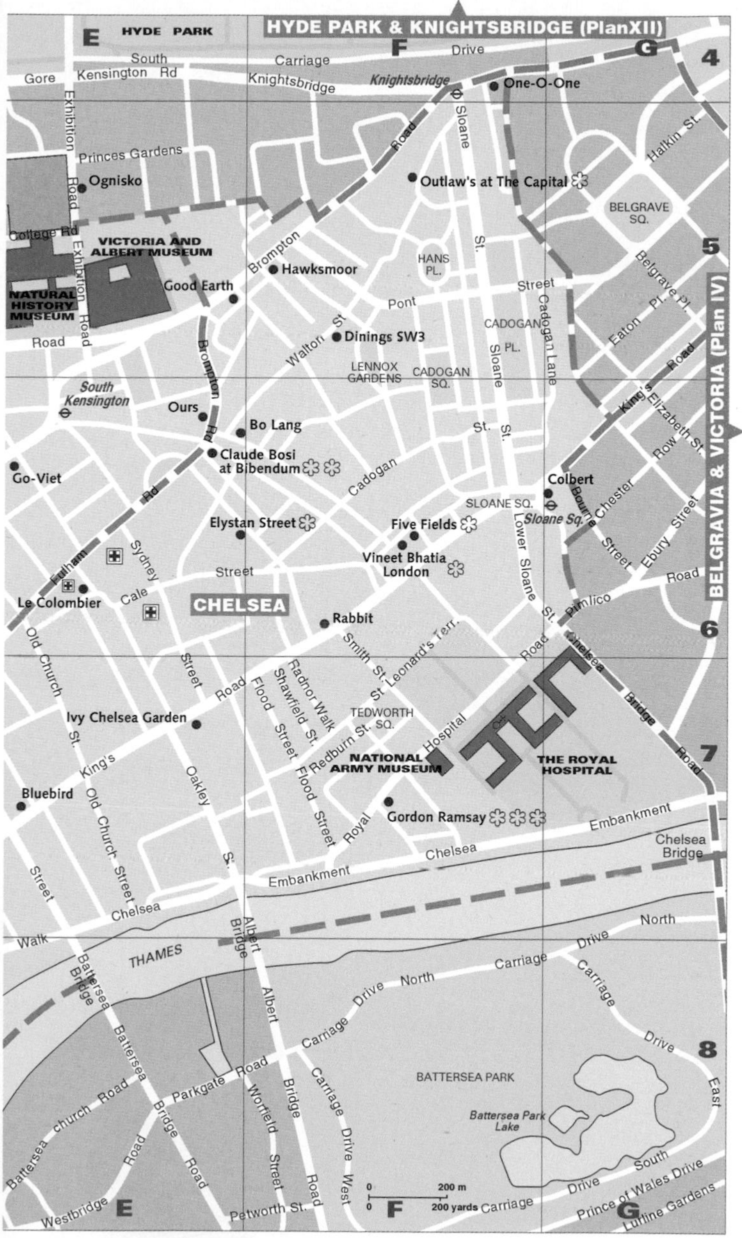

HYDE PARK & KNIGHTSBRIDGE (PlanXII)
BELGRAVIA & VICTORIA (Plan IV)
HYDE PARK
One-O-One
Ognisko
Outlaw's at The Capital
VICTORIA AND ALBERT MUSEUM
NATURAL HISTORY MUSEUM
Hawksmoor
Good Earth
Dinings SW3
Ours
Bo Lang
Claude Bosi at Bibendum
Go-Viet
Colbert
Elystan Street
Five Fields
Vineet Bhatia London
Le Colombier
CHELSEA
Rabbit
Ivy Chelsea Garden
NATIONAL ARMY MUSEUM
THE ROYAL HOSPITAL
Bluebird
Gordon Ramsay
THAMES
BATTERSEA PARK
Battersea Park Lake
BELGRAVE SQ.
HANS PL.
CADOGAN PL.
LENNOX GARDENS
CADOGAN SQ.
SLOANE SQ.
TEDWORTH SQ.
South Kensington
Knightsbridge
Sloane Sq.
200 m
200 yards

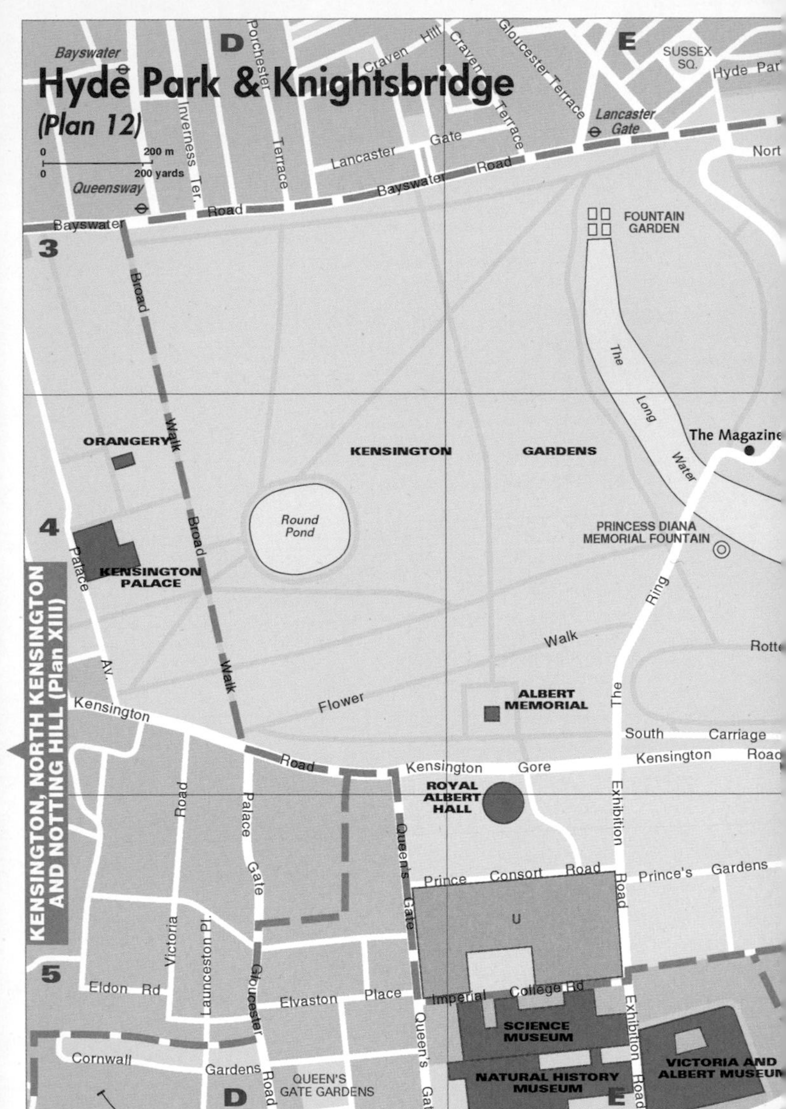
Hyde Park & Knightsbridge
(Plan 12)
0 200 m
0 200 yards
Bayswater
Queensway
Porchester
Craven Hill
Craven
Gloucester Terrace
Terrace
Inverness Ter.
Terrace
Lancaster Gate
Lancaster Gate
Bayswater Road
Bayswater Road
SUSSEX SQ.
Hyde Par
Nort
FOUNTAIN GARDEN
Broad Walk
Broad Walk
ORANGERY
KENSINGTON
GARDENS
The Long Water
The Magazine
Round Pond
PRINCESS DIANA MEMORIAL FOUNTAIN
KENSINGTON PALACE
Palace
Av.
The Ring
Walk
Flower
Rott
ALBERT MEMORIAL
Kensington
Road
South Carriage
Kensington Road
Kensington Gore
ROYAL ALBERT HALL
Road
Palace Gate
Queen's Gate
Exhibition Road
Prince Consort Road
Prince's Gardens
U
Victoria
Launceston Pl.
Gloucester Road
Eldon Rd
Elvaston Place
Imperial College Rd
SCIENCE MUSEUM
NATURAL HISTORY MUSEUM
VICTORIA AND ALBERT MUSEUM
Cornwall Gardens
QUEEN'S GATE GARDENS
D
E
3
4
5
KENSINGTON, NORTH KENSINGTON AND NOTTING HILL (Plan XIII)

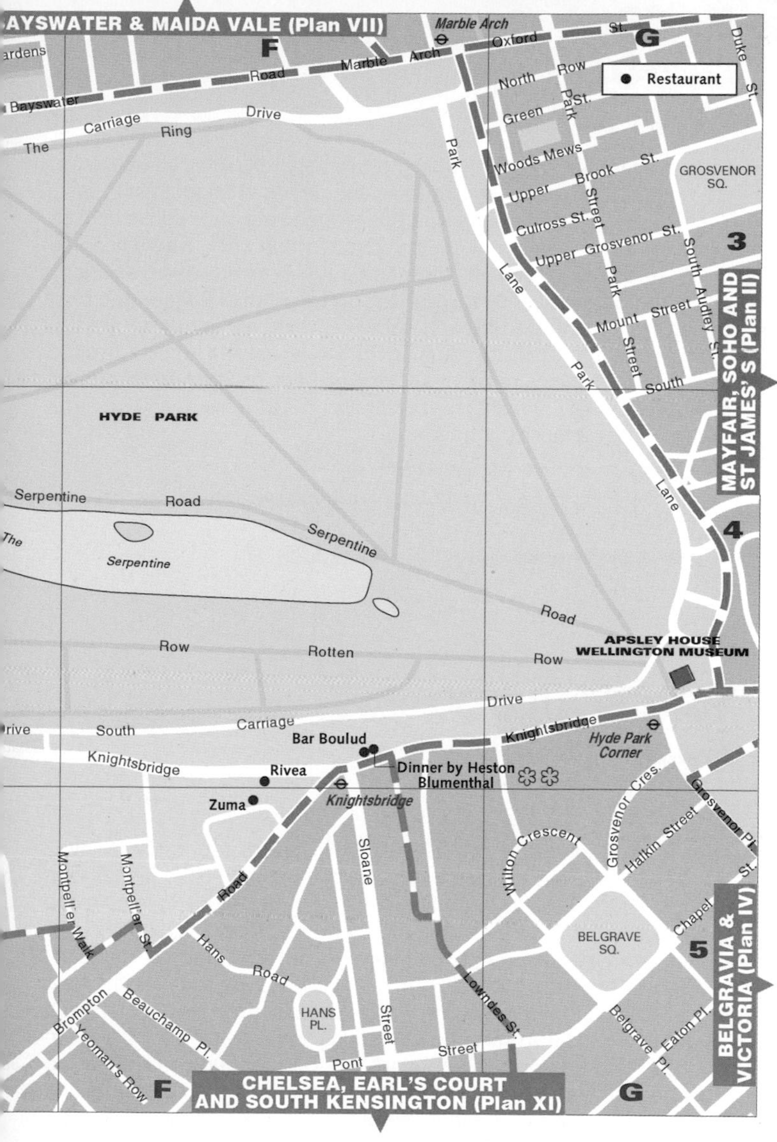

BAYSWATER & MAIDA VALE (Plan VII)
MAYFAIR, SOHO AND ST JAMES'S (Plan II)
BELGRAVIA & VICTORIA (Plan IV)
CHELSEA, EARL'S COURT AND SOUTH KENSINGTON (Plan XI)
Restaurant
HYDE PARK
Marble Arch
Oxford St.
Bayswater Road
The Ring
North Row
Green St.
Woods Mews
Upper Brook St.
Culross St.
Upper Grosvenor St.
Mount Street
South Audley St.
Park Street
Park Lane
South St.
Duke St.
GROSVENOR SQ.
Serpentine Road
The Serpentine
Rotten Row
South Carriage Drive
Knightsbridge
APSLEY HOUSE WELLINGTON MUSEUM
Hyde Park Corner
Bar Boulud
Rivea
Zuma
Dinner by Heston Blumenthal
Knightsbridge
Sloane Street
Wilton Crescent
Grosvenor Cres.
Halkin Street
Grosvenor Pl.
Chapel St.
BELGRAVE SQ.
Lowndes St.
Belgrave Pl.
Eaton Pl.
Montpellier Walk
Montpellier St.
Brompton Road
Hans Road
HANS PL.
Beauchamp Pl.
Yeoman's Row
Pont Street

BANDOL

Provençal • Design

MAP: 11-D7

Sister to Margaux in South Kensington, this stylishly dressed restaurant is named after the well-known town and region in South East France. There are seats at the gleaming copper-topped bar but if you're here on a date, head to the more intimate section further back, where hanging brass lamps cast a romantic glow and a 100 year old olive tree brings back memories of sunny days spent on the French Riviera; the best tables are the three to the left with their semi-circular banquettes. Sharing plates take centre stage on the Provençal and Niçoise inspired menu, with dishes like bouillabaisse or fillet of Saint-Pierre being generously sized and full of flavour. Seafood is a highlight and desserts like tarte Tatin pleasingly traditional.

- 6 Hollywood Rd ✉ SW10 9HY
  020 7351 1322 — **www**.barbandol.co.uk
  Earl's Court
- Menu £15 (weekday lunch) - Carte £26/57
  Closed 24-26 December and 1 January

BAR BOULUD

French • Brasserie

MAP: 12-F4

Lyon-born Daniel Boulud built his considerable reputation in New York and these two cities now inform the menu here at his London outpost. Order a plate of excellent charcuterie while you look at the menu; sausages are a highlight and there are plenty of classic French dishes, from fruits de mer to coq au vin, but it's the burgers that steal the show. Designed by Adam Tihany, the restaurant makes the best of its basement location which was previously used by the Mandarin Oriental Hotel as a storeroom. Don't think you'll be in exile if they lead you to a table around the corner: it's a good spot and you'll be facing the open kitchen. Service is fast and furious; prices are sensible and the place is noisy, fashionable and fun.

- Mandarin Oriental Hyde Park Hotel -
  66 Knightsbridge ✉ SW1X 7LA
  020 7201 3899 — **www**.mandarinoriental.com/london
  Knightsbridge
- Menu £19 (weekday lunch) - Carte £26/57

BLUEBIRD ЮО

Modern British • Design

MAP: 11-E7

This iconic building on the King's Road, originally built as a garage for the Bluebird Motor Company, was converted into a restaurant in the late 1990s by Sir Terence Conran, and taken over in the noughties by D&D London. There's an épicerie, a café, a terrace and even a clothes shop, but the highlight has to be the dimly lit first floor restaurant with its marble-topped horseshoe bar, steel roof girders, bold print banquettes and abundance of foliage. There's a Mediterranean slant to the menu, with dishes like quinoa tabbouleh, Greek salad or lamb rump with merguez and bulgar. It's tasty stuff but sides can soon cause the bill to rack up – not that this bothers the Chelsea set, who are glad to have their local back on song.

- 350 King's Rd. ✉ SW3 5UU
  ✆ 020 7559 1000 — **www**.bluebird-restaurant.co.uk
  ⊖ South Kensington
- Carte £30/55

BO LANG ЮО

Chinese • Trendy

MAP: 11-E6

It's all about dim sum at this diminutive Hakkasan wannabe and they get a lot of things right: the kitchen has a deft touch, the cocktails are very good, the service is polite, the look is cool and the lighting moody. While there are more substantially sized 'main courses' on the menu you're better off sticking with the dim sum, particularly the traditional steamed items, and sharing with friends to mitigate the effects of some fairly ambitious pricing. What doesn't quite work are those dishes made up of more unusual flavour combinations, the small tables – which are not particularly conducive to this style of eating –and the intrusively loud music which, in such a small space, hints at a lack of nerve on someone's part.

- 100 Draycott Ave ✉ SW3 3AD
  ✆ 020 7823 7887 — **www**.bolangrestaurant.com
  ⊖ South Kensington
- Menu £15 (lunch) - Carte £30/50

BOMBAY BRASSERIE

Indian • Exotic décor

MAP: 11-D6

One of the reasons why The Bombay Brasserie has been going strong since 1982 is that it always seems to have just finished - or to be just about to start - a programme of redecoration to keep it looking fresh. Plushness abounds, from the murals and huge chandeliers of the large main room to the show kitchen of the conservatory and the very smart bar. The staff look the part in their burgundy waistcoats and offer efficient and professional service. The menu isn't forgotten either and they've replaced the predictable with the more creative, while at the same time respecting traditional philosophies; influences are a combination of Bori, Parsi, Maharashtrian and Goan cuisine. The weekend buffet remains as hugely popular as ever.

- Courtfield Rd. ✉ SW7 4QH
  020 7370 4040 — **www**.bombayb.co.uk
  Gloucester Road
- Menu £27 (weekday lunch) - Carte £36/52
  Closed 25 December - bookings advisable at dinner

CAMBIO DE TERCIO

Spanish • Cosy

MAP: 11-D6

Never standing still is the key to the longevity of this Spanish restaurant - something the passionate and excitable staff take quite literally as they're forever bobbing between tables, engaging with their customers and generally adding to the energy in the room. Their recommendations are also worth following, especially on the wine list - which proves there is so much more to Spanish wines than rioja - and the sherry list, which is one of the best in town. The menu is a mix of the modern and the traditional - and it's best to mix the dishes up. Don't miss the El Bulli inspired Spanish omelette, or classics like roast suckling pig, and save room for the 'London Underground' dessert - you'll never look at your Oyster Card in the same way again.

- 163 Old Brompton Rd. ✉ SW5 0LJ
  020 7244 8970 — **www**.cambiodetercio.co.uk
  Gloucester Road
- Menu £45 - Carte £21/69 **s**
  Closed 2 weeks December and 2 weeks August

CAPOTE Y TOROS

Spanish • Tapas bar

MAP: 11-D6

From the owners of not-quite-next-door Cambio de Tercio comes the compact and vividly coloured Capote y Toros which celebrates sherry, tapas and ham. Named after the matador's cape and his foe, there are enough bullfighting references to satisfy enthusiasts of Hemingway proportions, including a large wall of photos. However, it is sherry that takes centre stage and there's a huge variety and choice on offer. Those as yet unmoved by this most underappreciated of wines should start by trying 5 varieties in a 'flight'. Meanwhile, the menu revolves around about 25 dishes; try 3 per person - the Iberico ham and the octopus are excellent. Bookings are now taken but you have a limited time at the table. A guitarist plays in the evenings.

157 Old Brompton Road ✉ SW5 0LJ
020 7373 0567 — **www**.cambiodetercio.co.uk
Gloucester Road

Carte £15/33
Closed 2 weeks Christmas, Sunday and Monday - (dinner only)

COLBERT

French • Brasserie

MAP: 11-G6

With its posters, chessboard tiles and red leather seats, Colbert bears more than a passing resemblance to a Parisian pavement café and there can't be a better spot for one than here on Sloane Square, next to the Royal Court. This is the old Oriel café and it was transformed by seasoned restaurateurs Chris Corbin and Jeremy King. It's an all-day, every day operation and the menu lists all the French classics; you can pop in for a croque monsieur, linger over a steak Diane or come for breakfast at any time of day. The best dishes are the simpler ones and if you haven't booked, try the bar. Despite the somewhat dispiriting sight of an anachronistic cover charge, this place feels set to become part of the local fabric for some time.

50-52 Sloane Sq ✉ SW1W 8AX
020 7730 2804 — **www**.colbertchelsea.com
Sloane Square

Carte £21/56
Closed 25 December - booking advisable

Ⓝ CLAUDE BOSI AT BIBENDUM ✿✿

French • Elegant

XXX A/C ✿ **MAP:** 11-E6

Michelin

FIRST COURSE: Frogs' legs with girolles and vin jaune. • Cornish cock crab with elderflower and sea herbs.

MAIN COURSE: Somerset kid, razor clams and sea beets sauce. • Cornish turbot 'Grenobloise'.

DESSERT: Pistachio soufflé with banana ice cream. • Wild strawberry vacherin with aged balsamic.

With a return to his French roots, Claude Bosi has breathed new life into Bibendum, on the first floor of the historic art deco building which was built as Michelin's London HQ in 1911. Thirty years after owner Sir Terence Conran first opened it as a restaurant, it now sports a cleaner, more contemporary look, and its handsome interior cannot help but impress. The iconic stained glass windows allow light to flood in – a fact best appreciated at lunch when the Michelin Man can be seen in all his glory; the loveable character can also be spotted throughout the restaurant, from the butter dish to the salt and pepper pots. Claude Bosi's food is much changed from his time at Hibiscus: expect high-end traditional French cooking but with creative modern touches – as in the pissaladière-flavoured olives served on arrival. Dishes are poised and well-balanced with bold, assured flavours; choose the à la carte menu for classics like frog's legs with girolles and vin jaune or turbot 'Grenobloise' – and don't miss the pistachio soufflé with banana ice cream.

- Michelin House, 81 Fulham Road ✉ SW3 6RD
  ✆ 020 7581 5817 — **www**.bibendum.co.uk
  ⊖ South Kensington
- Menu £37/85
  Closed dinner 24 -26 December, 2-4 January, Sunday dinner, Monday and Tuesday – booking essential

LE COLOMBIER

French • Neighbourhood

MAP: 11-E6

Le Colombier is as warm and welcoming as it is honest and reliable, and thereby offers proof that being a good neighbourhood restaurant takes more than just being in a good neighbourhood. French influences abound, from the accents of the staff and the menu content to the inordinate amount of double cheek kissing that occurs – most of the customers appear to know one another or feel they should like to know one another. In summer, when the full-length windows fold back, the terrace is the place to sit although the underfloor heating ensures the place is equally welcoming in winter. Oysters, game in season, veal in various forms and regional cheeses are the highlights, as are the classic desserts from crêpe Suzette to crème brûlée.

- 145 Dovehouse St. ✉ SW3 6LB
  ☏ 020 7351 1155 — **www**.le-colombier-restaurant.co.uk
  ⊖ South Kensington
- Menu £25 (lunch) - Carte £36/63

N DININGS SW3

Japanese • Intimate

MAP: 11-F5

This little sister to the Marylebone original can be found in a discreet mews location; head to the basement dining area with its closely spaced tables and brightly lit marble-topped bar – the best place to sit to enjoy the kitchen's signature sushi and sashimi. Executive chef and part-owner Masaki Sugisaki is a Nobu alumni and the Nobu influence is clear to see in the well-executed Japanese cooking, with dishes like sea bass carpaccio with truffle and ponzu jelly, and seared Wagyu tataki with porcini ponzu. The robata and Josper grills are used to good effect, and there's plenty of top quality sustainable seafood sourced mostly from UK waters; the bill can soon rack up, but this is unlikely to worry the Chelsea set who've made it their home.

- Walton House, Lennox Garden Mews (off Walton St.) ✉ SW3 2JH
  ☏ 020 7723 0666 — **www**.diningssw3.co.uk
  ⊖ Sloane Square
- Carte £19/65
  Closed 24-26, 31 December and 1 January - booking advisable

DINNER BY HESTON BLUMENTHAL ✿✿

Traditional British • Design

XXX A/C ⊡ ✿ **MAP:** 12-F4

Michelin

FIRST COURSE: Mandarin, chicken liver parfait and grilled bread (c.1500). • Savoury porridge with frogs' legs, girolles, garlic, parsley and fennel (c.1660).

MAIN COURSE: Hereford rib-eye with mushroom ketchup and triple cooked chips (c.1830). • Cod in cider with chard and flamed mussels (c.1940).

DESSERT: Tipsy cake with spit-roast pineapple (c.1810). • Raspberry tart with Jersey cream and raspberry & verbena sorbet (c.1800).

Don't come to this impeccably well-run restaurant at the Mandarin Oriental Hyde Park expecting Heston Blumenthal's 'molecular' alchemy. Instead, you'll find a menu that reads like a record of British kitchen triumphs through the ages, with the date of origin given to each dish and a fashionably terse list of its parts – on the reverse of the card you can read more about its historical provenance. A kitchen brigade of 45 works with obvious intelligence, calm efficiency and meticulous attention to detail to produce food that looks deceptively simple but tastes sublime. Many of the dishes have already gained near legendary status and thus enjoy a permanent presence on the menu, like 'Meat Fruit' (c.1500) which is a thing of beauty, and 'Rice & Flesh' (c.1390) – a variation of risotto alla Milanese with oxtail. The large, light room has quirky touches, like wall sconces shaped as jelly moulds, but the main focus is on the open kitchen, with its oversized watch mechanics powering the spit to roast the pineapple that goes with the Tipsy Cake (c.1810).

- Mandarin Oriental Hyde Park Hotel, 66 Knightsbridge, ✉ SW1X 7LA
  ✆ 020 7201 3833 — **www**.dinnerbyheston.com
  ⊖ Knightsbridge
- Menu £45 (weekday lunch) - Carte £58/121
  Closed 17-31 October

ELYSTAN STREET

Modern British • Elegant

MAP: 11-E6

Elystan Street

FIRST COURSE: Ravioli of langoustines with barbecue dressing, cabbage and pumpkin. • Tartare of veal with white peach, artichokes, burrata, girolles, fennel pollen and truffle.

MAIN COURSE: Breast and spring roll of duck with pistachio, cherries, turnip and greens. • Crumbed fillet of plaice with new potato & crab salad, runner beans and lemon.

DESSERT: Orange cheesecake with caramelised white chocolate and cardamom ice cream. • Bitter chocolate mousse with cocoa tuiles, milk ice cream and salted caramel.

After 25 years at the helm of The Square in Mayfair, Philip Howard took on a new project in 2016, in partnership with experienced restaurateur Rebecca Mascarenhas (with whom he also jointly owns Kitchen W8 and Sonny's Kitchen). They've both put their stamp on the place, with Rebecca supplying the contemporary artwork and Philip the modern sculptures; décor is elegant and understated with a blonde wood floor, oak and polished concrete tables, and large windows which let in plenty of light. Chairs come in air force blue and soft salmon, though the teal banquettes around the edges of the room are the best place to sit; this is a charming lunchtime spot which transmogrifies into an intimate dinner venue. Cooking is relaxed and unfussy, yet there's a vigour and an energy to it which suggests that it comes from the heart. Dishes have a classical base but there's a lightness of touch, as well as an increased focus on vegetables and salads. Many dishes have Mediterranean influences and flavours are well-defined and eminently satisfying. Desserts are a highlight.

- 43 Elystan St SW3 3NT
  020 7628 5005 — **www**.elystanstreet.com
  South Kensington
- Menu £43 (weekday lunch) - Carte £45/92
  Closed 25-26 December and 1 January - booking essential

L'ETRANGER

Modern French • Neighbourhood

MAP: 11-D5

Messing around with classic French cooking is considered sacrilegious in certain parts of France but L'Etranger has escaped the tyranny of tradition by locating itself in South Kensington, London's own little Gallic ward. It offers an eclectic mix of French dishes with Asian - and particularly Japanese - influences, so expect to see choices like slow-cooked chicken breast with wild mushroom fricassee and heirloom carrots alongside tuna tartar with ponzu sauce and spring onion. The room is dark and moody and better suited to evenings, while service is perhaps a little more formal than it need be. The clientele is a mix of well-heeled locals and homesick French and Japanese émigrés, who also appreciate the depth of the impressive wine list.

- 36 Gloucester Rd. SW7 4QT
  020 7584 1118 — **www**.etranger.co.uk
  Gloucester Road
- Menu £25/30 - Carte £30/57
  Booking essential

GO-VIET

Vietnamese • Contemporary décor

MAP: 11-E6

Go-Viet is brought to us by experienced chef Jeff Tan, formerly of Hakkasan ,and owner of Soho street-food restaurant Vietfood. As its name suggests, it also serves Vietnamese food - this time, elevating it to a higher level. The menu takes ingredients from Europe and combines them with vegetables from Vietnam; the result being interesting, flavourful dishes with a distinct modern edge. The relaxed lunchtime offering concentrates on classics like pho and bun, while dinner provides a more sophisticated experience, with dishes like inspired seafood salsa and 24-hour slow-cooked Black Gold beef cheek. There are only eight tables on the contemporary ground floor - this is the place to sit rather than the more modestly-furnished basement.

- 53 Old Brompton Rd SW7 3JS
  020 7589 6432 — **www**.vietnamfood.co.uk
  South Kensington
- Carte £20/74
  Closed 24-26 December

FIVE FIELDS ✿

Modern cuisine • Neighbourhood

XXX ♿ A/C ⊕ ✿ **MAP:** 11-F6

Five Fields

FIRST COURSE: Foie gras with shimeji mushrooms and beetroot. • Red mullet with lardo, fennel and strawberry.

MAIN COURSE: Roe deer with morels, artichoke and truffle. • Cod with cauliflower, capers and crayfish.

DESSERT: Apple with caramel, vanilla cream and panna cotta. • Chocolate, sesame and smoke.

Its name comes from that given to the neighbourhood by the 18C cartographer John Rocque, and over the years this charming Chelsea restaurant has certainly built up a loyal local following. It is a formally run yet intimate place, with a discreet atmosphere and a warm, comfortable feel. The room is luxuriously decorated in crisp creams and the smart, suited staff who work it are professional and engaging. The chef-owner – blessed with the great name of Taylor Bonnyman – has worked in some illustrious kitchens around the world and his cooking is very much in a modern style. His dishes are skilfully conceived, quite elaborate constructions; attractively presented and packed with flavour. Produce is top-notch and includes the occasional Asian ingredient, and many of the herbs and vegetables come from the restaurant's own kitchen garden in East Sussex. Alongside the classic burgundies and bordeaux, the extensive wine list also offers some more esoteric bottles from Eastern Europe and the Middle East. The tasting menu allows you to enjoy some interesting wine pairings.

8-9 Blacklands Terr ✉ SW3 2SP
☎ 020 7838 1082 — **www**.fivefieldsrestaurant.com
⊖ Sloane Square

Menu £65/85

Closed Christmas-mid January, 2 weeks August, Saturday-Sunday and bank holidays – booking essential – (dinner only)

GOOD EARTH

Chinese • Elegant

MAP: 11-E5

The menu might seem a little predictable but this long-standing Chelsea Chinese has always proved a reliable choice in an area where tourist-traps are not entirely unknown. Although there is no particular geographical bias, the cooking is fresh and carefully executed and dishes neatly presented and authentic. Shanghai chilli chicken and claypots are the popular choices; there's a decent selection of vegetarian dishes; and the kitchen uses some pretty high-end ingredients without charging the earth. The restaurant has a smart, slightly lighter look these days; choose between the larger, more comfortable basement and the ground floor room with its smart horseshoe bar for those who like counter dining.

- 233 Brompton Rd. SW3 2EP
  020 7584 3658 — **www**.goodearthgroup.co.uk
  Knightsbridge
- Menu £12 (weekday lunch) - Carte £26/46
  Closed 23-31 December

HAWKSMOOR

Meats and grills • Brasserie

MAP: 11-F5

The Hawksmoor people turned to the more rarefied surroundings of Knightsbridge for their fifth London restaurant and this meant a few subtle tweaks to their formula. Steak is obviously still the star of the show and the choice of 70% of customers, but the menu here also offers a decent selection of fish and seafood dishes which prove particularly popular at lunchtime. The customers in these parts are a sophisticated bunch - you're more likely to see negronis being ordered than shots - and they don't seem put off by the basement surroundings. To counter this, the restaurant comes with a degree of art deco elegance and the staff are a confident and engaging bunch who spend time getting to know their customers.

- 3 Yeoman's Row SW3 2AL
  020 7590 9290 — **www**.thehawksmoor.com
  South Kensington
- Menu £28 (weekday lunch) - Carte £23/69
  Closed 24-26 December and 1 January

GORDON RAMSAY ✿✿✿

French • Elegant

XXXX A/C 🍷 ✿ **MAP:** 11-F7

Michelin

FIRST COURSE: Pan-fried scallops with apple, walnuts, celery and cider. • Sautéed foie gras with cherries, almond and camomile.

MAIN COURSE: Poached halibut, king crab and lime with ras el hanout infused broth. • Roast pigeon with fennel, lavender, honey and apricot.

DESSERT: Earl Grey parfait, Yorkshire rhubarb and lemon balm. • Raspberry soufflé with almond ice cream.

Gordon Ramsay may have the highest media profile of any chef, as well as many restaurants around the world, but this one, tucked away in a corner of Chelsea, is the undoubted flagship of his company – and the seriousness with which he protects its reputation is palpable. Calmness rules the elegant room, thanks largely to the way it is run by Jean-Claude – the manager who has been here since the day it opened, some twenty years ago. The service from his team is very attentive, polished and professional, but it also comes with personality and this puts everyone at ease. The main reason everyone is here is for the food however, which is as good as ever following the promotion of Matt Abé to head chef. The style of cooking manages to bridge both classical and modern schools and is executed with enormous confidence and considerable poise. The attention to detail is exemplary and the component parts of each dish marry perfectly – it is this balance, coupled with an extraordinary lightness of touch, which makes them so effortlessly easy to enjoy.

- 68-69 Royal Hospital Rd. ✉ SW3 4HP
  ✆ 020 7352 4441 — **www.**gordonramsayrestaurants.com
  ⊖ Sloane Square
- Menu £65/110
  Closed 21-28 December, Saturday and Sunday - booking essential

IL TRILLO

Italian • Friendly

MAP: 11-D7

The Bertuccelli family have been making wine and running a restaurant in the Tuscan Hills for over 30 years. Two of the brothers are now in London, running this smart neighbourhood restaurant which showcases the produce and wine from their region. A third brother, who's an architect, designed the room and nearly everything was brought over from Italy, from the marble to the tables and chairs. Most of the ingredients are shipped over weekly too, either from their own farm or suppliers they've known for years. The cooking is gutsy and the breads and homemade pasta stand out, as does the signature dish of stuffed onions cooked in Vermentino. The courtyard has been transformed into a pleasant decked garden, complete with lemon trees.

- 4 Hollywood Rd ✉ SW10 9HY
  020 3602 1759 — **www**.iltrillo.net
  Earl's Court
- Menu £31 - Carte £36/60
  Closed Monday - (dinner only and lunch Saturday-Sunday)

IVY CHELSEA GARDEN

Traditional British • Fashionable

MAP: 11-E7

This Ivy spin-off is set right in the heart of Chelsea and its appeal is clear to see: the interior is cosy and sophisticated, the atmosphere distinctly animated, and the clientele strikingly glamorous. Stop off at the zinc-topped cocktail bar for a Sloane Ranger or an Ivy Garden Royale; the liveliest seats are up here, so for a more intimate table, head down to the Orangery or out into the garden. The menu covers all bases: from breakfast through to lunch, afternoon tea and dinner; there's brunch at weekends and even a 'light and healthy' section on the menu for supermodel appetites. Plump for classics like the fish cakes, the chicken Milanese or the rack of lamb - and be aware that bread, sides and sauces will push up your final bill.

- 197 King's Rd ✉ SW3 5ED
  020 3301 0300 — **www**.theivychelseagarden.com
  South Kensington
- Carte £27/61
  Booking essential

THE MAGAZINE

Modern cuisine • Design

MAP: 12-E4

Designed by the late Zaha Hadid, the Serpentine Sackler Gallery opened in 2013 and comprises a restored former 1805 gunpowder store – hence the name of its restaurant – and a stunning modern extension. Bright and distinctly stylish, The Magazine is a big open space with a bar down one side and what must surely be one of London's most striking open kitchens. The style of food with the unenviable task of competing with the impressive surroundings is light, easy to eat and keeps its influences largely within Europe; there's a focus on seasonality and the ingredients are allowed room to shine. The restaurant is open for breakfast through to afternoon tea, and also serves brunch at weekends.

- Serpentine Sackler Gallery, West Carriage Dr, Kensington Gardens ✉ W2 2AR
  020 7298 7552 — **www**.magazine-restaurant.co.uk
  Lancaster Gate
- Menu £26/35 - Carte £26/40
  Closed Monday except bank holidays - (lunch only)

MARGAUX

Mediterranean cuisine • Trendy

MAP: 11-D6

France and Italy are the primary culinary influences at this appealing modern bistro, with a menu that features classics like beef bourguignon and gnocchi alongside more unusual dishes such as yellowtail carpaccio with pomegranate and honey, or white miso and honey-glazed kingfish fillet with sweet and sour pak choi. Ingredients are top notch, cooking is careful and flavours plentiful – keen staff and a buzzing room full of locals further add to the experience. The wine list by the glass and carafe provides a good choice of varietals from quality producers along with plenty of gems from top growers. While the kitchen's influences are largely European, the ersatz industrial look of the place is far more Downtown Manhattan.

- 152 Old Brompton Rd ✉ SW5 0BE
  020 7373 5753 — **www**.barmargaux.co.uk
  Gloucester Road
- Menu £15 (weekday lunch) - Carte £32/57
  Closed 24-26 December, 1 January and lunch August

MAZE GRILL PARK WALK

Meats and grills • Fashionable

MAP: 11-D7

When Gordon Ramsay snapped up the lease here at Park Walk it came as no great surprise – this was the site of Aubergine, the restaurant where it all started for him back in the mid '90s. As Maze Grill it now follows the example set by the Mayfair original and specialises in steaks. The meats are dry-aged in-house and the selection includes native and rare breeds, along with grain-fed US and Japanese breeds. Having a basement kitchen ruled out a Josper so instead they use a big beast called a Montague grill which gets the job done by charbroiling the meat at 400°C. The restaurant is comfortable and well-organised, with a large bar the focal point of the room. There's another Maze Grill close by in Royal Hospital Road.

- 11 Park Walk SW10 0AJ
  020 7255 9299 — **www**.gordonramsayrestaurants.com/maze-grill-park-walk
  South Kensington
- Menu £19/40 - Carte £25/75

MEDLAR

Modern cuisine • Neighbourhood

MAP: 11-E7

Medlar is an established landmark at this end of Chelsea and the two young owners have shown that being alumni of Chez Bruce proves to be a pretty good blueprint for your own place. The two restaurants share a warm and welcoming atmosphere and a feeling of being a genuine neighbourhood spot – you sense that a majority of the customers on any given night all know one another. The young service team here in Chelsea get the tone right too: they do their job but are also willing to engage with their customers. The menu is nicely balanced and the ingredients are clearly good; preparation is done with obvious care and dishes deliver distinct flavours in relatively classic combinations.

- 438 King's Rd SW10 0LJ
  020 7349 1900 — **www**.medlarrestaurant.co.uk
  South Kensington
- Menu £35/49
  Closed 24-26 December and 1 January

OGNISKO

Polish • Elegant

MAP: 11-E5

Ognisko Polskie - The Polish Hearth Club - was founded in 1940 and became an important cultural centre for the Polish community in exile after the war. It is housed in the magnificent surroundings of a 1870s townhouse whose elegant restaurant is appealing in its simplicity. Head first to the bar for a quick sharpener provided by home-flavoured vodka, then plunge straight into the unapologetically traditional Eastern European menu, which celebrates cooking that is without pretence and truly from the heart. The dumplings are good and available as starters or mains, the roast duck is popular ,and the Krupnik or Bigos just perfect for a winter's day. On a summer's day ask for a table on the terrace overlooking Prince's Gardens.

- 55 Prince's Gate, Exhibition Rd ✉ SW7 2PN
  ✆ 020 7589 0101 — **www**.ogniskorestaurant.co.uk
  ⊖ South Kensington
- Menu £22 (lunch and early dinner) - Carte £27/37
  Closed 24-26 December and 1 January

ONE-O-ONE

Seafood • Intimate

MAP: 11-F4

Walking past the Park Tower Knightsbridge hotel, one of London's less majestic buildings, you'd never know there was a restaurant behind those heavy net curtains, and a rather good one to boot. Granted, the room size and shape can mean an animated atmosphere remains elusive - but the food is good and that food is mostly fish. There are tasting menus alongside an appealing à la carte so there is something for everyone and all occasions, whether that means sharing a whole turbot or just enjoying a bowl of bouillabaisse. Much of the produce comes from Brittany and Norway; the latter gives us the King crab legs which are the stars of the show. The kitchen is also unafraid of adding a little playfulness to its classical base.

- Park Tower Knightsbridge Hotel, 101 Knightsbridge ✉ SW1X 7RN
  ✆ 020 7290 7101 — **www**.oneoonerestaurant.com
  ⊖ Knightsbridge
- Menu £20 (lunch and early dinner) - Carte £43/106

OURS

Modern cuisine • Fashionable

MAP: 11-E6

For the French diaspora who have made this area of London their own, the name means 'bear', but it's actually meant to signify 'What's ours is yours'; a phrase highlighted in neon on the wall above the bar. Green banquettes, trees and a living plant wall of 1,200 flower pots give the place a back-to-nature feel. Its immense size means it can lack atmosphere at lunch so come in the evening for a livelier vibe, when the fairy lights twinkle and the mezzanine level bar-lounge fills up with fun-seekers. The modern menu offers seasonal, ingredient-led dishes with a fresh, light style. Portions are not large, so sides are needed which can push prices up. There's also a distinct lack of carbs - which no doubt appeals to the local fashionistas.

- 264 Brompton Rd ✉ SW3 2AS
  ✆ 020 7100 2200 — **www**.restaurant-ours.com
  ⊖ South Kensington
- Carte £35/77
  Closed 24-28 December, Sunday and Monday - booking advisable - (dinner only and Saturday lunch)

RABBIT

Modern British • Rustic

MAP: 11-F6

Following the success of The Shed, the Gladwin brothers turned to Chelsea for their second restaurant and took over the site occupied since the 1950s by Choys Chinese. The playful, rustic look, complete with tractor seats and corrugated iron panelling, works well in this locale as does the service which is youthful and full of easy-going charm. The menu shares the same concept as The Shed - small plates of earthy, robustly flavoured dishes using produce from their farm - but there are some differences too: Chelsea residents are, apparently, slightly less enthusiastic about sharing than their Notting Hill cousins but are keener on game which is appropriate considering the name. As you'd expect, the rabbit dishes really are the standouts.

- 172 King's Rd ✉ SW3 4UP
  ✆ 020 3750 0172 — **www**.rabbit-restaurant.com
  ⊖ Sloane Square
- Menu £14 (weekday lunch)/28 - Carte £21/31
  Closed 22 December-2 January - pre-book at weekends

OUTLAW'S AT THE CAPITAL ✿

Seafood • Intimate

XX A/C ⊡ 🍷 ✿ 🍸 **MAP:** 11-F5

Michelin

FIRST COURSE: Lobster risotto, orange and basil. • Red wine braised octopus with seaweed dressing and beans.

MAIN COURSE: John Dory, Porthilly sauce and cabbage. • Cod with devilled butter, brown shrimps and celeriac.

DESSERT: Strawberry ice cream sandwich with lime and elderflower. • Custard tart with rhubarb and ginger beer.

Nathan Outlaw's elegant yet informal restaurant is the perfect fit for this long-standing, personally run hotel; its understated style putting the emphasis not on the room itself, but on the highly accomplished cooking and the exceptional wine list. The seasonal menus are all about sustainable seafood, with fresh fish shipped up from Cornwall on a daily basis, and while the 5 course tasting menu shows off the kitchen's abilities, the excellent value lunch menu makes the perfect pit-stop after shopping at nearby Harrods. The modern, delicately flavoured cooking is ingredient-led with the spotlight firmly on the freshness of the fish - and the wine list is a wonderfully balanced tome of vinous delights and includes the refreshing and herbaceous Levin Sauvignon Blanc from the former owner's estate in the Loire. The room is good-looking, with the main feature being views into the kitchen through the large picture window. Service is relaxed yet attentive and the restaurant's many regulars are testament to the diligence of the staff.

- The Capital Hotel, 22-24 Basil St. ✉ SW3 1AT
  ✆ 020 7591 1202 — **www**.capitalhotel.co.uk
  ⊖ Knightsbridge
- Menu £29/62
  Closed Sunday - booking essential

RIVEA

Mediterranean cuisine • Design

MAP: 12-F4

In the basement, beneath the Bulgari Hotel's sleek bar, is the not-quite-so-sunny sister to the 'Rivea' restaurant in St Tropez; an elegantly appointed room where blues and whites make reference to warmer climes. Unfussy cooking also focuses on the French - and Italian - Riviera, offering an interesting range of small plates which are vibrant in both colour and flavour. Four or five dishes per person should suffice and sharing is the way to go for those who just can't quite decide. Alongside the must-try pasta dishes you'll find the likes of roasted duck with tender turnips and beetroots, and sea bass with violin courgettes and flowers. These are accompanied by an eclectic wine list which showcases varietals purely from the Med.

- Bulgari Hotel, 171 Knightsbridge ✉ SW7 1DW
  ☎ 020 7151 1025 — **www**.rivealondon.com
  ⊖ Knightsbridge
- Menu £26 (lunch) - Carte £39/51

YASHIN OCEAN HOUSE

Japanese • Chic

MAP: 11-D6

It seems you can't open a restaurant these days without it having a 'concept'. The USP of this modern Japanese restaurant - sister to Yashin in Kensington - is 'head to tail' eating, although, as there's nothing here for carnivores, perhaps 'fin to scale' would be more accurate. The stylish interior includes large cabinets of dry-aged fish to get you in the mood for this style of eating, which is actually pretty commonplace in Japan. Take a seat at the counter or grab a table opposite the curiously incongruous full-sized horse lampstand and get cracking with a few small dishes like mackerel bone and fish skin for a joyous umami hit. Some dishes work better than others so stick with the specialities, like the whole dry-aged sea bream.

- 117-119 Old Brompton Rd ✉ SW7 3RN
  ☎ 020 7373 3990 — **www**.yashinocean.com
  ⊖ Gloucester Road
- Carte £20/86
  Closed Christmas

Ⓝ VINEET BHATIA LONDON ✿

Indian • Elegant

XX A/C ⊡ |♡ **MAP:** 11-F6

Michelin

FIRST COURSE: Chilli cod. • Beet foie gras.

MAIN COURSE: Kapi lamb chop. • Patiala chicken.

DESSERT: Clementine kulfi. • Chocolate 'cure'.

The archetypal Chelsea townhouse that previously housed Rasoi has been given a comprehensive refurbishment and relaunched as Vineet Bhatia London; a hint, perhaps, of more to come from the eponymous chef who already boasts an international presence, with restaurants in Geneva, Bahrain, Mauritius, Dubai and Riyadh. The meal kicks off with a superb array of attention-grabbing, street food inspired snacks like Khari biscuit aubergine kut and idli-sambhar crab chutney, and flavours build as you proceed through the 7 course tasting menu, which features previous hits such as tandoori-spiced salmon as well as new creations like lamb chop marinated in coffee and jaggary. The cooking is informed by the owners' Mumbai heritage and global travels and dishes are detailed, delicately spiced and colourful, with a stunning array of textures and flavours. There's also a refreshing lack of carbs, which keeps things beautifully balanced and light. Go for the wine flights, which have been put together with some thought.

■ 10 Lincoln St ✉ SW3 2TS
✆ 020 7225 1881 — **www**.vineetbhatia.london
⊖ Sloane Square

■ Menu £105
Closed 25-27 December, 1-3 January and Monday - booking essential - (dinner only) - (tasting menu only)

ZUMA

Japanese • Fashionable

MAP: 12-F5

Zuma may have become a global brand, with branches stretching from Istanbul to Hong Kong, but this is the original and it's still giving its fashionable band of fans – which includes a high quotient of celebrities and enough footballers to make up a whole team – exactly what they want. Glamorous surroundings with an open kitchen, a great cocktail bar, intelligent service and easy-to-share modern Japanese food mean that the large, stylish space is rarely less than bursting, especially at night. The menu covers all bases but instead of sushi, sashimi or tempura your best bet is to head straight for the delicately presented, modern constructions as well as those dishes cooked on the robata grill, which range from beef to sea bass.

5 Raphael St ✉ SW7 1DL
020 7584 1010 — **www**.zumarestaurant.com
⊖ Knightsbridge

Menu £76/124 - Carte £26/193
Closed 25 December - booking essential

J. Castle/Loop Images/age fotostock

KENSINGTON · NORTH KENSINGTON · NOTTING HILL

It was the choking air of 17C London that helped put **Kensington** on the map: the little village lying to the west of the city became the favoured retreat of the asthmatic King William III who had Sir Christopher Wren build **Kensington Palace** for him. Where the king leads, the titled follow, and the area soon became a fashionable location for the rich. For over 300 years, it's had no problem holding onto its cachet, though a stroll down Kensington High Street is these days a more egalitarian odyssey than some more upmarket residents might approve of.

The shops here mix the everyday with the flamboyant, but for a real taste of the exotic you have to take the lift to the top of the Art Deco Barkers building and arrive at the Kensington Roof Gardens, which are open to all as long as they're not in use for a corporate bash. The gardens are now over seventy-five years old, yet still remain a 'charming secret'. Those who do make it up to the sixth floor discover a delightful woodland garden and gurgling stream, complete with pools, bridges and trees. There are flamingos, too, adding a dash of vibrant colour.

Back down on earth, Kensington boasts another hidden attraction in **Leighton House** on its western boundaries. The Victorian redbrick façade looks a bit forbidding as you make your approach, but step inside and things take a dramatic turn, courtesy of the extraordinary Arab Hall, with its oriental mosaics and tinkling fountain creating a scene like something from *The Arabian Knights.* Elsewhere in the building, the Pre-Raphaelite paintings of Lord Leighton, Burne-Jones and Alma-Tadema are much to the fore. Mind you, famous names have always had a hankering for W8, with a particular preponderance to dally in enchanting **Kensington Square,** where there are almost as many blue plaques as buildings upon which to secure them. William Thackeray, John Stuart Mill and Edward Burne-Jones were all residents.

One of the London's most enjoyable green retreats is **Holland Park,** just north of the High Street. It boasts the 400 year-old Holland House, which is a fashionable focal point for summer-time al fresco theatre and opera. Holland Walk runs along the eastern fringe of the park, and provides a lovely sojourn down to the shops; at the Kyoto Garden, koi carp reach hungrily for the surface of their pool, while elsewhere peacocks strut around as if they own the place.

Another world beckons just north of here – the seedy-cum-glitzy environs of **Notting Hill.** The main drag itself, Notting Hill Gate, is little more than a one-dimensional thoroughfare, but to its south are charming cottages with pastel shades in leafy streets, while to the north the appealing **Pembridge Road** evolves into the boutiques of Westbourne Grove. Most people heading in this direction are making for the legendary Portobello Road market – particularly on Saturdays, which are manic. The market stretches on for more than a mile, with a chameleon-like ability to change colour and character on the way: there are antiques at the Notting Hill end, followed further up by food stalls, and then designer and vintage clothes as you reach the Westway. Those who don't fancy the madding crowds of the market can nip into the Electric Cinema and watch a movie in supreme comfort: it boasts two-seater sofas and leather armchairs. Nearby there are another two film-houses putting the hip into the Hill – the Gate, and the Coronet, widely recognised as one of London's most charming 'locals'.

Hidden in a mews just north of **Westbourne Grove** is a fascinating destination: the Museum of Brands, Packaging and Advertising, which does pretty much what it says on the label. It's both nostalgic and evocative, featuring thousands of items like childhood toys, teenage magazines… and HP sauce bottles.

Incamerastock/Photononstop

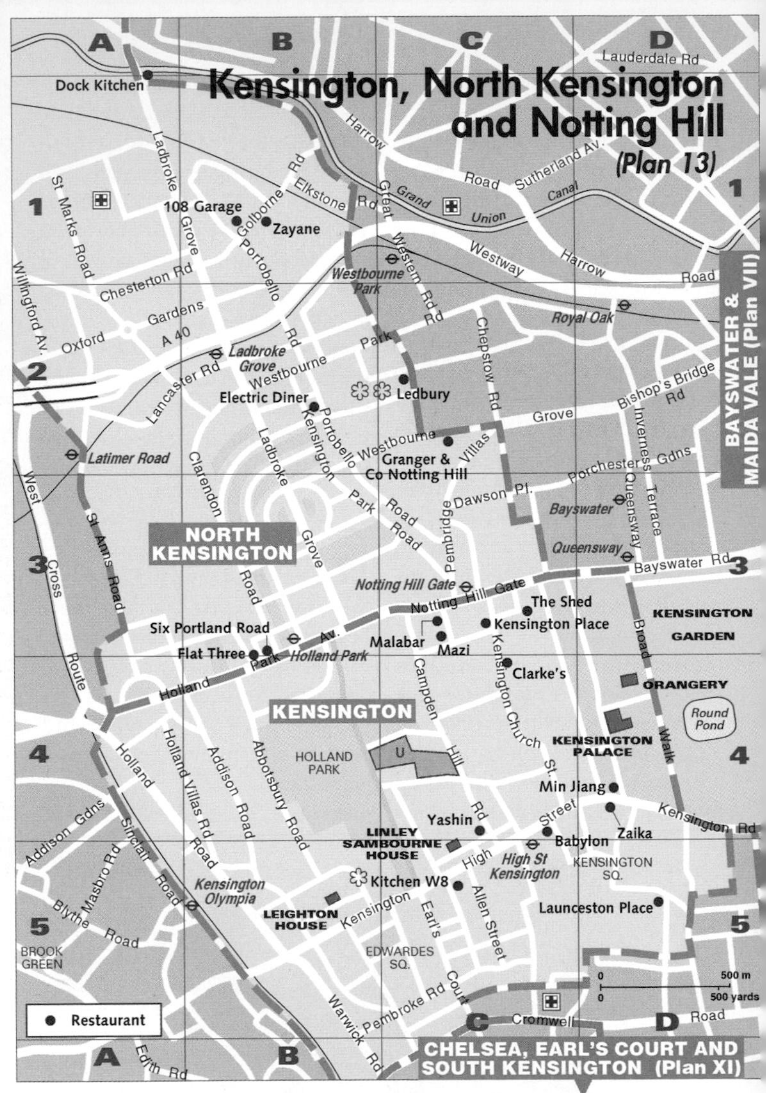
Kensington, North Kensington and Notting Hill
(Plan 13)
Dock Kitchen
108 Garage
Zayane
Ledbury
Electric Diner
Granger & Co Notting Hill
The Shed
Kensington Place
Malabar
Mazi
Six Portland Road
Flat Three
Clarke's
Min Jiang
Zaika
Yashin
Babylon
Kitchen W8
Launceston Place
NORTH KENSINGTON
KENSINGTON
HOLLAND PARK
KENSINGTON GARDEN
ORANGERY
Round Pond
KENSINGTON PALACE
LINLEY SAMBOURNE HOUSE
LEIGHTON HOUSE
EDWARDES SQ.
KENSINGTON SQ.
BROOK GREEN
Westbourne Park
Royal Oak
Ladbroke Grove
Latimer Road
Bayswater
Queensway
Notting Hill Gate
Holland Park
High St Kensington
Kensington Olympia
Restaurant
500 m
500 yards
BAYSWATER & MAIDA VALE (Plan VIII)
CHELSEA, EARL'S COURT AND SOUTH KENSINGTON (Plan XI)

BABYLON

Modern cuisine • Fashionable

MAP: 13-C4

Take the lift on Derry Street up to the 7th floor and you'll find yourself staring down at trees, shrubs and possibly even a flamingo in an amazing 1½ acre rooftop garden. The restaurant's terrace must surely be one of the city's best spots for a cocktail and a view, with the easterly skyline visible through the oak and fruit trees. However, be aware that private parties often have exclusive access. The food can't always compete with this bucolic scene and presentation can sometimes be at the expense of flavour but the menu does offer plenty of choice. Dishes are not too heavy, which is a plus for later as dinner at weekends entitles you to discounted access to The Club. You could also consider coming on a Tuesday as that's jazz night.

- The Roof Gardens, 99 Kensington High St (entrance on Derry St) W8 5SA
  020 7368 3993 — **www**.roofgardens.virgin.com
  High Street Kensington
- Menu £24 (weekday lunch) - Carte £38/59
  Closed 24-30 December, 1-2 January and Sunday dinner

CLARKE'S

Modern cuisine • Neighbourhood

MAP: 13-C4

Thirty-four years on and Sally Clarke has lost none of her passion for her Kensington kitchen; its pleasant, unhurried atmosphere, enthusiastic service and dedication to its regulars just a few of the many reasons why this restaurant has instilled such unwavering loyalty from so many for so long. There's a private dining room downstairs, the Bar Room is open all day for breakfast, coffee, light lunches and teas, and dinner is served in the relaxed yet elegant dining room. Sally's insistence on using the freshest seasonal ingredients has created a credible consistency to the cooking at Clarke's; there's a clear understanding of the less-is-more principle and dishes are confidently executed, with a pleasing lightness of touch.

- 124 Kensington Church St W8 4BH
  020 7221 9225 — **www**.sallyclarke.com
  Notting Hill Gate
- Menu £27/39 - Carte £40/60
  Closed 2 weeks August, Christmas-New Year, Sunday January-September and bank holidays - booking advisable

DOCK KITCHEN

Mediterranean cuisine • Design

MAP: 13-A0/1

This restaurant is set in a canalside former Victorian goods yard and the space is shared with designer Tom Dixon, some of whose furniture and lighting is showcased here. The open kitchen dominates one end of the room where steel girders and exposed brick add to the industrial aesthetic. The similarities to Moro, River Café and Petersham Nurseries are palpable, not just in the refreshing lack of ceremony and the fashionable crowds that flock here, but also in the cooking, where quality ingredients are a given and natural flavours speak for themselves. Look out for the themed set menus on the last Tuesday of each month; these could be based on any region from Jerusalem to Catalonia; Mexico to Sri Lanka.

- Portobello Dock, 342-344 Ladbroke Grove ✉ W10 5BU
  ✆ 020 8962 1610 — **www**.dockkitchen.co.uk
  ⊖ Ladbroke Grove
- Carte £25/40
  Closed Christmas, Sunday dinner and bank holidays

ELECTRIC DINER

Meats and grills • Rustic

MAP: 13-B2

Any cinema that's over 100 years old deserves to be shown respect, so treat your visit to the Electric Cinema as a special occasion and start, or finish, with a meal next door at the Electric Diner. It's a loud, fun and brash all-day operation with a simple but all-encompassing menu that changes daily. The long counter, red leather booths and low ceiling certainly create the mood and look of the classic American diner – even the music comes from a reel-to-reel. Au Cheval diner in Chicago has supplied most of the influences so be prepared for big portions that are heavy on flavour. The room fills with smoke from the grill; the steak and pork chops could easily feed two and the lemon meringue pie is of Desperate Dan dimensions.

- 191 Portobello Rd ✉ W11 2ED
  ✆ 020 7908 9696 — **www**.electricdiner.com
  ⊖ Ladbroke Grove
- Carte £17/34
  Closed 30-31 August and 25 December

FLAT THREE

Creative • Design

MAP: 13-B3/4

A restaurant blending the cuisines of Scandinavia, Korea and Japan needs planning and indeed, it was while living at Flat 3 that the owner first had the idea. It was also where she developed the menu and honed the cooking, along with the chef, by hosting supper clubs. Only an obsessive foodie with an encyclopaedic mind will recognise all the ingredients and while some dishes are more style over substance, there are others that do work well such as those involving the wood-fired oven. They make their own soy and miso, press their own juices and, needless to say, serve more foraged ingredients than you'll find in Ray Mears' pocket. Presentation is minimalist - rather like the basement room - and there's a menu specifically for vegans.

- 120-122 Holland Park Ave ✉ W11 4UA
  020 7792 8987 — **www**.flatthree.london
  Holland Park
- Carte £40/66
  Closed 21 December-4 January, 21 August-1 September, Sunday and Monday - (dinner only and lunch Friday-Saturday)

GRANGER AND CO. NOTTING HILL

Modern cuisine • Friendly

MAP: 13-C2

Having relocated from the sun of Sydney to the cool of Notting Hill, Bill Granger decided to open a local restaurant. He brought with him that disarmingly charming 'matey' service that only Australians can do, along with his breakfast sweetcorn fritters and ricotta hotcakes, and a zesty menu that features everything from pasta to pork chops. At dinner a BBQ section is added along with a daily fish dish, while various puds replace the cakes offered during the day. The room is bright and open, prices are reasonable and the Asian accents lend many of the dishes an easy-to-eat quality, which makes you feel healthier than when you arrived and allows you to forget that you probably had to queue for a table.

- 175 Westbourne Grove ✉ W11 2SB
  020 7229 9111 — **www**.grangerandco.com
  Bayswater
- Carte £19/41
  Closed August bank holiday weekend and 25 December - bookings not accepted

KENSINGTON PLACE

Seafood • Neighbourhood

MAP: 13-C3

2017 marked the 30th birthday of this iconic brasserie, which was at the vanguard of a new wave of restaurants at the time when London's dining scene changed forever – and it remains relevant in this more competitive age by being well run and authentic. Its owners – the D&D group – have wisely resisted the urge to change its appearance too much, save for a little freshening up here and there, and the room is bright and cheery like the young staff who serve the tables. Fish is the focus of the fairly priced menu which mixes classics like prawn cocktail and fish pie with more modern dishes such as cod with a seaweed dressing. The selection of the day's fish from the market is often the best choice, which you can have grilled or roasted.

- 201-209 Kensington Church St. W8 7LX
  020 7727 3184 — **www**.kensingtonplace-restaurant.co.uk
  Notting Hill Gate
- Menu £20 (lunch and early dinner) - Carte £25/52
  Closed Sunday dinner, Monday lunch and bank holidays

LAUNCESTON PLACE

Modern cuisine • Neighbourhood

MAP: 13-D5

There are a number of features of this longstanding Kensington restaurant that really engender it to diners: it has a palpable sense of neighbourhood, boasts one of the prettiest façades around, and is divided into various nooks and crannies so makes an ideal choice for trysts or tête-à-têtes. It is run with perhaps a greater degree of formality than is really needed but the suited and booted team do at least know when to leave their guests alone. The menu is fashionably terse, merely listing the main components of each dish on the two menus – the set menu and the Tasting menu. The cooking is elaborate in style, with the kitchen using lots of modern techniques; dishes are big on originality and artfully presented.

- 1a Launceston Pl W8 5RL
  020 7937 6912 — **www**.launcestonplace-restaurant.co.uk
  Gloucester Road
- Menu £25/75
  Closed 25-30 December, 1 January, Tuesday lunch and Monday – bookings advisable at dinner

KITCHEN W8 ✿

Modern cuisine • Neighbourhood

XX A/C

MAP: 13-C5

Michelin

FIRST COURSE: Smoked eel with grilled mackerel, golden beetroot and sweet mustard. • Breast and leg of quail with charred white asparagus, peas and truffle pesto.

MAIN COURSE: Roast rump of veal with bulgur wheat, charred lettuce, hazelnuts and shiitake. • Fillet of turbot with courgette, broad beans, artichoke, spiced almonds and mint.

DESSERT: Muscovado financiers with salted peanut ice cream, bitter chocolate and banana. • Elderflower custard with baked strawberry ice cream and 'Jammie Dodger'.

Kitchen W8 is the sort of restaurant every neighbourhood should have because it succeeds on so many levels. Whether you're here for a special occasion on a Saturday night or a quick bite for lunch during the week, the staff will get the tone of the service just right and the food will be meticulously prepared yet very easy to eat. The restaurant is a joint venture between experienced restaurateurs Rebecca Mascarenhas and Philip Howard and their influence is clear to see. Head Chef Mark Kempson puts as much care into the great value lunch and early evening menu as he does the main à la carte; both are produce driven and his confident cooking delivers great flavours and subtle degrees of originality so that the dishes have personality and depth. The restaurant may not be quite as informal as the name suggests but it is certainly free of pomp or pomposity. On Sunday the restaurant entices even more locals in by making it a corkage free night which encourages them to open up their own cellars.

- 11-13 Abingdon Rd ✉ W8 6AH
  ✆ 020 7937 0120 — **www**.kitchenw8.com
  ⊖ High Street Kensington
- Menu £28/30 (early weekday dinner) - Carte £40/55
  Closed 24-26 December and bank holidays

LEDBURY ✿✿

Modern cuisine • *Neighbourhood*

XXX   A/C   **MAP:** 13-C2

Michelin

FIRST COURSE: Clay-baked golden beetroot with English caviar, smoked and dried eel. • Grilled cuttlefish with garlic and cracked wheat.

MAIN COURSE: Dorset Sika deer with hen-of-the-wood, pickled wild hops and smoked bone marrow. • John Dory with artichokes and lemon.

DESSERT: Chocolate, dark chocolate Chantilly and mint. • Pear in brown butter with goat's milk caramel and malt.

Brett Graham is a chef who understands his ingredients. His deep-rooted knowledge of husbandry and his close working relationship with his suppliers are revealed through his menus and reflected on the plate. The quality of the produce really shines through and the kitchen's ability and deft touch mean that the strikingly original flavour combinations will linger long in the memory. Lovers of game have much to savour in the season and it is not unknown for Brett to head up to Norfolk after service to shoot some venison. The wine list offers good value at all levels, is strong across the regions and includes a great selection by the glass. The Ledbury has always had to work hard to attract lunchtime business so the fixed price lunch menu represents excellent value and often includes some unexpectedly luxurious ingredients, like Red Ruby beef or hand-dived scallops; at weekends, only a tasting menu is offered for dinner. Whenever you come, you'll find this a smart yet unshowy restaurant with a satisfying hum and smooth, engaging service.

■ 127 Ledbury Rd. ✉ W11 2AQ
✆ 020 7792 9090 — **www**.theledbury.com
⊖ Notting Hill Gate

■ Menu £75/145
Closed 25-26 December, August bank holiday and lunch Monday-Tuesday

MALABAR

Indian • Neighbourhood

MAP: 13-C3

One of the reasons why Malabar has been going strong since 1983 is that it has kept on top of its appearance, as, it seems, do most of its Notting Hill customers. These days the front has a sleek, understated look; the interior is a fashionable grey; and the staff do their bit by dressing in black. What doesn't change is the quality of the food, from the breads to the piping hot thalis. The favourites remain but the seafood section has been beefed up with the addition of a monkfish curry and a whole gilt-head bream; and just because the tandoori dishes sit beside the starters on the menu, don't assume they come in starter sizes. The excellent value Sunday buffet lunch, when children under 12 eat for free, still packs them in.

- 27 Uxbridge St. W8 7TQ
  020 7727 8800 — **www**.malabar-restaurant.co.uk
  Notting Hill Gate
- Carte £18/37 **s**
  Closed 1 week Christmas - (dinner only and lunch Saturday-Sunday)

MAZI

Greek • Friendly

MAP: 13-C3

Apart from one or possibly two exceptions, Greek restaurants in the capital have been less than inspiring over the years - but that may start to change thanks to Mazi, which means 'together'. The kitchen seeks inspiration from traditional recipes then adds contemporary twists to create vibrant, colourful and fresh tasting dishes. It's all about sharing here, with cold dishes such as tarama with lemon confit served in glass jars; bigger, more robust dishes include braised saddle of lamb with its shoulder, and rabbit ragout with pasta. The wine list is exclusively Greek and much of the imported produce is available to buy. The simple room is bright and fresh and there are few more charming spots than the garden terrace at the back.

- 12-14 Hillgate St W8 7SR
  020 7229 3794 — **www**.mazi.co.uk
  Notting Hill Gate
- Menu £15 (weekday lunch) - Carte £28/43
  Closed 24-25 December and 1-2 January

MIN JIANG

Chinese • Elegant

MAP: 13-D4

It's got great views of Kensington Palace and Gardens (ask for tables 11 or 16) but because of its own good looks and its collection of vases influenced by the Ming Dynasty, this stylish Chinese restaurant on the 10th floor of the Royal Garden hotel can more than hold its own. The speciality is wood-fired Beijing duck in two servings - order it in advance; its glistening meat is carved at the table and one then has the difficult task of choosing one of the four options offered for the second serving. The cuisine covers all provinces, although Cantonese and Sichuanese are the most dominant. Signature dishes include sea bass with shredded chicken, sautéed Gong Bao chicken and spicy pork belly with leeks.

■ Royal Garden Hotel, 2-24 Kensington High St (10th Floor) ✉ W8 4PT
✆ 020 7361 1988 — **www**.minjiang.co.uk
⊖ High Street Kensington
■ Menu £40/80 - Carte £30/99

N 108 GARAGE

Modern British • Neighbourhood

MAP: 13-B1

It's got an urban, utilitarian look that's more Hackney than Kensington, with bare brick, exposed ducting and a polished concrete floor; chairs are metal mesh, crockery comes from junk shops on Portobello Road and counter and communal dining both feature. Sit on a stool and chat to the affable chef; if you're here on a date, curious artefacts like a framed collection of water pipes or an out-sized oil of Henry IV could prove useful should the conversation falter. Modern dishes are vibrant and tasty and change according to the ingredients fresh in. A heavenly sourdough kicks things off, a BBQ monkfish from the 'Green Egg' comes with salty olives and seasonal artichokes, and the Jacob's Ladder is another popular choice.

■ 108 Golborne Rd ✉ W10 5PS
✆ 020 8969 3769 — **www**.108garage.com
⊖ Westbourne Park
■ Menu £35/45 - Carte £28/46
Closed 2 weeks August, 2 weeks Christmas, Sunday and Monday - booking essential

THE SHED

Modern British • Rustic

MAP: 13-C3

Names add to expectations, so if you call your place the Grand Palace it really doesn't give you anywhere to hide. The Gladwin brothers behind The Shed instead opted for understatement and it works a treat. This is the old Ark restaurant and is obviously more than just a shed, even though it comes with a healthy dose of the outdoors. There are farming tools, upturned barrels for tables and even an old tractor engine, all adding to its higgledy-piggledy charm. One brother cooks, one manages, and the third runs the farm in West Sussex from where much of the produce comes. The cooking is appropriately British, earthy and satisfying, with the small plates divided into 'slow' or 'fast': a reference to the cooking process.

- 122 Palace Gardens Terr ✉ W8 4RT
  020 7229 4024 — **www**.theshed-restaurant.com
  ⊖ Notting Hill Gate
- Carte £21/32
  Closed Monday lunch and Sunday

SIX PORTLAND ROAD

French • Neighbourhood

A/C

MAP: 13-B3

If North Kensington is your hood, then this is a neighbour who'll soon become a firm friend. A cosy, intimate place, it's owned by Oli Barker, who brought his head chef along with him when he left Terroirs in the Strand. He personally welcomes his regulars – of which there are many – and has found a relaxed and friendly team of servers who clearly know their stuff. The seasonal menu changes frequently and has a strong French accent; dishes are reassuringly recognisable, skilfully constructed and very tasty. Start with half a dozen of County Waterford's best oysters or a robust pork and pistachio terrine; a satisfying main of turbot comes with broad beans, mousserons and beurre blanc, while griottines add a kick to a silky chocolate mousse.

- 6 Portland Rd ✉ W11 4LA
  020 7229 3130 — **www**.sixportlandroad.com
  ⊖ Holland Park
- Menu £19 (weekday lunch) – Carte £30/52
  Closed Christmas-New Year, last 2 weeks August, Sunday dinner and Monday

YASHIN

Japanese • Design

MAP: 13-C4

Two experienced sushi chefs joined forces to create this contemporary restaurant with its crisp, appealing black and white theme. Their worthy ambition to wean diners off fermented soya bean is reflected in their grammatically challenging but charmingly equitable slogan: "without soy sauce... but if you want to". There are three omakase choices offering 8, 11 or 15 pieces of sushi selected by the chefs and served together. The quality of the fish is clear and originality comes in the form of minuscule garnishes adorning each piece and the odd bit of searing. Service is knowledgeable and endearing but be sure to ask for a counter seat, as one of the joys of sushi comes from watching the chefs' dextrous knife skills and their deft handling of the fish.

- 1a Argyll Rd. W8 7DB
  020 7938 1536 — **www**.yashinsushi.com
  High Street Kensington
- Carte £45/89
  Closed 24, 25 and 31 December and 1 January - booking essential

ZAIKA

Indian • Exotic décor

MAP: 13-D4

After a short-lived and rather curious venture into modern European cooking, the Tamarind Collection wisely returned their Kensington outpost to what it did best and re-opened it as Zaika. The cooking focuses on the North of India and the influences of Mughal and Nawabi, so you can expect rich, satisfying and fragrantly spiced dishes that include tandoor-cooked kebabs and succulent Gosht Dum biryani. With its wood-panelled walls and ornate ceiling, it comes as no surprise that this softly-lit room was once a bank, but the sepia prints now add a hint of colonialism and the cocktail bar lends a touch of modernity. Factor in the friendly and attentive service and you have a restaurant that should never have gone away.

- 1 Kensington High St. W8 5NP
  020 7795 6533 — **www**.zaikaofkensington.com
  High Street Kensington
- Menu £19 (lunch) - Carte £32/67
  Closed 25-26 December, 1 January and Monday lunch

ZAYANE

Moroccan • Neighbourhood

MAP: 13-B1

This intimate neighbourhood restaurant is a delight for the senses: the scent of exotic spiced candles hits you as you walk in, modern African music pumps from the speakers, hanging lamps cast an atmospheric glow and colourful crockery and a framed national dress provide a visual treat. And then there's the food: the Moroccan cooking comes with modern techniques and authentic flavours; Casablanca-born owner Meryem tastes each dish personally and the chef adjusts them accordingly. Start with warm bread and fresh, zingy olives; starters might include pan-fried scallops chermoula with chickpeas or a smoked octopus salad; main courses could be a full-flavoured poussin tangine or, the fast-becoming-a-cult-dish, Morrocan-spiced short rib of beef.

- 91 Golborne Rd W10 5NL
  020 8960 1137 — **www**.zayanerestaurant.com
  Westbourne Park
- Menu £25 - Carte £24/38
  Closed 26 August-3 September

GREATER LONDON

londongal_/iStock (bottom) • Eviled/Shutterstock.com (top)

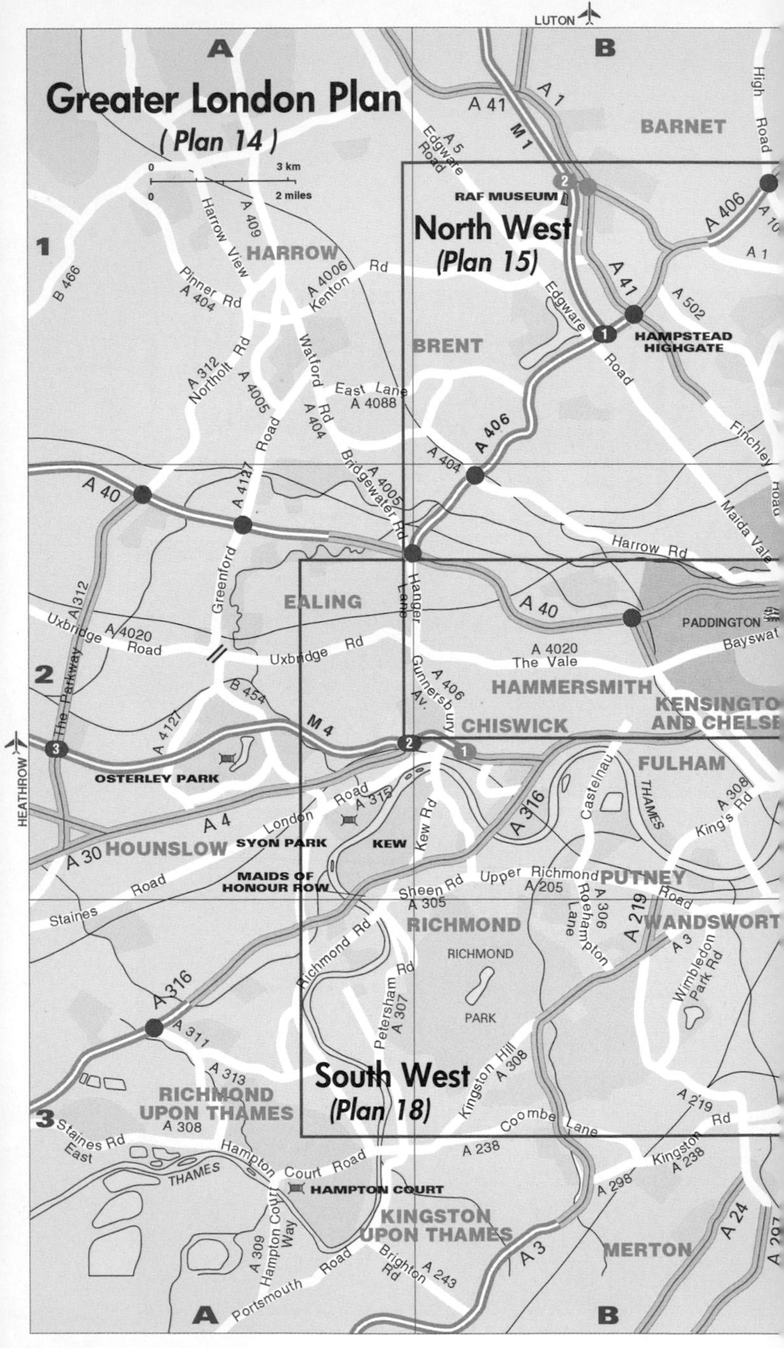

LUTON
Greater London Plan
(Plan 14)
0 3 km
0 2 miles
A
B
1
2
3
BARNET
RAF MUSEUM
North West
(Plan 15)
HARROW
BRENT
HAMPSTEAD
HIGHGATE
EALING
PADDINGTON
HAMMERSMITH
KENSINGTON AND CHELSEA
CHISWICK
FULHAM
OSTERLEY PARK
HOUNSLOW
SYON PARK
KEW
MAIDS OF HONOUR ROW
PUTNEY
WANDSWORTH
RICHMOND
RICHMOND PARK
South West
(Plan 18)
RICHMOND UPON THAMES
HAMPTON COURT
KINGSTON UPON THAMES
MERTON
HEATHROW
THAMES

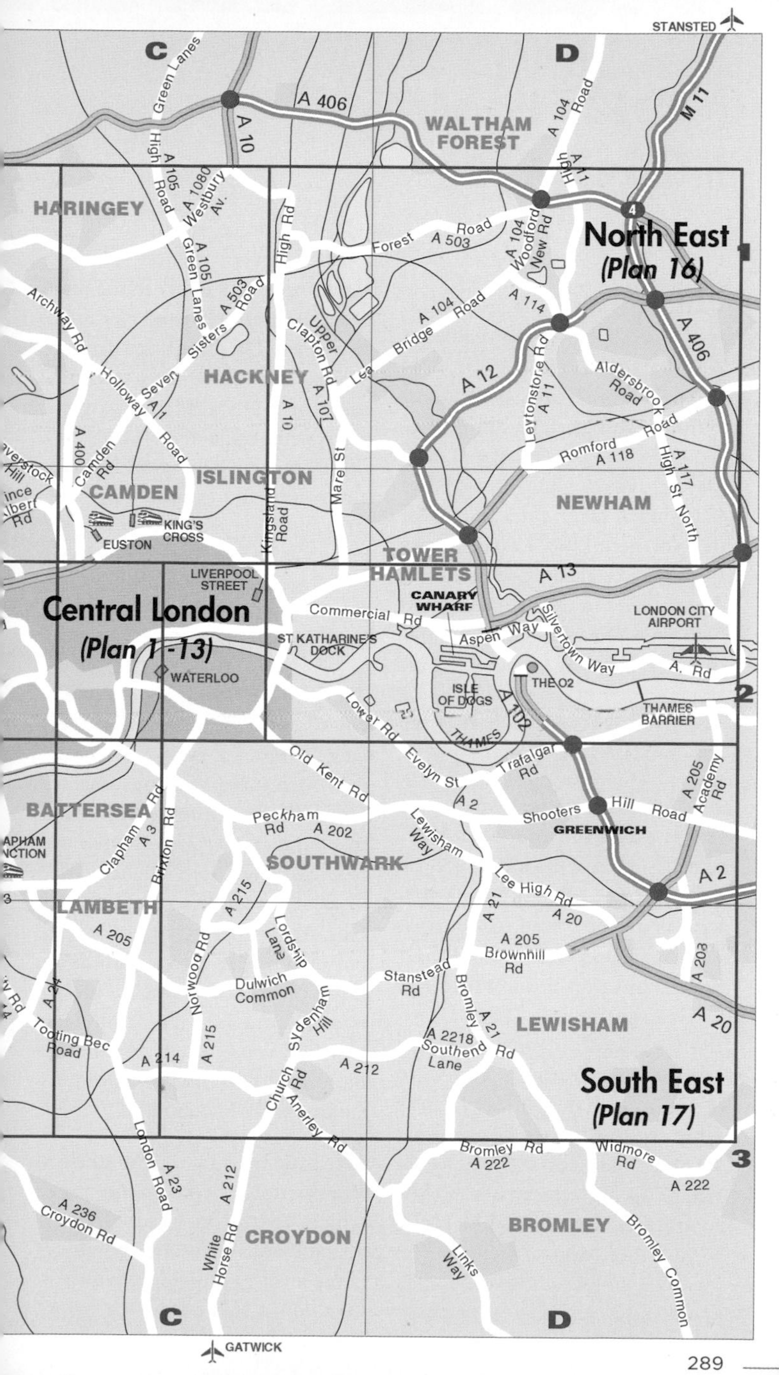
STANSTED
C
D
Green Lanes
A 406
A 10
WALTHAM FOREST
A 104 Road
M 11
High Road A 105
A 1080 Westbury Av.
High A 11
HARINGEY
High Rd
Forest Road A 503
A 104 Woodford New Rd
North East
(Plan 16)
A 105 Green Lanes
Seven Sisters A 503 Road
Archway Rd
Upper Clapton Rd A 107
A 104 Lea Bridge Road
A 114
A 12
Leytonstone Rd A 11
A 406
Aldersbrook Road
HACKNEY
Holloway A 1 Road
A 10
Mare St
Romford A 118 Road
High St North A 117
A 400 Camden Rd
ISLINGTON
CAMDEN
NEWHAM
KING'S CROSS
EUSTON
Kingsland Road
TOWER HAMLETS
LIVERPOOL STREET
A 13
CANARY WHARF
Central London
(Plan 1-13)
Commercial Rd
LONDON CITY AIRPORT
ST KATHARINE'S DOCK
Aspen Way
Silvertown Way
A. Rd
WATERLOO
THE O2
ISLE OF DOGS
A 102
Lower Rd
THAMES
THAMES BARRIER
2
Old Kent Rd
Evelyn St
Trafalgar Rd
A 205 Academy Rd
BATTERSEA
Clapham A 3 Rd
Brixton Rd
Peckham Rd A 202
Lewisham Way
A 2
Shooters Hill Road
GREENWICH
SOUTHWARK
Lee High Rd
A 2
LAMBETH
A 215
A 21
A 20
A 205
Lordship Lane
A 205 Brownhill Rd
A 203
Norwood Rd
Dulwich Common
Stanstead Rd
Bromley A 21 Rd
A 24
Sydenham Hill
A 20
Tooting Bec Road
A 215
LEWISHAM
A 214
A 2218 Southend Lane
A 212
South East
(Plan 17)
Church Rd
Anerley Rd
London Road A 23
Bromley Rd A 222
Widmore Rd
3
A 212
A 222
A 236 Croydon Rd
White Horse Rd
CROYDON
BROMLEY
Links Way
Bromley Common
C
D
GATWICK

NORTH-WEST LONDON

Heading north from London Zoo and Regent's Park, the green baton is passed to two of the city's most popular and well-known locations: Hampstead Heath and Highgate Wood. In close proximity, they offer a favoured pair of lungs to travellers emerging from the murky depths of the Northern Line. Two centuries ago, they would have been just another part of the area's undeveloped high ground and pastureland, but since the building boom of the nineteenth century, both have become prized assets in this part of the metropolis.

People came to seek shelter in **Hampstead** in times of plague, and it's retained its bucolic air to this day. Famous names have always enjoyed its charms: Constable and Keats rested their brush and pen here, while the sculptors Henry Moore and Barbara Hepworth were residents in more recent times. Many are drawn to such delightful places as Church Row, which boasts a lovely Georgian Terrace. You know you're up high because the thoroughfares bear names like Holly Mount and Mount Vernon. The Heath is full of rolling woodlands and meadows; it's a great place for rambling, particularly to the crest of **Parliament Hill** and its superb city views. There are three bathing ponds here, one mixed, and one each for male and female swimmers, while up on the Heath's northern fringes, **Kenwood House,** along with its famous al fresco summer concerts, also boasts great art by the likes of Vermeer and Rembrandt. And besides all that, there's an ivy tunnel leading to a terrace with idyllic pond views.

Highgate Wood is an ancient woodland and conservation area, containing a leafy walk that meanders enchantingly along a former railway line to **Crouch End,** home to a band of thespians. Down the road at Highgate Cemetery, the likes of Karl Marx, George Eliot, Christina Rossetti and Michael Faraday rest in a great entanglement of breathtaking Victorian over-decoration. The cemetery is still in use – recent notables to be buried here include Douglas Adams and Malcolm McLaren.

Next door you'll find **Waterlow Park,** another fine green space, which, apart from its super views, also includes decorative ponds on three levels. Lauderdale House is here, too, a 16C pile which is now an arts centre; more famously, Charles II handed over its keys to Nell Gwynn for her to use as her North London residence. Head back south from here, and **Primrose Hill** continues the theme of glorious green space: its surrounding terraces are populated by media darlings, while its vertiginous mass is another to boast a famously enviable vista.

Of a different hue altogether is **Camden Town** with its buzzy edge, courtesy of a renowned indie music scene, goths, punks, and six earthy markets selling everything from tat to exotica. Charles Dickens grew up here, and he was none too complimentary; the area still relishes its seamy underside. A scenic route out is the **Regent's Canal,** which cuts its way through the market and ambles to the east and west of the city. Up the road, the legendary Roundhouse re-opened its arty front doors in 2006, expanding further the wide range of Camden's alt scene.

One of the music world's most legendary destinations, the **Abbey Road** studios, is also in this area and, yes, it's possible to join other tourists making their way over that zebra crossing. Not far away, in Maresfield Gardens, stands a very different kind of attraction. The Freud Museum is one of the very few buildings in London to have two blue plaques. It was home to Sigmund during the last year of his life and it's where he lived with his daughter Anna (her plaque commemorates her work in child psychiatry). Inside, there's a fabulous library and his working desk. But the pivotal part of the whole house is in another corner of the study – the psychiatrist's couch!

s4svisuals/Shutterstock.com

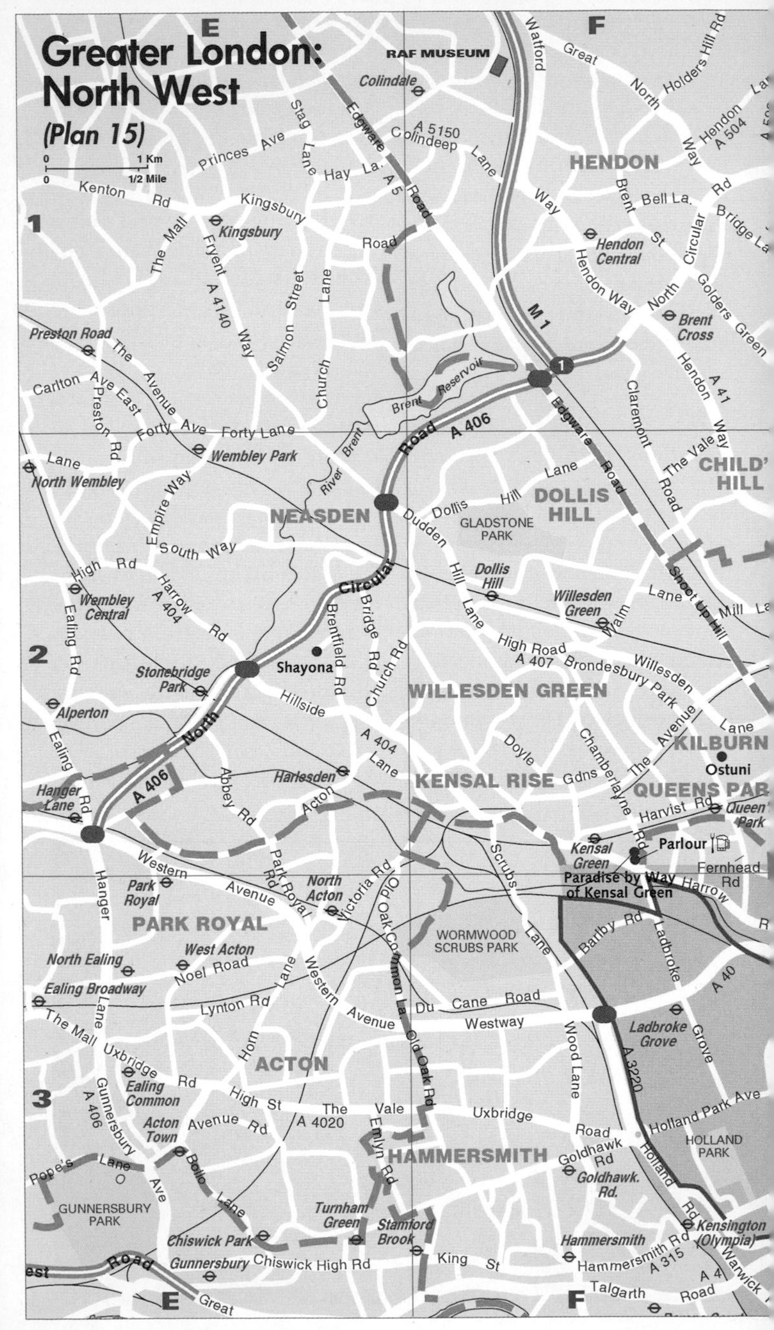
Greater London: North West
(Plan 15)
0 1 Km
0 1/2 Mile
E
F
1
2
3
RAF MUSEUM
Colindale
HENDON
Hendon Central
Brent Cross
Kingsbury
Preston Road
Wembley Park
North Wembley
NEASDEN
GLADSTONE PARK
DOLLIS HILL
CHILD'S HILL
Dollis Hill
Willesden Green
Wembley Central
Stonebridge Park
Shayona
WILLESDEN GREEN
Alperton
Hanger Lane
Harlesden
KENSAL RISE
KILBURN
Ostuni
QUEENS PARK
Queen's Park
Kensal Green
Parlour
Paradise by Way of Kensal Green
Park Royal
North Acton
PARK ROYAL
WORMWOOD SCRUBS PARK
North Ealing
West Acton
Ealing Broadway
Ladbroke Grove
ACTON
Ealing Common
Acton Town
HAMMERSMITH
Goldhawk Rd.
HOLLAND PARK
GUNNERSBURY PARK
Turnham Green
Stamford Brook
Chiswick Park
Gunnersbury
Hammersmith
Kensington (Olympia)
Brent Reservoir
River Brent
M1
A 406
North Circular Road
Edgware Road A 5
A 5150 Colindeep Lane
Watford Way
Great North Way
Holders Hill Rd
Hendon Way A 504
A 41
Kenton Rd
Princes Ave
Stag Lane
Hay La.
Kingsbury Road
The Mall
Fryent Way A 4140
Salmon Street
Church Lane
The Avenue
Carlton Ave East
Preston Rd
Forty Ave
Forty Lane
Empire Way
South Way
High Rd
Harrow Rd A 404
Ealing Rd
Brentfield Rd
Bridge Rd
Church Rd
Dudden Hill Lane
Dollis Hill Lane
Claremont Road
The Vale
Shoot Up Hill
Mill Lane
Walm Lane
High Road A 407
Brondesbury Park
Willesden Lane
Hillside
A 404
Acton Lane
Abbey Rd
Doyle Gdns
Chamberlayne Rd
The Avenue
Harvist Rd
Fernhead Rd
Harrow Rd
Scrubs Lane
Western Avenue
Park Royal Rd
Victoria Rd
Old Oak Common La.
Old Oak Rd
Barlby Rd
Ladbroke Grove
A 40
Hanger Lane
Noel Road
Horn Lane
Lynton Rd
Du Cane Road
Westway
Wood Lane
A 3220
The Mall
Uxbridge Rd
High St
The Vale A 4020
Uxbridge Road
Holland Park Ave
Emlyn Rd
Gunnersbury Ave
A 406
Avenue Rd
Bollo Lane
Pope's Lane
Goldhawk Rd
Holland Rd
Chiswick High Rd
King St
Hammersmith Rd A 315
Talgarth Road A 4
Great West Road
Warwick
Bell La.
Brent St
Circular Rd
Bridge La.
Hendon Way
North Circular
Golders Green
Hendon Way A 41
Edgware Road
Dollis Hill Lane
Lane

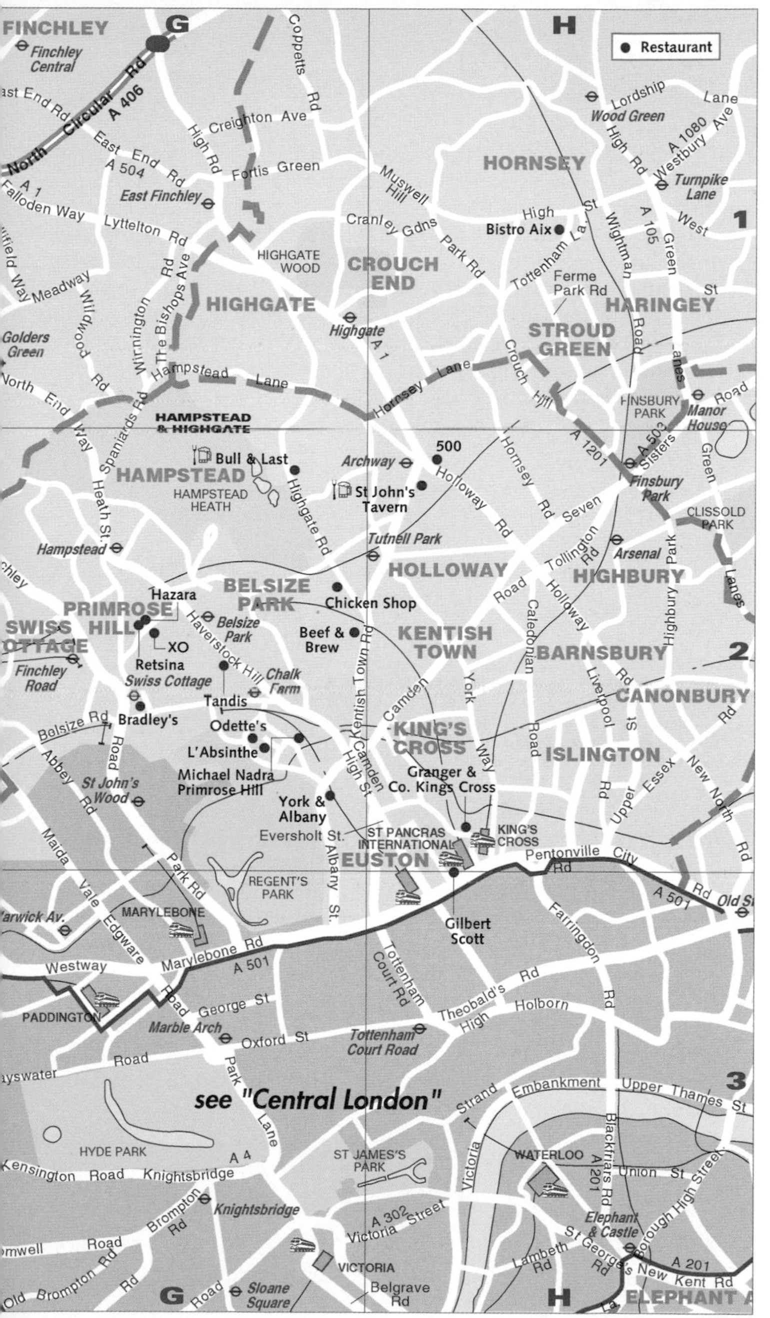
G
H
Restaurant
1
2
3
FINCHLEY
Finchley Central
East End Rd
North Circular Rd
A 406
A 504
A 1
Falloden Way
Lyttelton Rd
East Finchley
Creighton Ave
High Rd
Fortis Green
Coppetts Rd
Muswell Hill
Cranley Gdns
Park Rd
HIGHGATE WOOD
CROUCH END
HIGHGATE
Highgate
A 1
Meadway
Wildwood Rd
Winnington Rd
The Bishops Ave
Golders Green
North End Way
Hampstead Lane
Hornsey Lane
Spaniards Rd
HAMPSTEAD & HIGHGATE
HORNSEY
Lordship Lane
Wood Green
High Rd
A 1080
Westbury Ave
Turnpike Lane
West Green
A 105
Bistro Aix
High St
Tottenham La.
Wightman Road
Ferme Park Rd
HARINGEY
St
STROUD GREEN
Crouch Hill
Lanes
FINSBURY PARK
Manor House
Road
Green Lanes
A 1201
A 503
Seven Sisters
Finsbury Park
CLISSOLD PARK
Bull & Last
HAMPSTEAD
HAMPSTEAD HEATH
Heath St.
Highgate Rd
Archway
500
St John's Tavern
Holloway Rd
Hornsey Rd
Seven
Tutnell Park
HOLLOWAY
Tollington Rd
Arsenal
HIGHBURY
Hampstead
BELSIZE PARK
Chicken Shop
Road
Holloway
Caledonian Road
Highbury Park
Hazara
PRIMROSE HILL
SWISS COTTAGE
XO
Retsina
Belsize Park
Haverstock Hill
Beef & Brew
Kentish Town Rd
KENTISH TOWN
BARNSBURY
Finchley Road
Swiss Cottage
Chalk Farm
Tandis
Camden
York Way
Liverpool Rd
CANONBURY
Rd
Belsize Rd
Bradley's
Odette's
L'Absinthe
Michael Nadra Primrose Hill
KING'S CROSS
ISLINGTON
St
Abbey Rd
Road
St John's Wood
Camden High St
Granger & Co. Kings Cross
York & Albany
Upper Essex Rd
New North Rd
Maida Vale
Eversholt St.
ST PANCRAS INTERNATIONAL
KING'S CROSS
EUSTON
Pentonville Rd
City Rd
Park Rd
REGENT'S PARK
Albany St.
A 501
Old St
Warwick Av.
Edgware
MARYLEBONE
Gilbert Scott
Farringdon Rd
Westway
Marylebone Rd
A 501
Tottenham Court Rd
PADDINGTON
Road
George St
Theobald's Rd
Holborn
High
Marble Arch
Oxford St
Tottenham Court Road
Bayswater Road
Park Lane
see "Central London"
Strand
Embankment
Upper Thames St
HYDE PARK
A 4
ST JAMES'S PARK
WATERLOO
Victoria
Blackfriars Rd
A 201
Union St
Kensington Road
Knightsbridge
Brompton Rd
Knightsbridge
A 302
Victoria Street
Elephant & Castle
Borough High Street
Cromwell Road
St George's Rd
Lambeth Rd
New Kent Rd
A 201
Old Brompton Rd
Rd
Road
VICTORIA
Sloane Square
Belgrave Rd
ELEPHANT

500

Italian • Friendly

MAP: 15-H2

It's named after the cute little Fiat and that couldn't be more appropriate because here is a restaurant which is small, fun, well-priced and ideal for London. The owner is an ebullient fellow who takes an active role in the service, as does the chef who likes to see the look of satisfaction on his customers' faces. Their shared passion is evident in the cooking: homemade breads and pastas are very good; the fluffy gnocchi with sausage ragu delivers a kick; the tender veal chop is a winner, and the rabbit is the house special. The menu, which has occasional Sardinian leanings, changes regularly and the sheet of daily specials includes great little snacks to have with a drink. Black and white photos of old Holloway are the only incongruity.

- **Archway** — 782 Holloway Rd ✉ N19 3JH
  ✆ 020 7272 3406 — **www**.500restaurant.co.uk
  ⊖ Archway
- Carte £26/34
  Closed 2 weeks summer and 2 weeks Christmas-New Year - booking essential - (dinner only and lunch Friday-Sunday)

ST JOHN'S TAVERN

Modern cuisine • Pub

MAP: 15-H2

A Junction Road landmark, St John's Tavern has been providing sustenance to the good people of Islington since the 1860s - generally in the form of beer. Tapas is a rather more modern addition - these days served in the front bar - so choose from such delights as plaice goujons, globe artichoke, patatas bravas and jamon croquetas. For a more structured meal, head to the vast and hugely appealing rear dining room with its art and lithographs. The well-crafted dishes are mainly British with a nod to the Med, and could include pig's head terrine with piccalilli, octopus risotto or pork belly with quince aioli. Add in friendly service and a great selection of artisan beers and you'll see why this is still very much a favourite with the locals.

- **Archway** — 91 Junction Rd ✉ N19 5QU
  ✆ 020 7272 1587 — **www**.stjohnstavern.com
  ⊖ Archway.
- Carte £21/36
  Closed 25-26 December and Monday lunch - booking advisable

HAZARA ℩O

Indian • Neighbourhood

XX A/C MAP: 15-G2

He trained as a lawyer and spent eight years as a teacher but Tajinder, the owner, realised a long held ambition when he opened his own restaurant. He named it after his grandfather and staffed it with conscientious waiting team and chefs who trained with the Taj Group and had experience of cooking specialities from all regions of India. The extensive menu does offer a few old classics but the more adventurous diner will be faced with an appealing choice, including dishes which make good use of game in season; fish dishes are also particularly good and Tajinder goes personally to Smithfield and Billingsgate to ensure the quality of the produce. The brighter, modern ground floor is the better place to sit.

- **Belsize Park** — 44 Belsize Ln ✉ NW3 5AR
  ✆ 020 7433 1147 — **www**.hazararestaurant.com
  ⊖ Belsize Park
- Menu £20 - Carte £16/31
  Closed 25-26 December and 1 January - (dinner only and lunch Saturday-Sunday)

RETSINA ℩O

Greek • Rustic

X A/C MAP: 15-G2

As private equity companies and international conglomerates continue on the path to world domination, there's something very reassuring about finding a restaurant that's still family-owned and part of the neighbourhood. It's quite a simple-looking place - bright, airy and enlivened with some modern artwork. Regulars across all age groups are literally welcomed with open arms and, with a little wishful thinking and a touch of imagination, one could almost be eating with the locals on a Greek island. The menu has all the Greek classics, from dolmathes to spanakopita, kleftico to moussaka but, bearing in mind they have a proper charcoal grill in the kitchen, the kebabs, cutlets and souvla are worthy choices.

- **Belsize Park** — 48-50 Belsize Ln ✉ NW3 5AR
  ✆ 020 7431 5855 — **www**.retsina.squarespace.com
  ⊖ Belsize Park
- Carte £24/34
  Closed 25-26 December, 1 January, Monday lunch and bank holidays

TANDIS

World cuisine • Neighbourhood

MAP: 15-G2

The appeal of Tandis and its enticing Persian and Middle Eastern cooking stretches way beyond the Iranian diaspora - plenty of locals were also seduced as soon as they tasted the traditional flat bread baked in a clay oven and the Masto Khiyar. Start with the complex flavours of Kashke Badem, then move on to an invigorating khoresh stew, such as lamb and split peas, or try a succulent kabab; vegetarians are also well catered for. Newcomers shouldn't be afraid to ask for a little guidance; dishes are substantial and sharing is the key - and make sure you finish with the refreshing Persian sorbet with rosewater. A very successful takeaway service doesn't seem to affect the efficiency with which it is run.

■ **Belsize Park** — 73 Haverstock Hill ✉ NW3 4SL
020 7586 8079 — **www**.tandisrestaurant.com
Chalk Farm

■ Carte £19/31
Closed 25 December

YORK & ALBANY

Modern cuisine • Inn

MAP: 15-G2

This 1820s John Nash coaching inn is a handsome fellow. Rescued by Gordon Ramsay a few years back after lying almost derelict, its reputation now brings customers from all parts of northwest London. It's a moot point, though, whether it still qualifies as an inn or is more of a restaurant these days; granted, you can drop in for a drink at the bar but then that's after you've been welcomed by a hostess at the door. The food certainly veers more towards a restaurant style: instead of burgers and pasta, there are seared scallops with celeriac or red leg partridge with barley, although you can get quite robust dishes like ox cheeks and steaks. The bright, apron-wearing staff provide confident, breezy service and there are bedrooms available.

■ **Camden Town** — 127-129 Parkway ✉ NW1 7PS
020 7592 1227 — **www**.gordonramsayrestaurants.com/york-and-albany
Camden Town

■ Menu £25 (weekday lunch) - Carte £27/56

SHAYONA

Indian • Family

MAP: 15-E2

Shayona sits in the shadow of Neasden's remarkable Shri Swaminarayan Mandir and is actually owned by the temple. In contrast to the splendour of this Hindu gem, the restaurant is housed within a supermarket - but head past the sweet counter and you'll find yourself in a comfortable and vibrantly decorated room. The fresh, balanced cooking here is sattvic, which means it is vegetarian and 'pure' and so avoids certain foods like onion or garlic. The varied menu covers all parts of India and includes curries from the north, dosas from the south and street snacks from Mumbai - and prices mean you can experiment and share dishes, without worrying too much about their cost. There is no alcohol available so choose a refreshing lassi instead.

- **Church End** — 54-62 Meadow Garth ✉ NW10 8HD
  ✆ 020 8965 3365 — **www**.shayonarestaurants.com
  ⊖ Stonebridge Park
- Menu £10 (weekday lunch) - Carte approx. £19
  Closed 7-8 November and 25 December

BISTRO AIX

French • Bistro

MAP: 15-H1

Bistro Aix has enough local followers that it doesn't need to entice passers-by, which is just as well as there aren't usually too many boulevardiers wandering Tottenham Lane in search of duck confit. It's easy to see why Crouch Enders have taken this bistro to their hearts: the atmosphere is unpretentious and welcoming, the French food is unfussy and dependable, the wine list is competitively priced, and the surroundings rustic and relaxed with Degas-inspired paintings and colourful murals a fitting backdrop. The seasonally changing menu offers bags of choice, with around 20 starters and just as many main courses, and the kitchen does the classics, like snails, onion soup, rabbit with mustard, and tarte Tatin, particularly well.

- **Crouch End** — 54 Topsfield Par, Tottenham Ln ✉ N8 8PT
  ✆ 020 8340 6346 — **www**.bistroaix.co.uk
  ⊖ Crouch Hill
- Menu £19/24 - Carte £25/50
  Closed 24, 26 December and 1 January - (dinner only and lunch Saturday-Sunday)

BULL & LAST

Traditional British • Neighbourhood

MAP: 15-G2

This Victorian corner pub is well loved by the locals and it's easy to see why. It's full of character and life – and the food is gloriously robust and wholesome. Stay on the ground floor as it has more character than upstairs; if you haven't booked, it's worth trying your luck anyway as they keep the odd table back – mind you, with enticing bar snacks like ham and corn croquettes and buttermilk chicken wings, you may simply find happiness at the bar ordering these with a pint. The daily menu can sometimes change between services, depending on what ingredients come in. The kitchen knows its way around an animal – the charcuterie boards and terrines are very good, and game in season is not to be missed. They do a pretty good breakfast too.

■ **Dartmouth Park** — 168 Highgate Rd ✉ NW5 1QS
✆ 020 7267 3641 — **www**.thebullandlast.co.uk
⊖ Tufnell Park.

■ Carte £32/42
Closed 23-25 December - booking essential

PARADISE BY WAY OF KENSAL GREEN

Modern British • Pub

MAP: 15-F2

Calling 'Paradise' a pub hardly does it justice – this is a veritable fun palace. Named after a line from a GK Chesterton poem, this gloriously bohemian place is spread over three floors and means different things to different people: some come along for comedy nights and cocktails or party nights and DJs; others pop in for drinks in the Reading room or snacks in the bar; many come to eat in the restaurant; and you can even get married here. The food is a reassuring mix of British favourites and European themed dishes, all made using good ingredients from trusted suppliers and prepared with obvious care. The surroundings are wonderfully quirky and idiosyncratic, the staff are contagiously enthusiastic and the vibe, effortlessly cool.

■ **Kensal Green** — 19 Kilburn Ln ✉ W10 4AE
✆ 020 8969 0098 — **www**.theparadise.co.uk
⊖ Kensal Green.

■ Carte £28/41
(dinner only and lunch Saturday-Sunday)

PARLOUR

Modern British • Pub

MAP: 15-F2

It may not quite be a pub but nor is it a restaurant, so let's focus more on what Parlour actually is – a fun, warmly run and slightly quirky neighbourhood hangout. Open from breakfast until late, it has one room dominated by a large bar and the other, with an appealingly higgledy-piggledy look, set up for eating. They do a decent cocktail and a great range of beers and the menu is a wonderfully unabashed mix of tradition, originality and reinvention. Ingredients are beautifully fresh, flavours are distinct, combinations work well – and it's all such good value. Approaching legendary status is their cow pie which even Dan, however Desperate, would struggle to finish. On warm nights ask for one of the cabanas in the garden.

- **Kensal Green** — 5 Regent St ✉ NW10 5LG
  ✆ 020 8969 2184 — **www.**parlourkensal.com
  ⊖ Kensal Green
- Menu £15/25 - Carte £20/41
  Closed 1 week late August, 1 week Christmas-New Year and Monday

BEEF & BREW

Meats and grills • Simple

A/C

MAP: 15-G2

The name really tells you all you need to know. The steaks here tend to be less familiar cuts, like onglet or flat iron, which keep the prices down, and the beers are from small artisan brewers, the nearest of which is Camden Brewery just down the road. The simple, pared-down look makes it appear not unlike a butcher's shop, where the only decorative feature is an image of a cow displaying the various cuts. Kick off with the lip-smacking brisket jam nuggets, which have become something of a signature, and then have a steak or something in a bun like the intensely-flavoured beef cheek. Beer is not just offered to drink – it can also feature in the cheese, the ice cream or as a porter sauce for the Brewer's Mess dessert.

- **Kentish Town** — 323 Kentish Town Rd ✉ NW5 2TJ
  ✆ 020 7998 1511 — **www.**beef-and-brew.co.uk
  ⊖ Kentish Town
- Carte £18/31
  Closed Monday lunch - bookings advisable at dinner

CHICKEN SHOP

Meats and grills • Rustic

MAP: 15-G2

The concept is so simple, you'll leave wondering why you didn't think of it yourself. There's no menu, just chicken - marinated, steamed and then finished over wood and charcoal. You simply order a quarter, half or whole bird, choose a side from crinkle-cut chips, proper coleslaw, sweetcorn or salad and it's quickly delivered on enamel plates. The chicken is great: the skin is crisp and the meat beneath it moist and succulent. Pudding is just as straightforward - a brownie or a slice of cheesecake or apple pie. It all happens in a noisy, mildly chaotic basement but it's great fun and good value - look out for the hessian bag on the front door or you'll never find it. Queuing is a certainty unless you arrive ridiculously early.

- **Kentish Town** — 79 Highgate Rd ✉ NW5 1TL
  020 3310 2020 — **www**.chickenshop.com
  ⊖ Kentish Town
- Carte £16/21
  Bookings not accepted - (dinner only and lunch Saturday-Sunday)

GILBERT SCOTT

Traditional British • Brasserie

MAP: 15-H2/3

Britain's less than stellar reputation for the quality of its food won't change until more people come and see what's cooking in our kitchens, so snaring those tourists as soon as they step off the Eurostar is no bad thing. Run under the aegis of Marcus Wareing and named after the architect who designed this Gothic masterpiece of a hotel in 1873, the restaurant has the splendour of a Grand Salon but the buzz of a busy brasserie. Ask to sit under one of the tall windows before studying the appealing menu; the kitchen celebrates British produce whilst also incorporating influences from further afield, so expect dishes like ceps with black pudding and truffle, Iberico pork with fennel and romesco and blood peach with yoghurt sorbet and madeleines.

- **King's Cross St Pancras** — St Pancras Renaissance Hotel, Euston Rd ✉ NW1 2AR
  020 7278 3888 — **www**.thegilbertscott.co.uk
  ⊖ King's Cross St Pancras
- Menu £21 (lunch) - Carte £28/61

GRANGER & CO. KING'S CROSS ꟷ

Modern cuisine • *Friendly*

MAP: 15-H2

This is the third London outpost for Australian chef Bill Granger, and – as with the others – you know as soon as you walk through the door that you're in for a good time. The welcome is warm enough to bring some Aussie sunshine to the dullest of British days, and the buzz of happy customers is all around. Yes, you may need to wait, but that just gives you the opportunity to indulge in a couple of ripper cocktails. The menu is a clever mix of small plates, barbecue dishes, and bowls and grains, with plenty of South East Asian flavours for good measure. Dishes like prawn and bok choi pot-stickers and parmesan-crumbed chicken schnitzel are vibrant, fresh and uplifting – and the wine list is one of the most fairly priced in town.

- **King's Cross St Pancras** — Stanley Building, 7 Pancras Sq. ✉ N1C 4AG
  ✆ 020 3058 2567 — **www**.grangerandco.com
  ⊖ King's Cross St Pancras
- Carte £18/39
  Closed 25 December

L'ABSINTHE

French • Bistro

MAP: 15-G2

In thoroughly English-sounding Primrose Hill is a bistro so Gallic you'll find yourself unwittingly summoning the spirit of Serge Gainsbourg or at least contemplating an affair. The menu has all the great classics, from cassoulet to onion soup, steak frites to duck confit. Okay, so the execution doesn't always quite live up to the promise of the menu but no one seems to mind because the wine list is terrific - the owner just charges corkage on the retail price - and the atmosphere's great, although do try to get a table on the ground floor as it's more appealing than downstairs. Next door you'll find their traiteur, an ideal spot for morning coffee or a lunchtime plat du jour - or for a bottle of wine at any time.

- **Primrose Hill** — 40 Chalcot Rd ✉ NW1 8LS
  ✆ 020 7483 4848 — **www**.labsinthe.co.uk
  ⊖ Chalk Farm
- Carte £20/30
  Closed 1 week Christmas, Sunday and dinner Monday

MICHAEL NADRA PRIMROSE HILL

Modern cuisine • Neighbourhood

MAP: 15-G2

When you have a successful restaurant in Chiswick, opening a second branch in Primrose Hill would suggest that not only have you recognised similarities between the two neighbourhoods but also that you know a pretty decent shortcut to get you across town. Michael Nadra took over the old Sardo Canale premises in 2012; it's a modern space which comes with lots of glass, judicious lighting, a pleasant terrace and a comfortable bar which offers a selection of over 20 martinis. His menu closely resembles the one in Chiswick, which means that flavours from the Mediterranean feature widely but he's not averse to introducing the occasional Asian accent and his cooking shows a careful hand when balancing flavours.

- **Primrose Hill** — 42 Gloucester Ave ✉ NW1 8JD
  ✆ 020 7722 2800 — **www**.restaurant-michaelnadra.co.uk/primrose
  ⊖ Camden Town
- Menu £23/39
  Closed 24-28 December and 1 January

ODETTE'S

Modern cuisine • Neighbourhood

MAP: 15-G2

It's amazing what a window can do: they installed a big one at the front of the restaurant and it opened the whole place up and made it feel far more welcoming. Locals used to regard Odette's as being a little bit standoffish but service is now a lot chattier and the atmosphere more relaxed, which in turn makes it feel more a part of the community. The cooking is also a little less complicated than it was and is all the better for it, although there is still depth to the dishes. Flavours are robust and braised dishes a highlight; the owner clearly has a passion for his Welsh roots. The lunch and early evening menus are a steal and change every fortnight; there are also tasting and vegetarian menus alongside the à la carte.

- **Primrose Hill** — 130 Regent's Park Rd. ✉ NW1 8XL
  020 7586 8569 — **www**.odettesprimrosehill.com
  Chalk Farm
- Menu £22 (lunch) - Carte £31/53
  Closed Christmas-New Year, Monday and dinner Sunday

OSTUNI

Italian • Neighbourhood

MAP: 15-F2

The cuisine of Puglia, the red hot heel in Italy's boot, is celebrated at Ostuni – which now also has a sister in Highgate. Start with olives or taralli, then order the creamy burrata or mackerel before heading to the orecchiette – the region's ear-shaped pasta made from durum wheat. For the main course, carnivores should look no further than the sausages or bombette (cheese encased in pork) from the charcoal oven, or the ox cheek which comes with another speciality – fava bean purée. Even dessert celebrates all things Pugliese: the panna cotta is topped with a sweet reduction of Primitivo. The room has an appealing, rustic look and a large terrace; seats at the bar and at the counter of the open kitchen are kept for locals who haven't booked.

- **Queens Park** — 43-45 Lonsdale Rd ✉ NW6 6RA
  020 7624 8035 — **www**.ostuniristorante.co.uk
  Queen's Park
- Carte £16/40
  Closed 25 December

BRADLEY'S ⑩

Modern cuisine • Neighbourhood

XX A/C ⑰ 🎭 **MAP:** 15-G2

For over 20 years Simon Bradley's well-liked restaurant has been a stalwart of the Swiss Cottage dining scene. His loyal followers are always guaranteed a warm welcome and ticket holders to Hampstead Theatre won't find a more convenient spot for a bite before curtain up. The room has a fairly contemporary feel, with the tables at the large window always in demand, along with the two cosy booths. The array of menus on offer can be a little bewildering but always includes a competitively priced set menu and an extensive à la carte. Many head for the tried-and-tested classics like Mediterranean fish soup or veal Holstein, while others prefer the more ambitious dishes like foie gras with onion confit.

- **Swiss Cottage** — 25 Winchester Rd. ✉ NW3 3NR
  ✆ 020 7722 3457 — **www**.bradleysnw3.co.uk
  ⊖ Swiss Cottage
- Menu £24 (lunch and early dinner) - Carte £34/44
  Closed Sunday dinner and bank holidays

W. Bibikow/AWL Images/Getty Images

NORTH-EAST LONDON

If northwest London is renowned for its leafy acres, then the area to its immediate east has a more urban, brick-built appeal. Which has meant, over the last decade or so, a wholesale rebranding exercise for some of its traditionally shady localities. A generation ago it would have been beyond the remit of even the most inventive estate agent to sell the charms of Islington, Hackney or Bethnal Green. But then along came Damien Hirst, Tracey Emin et al, and before you could say 'cow in formaldehyde' the area's cachet had rocketed.

Shoreditch and **Hoxton** are the pivotal points of the region's hip makeover. Their cobbled brick streets and shabby industrial remnants were like heavenly manna to the artists and designers who started to colonise the old warehouses thirty years ago. A fashionable crowd soon followed in their footsteps, and nowadays the area around **Hoxton Square** positively teems with clubs, bars and galleries. Must-sees include Rivington Place, a terrific gallery that highlights visual arts from around the world, Deluxe (digital installations) and Hales (contemporary art). Before the area was ever trendy, there was the Geffrye Museum. A short stroll up Hoxton's **Kingsland Road,** it's a jewel of a place, set in elegant 18C almshouses, and depicting English middle-class interiors from 1600 to the present day. Right behind it is St. Mary's Secret Garden, a little oasis that manages to include much diversity including a separate woodland and herb area, all in less than an acre. At the southern end of the area, in Folgate Street, Dennis Severs' House is an original Huguenot home that recreates 18 and 19C life in an original way – cooking smells linger, hearth and candles burn, giving you the impression the owners have only just left the place. Upstairs the beds remain unmade: did a certain local artist pick up any ideas here?

When the Regent's Canal was built in the early 19C, **Islington's** fortunes nose-dived, for it was accompanied by the arrival of slums and over-crowding. But the once-idyllic village managed to hold onto its Georgian squares and handsome Victorian terraces through the rough times, and when these were gentrified a few years ago, the area ushered in a revival. **Camden Passage** has long been famed for its quirky antique emporiums, while the slinky Business Design Centre is a flagship of the modern Islington. Cultural icons established themselves around the Upper Street area and these have gone from strength to strength. The **Almeida** Theatre has a habit of hitting the production jackpot with its history of world premieres, while the King's Head has earned itself a reputation for raucous scene-stealing; set up in the seventies, it's also London's very first theatre-pub. Nearby, the Screen on the Green boasts a wonderful old-fashioned neon billboard.

Even in the 'bad old days', Islington drew in famous names, and at Regency smart **Canonbury Square** are the one-time homes of Evelyn Waugh (no.17A) and George Orwell (no.27). These days it houses the Estorick Collection of Modern Italian Art; come here to see fine futuristic paintings in a Georgian villa. To put the history of the area in a proper context, head to St. John Street, south of the City Road, where the Islington Museum tells the story of a colourful and multi-layered past.

Further up the A10, you come to **Dalston,** a bit like the Islington of old but with the buzzy Ridley Road market and a vibrant all-night scene including the blistering Vortex Jazz Club just off Kingsland Road. A little further north is **Stoke Newington,** referred to, a bit unkindly, as the poor man's Islington. Its pride and joy is Church Street, which not only features some eye-catching boutiques, but also lays claim to Abney Park Cemetery, an enchanting old place with a wildlife-rich nature reserve.

Dosfotos/Design Pics/Photononstop

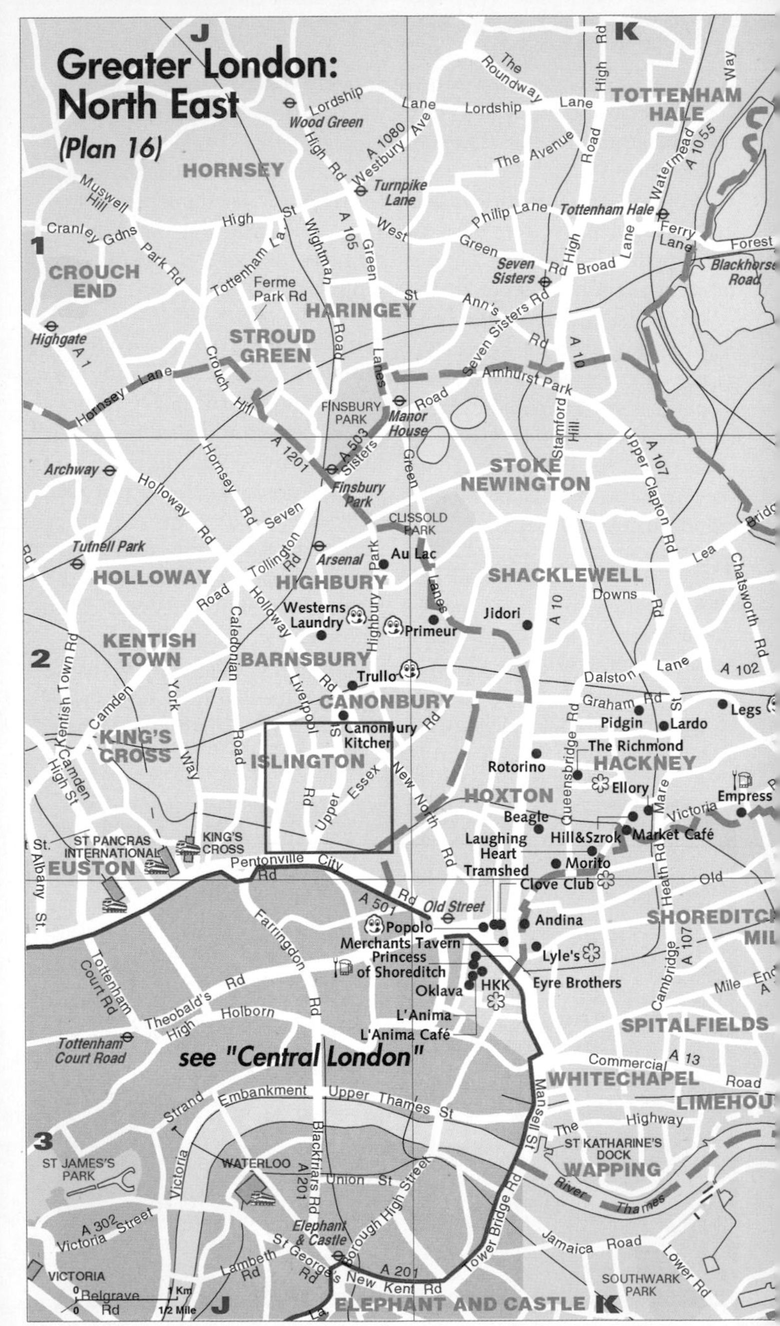
Greater London: North East
(Plan 16)
HORNSEY
CROUCH END
Highgate
STROUD GREEN
HARINGEY
Wood Green
Turnpike Lane
TOTTENHAM HALE
Tottenham Hale
Seven Sisters
Blackhorse Road
FINSBURY PARK
Manor House
Archway
Finsbury Park
STOKE NEWINGTON
CLISSOLD PARK
Tufnell Park
HOLLOWAY
Arsenal
HIGHBURY
SHACKLEWELL
Au Lac
Westerns Laundry
Primeur
Jidori
KENTISH TOWN
BARNSBURY
Trullo
CANONBURY
Canonbury Kitchen
KING'S CROSS
ISLINGTON
Legs
Pidgin
Lardo
The Richmond
Rotorino
HACKNEY
Ellory
Empress
HOXTON
Beagle
Hill&Szrok
Market Café
Laughing Heart
Tramshed
Morito
Clove Club
ST PANCRAS INTERNATIONAL
KING'S CROSS
EUSTON
Old Street
Popolo
Andina
Merchants Tavern
Princess of Shoreditch
Lyle's
Oklava
HKK
Eyre Brothers
L'Anima
L'Anima Café
SHOREDITCH
SPITALFIELDS
Tottenham Court Road
see "Central London"
WHITECHAPEL
LIMEHOU
ST KATHARINE'S DOCK
WAPPING
River Thames
ST JAMES'S PARK
WATERLOO
Elephant & Castle
VICTORIA
SOUTHWARK PARK
ELEPHANT AND CASTLE
0 1 Km
0 1/2 Mile
J
K
1
2
3

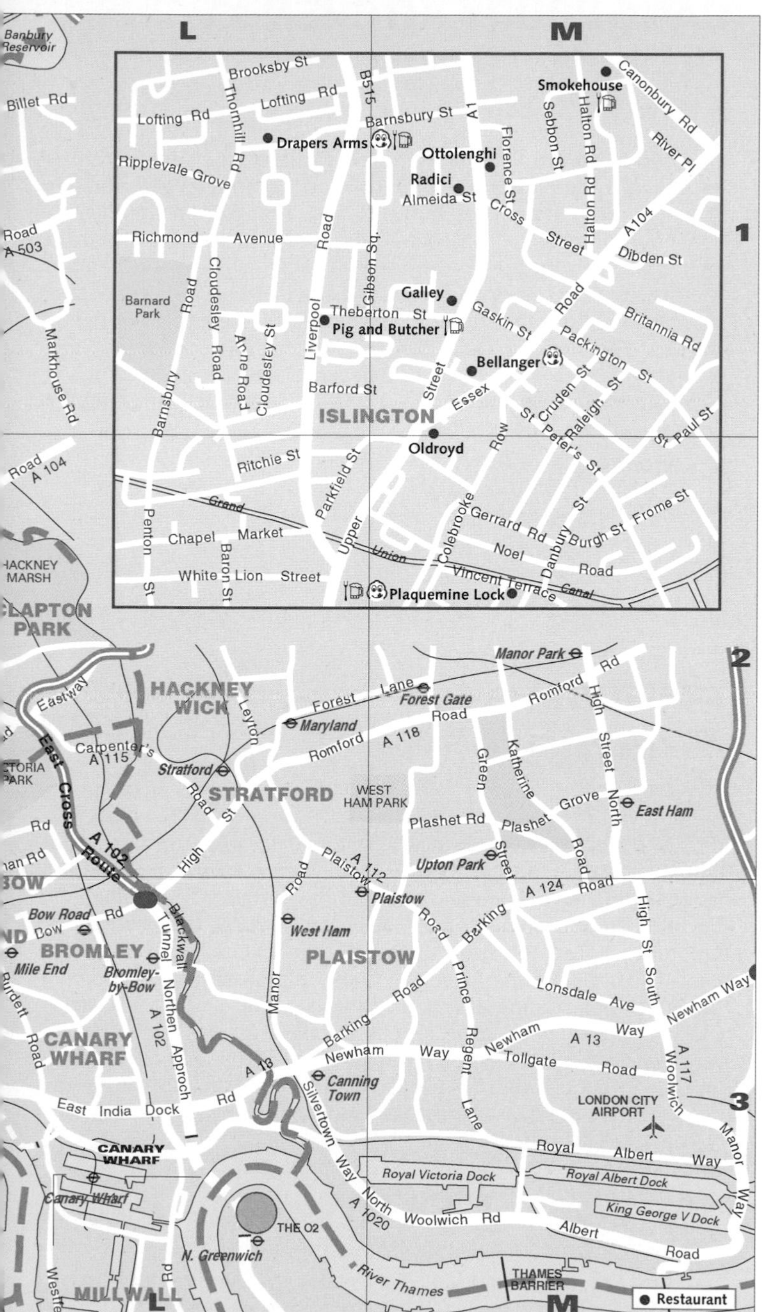
L
M
1
2
3
Smokehouse
Drapers Arms
Ottolenghi
Radici
Galley
Pig and Butcher
Bellanger
Oldroyd
Plaquemine Lock
ISLINGTON
Brooksby St
Lofting Rd
Barnsbury St
Thornhill Rd
Ripplevale Grove
Richmond Avenue
Barnard Park
Cloudesley Road
Liverpool Road
Gibson Sq.
Theberton St
Almeida St
Florence St
Cross Street
Canonbury Rd
River Pl
Sebbon St
Halton Rd
Dibden St
Gaskin St
Britannia Rd
Packington St
Essex Road
Barford St
Ritchie St
Parkfield St
Upper Street
Chapel Market
White Lion Street
Penton St
Baron St
Grand Union Canal
Colebrooke Row
Gerrard Rd
Noel Road
Vincent Terrace
Danbury St
Burgh St
Frome St
St Peter's St
Cruden St
Raleigh St
St Paul St
HACKNEY WICK
STRATFORD
WEST HAM PARK
PLAISTOW
BROMLEY
CANARY WHARF
MILLWALL
CLAPTON PARK
HACKNEY MARSH
BOW
Manor Park
Forest Gate
Maryland
Stratford
East Ham
Upton Park
Plaistow
West Ham
Bow Road
Mile End
Bromley-by-Bow
Canning Town
N. Greenwich
THE O2
LONDON CITY AIRPORT
Royal Victoria Dock
Royal Albert Dock
King George V Dock
River Thames
THAMES BARRIER
East Cross Route
A 102
Blackwall Tunnel Northen Approch
East India Dock Rd
Newham Way
A 13
Barking Road
Romford Road
A 118
High Street North
Plashet Grove
Katherine Road
Green Street
Prince Regent Lane
Silvertown Way
North Woolwich Rd
Albert Road
Royal Albert Way
Manor Way
Tollgate Road
Lonsdale Ave
High St South
A 117 Woolwich
Restaurant

CANONBURY KITCHEN

Italian • Neighbourhood

MAP: 16-J2

Inserting the word 'kitchen' into the name of one's restaurant is becoming more and more common as it instantly evokes images of simple food and unpretentious dining. That certainly applies to Canonbury Kitchen, which comes with an appropriately light, fresh look, thanks to its exposed brick walls, high ceiling and painted floorboards. With seating for just forty it also feels like the very epitome of a neighbourhood restaurant. Owner Max and his team provide gently reassuring service and the kitchen - on-view at the far end - sensibly keeps things simple. That includes an ever-popular fritto misto made with cuttlefish and octopus, pan-fried hake with herbs, and a lemon tiramisu with limoncello replacing the marsala.

- **Canonbury** — 19 Canonbury Ln ✉ N1 2AS
  020 7226 9791 — **www**.canonburykitchen.com
  Highbury & Islington
- Menu £14 - Carte £27/37
  Closed Sunday dinner - (dinner only and lunch Saturday-Sunday)

PRIMEUR

Modern cuisine • Simple

MAP: 16-K2

A relaxed restaurant where locals can pop in for a few small plates of unfussy seasonal food, with no standing on ceremony: this was the vision held by its owners and one that has certainly been fulfilled in the creation of this neighbourhood restaurant. The 'Barnes Motors' sign tells you that this used to be a garage and its huge concertina doors fold back to reveal an equally quirky interior with counter seating around the edges and a large communal table. The blackboard is chalked up daily with a dozen or so dishes; these are matched with wines which are all available by the glass. Plates are small and designed for sharing; understated but packed with flavour - simplicity is the key here, allowing the quality ingredients to really shine.

- **Canonbury** — 116 Petherton Rd ✉ N5 2RT
  020 7226 5271 — **www**.primeurn5.co.uk
  Canonbury
- Menu £30/35 - Carte £16/33
  Closed Christmas, Sunday dinner, Monday and Tuesday-Thursday lunch

SMOKEHOUSE

Modern cuisine • Pub

MAP: 16-M1

If, to you, barbecuing means a burnt chicken leg, warm wine and a wet garden then a visit to Smokehouse will set you straight. You can smell the oak chips in the smoker as you approach this warm, modern pub, which was previously called The House. Meat is the mainstay of the very appealing menu – the peppered ox cheeks have understandably become a firm favourite – but whilst the flavours are undeniably gutsy, the smoking and barbecuing manages to add a little something to the ingredients without ever overpowering them. With portion sizes to appease Desperate Dan, only the committed may make it to dessert but chocolate lovers should try the Friday pie. The pub is enthusiastically run and staff are eager to recommend dishes.

Canonbury — 63-69 Canonbury Rd ✉ N1 2DG
020 7354 1144 — **www**.smokehouseislington.co.uk
⊖ Highbury & Islington.

Carte £28/35
Closed 24-26 December and lunch Monday-Thursday except bank holidays – booking advisable

TRULLO

Italian • Neighbourhood

MAP: 16-J2

This neighbourhood gem is split over two floors: the homely, well-worn ground floor with its open kitchen has the feel of a traditional osteria, while the basement has a dark, subterranean feel, with exposed brick, industrial ducting, and several sought-after booths. The ingredient-led, resolutely Italian menu is written daily and the quality produce is treated with respect and reverence. Harmonious, tried-and-tested combinations create rustic, full-flavoured dishes, including meats and fish cooked on the charcoal grill and – the highlight – fresh pasta, hand-rolled before each service. Add in moreish puddings, an all-Italian wine list and eager-to-please staff and this is somewhere you'll want to come back to time and time again.

Canonbury — 300-302 St Paul's Rd ✉ N1 2LH
020 7226 2733 — **www**.trullorestaurant.com
⊖ Highbury & Islington

Carte £28/45
Closed 25-26 December and Sunday dinner – booking essential

JIDORI

Japanese • Bistro

MAP: 16-K2

This sweet neighbourhood restaurant models itself on traditional Japanese yakitori-ya: small, unadorned places serving succulent skewers of grilled chicken. The first section of the menu offers small plates such as sesame and chilli marinated cucumber or a spicy curry scotch egg to spike the tastebuds; the second, the yakitori, features different parts of the chicken - wing with shiso and grilled lemon; thigh with spring onion or perhaps the parson's nose. The charming staff recommend two plates from each section; there are two yakitori skewers per plate and these are cooked quickly on the charcoal-fired Kama-Asa Shoten grill to give a charred exterior to the juicy meat. There's a good selection of cocktails, sake and craft beers too.

- **Dalston** — 89 Kingsland High St ✉ E2 8BP
  020 7686 5634 — **www**.jidori.co.uk
  ⊖ Dalston Kingsland
- Carte £17/28
  Closed 25-26 December, 1 January, bank holiday Mondays and Sunday - bookings not accepted - (dinner only and lunch Wednesday-Friday)

THE RICHMOND

Modern British • Neighbourhood

MAP: 16-K2

This used to be a pub and what was formerly the bar is now a counter where you might well see someone shucking oysters. Seafood - notably raw seafood - is the focus here, so expect to see Palourde clams, Brixham scallops and Cornish mussels on the seasonally driven menus; they also offer plenty to please carnivores, so there will be dishes like pheasant with caramelised figs and salsify alongside the Richmond burger and 35 day aged Longhorn steaks. Chef-owner Brett Redman also runs Elliot's in Borough Market and unsurprisingly insists on only the best ingredients; little is required to embellish produce when it's a fresh as this. Bold red décor gives the place a fashionable look, prices are sensible and staff are charm personified.

- **Dalston** — 316 Queensbridge Rd ✉ E8 3NH
  020 7241 1638 — **www**.therichmondhackney.com
  ⊖ Dalston Junction
- Carte £21/35
  Closed 25-26 December - booking advisable - (dinner only and lunch Saturday-Sunday)

ROTORINO

Italian • Simple

MAP: 16-K2

There are some restaurants you warm to straight away - and this stylish yet down to earth Italian on Kingsland Road is one of them. There's lots of texture to the decoration, which includes bare brick and plaster, wood and some wonderful tiles. Start with a glass of wine at the zinc-topped bar; the long table you notice when you walk in is for those who've failed to book, while those who do like to plan ahead should ask for one of the prized booths at the back. Wherever you sit, the staff will make you feel welcome and will impress you with their knowledge of the menu. The kitchen offers fresh tasting and good value Southern Italian specialities, such as caponata, gnudi, Sasso chicken - and possibly the cheapest hanger steak in town.

- **Dalston** — 434 Kingsland Rd ✉ E8 4AA
  020 7249 9081 — **www**.rotorino.com
  Dalston Junction
- Menu £15 (early dinner) - Carte £18/33
  Closed 23 December-2 January - (dinner only and Saturday-Sunday lunch)

N LAUGHING HEART

Modern cuisine • Wine bar

MAP: 16-K2

Think 'wine bar' and you think the '80s, bad wine and even worse food. Thankfully, the avuncular Aussie Charlie Mellor has created a wine bar for our age and it's a truly joyful place. The staff are a delight, the vibe is great, it's open until the wee small hours and the look - with the specially commissioned tables with cutlery draws - works perfectly. The food, from the open kitchen, is also thoroughly contemporary, with its clever sourcing of seasonal ingredients, its innovative pairings and occasional addition of Asian flavours. The menu is a flexible affair, with dishes designed for sharing. Natural wines are the focus on the thoughtfully compiled list - and you'll find them for sale downstairs is the small wine shop.

- **Hackney** — 277 Hackney Rd ✉ E2 8NA
  020 7686 9535 — **www**.thelaughingheartlondon.com
  Hoxton
- Carte £19/40
  (dinner only and Sunday lunch)

LEGS

Modern British • Neighbourhood

MAP: 16-K2

This urban, no-frills bistro has been brought to life by Magnus Reid, an Australian-born former tattoo artist. Reid spends time ensuring that the quality of his produce is top-notch, and his food is bursting with freshness and flavour. He also shows equal respect for his customers and you get the feeling that the friendly staff here really enjoy what they do. Lunch offers some interesting sandwiches - they also offer brunch on Saturdays - while dinner means a daily changing selection of about 10 vibrant small plates designed for sharing. Time has evidently also been spent on the wine list, which focuses on organic wines from small producers; 'Legs' refers to the residual wine left on a glass - an indicator of its sugar and alcohol content.

Hackney — 120 Morning Ln ✉ E9 6LH
✆ 020 3441 8765 — **www**.legsrestaurant.com
⊖ Hackney Central

Carte £19/36
Closed Sunday dinner, Monday and Tuesday

AU LAC

Vietnamese • Friendly

MAP: 16-J2

It's unlikely to ever attract passers-by on looks alone but fortunately enough people know about this long-standing Vietnamese restaurant, run by two brothers, to ensure that its phone rings red hot most nights. The comforts inside may also be fairly unremarkable but that just allows everyone to focus their attention on the lengthy menu, to which new dishes are added regularly. The pho noodle soup is a favourite but along with the traditional dishes there are plenty of more contemporary creations, all exhibiting the same freshness and lively flavours. The prices are kept honest, especially as the generous portion sizes mean that you don't have to order too many dishes to feel satisfied. They also do a roaring trade in takeaways.

Highbury — 82 Highbury Park ✉ N5 2XE
✆ 020 7704 9187 — **www**.aulac.co.uk
⊖ Arsenal

Carte £12/24
Closed 24-26 December, 1-2 January and 1 week early August - (dinner only and lunch Thursday-Friday)

Ⓝ WESTERNS LAUNDRY

Seafood • Fashionable

MAP: 16-J2

Set on the ground floor of a former laundry close to the Emirates Stadium, this little sister to Primeur has the same industrial-chic styling and daily menu of small plates, but this time the focus is on fish. Choose from such delights as Jersey oysters, fried cod tongues, hake with saffron or turbot with ginger: these are confident, well-executed dishes which use the freshest ingredients and are full of flavour. Floor-to-ceiling doors open onto a pleasant terrace with a couple of olive trees; take a seat at the kitchen counter or at one of the communal tables, where your name will be scrawled in chalk. In what some might say is a brave move, all of their wines are natural; ask one of the cheery staff for a recommendation.

- **Holloway** — 34 Drayton Pk ✉ N5 1PB
  ☎ 020 7700 3700 — **www**.westernslaundry.com
  ⊖ Holloway Road
- Carte £25/33
  Closed Monday, lunch Tuesday-Thursday and Sunday dinner - booking essential

BEAGLE

Traditional British • Rustic

MAP: 16-K2

Occupying three converted railway arches, and named after the steam train that ran on the line above, Beagle is a big, bustling operation. One arch is used as a bar; one as the dining room; and the third is a kitchen and private dining room. Lots of brick, reclaimed materials and clever lighting add to the atmosphere and the terrace, overlooking The Geffrye, is a good spot to enjoy one of their cocktails. The British menu changes twice a day and its contents are largely determined by whatever seasonal produce arrives at the kitchen door - the descriptions are derivatively terse. There are occasional Italian touches, like a braised beef shin pappardelle, and blackboards announce the dishes for two, such as whole steamed sea bass.

- **Hoxton** — 397-400 Geffrye St ✉ E2 8HZ
  ☎ 020 7613 2967 — **www**.beaglelondon.co.uk
  ⊖ Hoxton
- Carte £27/46
  Closed Sunday dinner

MORITO

Spanish • Simple

MAP: 16-K2

Sam and Sam Clark have branched out with their third restaurant - a second Morito - this time bringing their brand of Moorish cuisine to the vibrant East London dining scene. The Hackney Road offshoot has all the utilitarianism of its older sister but much more space; a horseshoe bar takes centre stage and there are several counters, including one in the window. The menu features small plates under the headings para picar, vegetables, fish, meat and dulce and dishes draw their influences not only from Spain, but also from North Africa and the Eastern Mediterranean, including chef Marianna's homeland, Crete. Choose around 3 dishes each - these will come when they're ready, which can make for a mixed up meal but adds to the fun of this lively spot.

- **Hoxton** — 195 Hackney Rd E2 8JL
  020 7613 0754 — **www**.moritohackneyroad.co.uk
  Hoxton
- Carte £25/40
  Closed Christmas, Monday lunch and bank holidays

SARDINE

French • Fashionable

MAP: 16-K2

It's named for the food, which focuses on Southern France, but it could equally be a reference to how you feel squeezed into such a compact space. This trendy restaurant is set within the Parasol Art Gallery and has a communal table at the heart of proceedings; counter seats are available at the open kitchen and the bar and staff move between tables with the grace of ballerinas. Chef-owner Alex Jackson's cooking comes from the heart: this is food he loves and respects, and dishes like soupe au pistou; red mullet, pastis and courgettes; mussels en papillote; and apricot galette are rustic, unfussy and incredibly tasty. Stand-outs include the lamb à la ficelle: leg of lamb tied on a string and cooked over an open fire.

- **Hoxton** — Parasol Art Gallery, 15 Micawber St N1 7TB
  020 7490 0144 — **www**.sardine.london
  Old Street
- Carte £26/40
  Closed Christmas-New Year and Monday lunch - booking essential

BELLANGER

French • Brasserie

MAP: 16-M1

Corbin and King evidently have another success on their hands; this time in the form of an all-day brasserie, modelled on those opened in Paris by the Alsatians at the turn of the century. No stone has been left unturned in the desire to recreate the sumptuous style of an authentic grand café and the long, high ceilinged room features wood panelling, spacious booths and a bar with counter seating - even the toilets have been given the star treatment! Regional French and particularly Alsatian-inspired fare is served from breakfast until late and there's some good value to be had with dishes like the celeriac remoulade or sausages with braised lentils - as well as sharing dishes like coq au Riesling for up to four to share.

- **Islington** — 9 Islington Grn ✉ N1 2XH
  ✆ 020 7226 2555 — **www**.bellanger.co.uk
  ⊖ Angel
- Menu £18 (lunch) - Carte £21/43
  Bookings advisable at dinner

DRAPERS ARMS

Traditional British • Neighbourhood

MAP: 16-L1

This pub is leased from one of London's Great Twelve livery companies, the Drapers Company, which explains both its name and its imposing façade. It's set in a residential area, and is all you could want from your local, with warming fires, shabby-chic styling, a relaxed, unpretentious feel, a bevy of eager-to-please staff and even a courtyard garden. Add to this a great selection of regional ales, a well-thought-out wine list, and a choice of gutsy and satisfying British dishes and you can see why it's often packed to the rafters. Seasonal menus use the best produce available, with offal a highlight; choose from hearty dishes such as jugged hare and mashed potato, venison haunch with beetroot or slow-cooked shoulder of lamb to share.

- **Islington** — 44 Barnsbury St ✉ N1 1ER
  ✆ 020 7619 0348 — **www**.thedrapersarms.com
  ⊖ Highbury & Islington.
- Carte £22/34
  Closed 25-26 December - bookings advisable at dinner

GALLEY ıIO

Seafood • Brasserie

MAP: 16-M1

Chef-owner Marcel spent many years working at Randall and Aubin, before joining forces with his sister Oriona to create this refreshingly different fish restaurant (she's in charge of interior design and has created a smart, colourful space with the feel of a brasserie). There's a bar at the front and a few prized booths, but the best seats in the house are those at the counter of the galley kitchen, where you can chat to the chefs and watch their craft close-up. This is a place that's serious about seafood; its all-day menu led by what is available, fresh from the day boats. Small plates might mean galley fish stew; large plates, lobster pappardelle; oysters are always a good bet, and the hot or cold seafood platters are great to share.

- **Islington** — 105-106 Upper St ✉ N1 1QN
  ✆ 020 3670 0740 — **www**.galleylondon.co.uk
  ⊖ Highbury & Islington
- Menu £15 (weekday lunch) - Carte £22/57
  Closed 1 January

OLDROYD ıIO

Modern British • Intimate

MAP: 16-M1

This is one of those places where you leave feeling satisfied by both the food that you've eaten and the size of the bill you've just paid. The eponymous Oldroyd is Tom, who left his role with the Polpo group to open this little bistro in what was previously a deli. It's all about small plates, with one main ingredient always taking centre stage. The ingredients are largely British, influences are from within Europe and the dishes are very easy to eat - five plates between two should be enough. The meatballs are always popular, the mackerel is great and the zucchini fries are worth the price of admission alone. The place is open all day every day, which seems to be the only way to cope with the huge demand for seats.

- **Islington** — 344 Upper St ✉ N1 0PD
  ✆ 020 8617 9010 — **www**.oldroydlondon.com
  ⊖ Angel
- Menu £19 (weekday lunch) - Carte £20/31
  Closed 25-26 December

OTTOLENGHI

Mediterranean cuisine • Fashionable

MAP: 16-M1

It's common for customers to bump into each other in the entrance to Ottolenghi, so drawn are their eyes to the fresh, vibrantly coloured salads and the how-can-one-possibly-choose cakes on display. Two communal tables form the centrepiece of this coolly decorated restaurant, and a seat at one of these makes you feel you could be sitting in a friend's kitchen. Yotam Ottolenghi has done more travelling than Gulliver and the frequently changing menu reflects this. Different sections list dishes from the counter and the kitchen; three each is a good amount - although you'll probably find yourself ordering more once you've tasted your first mouthful! Don't worry about saving room for pudding, as you can always buy a few treats to take home with you.

Islington — 287 Upper St. ✉ N1 2TZ
020 7288 1454 — **www**.ottolenghi.co.uk
Highbury & Islington

Carte £23/45
Closed 25-26 December, Sunday dinner and bank holidays - booking essential

PIG AND BUTCHER

Traditional British • Pub

MAP: 16-L1

This corner pub dates from the mid-19C, when cattle drovers taking their livestock to Smithfield Market would stop for a swift one. Now sympathetically restored, it enjoys the same ownership as the Princess of Shoreditch as well as Islington and Chiswick's 'Smokehouse's. The busy bar offers an impressive number of bottled beers, while the dining room is secreted behind shelves of bric-a-brac. There's a strong British element to the menu and not just because they use words like 'Beeton' and 'Mrs'. Meat comes straight from the farm and is butchered and smoked in-house; fish comes from day boats off the south coast. Roasts take centre stage on Sundays; "just like your mother's" they claim, which presumably means something different to us all.

Islington — 80 Liverpool Rd ✉ N1 0QD
020 7226 8304 — **www**.thepigandbutcher.co.uk
Angel.

Carte £28/50
Closed 24-26 December - booking advisable - (dinner only and lunch Friday-Sunday)

PLAQUEMINE LOCK

Creole • Cosy

MAP: 16-M2

Plaquemine Lock – the brainchild of restaurateur and chef Jacob Kenedy, of Bocca di Lupo fame – is set on the Regents Canal in Angel and is named after a small city in Louisiana, once home to Kenedy's great-grandmother. Maps and prints hang on the walls of this unique and very colourful pub, and two bright murals, painted by Kenedy's mother depict scenes from the Deep South. Cooking is centred around Creole and Cajun traditions, and dishes like gumbo with okra, blackened chicken, and crawfish with corn and potatoes are carefully cooked and packed with flavour. Po'boys – sub-style sandwiches – are popular, the awesome oysters go flying out of the kitchen, puds like pecan pie make a great end to your meal and Big Easy style cocktails add to the fun.

- **Islington** — 139 Graham St ✉ N1 8LB
  020 7688 1488 — **www**.plaqlock.com
  Angel
- Carte £20/30
  Closed 25 December

RADICI

Italian • Rustic

MAP: 16-M1

Radici means roots and it's an appropriate moniker since the cooking is based around hearty Southern Italian classics inspired by chef Francesco Mazzei's childhood in Calabria. Charred mackerel with fregola and tomatoes; creamy burrata with anchovy and broccoli; spicy chicken calabrese; and a moreish mountain of zucchini fritti – this is comfort food at its best and will leave you with a satisfied smile. What was previously Almeida has been given more of a rustic look by owners D&D, with a central bar, a wood-fired oven for pizzas and a wine lounge packed with Italian bottles. The proximity of the Almeida Theatre suggests that this is a place which will never want for customers – the well-priced, tasty dishes guarantee it.

- **Islington** — 30 Almeida St ✉ N1 1AD
  020 7354 4777 — **www**.radici.uk
  Angel
- Menu £18 (lunch and early dinner) – Carte £21/41
  Closed 25 December, Sunday dinner and Monday

ELLORY ❀

Modern cuisine • Simple

MAP: 16-K2

FIRST COURSE: Chicory with walnut and Ossau-Iraty cheese. • Cuttlefish with fennel and lardo.

MAIN COURSE: Brill with lovage and parsley root. • Pork loin, radicchio, red wine and anchovy.

DESSERT: Pear sorbet, parmesan and olive oil. • Rice pudding with apple and pistachio.

Located on the ground floor of Netil House – a 1950s warehouse turned creative commune – this East London restaurant is an unpretentious, stripped back place: all skimmed concrete, exposed ducting and bare lightbulbs – and given these unadorned surroundings, the depth in the cooking comes as something of a surprise. There aren't many choices on the no-frills weekly changing menu, nor many ingredients making up the modern, Mediterranean-influenced small plates – but those that do are top quality, perfectly balanced and packed with intense flavours; examples being purple sprouting broccoli with miso and chilli, or cuttlefish with fennel and lardo. As you might expect with two young sommeliers at the helm, the well-priced European wine list makes for an interesting read, with a good selection by the glass; go for the wine pairings or ask for recommendations, which the personable staff are only too pleased to give. A bar for drinkers and diners, an open kitchen and a turntable add to the cool, relaxed vibe.

- **London Fields** — Netil House, 1 Westgate St ✉ E8 3RL
  ✆ 020 3095 9455 — **www.**ellorylondon.com
  ⊖ London Fields
- Menu £30/42 - Carte £32/43
  Closed 23 December-3 January - (dinner only and lunch Saturday-Sunday)

HILL & SZROK

Meats and grills • Neighbourhood

MAP: 16-K2

Butcher's shop by day; unpretentious, meat-focused restaurant by night: Hill & Szrok is the ultimate carnivore's dream. At the end of the working day, most of the meat is cleared away, and the central marble-topped counter becomes a communal table, with seats round the edge of the room adding space for a few more diners. The staff are friendly, the atmosphere is buzzing, but bookings aren't taken, so you may have to queue up. The daily menu offers around 3 starters – perhaps pan-fried chicken livers or a plate of cured ham – but it's the main courses which really excite, particularly the top quality steaks, which are aged for a minimum of 60 days. If you're here with friends, go for the chateaubriand.

- **London Fields** — 60 Broadway Market ✉ E8 4QJ
  ✆ 020 7254 8805 — **www**.hillandszrok.co.uk
  ⊖ Bethnal Green
- Carte £20/57
  Closed 23 December-3 January - bookings not accepted - (dinner only and Sunday lunch)

LARDO

Italian • Bistro

MAP: 16-K2

Evidence of Hackney's nascent gentrification comes in the form of this delightful Italian eatery. It's housed within the striking 1930s Arthaus building, and though it may boast the ubiquitous faux industrial look, there's no artifice when it comes to the cooking. As hinted by the name, they cure their own meats so the daily changing menu of small plates may include fennel pollen salami or lardy loin. The well-priced dishes really hit the spot - try a creamy burrata, white bean bruschetta, or sweet and sour sardines and be sure to leave room for the torta del giorno. The gas-fired oven - which resembles a giant glitter ball - does sterling work in the open kitchen and pizzas, including those of the gluten free variety, are another major draw.

- **London Fields** — 197-205 Richmond Rd ✉ E8 3NJ
  ✆ 020 8985 2683 — **www**.lardo.co.uk
  ⊖ Hackney Central
- Carte £26/43
  Closed 24 December-2 January

MARKET CAFE

Mediterranean cuisine • Neighbourhood

MAP: 16-K2

Forget data studies and economic analysis – an area's gentrification can be largely gauged by the arrival of two things: delis and restaurants. Broadway Market's steady advance towards middle class hipdom was given a nudge by the opening of Market Cafe, a former pub beside the canal. Research was clearly done because it ticks all the zeitgeist boxes, from the Formica table tops to the salvaged chairs, the pierced-and-inked young staff to the terse menu descriptions. There's a distinct Italian accent to many of the dishes, with homemade pastas a feature. The kitchen uses the local market for its meat, bread and coffee, the cooking is fresh and generous and the prices fair – especially the 'workers lunch'. Weekend brunches are very popular.

- **London Fields** — 2 Broadway Mkt ✉ E8 4QG
  020 7249 9070 — **www**.market-cafe.co.uk
  Bethnal Green
- Carte £19/31
  Closed 25 December

PIDGIN

Modern British • Neighbourhood

MAP: 16-K2

Pidgin is a grammatically simplified form of a language and this cosy, single room restaurant, tucked away on a residential Hackney street, is all about simplicity. Décor is understated, with the only adornments on the plain walls being a few dried branches and some shelves of wine. And then there's the menu: a no-choice four courser which changes weekly – as do the cocktails and the equally concise wine list. Modern British dishes might include lamb rib, skyr, miso and black olive oreo; or salted lemon, candied kombu and yuzu kosho curd; the simpler ones, with a focus on fewer flavours, are the best. Service is relaxed and friendly, and the closely packed tables and many regulars make for a lively, convivial atmosphere.

- **London Fields** — 52 Wilton Way ✉ E8 1BG
  020 7254 8311 — **www**.pidginlondon.com
  Hackney Central
- Menu £45
  Closed Christmas-New Year, Monday and Tuesday – booking essential – (dinner only and lunch Saturday and Sunday) – (tasting menu only)

ANDINA

Peruvian • Simple

MAP: 16-K3

Andina may be smaller and slightly more chaotic that its sister Ceviche, but this picantería with its Peruvian specialities and live music is proving equally popular. The friendly staff are keen to share their knowledge and offer sound advice - and if you come for lunch you're rewarded with a steal of a menu. Start off with some crunchy corn or Cancha; then head for the ceviche - there are usually around six types to choose from and they pack a punch. The skewers are also popular and the salads are excellent; veggies and vegans will also find they have plenty of choice. If you can muster enough friends, the Music Room at the back is a great place for a private dinner surrounded by an interesting collection of LPs.

- **Shoreditch** — 1 Redchurch St ✉ E2 7DJ
  020 7920 6499 — **www.**andinalondon.com
  Shoreditch High Street
- Carte £13/28
  Booking essential

L'ANIMA

Italian • Fashionable

MAP: 16-K3

You know you've got a successful restaurant on your hands when the live music in the bar is barely audible above the noise being made by your contented diners. With its limestone walls, impeccably laid tables, white leather chairs and clever lighting, L'Anima is an extremely handsome restaurant, and one that looks as though it should be located somewhere slightly more glamorous than the edge of The City. The kitchen team hail from all parts of Italy and their à la carte menu offers a mix of the classic and the more unusual - look out for the lesser known varieties of pasta or an occasional Moorish influence; there's also a good value midweek menu. It's worth asking for a window table or one on the raised section at the back.

- **Shoreditch** — 1 Snowden St, Broadgate West ✉ EC2A 2DQ
  020 7422 7000 — **www.**lanima.co.uk
  Liverpool Street
- Carte £36/70
  Closed 25-26 December, Sunday and bank holidays - booking essential

L'ANIMA CAFÉ

Italian • Brasserie

MAP: 16-K3

The name succeeds in conveying the fact that this is a baby sister to L'Anima around the corner, but calling it a 'café' does it something of an injustice because it is so much more than that. This is a big, bright restaurant with a fashionable bar that pulls in the after-work crowd and a busy deli for those wanting something to cook at home; there are even DJs on Thursday and Friday nights to help celebrate the end of the working week. The pizzas are popular and done well, although look closely at that large pizza oven and you'll see it's gas-fired; the rest of the menu has its roots in southern Italy and includes a decent selection of well-made pasta dishes; the prices are fair and the cooking, straightforward and tasty.

- **Shoreditch** — 10 Appold St ✉ EC2A 2AP
  ✆ 020 7422 7080 — **www**.lanimacafe.co.uk
  ⊖ Liverpool Street
- Carte £15/32
  Closed Saturday, Sunday and bank holidays

EYRE BROTHERS

Spanish • Elegant

MAP: 16-K3

Thanks to their pioneering pub, The Eagle, the Eyre name will be forever linked to the rise of the gastropub, but this sleek and confidently run 100-seater shows that they know how to do restaurants as well. The menu celebrates all things Iberian and draws on memories of their upbringing in Mozambique. Tiger prawns piri-piri has been on since day 1; the 'Cinco Jotas' ham is deliciously sweet and the meats are all cooked over lumpwood charcoal, which adds a wonderful aroma to proceedings. If you're in a larger party, pre-order paella or a whole suckling pig. The wine list is Iberian too, with Riojas for every pocket and a great selection of Madeira and Jerez. Everyone leaves feeling satisfied, even if you've just popped in for tapas at the bar.

- **Shoreditch** — 70 Leonard St ✉ EC2A 4QX
  ✆ 020 7613 5346 — **www**.eyrebrothers.co.uk
  ⊖ Old Street
- Carte £29/54
  Closed 24 December-4 January, Saturday lunch, Sunday and bank holidays

CLOVE CLUB ✿

Modern cuisine • Trendy

MAP: 16-K3

Michelin

FIRST COURSE: Raw Orkney scallop with mandarin, hazelnut and Périgord truffle. • Warm chestnut and oyster broth with wild Scottish seaweed.

MAIN COURSE: Grilled red mullet with new season onions, cinnamon and curry leaf sauce. • Mallard with fermented cabbage, beetroot and blackcurrant.

DESSERT: Amalfi lemonade and Kampot pepper ice cream. • Tarte Tatin with sour cream.

'Crowdfunded' into existence by a trio of young chefs who made their names in pop-ups, the Clove Club has once more pulled off a maverick manoeuvre with the introduction of its online prepay booking system. Said chefs perform centre stage in the smart, blue-tiled kitchen of the Grade II listed Shoreditch Town Hall, whose sparse dining room has been softened slightly by the introduction of window blinds and foliage; sit here rather than in the adjacent bar so you don't miss out on the buzz. Cooking has a Scandic touch, with a set menu at dinner – this is a kitchen fanatical about sourcing top-notch British produce so expect scallops from Orkney, mackerel from Cornwall and veal from Dorset. The meal starts with a few canapés which set the tone: there is originality, verve and flair but flavours are always expertly judged and complementary, with seafood dishes a highlight. Wonderfully simple-looking dishes often have a deceptive depth to them, with full-on flavours extracted from the humblest of produce.

- **Shoreditch** — 380 Old St ✉ EC1V 9LT
  ✆ 020 7729 6496 — **www**.thecloveclub.com
  ⊖ Old Street
- Menu £75/110 - Carte lunch £35/56
  Closed 2 weeks Christmas-New Year, August bank holiday, Monday lunch and Sunday - bookings advisable at dinner

HKK ✿

Chinese • Elegant

XX ♿ A/C ⊕ 🍷 **MAP:** 16-K3

FIRST COURSE: Dim Sum Platter. • Quail's egg with beef tongue, cinnamon, mirin and mustard.

MAIN COURSE: Jasmine tea-smoked Chilean wagyu beef. • Native lobster with black bean, rice cake, kumquat foam and crispy vermicelli.

DESSERT: Century egg with hazelnut, sesame and coffee. • Mango semifreddo.

Cantonese has always been considered the finest of the Chinese cuisines and here at HKK it is given an extra degree of refinement. The kitchen examines the seasonal ingredients available, considers what is being served in China and then designs a dish around them. The result is intriguing and original, with flavours that are sharp and well-defined and combinations that are well-judged. A perennial highlight is the duck: roasted to order in a cherry wood fired oven, it is expertly carved and served in three different ways. The presentation of all of the dishes is sublime and they also come with well-chosen wine pairings. The room is understated, elegant and graceful, and the service smooth, assured and unobtrusive. As time is money in this part of town, the lunch menu has been designed with consideration towards those who have to return to work - to really experience what HKK is all about, come for dinner when you're presented with their well-balanced 8 course menu, which evolves on a monthly basis.

■ **Shoreditch** — 88 Worship St ✉ EC2A 2BE
✆ 020 3535 1888 — **www.**hkklondon.com
⊖ Liverpool Street

■ Menu £94 (dinner) - Carte lunch £30/65
Closed Sunday and bank holidays

LYLE'S ✿

Modern British • Simple

✗ A/C **MAP:** 16-K3

Michelin

FIRST COURSE: Monkfish liver with blood orange. • Tomatoes, courgettes and fennel pollen.

MAIN COURSE: Red mullet with cured roe and turnip tops. • Dexter rib with pickled walnuts and beetroot.

DESSERT: Sleightlett cheese ice cream with burnt pear and goat's whey. • Russet apple, yeast and brioche.

The building was once owned by Lipton, the tea people, and the pared-down, ersatz industrial look is bang on trend. With its tiles and concrete floor, the space may be more about functionality than comfort but help is at hand from the open kitchen which is very much part of the room and adds colour and animation. Warmth and personality also come from the young service team, who share the passion of the kitchen, offer great advice and really know their menu. One glance at that menu tells immediately of the influence of Fergus Henderson - and sure enough, the young chef-owner previously ran the kitchen at St John Bread and Wine. Cooking is refreshingly unadorned and the use of superb seasonal British ingredients results in flavours that are clean, natural, unadulterated and a joy to experience. Only a set menu is offered at dinner but at lunch you can choose from an array of dishes in smaller sizes. Combinations are largely classically based but come with a modern touch.

- **Shoreditch** — Tea Building, 56 Shoreditch High St ✉ E1 6JJ
  ✆ 020 3011 5911 — **www**.lyleslondon.com
  ⊖ Shoreditch High Street
- Menu £55 (dinner) - Carte lunch £37/47
  Closed Sunday and bank holidays - (set menu only at dinner)

MERCHANTS TAVERN

Traditional British • Brasserie

MAP: 16-K3

It sounds like a pub, looks like one and even feels like one, but once you're settled in you'll soon realise there's more to this place than you initially thought. The 'pub' part – a Victorian warehouse – morphs into a big restaurant with an open kitchen and some very appealing booths beneath a skylight, which are the prized seats. Neil Borthwick and his partner Angela Hartnett are part-owners, along with the founders of Canteen, and the cooking is based on the simple yet sublime pleasures of seasonal British cooking. The kitchen has the confidence to stick to recognisable combinations in order to deliver flavours that are reassuringly familiar and satisfying, like trotters on toast, roast chicken with sweetcorn or gingerbread with caramel sauce.

- **Shoreditch** — 36 Charlotte Rd ✉ EC2A 3PG
  ✆ 020 7060 5335 — **www**.merchantstavern.co.uk
  ⊖ Old Street
- Carte £29/48
  Closed 25-26 December and 1 January

OKLAVA

Turkish • Bistro

MAP: 16-K3

With its concrete floor and its grey iron girders; its open kitchen and its counter dining, there's not much to distinguish this restaurant from many others in the area. Apart from the food, that is. An oklava is a traditional Turkish rolling pin used to make pastries and pides, both of which appear on the menu; for the chef is a Turkish Cypriot and cooks her interpretations of classic dishes from these countries. 3 or 4 of the well-priced small plates constitute a satisfying meal – the most popular are those cooked in the stone oven, like the filled flatbreads, or over the flaming charcoal grill, like the crispy lamb's breast with yoghurt. Sociable staff are happy to explain dishes or to recommend wines from the small, exclusively Turkish list.

- **Shoreditch** — 74 Luke St ✉ EC2A 4PY
  ✆ 020 7729 3032 — **www**.oklava.co.uk
  ⊖ Old Street
- Menu £18 (weekday lunch) - Carte £17/30
  Closed Saturday lunch, Sunday dinner, Monday and bank holidays - booking essential

Ⓝ POPOLO

Mediterranean cuisine • Trendy

MAP: 16-K3

With its rough-and-ready exterior, Popolo fits right in to its Shoreditch surroundings; its skimmed concrete floors, exposed brick walls and poured concrete counter adding to the utilitarian feel. Upstairs the rustic dining room has table seating but stick with the counter for a much more interesting experience, chatting to the chefs as they work. Chef-owner Jon Lawson is a Theo Randall alumnus so the Italian influences come as no surprise on the menu of small plates - Spain and North Africa also offer rich veins of inspiration. The concise menu evolves constantly and the classic, simply cooked dishes - 'food of the peasants' (or 'popolo') - allow the ingredients to shine. Choose 3 or 4 dishes - and make sure one of them is a plate of pasta.

- **Shoreditch** — 26 Rivington St ✉ EC2A 3DU
  ✆ 020 7729 4299 — **www**.popoloshoreditch.com
  ⊖ Old Street
- Carte £22/35
  Closed Sunday and Monday - bookings not accepted

PRINCESS OF SHOREDITCH

Traditional British • Pub

MAP: 16-K3

Apparently there has been a pub on this corner site since 1742 but it is doubtful many of the previous incarnations were as busy or as pleasant as the Princess is today. The owners have always been very hands-on and their welcoming attitude has rubbed off on their friendly staff; the pub comes with an appealing buzz and, to cap it all off, the prices are more than fair. It's set over two floors and the same menu is served throughout - although you can book upstairs. The menu changes daily, and sometimes between services; the food appears quite simple but the best dishes are those that come with a satisfyingly rustic edge, whether that's the buttery goose rillettes, the chicken pie with terrific mash or the tender pulled pork.

- **Shoreditch** — 76-78 Paul St ✉ EC2A 4NE
  ✆ 020 7729 9270 — **www**.theprincessofshoreditch.com
  ⊖ Old Street
- Menu £25/32 - Carte £26/38
  Closed 24-26 December - booking essential

TRAMSHED

Meats and grills • Brasserie

MAP: 16-K3

A Grade II listed warehouse, built in 1905 to house the generators for the trams, provides the backdrop to Mark Hix's impressive brasserie which is best enjoyed, like most things in life, in the company of friends. The striking piece of work by Damien Hirst of a tank containing a Hereford cow and a cockerel in formaldehyde is not just an impressive feature in the cavernous room, but also a clue as to what's on the menu. The Swainson House Farm chickens and the various cuts of Glenarm beef are accurately cooked and delicious; sides are good too and there are regularly changing starters and puds. The best seats are the booths around the wall. Service is alert and capable and they cope well with the numbers.

- **Shoreditch** — 32 Rivington St ✉ EC2A 3LX
  ✆ 020 7749 0478 — **www**.chickenandsteak.co.uk
  ⊖ Old Street
- Carte £20/65
  Closed 25 December

EMPRESS

Traditional British • Pub

MAP: 16-K2

This corner site pub used to be known as the Empress of India but was changed after people came expecting chicken tikka - information which will dishearten history teachers everywhere. Queen Victoria was then demoted to Empress E9, and eventually ended up as plain old Empress. Don't be surprised to see locals sprawled on the sofas or out on the pavement terrace enjoying a drink, as this is a neighbourhood pub at heart. The menu is short, simple and pleasingly seasonal, with traditional British dishes like Barnsley chop, rabbit pie for 2 and steak and chips, as well as the occasional Mediterranean influence in dishes like burrata with peach and almonds. Service is friendly and you can bring your own bottle on Tuesday nights.

- **South Hackney** — 130 Lauriston Rd, Victoria Park ✉ E9 7LH
  ✆ 020 8533 5123 — **www**.empresse9.co.uk
  ⊖ Homerton.
- Carte £24/34
  Closed 25-27 December and Monday lunch except bank holidays

Ⓝ GRAND TRUNK ROAD

Indian • Contemporary décor

This smart restaurant is a collaboration between an experienced chef and the manager of some of the city's best Indian restaurants, so it's no surprise that it stands out for both its cooking and its service. Dayashankar Sharma and Rajesh Suri named their restaurant after one of Asia's oldest and longest routes, which runs from Bangladesh to Afghanistan via India and Pakistan; a route they took time out to travel together, and which provided the inspiration for the cooking techniques, flavours and spices for their menu. Dishes are well-balanced and original with a modern touch; breads come from a charcoal-fired tandoor, vegetable dishes are a highlight - and the Peshawar ki lamb chops and slow-cooked lamb shanks have fast become favourites.

- **South Woodford** — 219 High Rd ✉ E18 2PB
  ✆ 020 8505 1965 — **www**.gtrrestaurant.co.uk
  ⊖ South Woodford
- Menu £23 (weekday lunch) - Carte £27/57
  Closed 25-26 December, 1 January and Monday - booking essential at dinner

PROVENDER

French • Bistro

Wanstead High Street may not necessarily be the first place one would expect to find great French bourgeois cooking but the locals must be mightily glad that Max Renzland decided to pitch up in their arrondissement. Max's reputation for creating terrific French restaurants was forged in the suburbs, albeit at the opposite end of town, and Provender has his stamp all over it. That means you can expect authentic and satisfying food; plenty of choice; and prices, for the menus and the exclusively French wine list, that are very competitive. The fish is good here, as are the charcuterie boards, and there are dishes to share and even a separate menu for 'les enfants'. It's no wonder the split-level room hums with the sound of contentment.

- **Wanstead** — 17 High St ✉ E11 2AA
  ✆ 020 8530 3050 — **www**.provenderlondon.co.uk
  ⊖ Snaresbrook
- Menu £17 (lunch and early dinner) - Carte £20/45

C. S. Pereyra/age fotostock

SOUTH-EAST LONDON

Once considered not only the wrong side of the tracks, but also most definitely the wrong side of the river, London's southeastern chunk has thrived in recent times courtesy of the Docklands Effect. As the gleaming glass peninsula of **Canary Wharf** (ironically, just north of the Thames) sprouted a personality of its own – with bars, restaurants, slinky bridges and an enviable view, not to mention moneyed residents actually putting down roots – the city's bottom right hand zone began to achieve destination status on a par with other parts of London. You only have to stroll around the glossy and quite vast **Limehouse Basin** – a slick marina that was once a hard-grafting East End dock – to really see what's happened here.

Not that the area hasn't always boasted some true gems in the capital's treasure chest. **Greenwich,** with fabulous views across the water to the docklands from its delightfully sloping park, has long been a favourite of kings and queens: Henry VIII and Elizabeth I resided here. The village itself bustles along with its market and plush picturehouse, but most visitors make their way to the standout attractions, of which there are many. The **Royal Observatory** and the Meridian Line draw star-gazers and hemisphere striders in equal number, while the palatial Old Royal Naval College is a star turn for lovers of Wren, who designed it as London's answer to Versailles. On the northern edge of Greenwich Park, the **National Maritime Museum** has three floors of sea-faring wonders; down by the pier, the real thing exists in the shape of the **Cutty Sark**. Up on the peninsula, the O2 Arena's distinctive shape has become an unmistakable landmark, but if you fancy a contrast to all things watery, the Fan Museum on Crooms Hill has more hand-held fans (over 3,000 of them) than anywhere else on earth. Strolling south from Greenwich park you reach **Blackheath,** an alluring suburban village, whose most striking feature is the towering All Saints' Church, standing proud away from the chic shops and restaurants.

Of slightly less spectacular charms, but a real crowd-pleaser nevertheless, is **Dulwich Village,** hidden deeper in the southeastern enclaves. It's a leafy oasis in this part of the world, with a delightful park that boasts at its western end, next to the original buildings of the old public school, the Dulwich Picture Gallery. This was designed in 1811, and its pedigree is evident in works by the likes of Rembrandt, Rubens, Van Dyck and Canaletto. Half an hour's walk away across the park is the brilliant Horniman Museum, full of natural history and world culture delights – as well as a massive aquarium that seems to take up much of southeast London.

A bit further east along the South Circular, there's the unexpected gem of Eltham Palace, originally the childhood home of Henry VIII with a magnificent (and still visible) Great Hall. What makes it unique is the adjacent Art Deco mansion built for millionaires in the 1930s in Ocean Liner style. It's the closest you'll ever get to a setting fit for hog roast and champagne. Heading back towards London, a lifestyle of bubbly and banquets has never really been **Peckham**'s thing, but it boasts a couple of corkers in the shape of the South London Gallery with its zeitgeist-setting art shows, and the Peckham Library, a giant inverted 'L' that looks like a lot of fun to go into.

Back in the luxury flat-lands of the **Docklands, Wapping** has become an interesting port of call, its new-build architecture mixing in with a still Dickensian feel, in the shape of glowering Victorian warehouses and Wapping New Stairs, where the bodies of pirates were hanged from a gibbet until seven tides had showered their limp bodies. You can catch a fascinating history of the whole area in the nearby Museum Of London Docklands.

I. Dimitrov/age fotostock

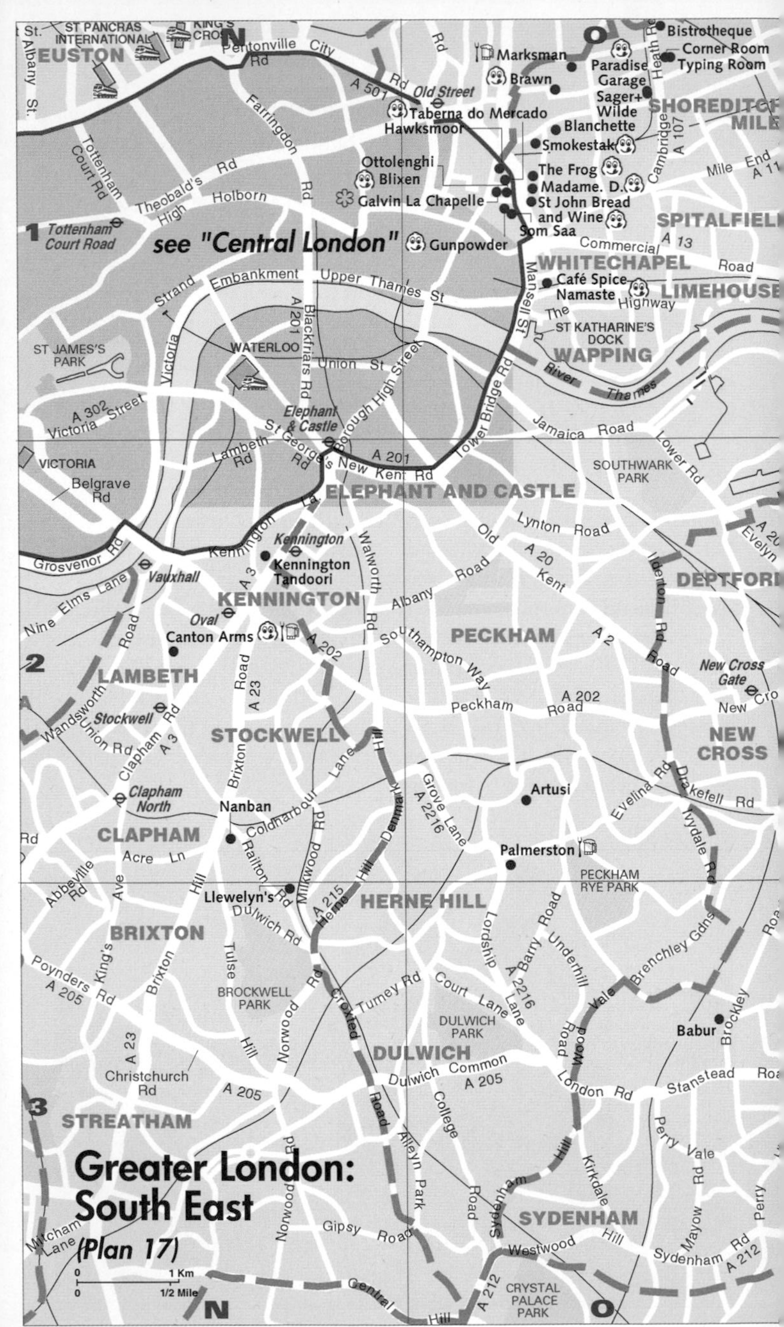
Greater London:
South East
(Plan 17)
see "Central London"
ST PANCRAS INTERNATIONAL
KING'S CROSS
EUSTON
Pentonville Rd
City Rd
A 501
Old Street
Farringdon Rd
Tottenham Court Rd
Theobald's Rd
High Holborn
Tottenham Court Road
Marksman
Brawn
Taberna do Mercado
Hawksmoor
Ottolenghi
Blixen
Galvin La Chapelle
Gunpowder
Bistrotheque
Corner Room
Typing Room
Paradise Garage
Sager+ Wilde
Blanchette
Smokestak
The Frog
Madame. D.
St John Bread and Wine
Som Saa
Café Spice Namaste
SHOREDITCH
MILE
Mile End
Cambridge
A 107
Heath Rd
SPITALFIELDS
Commercial Road
A 13
WHITECHAPEL
The Highway
LIMEHOUSE
Mansell St
ST KATHARINE'S DOCK
WAPPING
River Thames
Strand
Embankment
Upper Thames St
A 201
Blackfriars Rd
WATERLOO
Union St
Borough High Street
Tower Bridge Rd
ST JAMES'S PARK
Victoria
A 302
Victoria Street
Elephant & Castle
St George's Rd
Lambeth Rd
A 201
New Kent Rd
Jamaica Road
Lower Rd
SOUTHWARK PARK
VICTORIA
Belgrave Rd
ELEPHANT AND CASTLE
Grosvenor Rd
Kennington La.
Kennington
Kennington Tandoori
Walworth Rd
Lynton Road
Old Kent Road
A 20
A 2
Vauxhall
Nine Elms Lane
A 3
KENNINGTON
Albany Road
Oval
Canton Arms
A 202
Southampton Way
PECKHAM
Ilderton Rd
Road
DEPTFORD
A 20
Evelyn
New Cross Gate
New Cross
NEW CROSS
LAMBETH
Road
Road A 23
Wandsworth Road
Stockwell
Union Rd
Clapham Rd A 3
STOCKWELL
Peckham Road
A 202
Brixton
Lane
Hill
Clapham North
Nanban
Coldharbour
Grove Lane
A 2216
Denmark Hill
Artusi
Evelina Rd
Drakefell Rd
CLAPHAM
Acre Ln
Railton Rd
Milkwood Rd
Palmerston
Ivydale Rd
PECKHAM RYE PARK
Abbeville Rd
Ave
Hill
Llewelyn's
Dulwich Rd
A 215
Herne Hill
HERNE HILL
Barry Road
Lordship Lane
A 2216
Underhill
BRIXTON
King's
Poynders Rd
A 205
Brixton
Tulse Hill
BROCKWELL PARK
Norwood Rd
Croxted Road
Tumey Rd
Court Lane
DULWICH PARK
Wood Vale
Brenchley Gdns
Babur
Brockley
A 23
Christchurch Rd
A 205
DULWICH
Dulwich Common
A 205
College Road
London Rd
Stanstead Road
Perry Vale
STREATHAM
Norwood Rd
Alleyn Park
Sydenham Hill
Kirkdale
Mayow Rd
Perry
SYDENHAM
Gipsy Road
Westwood Hill
Sydenham Rd
A 212
Mitcham Lane
Central Hill
A 212
CRYSTAL PALACE PARK
0 1 Km
0 1/2 Mile
N
O
1
2
3

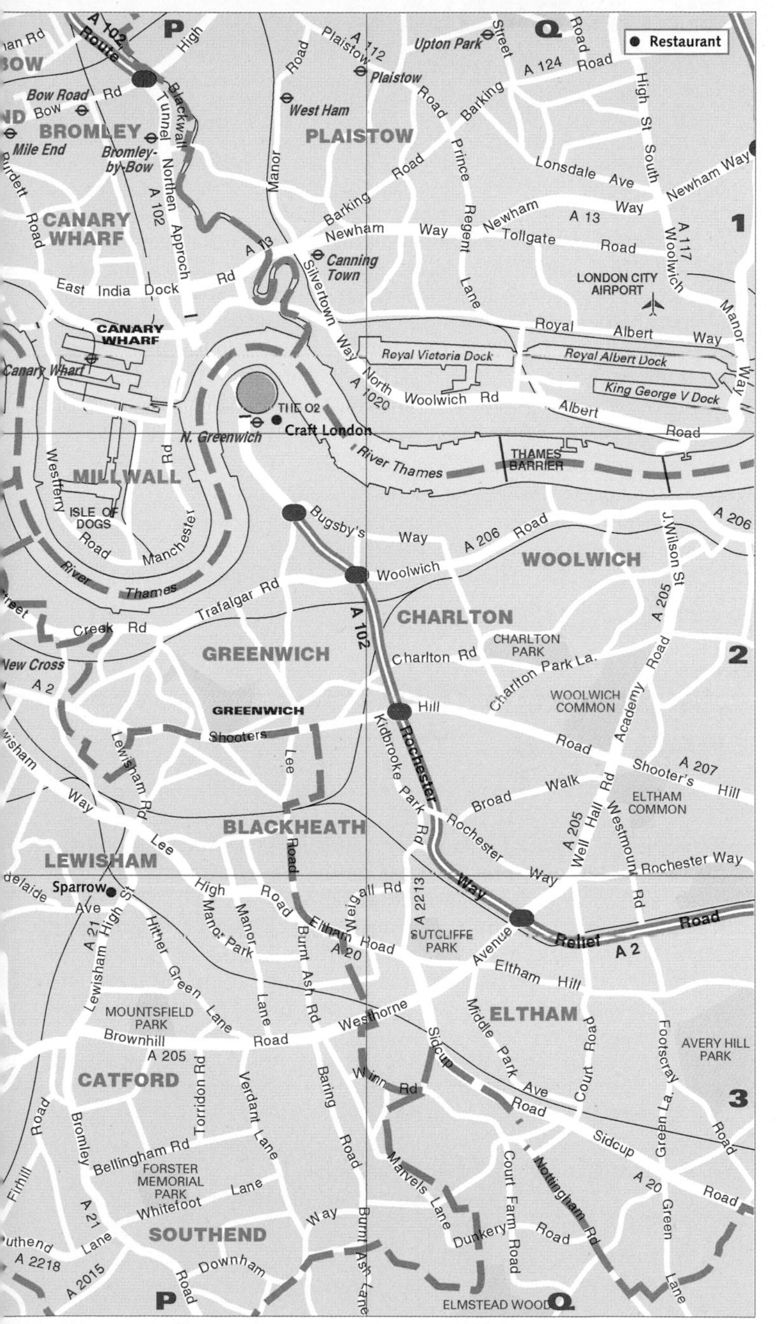
Restaurant
P
Q
1
2
3
BOW
BROMLEY
CANARY WHARF
PLAISTOW
MILLWALL
ISLE OF DOGS
WOOLWICH
CHARLTON
GREENWICH
BLACKHEATH
LEWISHAM
ELTHAM
CATFORD
SOUTHEND
CHARLTON PARK
WOOLWICH COMMON
ELTHAM COMMON
SUTCLIFFE PARK
MOUNTSFIELD PARK
FORSTER MEMORIAL PARK
AVERY HILL PARK
ELMSTEAD WOOD
LONDON CITY AIRPORT
THAMES BARRIER
THE O2
Craft London
Sparrow
Upton Park
Plaistow
West Ham
Bow Road
Bow
Mile End
Bromley-by-Bow
Canning Town
Canary Wharf
N. Greenwich
New Cross
River Thames
Royal Victoria Dock
Royal Albert Dock
King George V Dock
Blackwall Tunnel Northern Approch
A 102
East India Dock Rd
Newham Way
A 13
Barking Road
Tollgate Road
Royal Albert Way
Woolwich Rd
Albert Road
Silvertown Way
North Woolwich Rd
A 1020
Bugsby's Way
A 206
Woolwich Road
Trafalgar Rd
Creek Rd
Charlton Rd
Charlton Park La.
Shooters Hill Road
A 207
Rochester Way
Kidbrooke Park Rd
Broad Walk
Well Hall Rd
A 205
Westmount Rd
Academy Road
J. Wilson St
Relief Road
A 2
Eltham Hill
Eltham Road
A 20
Westhorne Avenue
Sidcup Road
Lewisham High St
A 21
Lewisham Way
Lee High Road
Lewisham Rd
Lee Road
Burnt Ash Rd
Burnt Ash Lane
Brownhill Road
Bellingham Rd
Whitefoot Lane
Downham Way
Verdant Lane
Torridon Rd
Baring Road
Winn Rd
Marvels Lane
Dunkery Road
Court Farm Road
Court Road
Nottingham Rd
Middle Park Ave
Footscray Road
Green La.
Green Lane
Westferry Road
Manchester Rd
Manor Road
Prince Regent Lane
High St South
A 117
Woolwich Manor Way
Lonsdale Ave
A 124
Plaistow Road
A 112
Weigall Rd
A 2213
Hither Green Lane
Manor Park
Manor Lane
Bromley Road
Firhill Road
Southend Lane
A 2218
A 2015
Adelaide Ave
Burdett Road

BISTROTHEQUE

French • Neighbourhood

MAP: 17-01

When a restaurant has an exterior as irredeemably bleak as this, it can only mean one thing: it's going to be painfully cool inside. Converted from an old sweatshop, the owners purposely left the exterior bereft of any sign of gastronomic life – just head past the anguished graffiti and take the stairs in the courtyard up to the 1st floor. Here you'll find a warmly run, wonderfully bustling industrial-looking space, with beams and girders, ducting and concrete. It's all great fun, especially as the restaurant rubs shoulders with a bar and cabaret. The menu is predominantly French bistro in style with some British classics thrown in. A good value set menu is offered early and late in the evening and weekend brunch comes with live music.

- **Bethnal Green** — 23-27 Wadeson St ✉ E2 9DR
  020 8983 7900 — **www.**bistrotheque.com
  Bethnal Green
- Menu £25 (early dinner) - Carte £31/50
  Closed 24-26 December - booking advisable - (dinner only and lunch Saturday-Sunday)

N BLANCHETTE

French • Bistro

MAP: 17-01

It's got its fair share of Balti houses but Brick Lane now also boasts a Blanchette, bringing French 'tapas' to this famous street. It's run by three brothers and, like the Soho original, is named after their mother. It's got the lively buzz, the funky music and the tasty French dishes to share, but this time the menu heads further south and there's a few North African influences too, so expect lamb tagine and cassoulet alongside seared onglet with snails. 3 or 4 plates per person should suffice: start with snacks and some top quality charcuterie before moving onto fish, meat, cheese and desserts. Add to this an interesting wine list, some colourful artwork and a friendly young team and you can see why this place is plein à craquer.

- **Bethnal Green** — 204 Brick Ln ✉ E1 6SA
  020 7729 7939 — **www.**blanchettelondon.co.uk
  Shoreditch High Street
- Menu £15 (lunch) - Carte £14/38
  Closed 24-26 December - booking advisable

BRAWN

Modern cuisine • Neighbourhood

MAP: 17-01

Found in a Victorian former furniture warehouse, away from the West End, this terrific neighbourhood restaurant is simply kitted out, with wooden tables and white brick walls hung with local artists' work. The name really captures the essence of the cooking perfectly: it is rustic and muscular, follows a nose-to-tail ethos and makes particularly good use of pig. Order about four dishes per person such as prosciutto or rillettes; mussels or prawns; something raw like Tuscan beef; and something slow-cooked like duck confit. It's all immeasurably satisfying and the polite young staff appear genuinely proud of the menu and happily proffer advice. The interesting wine list has an emphasis on natural and organic wines.

- **Bethnal Green** — 49 Columbia Rd. ✉ E2 7RG
  ✆ 020 7729 5692 — **www**.brawn.co
  ⊖ Bethnal Green
- Carte £25/44
  Closed Christmas-New Year, Sunday dinner, Monday lunch and bank holidays

CORNER ROOM

Creative • Intimate

MAP: 17-01

Hidden away above the Typing Room in the old town hall is a warm and intimate space called the Corner Room - and it's somewhere that is just a little bit different. The narrow room features wood panelling juxtaposed with bright white tiles and a backdrop of ornate and antique hanging light fittings for an extra bit of whimsy. From a small menu, the kitchen uses all sorts of modern techniques to produce dishes that are assured and very effective - there is originality here but also an avoidance of any needless elaboration; flavours are distinct and you feel you're getting a real taste of nature. The core ingredient of each dish is British, be it Longhorn beef or Tamworth pork.

- **Bethnal Green** — Town Hall Hotel, Patriot Sq ✉ E2 9NF
  ✆ 020 7871 0461 — **www**.cornerroom.co.uk
  ⊖ Bethnal Green
- Carte £28/35
  Bookings advisable at dinner

MARKSMAN

Traditional British • Friendly

MAP: 17-01

With its quirky, brown-tiled façade, the Marksman has long been a local landmark. Inside, it's a place of two halves: the wood-panelled bar retains the cosy, unaffected feel of a traditional boozer, while the first floor dining room is far more modern. There's a roof terrace for alfresco dining and the friendly atmosphere really adds to the pub's appeal. Owners Tom Harris and Jon Rotheram are St John alumni and their considerable experience is evident in the food. The simply cooked, seasonal dishes are wonderfully fresh, perfectly balanced and full of flavour – we're talking proper British cooking with the likes of devilled mussels on toast, skate with shrimps and turnip tops, or pheasant and trotter pie for two.

- **Bethnal Green** — 254 Hackney Rd ✉ E2 7SJ
  ✆ 020 7739 7393 — **www**.marksmanpublichouse.com
  ⊖ Hoxton.
- Carte £30/40
  Closed 25 December and 1 January – (dinner only and lunch Saturday-Sunday)

PARADISE GARAGE

Traditional British • Bistro

MAP: 17-01

This north-of-the-river sister to Clapham's Manor and Dairy is set under the railway arches in lively Bethnal Green and shares a menu format with its older siblings. When they're open, the oversized folding doors give the feeling you're dining alfresco, but there's counter dining too for those who like to watch chefs doing their thing. The constantly evolving collection of small plates are British at heart and, refreshingly, arrive in the sequence you ordered them. An excellent rustic sourdough paired with whisky-smoked butter kicks things off nicely and dishes like a wonderful scorched venison tartare are artfully presented and come with compelling contrasts in temperature, texture and flavour. The set 4 course midweek lunch menu is a steal.

- **Bethnal Green** — Arch 254, Paradise Row ✉ E2 9LE
  ✆ 020 7613 1502 — **www**.paradise254.com
  ⊖ Bethnal Green
- Menu £20 (weekdays) - Carte £26/39
  Closed 2 weeks Christmas-New Year, Sunday dinner, Monday and lunch Tuesday-Friday

SAGER + WILDE

Mediterranean cuisine • Rustic

MAP: 17-01

There's a friendly neighbourhood buzz to this rustic restaurant, set under a railway arch in busy Bethnal Green, and the regular rumble of trains overhead only adds to its appeal. It started life as a wine bar, like its Hackney sister, and some people do just pop in for a glass of wine or a cocktail, but it's worth staying to eat, even if just to enjoy bar nibbles like pickled Tokyo turnip or salt-baked celeriac. Tasty, well-priced, creative dishes have a Mediterranean heart and an eye-catching modern style, with some interesting – and sometimes challenging – combinations of ingredients, like baked artichoke with caramelised yoghurt or langoustine with millet and rice porridge. The wine list is thoughtfully chosen and mark-ups, modest.

- **Bethnal Green** — 250 Paradise Row ✉ E2 9LE
  020 7613 0478 — **www**.sagerandwilde.com
  ⊖ Bethnal Green
- Carte £19/33
  Closed Monday - (dinner only and lunch Friday-Sunday)

N SMOKESTAK

Meats and grills • Rustic

MAP: 17-01

You smell the aromas from this barbecue restaurant before you catch sight of its smoke-stained windows; once inside, the lively chatter of an excitable crowd competes with the clatter of pots and pans, amplified by an industrial backdrop of exposed metal. Chef-owner David Carter is an alumnus of some notable restaurants and his love of cooking – and specifically barbecue – comes from his Barbadian roots. He's a charming host and employs some equally affable serving staff who are happy to recommend dishes. Menu highlights include the brisket and ribs; these are brined before being left in the English Oak smoking oven overnight, then coated with a sticky sweet and sour BBQ sauce and chargrilled – the results being unctuous and incredibly satisfying.

- **Bethnal Green** — 35 Sclater St ✉ E1 6LB
  020 3873 1733 — **www**.smokestak.co.uk
  ⊖ Shoreditch High Street
- Carte £18/30

TYPING ROOM ɪıO

Modern cuisine • Fashionable

XX A/C

MAP: 17-01

The first thing you notice is the colony of chefs beavering away in the open kitchen – this remains the focal point of the room, which was once home to the erstwhile town hall's typing pool. There is a simpler menu available at lunchtime but most diners are here to enjoy the 5 course menus, as well as the thoughtful wine pairings that accompany them. Heavily influenced by new Nordic cuisine, the kitchen adopts plenty of techniques, like fermenting and smoking, to create dishes that are earthy, elaborate and feature lots of contrasting textures. The snacks that kick things off are excellent, as is the IPA sourdough bread. The tone and style of the clued-up service suits the place perfectly.

- **Bethnal Green** — Town Hall Hotel, Patriot Sq ✉ E2 9NF
  020 7871 0461 — **www**.typingroom.com
  Bethnal Green
- Menu £27 (weekdays)/65
  Closed Sunday dinner, Monday and lunch Tuesday/Wednesday

PALMERSTON ɪıO

Mediterranean cuisine • Pub

MAP: 17-02

The Palmerston has long realised that success for any pub lies in being at the heart of the local community. Since its last makeover, this Victorian pub has been popular with families – just look at all those highchairs – and local artists' work decorates the walls. It has a comfortable, lived-in feel, along with a snug, wood-panelled rear dining room with an original and quite beautiful mosaic floor. The menu is as reassuring as the service and the cooking has a satisfying, gutsy edge. There's plenty of choice, from chowders and soups to well-judged fish dishes but it's the meat dishes that stand out, like the mature steaks or lamb chops – and if they have grouse on the menu, then forsake all others and get in quick.

- **East Dulwich** — 91 Lordship Ln ✉ SE22 8EP
  020 8693 1629 — **www**.thepalmerston.co.uk
  East Dulwich (Rail).
- Menu £14 (weekday lunch) - Carte £26/44
  Closed 25-26 December and 1 January

BABUR ℗

Indian • Neighbourhood

XX A/C MAP: 17-O3

It's not just its good looks and innovative cooking that set Babur apart – this long-standing Indian restaurant is also run with great passion and enthusiasm. Regular customers are invited to tastings and can even have an input on the quarterly changing menus – and the make-up of each dish is fully explained when dishes are presented at the table. The south and north-west of India feature most predominantly on the menu but there are also Western-influenced dishes available, like crab claws with asparagus and saffron. Seafood is certainly a highlight, so look out for the periods of the year when the separate 'Treasures of the Sea' menu appears. You'll find suggested wine pairings for each dish, along with some inventive cocktails.

- **Forest Hill** — 119 Brockley Rise ✉ SE23 1JP
  ✆ 020 8291 2400 — **www**.babur.info
  ⊖ Honor Oak Park
- Menu £32/56 - Carte £28/36
  Closed 26 December

CRAFT LONDON ℗

Modern British • Design

X ♿ A/C 🍸 MAP: 17-P1

On the doorstep of the O2 arena is a building bursting with activity and full of the seductive smell of roasting and charred wood. Chef Stevie Parle, in conjunction with long-time collaborator and designer Tom Dixon, has created a striking space which includes a coffee shop serving light snacks on the ground floor, a cocktail bar upstairs with views and a terrace, and a restaurant championing the most British of produce. They do their own curing of meats, roasting of coffee, and their own pickling and smoking; they also grow their own herbs and even get their honey from bees in the nearby grounds. The food is modern, interesting and a little different – try the well-judged smoked eel with layers of flavour or the juicy pork loin.

- **Greenwich** — Peninsula Sq ✉ SE10 0SQ
  ✆ 020 8465 5910 — **www**.craft-london.co.uk
  ⊖ North Greenwich
- Menu £35 - Carte £32/50
  Closed Christmas-New Year, Sunday and Monday - (dinner only and Saturday lunch)

Ⓝ LLEWELYN'S ⑩

Traditional British • Neighbourhood

MAP: 17-N3

Llewelyn's village-like location is a huge part of its pull; it's set across from the station looking onto a small piazza and in summer the tables and chairs spill outside, giving it some seriously continental vibes. Cooking is British with Mediterranean influences; the short, daily changing menu moves with the seasons and dishes to share are a feature. The key players here have come from the likes of St John and Anchor & Hope, so expect quality ingredients in hearty portions, with no unnecessary elaboration. Come in the morning for coffee and pastries, mid-afternoon for charcuterie and wine, and on Sundays for a proper roast accompanied by the sights and sounds of the local farmers' market. Service is friendly, if a little fraught at times.

■ **Herne Hill** — 293-295 Railton Rd ✉ SE24 0JP
020 7733 6676 — **www**.llewelyns-restaurant.co.uk
⊖ Herne Hill

■ Carte £24/33
Closed 22 December-4 January, Sunday dinner and Monday – bookings advisable at dinner

KENNINGTON TANDOORI ⑩

Indian • Neighbourhood

MAP: 17-N2

One of the best things about this contemporary looking Indian restaurant is that even on your first visit you get the impression you'll be remembered the next time you turn up. Kowsar Hoque runs it with enormous pride and this filters through to the staff who display great care and enthusiasm. As a result, the place is usually home to quite a number of regulars on any given evening, be they MPs, cricket fans or locals, and many of them no longer bother reading a menu and just order their 'usual'. For newcomers, the menu is quite a long affair but it's worth taking a look at the loose page of seasonal specialities. The curries have depth and the side dishes and breads are prepared with equal care.

■ **Kennington** — 313 Kennington Rd ✉ SE11 4QE
020 7735 9247 — **www**.kenningtontandoori.com
⊖ Kennington

■ Carte £20/34
Closed 25-26 December – booking advisable – (dinner only and lunch Saturday and Sunday)

Ⓝ SPARROW ℩O

Modern British • Friendly

MAP: 17-P3

Chef-owners Yohini Nandakumar and Terry Blake originally met at St John and its influence is clear to see here at their first venture together; between them, they've also worked at various notable restaurants including Bao, Pollen Street Social and The Square. For Sparrow, they've flown south of the river to lucky Lewisham – its name symbolising the culinary diversity of their menus, as well as Yohini's Sri Lankan heritage. Choose from a truly joyous selection of globally influenced sharing plates; maybe Devon crab with Thai spices, lamb chops with tomato and hazelnut salsa or Massaman beef brisket with scorched rice. Weekends mean brunch, with choices as varied as mince on dripping toast, bacon sandwiches and appams – a type of Sri Lankan pancake.

- **Lewisham** — 2 Rennell St ✉ SE13 7HD
  ✆ 020 8318 6941 — **www**.sparrowlondon.co.uk
  ⊖ Lewisham
- Carte £22/33
  Closed 2 weeks August, Christmas, Sunday dinner and Monday – (dinner only and weekend brunch)

ARTUSI ℩O

Italian • Neighbourhood

MAP: 17-O2

Whether the 'Bellenden Village' moniker for this part of Peckham will ever catch on is a moot point; what is sure is that places like Artusi are a clear indication of a neighbourhood on the move. This Italian restaurant is named after Pellegrino Artusi who wrote a seminal work, "The Science of Cooking and the Art of Fine Dining", in 1891. The seasonal blackboard menu is quite short which helps keep costs and prices down and there's something very honest about the cooking. It is clear the kitchen has respect for the ingredients, with dishes a blend of the traditional and the modern; pasta, gelato and bread are all made in-house. Service is knowledgeable and keen, and if you're with a few friends ask for the long table by the pass.

- **Peckham** — 161 Bellenden Rd ✉ SE15 4DH
  ✆ 020 3302 8200 — **www**.artusi.co.uk
  ⊖ Peckham Rye
- Carte £20/40
  Closed 1 week Christmas – booking essential at dinner

BLIXEN

Mediterranean cuisine • Design

MAP: 17-01

It is clear that someone with an eye for detail was involved with the interior design of this former bank, because this is a very good-looking restaurant. There's lots of natural light and plenty of choice of where to sit, from the leather banquettes to the kitchen counter; head to the rear to sit in a plant-filled conservatory overlooking the market. When it comes to the largely European menu, you'll be hard pressed not to find something that appeals. Unfussy modern dishes like crumbed ox tongue with remoulade and mushroom pappardelle are not only prepared with care, but also offered at a very fair price. Staff are charming, the atmosphere's buzzing and you'll want to return for breakfast, or cocktails in the basement bar.

- **Spitalfields** — 65a Brushfield St ✉ E1 6AA
  020 7101 0093 — **www**.blixen.co.uk
  Liverpool Street
- Menu £24 (lunch) - Carte £23/38
  Closed Sunday dinner

GUNPOWDER

Indian • Simple

MAP: 17-01

This Indian restaurant exploded onto the Spitalfields food scene with a bang; a loud buzzy place with just ten, tightly packed tables serving vibrant small plates from across the Indian regions. Arrive within ten minutes of opening or you will have to wait; they take your number and text you when a table becomes available, so you're free to enjoy a drink elsewhere. The name is a reference to the chef's daily-made spice mix and his menu takes its influence from old family recipes. Dishes like spicy venison doughnut and sigri-grilled mustard broccoli are worth trying, while standouts include deep-fried soft shell crab and the crispy pork ribs with layer upon layer of flavour. 3 dishes are sufficient - and give pud a miss.

- **Spitalfields** — 11 White's Row ✉ E1 7NF
  020 7426 0542 — **www**.gunpowderlondon.com
  Liverpool Street
- Carte £15/31
  Closed Sunday - bookings not accepted

GALVIN LA CHAPELLE ✿

French • Elegant

XXX MAP: 17-01

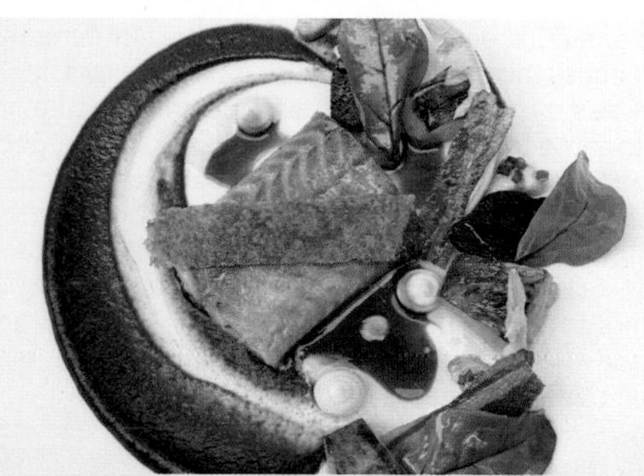

Galvin La Chapelle

FIRST COURSE: Lasagne of Dorset crab with beurre Nantais. • Terrine of Goosnargh chicken with Bayonne ham and sauce gribiche.

MAIN COURSE: Tagine of Bresse pigeon with couscous and harissa sauce. • Fillet of halibut with shellfish marinière and sea purslane.

DESSERT: Tarte Tatin with crème fraîche. • Rhubarb soufflé with vanilla ice cream.

The Galvin brothers are creating an empire of Romanesque proportions and it continues to expand at a rate of knots. Built in 1890 as a girls' school, this splendid Grade II listed structure with its vaulted ceiling, arched windows and marble pillars was an inspired choice for a venue, and remains as impressive now as when it first opened back in 2009. It lends itself effortlessly to its role as a glamorous restaurant: a magnificent open space with a mezzanine for private dining, and plenty of tables, whether in booths, in the wings or right in the middle of the action. The sommelier is knowledgeable, service is professional and the atmosphere, relaxed and unstuffy. Cooking is assured and precise, with a classical French foundation and a sophisticated modern edge. There are no unnecessary fripperies - just three courses of reassuringly familiar combinations with the emphasis on bold, harmonious flavours and, whilst dishes may sound complicated, they are anything but. Must-tries include the tagine of Bresse pigeon and the apple tarte Tatin.

- **Spitalfields** — 35 Spital Sq ✉ E1 6DY
  ✆ 020 7299 0400 — **www**.galvinrestaurants.com
  ⊖ Liverpool Street
- Menu £35 (lunch and early dinner) - Carte £48/76
  Closed 25-26 December and 1 January

HAWKSMOOR

Meats and grills • Friendly

MAP: 17-O1

Hawksmoor was a 17C architect and a student of Sir Christopher Wren so you could expect this steakhouse to be found in a building of note rather than in this modern edifice of little aesthetic value. Inside is equally unremarkable but no matter because this place is all about beef and, more specifically, British beef which has been hung for 35 days. It comes from Longhorn cattle raised by the Ginger Pig Co in the heart of the North Yorkshire Moors and the quality and depth of flavour is exceptional. Just choose your preferred weight - go for 400g if you're hungry. Starters and puds don't come close in quality but again, no matter, because when you've got some fantastic red meat in front of you, all you need is a mate and a bottle of red wine.

- **Spitalfields** — 157a Commercial St ✉ E1 6BJ
  ✆ 020 7426 4850 — **www**.thehawksmoor.com
  ⊖ Shoreditch High Street
- Menu £25 (lunch and early dinner) - Carte £23/75
  Closed 24-26 December - booking essential

N MADAME. D.

World cuisine • Simple

MAP: 17-O1

Sister to the successful Gunpowder, Madame. D. comes with a focus on Himalayan cuisine, including dishes from Nepal, Tibet, Northern India and China - its name being a reference to a Chinese woman who travelled the Himalayas, selling opium and collecting spices and recipes as she went. Being small, this simply furnished two-floor restaurant is always busy and tables, like dishes, are for sharing. Bright and breezy service keeps up with the fast pace of proceedings and the atmosphere is loud and buzzy. The concise menu is made up of great-tasting, nicely spiced small plates - five between two being more than enough; perhaps a moreish naga chilli beef puff, unctuous Tibetan pan-fried duck leg, Himalayan fried chicken or masala lamb noodles.

- **Spitalfields** — 76 Commercial St ✉ E1 6LY
  ✆ 020 7247 1341 — **www**.madame-d.com
  ⊖ Liverpool Street
- Carte £15/30
  Closed Monday - bookings not accepted - (dinner only)

OTTOLENGHI

Mediterranean cuisine • Design

MAP: 17-01

The development of the Ottolenghi 'brand' continues apace with this hugely popular spot a stone's throw from Spitalfield Market. It's something of a cross between the original shop in Upper Street where it all started and Nopi, their restaurant in Soho. The bright white look of the room works well in reminding you that this is food that's all about freshness. Largely Mediterranean, the dishes are as flavoursome as they are colourful, show respect for the ingredients and benefit from simple cooking techniques - starters come from the display counter and are cold. Sharing is the norm as everything comes on small plates - you can even share a table if you want. For dessert, you might just want to buy one of their vast meringues to take home.

- **Spitalfields** — 50 Artillery Ln ✉ E1 7LJ
  020 7247 1999 — **www**.ottolenghi.co.uk
  Liverpool Street
- Carte £26/67
  Closed dinner 24-27 and 31 December, 1-2 January, 2 April and Sunday dinner - booking essential

ST JOHN BREAD AND WINE

Traditional British • Bistro

MAP: 17-01

Less famous but by no means less loved than its sibling, this English version of a classic comptoir is the sort of place we would all like to have at the end of our road. Breakfast is served every day and includes a wonderful rare breed bacon sandwich, while the main menu changes twice a day and depends on what's in season. Dishes are starter-sized and perfect for sharing, and the Britishness of their ingredients and their promotion of forgotten recipes will enthuse everyone, not just culinary genealogists. There's plenty of man-food like roast pig spleen or 'raw Angus' on the menu, but also lighter dishes such as plaice with samphire or roast tomato with goat's curd and mint. For dessert, the Eccles cakes are a must.

- **Spitalfields** — 94-96 Commercial St ✉ E1 6LZ
  020 7251 0848 — **www**.stjohngroup.uk.com
  Liverpool Street
- Carte £26/40
  Closed 25-26 December and 1 January

SOM SAA

Thai • Rustic

MAP: 17-01

What began as a pop-up became a permanent fixture in 2016; the result of a collaboration between two chefs who first met at former Belgravia restaurant, Nahm, back in the noughties. It has a rustic, industrial look and as lively an atmosphere as its precedent pop-up; there are a few bookable booths and tables but most are communal and kept for walk-ins. Dishes from the north of Thailand and its borders are a feature, but their desire to showcase the diversity of Thai cuisine means that you'll find lesser known dishes from all over the country on the menu. Signature dishes include Burmese-style pork curry and whole deep-fried sea bass with roasted rice. 4 or 5 dishes between two are recommended - and don't forget to try a cocktail or two!

- **Spitalfields** — 43a Commerical St ✉ E1 6BD
  ✆ 020 7324 7790 — **www**.somsaa.com
  ⊖ Aldgate East
- Carte £18/31
  Closed Christmas, bank holiday Mondays, Sunday and Monday lunch - bookings advisable at dinner

TABERNA DO MERCADO

Portuguese • Simple

MAP: 17-01

Despite - or perhaps because of - the simplicity of Nuno Mendes' second restaurant, this modest little place in Old Spitalfields serving small plates of Portuguese classics has fast become a destination restaurant in itself. Grab a seat on the terrace (which is actually still inside the market hall): here, you can enjoy ethereal scents from the open kitchen and build up an appetite watching the chargrilling of the breads. The menu lists charcuterie and cheese as well as traditional offerings, but look closer and you'll see staples elevated to a higher level: alheira, Bísaro pork and prawn rissois all deliver wonderful flavours, as does the Abade de Priscos - and the specials are just that. The wine, staff and crockery are all Portuguese too.

- **Spitalfields** — Old Spitalfields Market, 107b Commercial St ✉ E1 6BG
  ✆ 020 7375 0649 — **www**.tabernamercado.co.uk
  ⊖ Liverpool Street
- Menu £15 (weekday lunch) - Carte £16/38
  Closed 24 December-3 January - (Bookings not accepted at dinner)

THE FROG

Modern cuisine • Neighbourhood

MAP: 17-O1

Ambitious young chef Adam Caxton is making a splash with his restaurant, set in the old Truman brewery; a space full of indy shops, cafés and bars. As is de rigueur for any E1 eatery worth its salt, the décor comes in a nice shade of neutral; the floor is an expanse of concrete and the kitchen is well and truly open. Small plates are listed under sections entitled 'snacks', 'garden', 'sea', 'land', 'cheese' and 'desserts', with 3 or 4 per person about right. Dishes are modern, creative and quite intricate, with vibrant flavour and texture combinations; some – like the nitro salmon, peas and wasabi; the bread with chicken butter; and the cheese, doughnut and truffle – incorporate playful elements. Craft beers and cocktails add to the fun.

- **Spitalfields** — 2 Ely's Yard, Old Truman Brewery, Hanbury St. ✉ E1 6QR
  ✆ 020 3813 9832 — **www**.thefrogrestaurant.com
  ⊖ Shoreditch High Street
- Carte £17/32
  Closed Sunday and Monday – booking essential

CANTON ARMS

Traditional British • Pub

MAP: 17-N2

Its appreciative audience proves that the demand for fresh, honest, seasonal food is not just limited to smart squares in Chelsea or Islington. The oval-shaped bar dominates the room; the front half busy with drinkers and the back laid up for diners, although it's all very relaxed and you can eat where you want. The kitchen's experience in places like the Anchor & Hope and Great Queen Street is obvious on their menu which features rustic, earthy British food, of the sort that suits this environment so well. Lunch could be a kipper or tripe and chips; even a reinvented toasted sandwich. Dinner sees a short, no-nonsense menu offering perhaps braised venison or grilled haddock, with daily specials like steak and kidney pie for two.

- **Stockwell** — 177 South Lambeth Rd ✉ SW8 1XP
  ✆ 020 7582 8710 — **www**.cantonarms.com
  ⊖ Stockwell.
- Carte £19/33
  Closed Christmas-New Year, Monday lunch, Sunday dinner and bank holidays – bookings not accepted

PHARMACY 2

Modern British • Design

MAP: 4-J6

The name will induce nods of recognition from those who remember their '90s restaurants: Pharmacy was the place to be for a while, yet was never destined to last. In 2016 Damien Hirst revived the name for the restaurant on the first floor of his Newport Street Gallery, where you'll find much of his work. Like hearing a decent cover version of a much-loved song, the medicinally-themed decoration is at once new yet familiar, although this time everything just seems a little more vivid. When it came to the food, he paired up with Mark Hix, so there is a distinct seasonal feel to the menu. Brunch is an all-day affair and the best dishes are the more British sounding ones. The mini-sized desserts allow you to try two.

■ **Vauxhall** — Newport Street Gallery, Newport St ✉ SE11 6AJ
020 3141 9333 — **www.**pharmacyrestaurant.com
Vauxhall

■ Carte £29/65
Closed Christmas, Sunday dinner and Monday

CAFE SPICE NAMASTE

Indian • Neighbourhood

MAP: 17-O1

Cyrus Todiwala has built up quite a following since opening in this former Victorian magistrate's court back in 1995. In that time he's also cooked for the Queen, grown a little empire and collected an OBE – not bad for someone who only planned on staying in the UK for 5 years. The menu here is extensive and appealing and makes good use of seasonal British ingredients. The Parsee and tandoor dishes are specialities; there are dishes to share; and vegetables get their own special menu. There may be no artificial colouring in the food but they certainly went to town on the room which is awash with bright yellows and blues – even the jaunty waistcoats of the staff catch your eye. Cyrus' wife Pervin oversees the service and she rarely misses a thing.

■ **Whitechapel** — 16 Prescot St. ✉ E1 8AZ
020 7488 9242 — **www.**cafespice.co.uk
Tower Hill

■ Carte £24/35
Closed Saturday lunch, Sunday and bank holidays

J. Sweeney/ The Image Bank/Getty Images

SOUTH-WEST LONDON

Meandering like a silver snake, **The Thames** coils serenely through south-west London, adding definition to the area's much-heralded middle-class enclaves and leafy suburbs. It's the focal point to the annual **university boat race** from **Putney** to **Mortlake,** and it serves as the giant glass pond attractively backing countless bank-side pubs. This area has long been regarded as the cosy bourgeois side of town, though within its postcode prowls the lively and eclectic **Brixton,** whose buzzing street markets and lauded music venues add an urban lustre and vibrant edge.

In most people's minds, though, south-west London finds its true colours in the beautiful terrace view from the top of **Richmond Hill,** as the river bends majestically through the meadows below. Or in the smart **Wimbledon Village,** its independent boutiques ranged prettily along its own hill, with the open spaces of the Common for a back garden. Or, again, in the Italianate architecture that makes **Chiswick House** and grounds a little corner of the Mediterranean close to the Great West Road.

Green space is almost as prolific in this zone as the streets of Victorian and Edwardian villas. **Richmond Park** is the largest royal park in the whole of London and teems with kite flyers, cyclists and deer – though not necessarily in that order. From here, round a southerly bend in the river, delightful grounds surround **Ham House,** which celebrated its 400th birthday in 2010, although not so excessively as during the seventeenth century when it was home to Restoration court life. Head slightly north to **Kew Gardens** whose world famous 300 acres can be viewed from above – the treetop walkway, takes you 60 feet up to offer some breath-taking views. Just across the river from here is another from the historical hitlist: **Syon Park,** which boasts water meadows still grazed by cattle, giving it a distinctly rural aspect. Syon House is considered one of architect Robert Adam's finest works; it certainly appealed to Queen Victoria, who spent much of her young life here. Up the road in bourgeoning Brentford, two unique museums bring in hordes of the curious: the Musical Museum includes a huge Wurlitzer theatre organ (get lucky and watch it being played), while almost next door, the London Museum of Water & Steam shows off all things steamy on a grand scale, including massive beam engines which pumped London's water for over a century.

Hammersmith may be known for its bustling Broadway and flyover, but five minutes' walk from here is the Upper Mall, which has iconic riverside pubs and Kelmscott House, the last home of artistic visionary William Morris: down in the basement and coach house are impressive memorabilia related to his life plus changing exhibitions of designs and drawings. From here, it's just a quick jaunt across **Hammersmith Bridge** and down the arrow-straight Castelnau to the Wetland Centre in Barnes, which for nearly two decades has lured wildlife to within screeching distance of the West End. **Barnes** has always revelled in its village-like identity – it juts up like an isolated peninsula into the Thames and boasts yummy boutiques and well-known restaurants. The Bulls Head pub in Lonsdale Road has featured some of the best jazz in London for over half a century.

In a more easterly direction, the urbanised areas of **Clapham** and **Battersea** have re-established themselves as desirable places to live over the last decade. **Clapham Common** is considered prime southwest London turf, to the extent that its summer music festivals are highly prized. It's ringed by good pubs and restaurants, too. Battersea used to be famous for its funfair, but now the peace pagoda in the park lends it a more serene light. And if you're after serenity on a hot day, then a cool dip in the wondrous **Tooting** Lido is just the thing.

vladyan/iStock

Greater London: South West

(Plan 18)

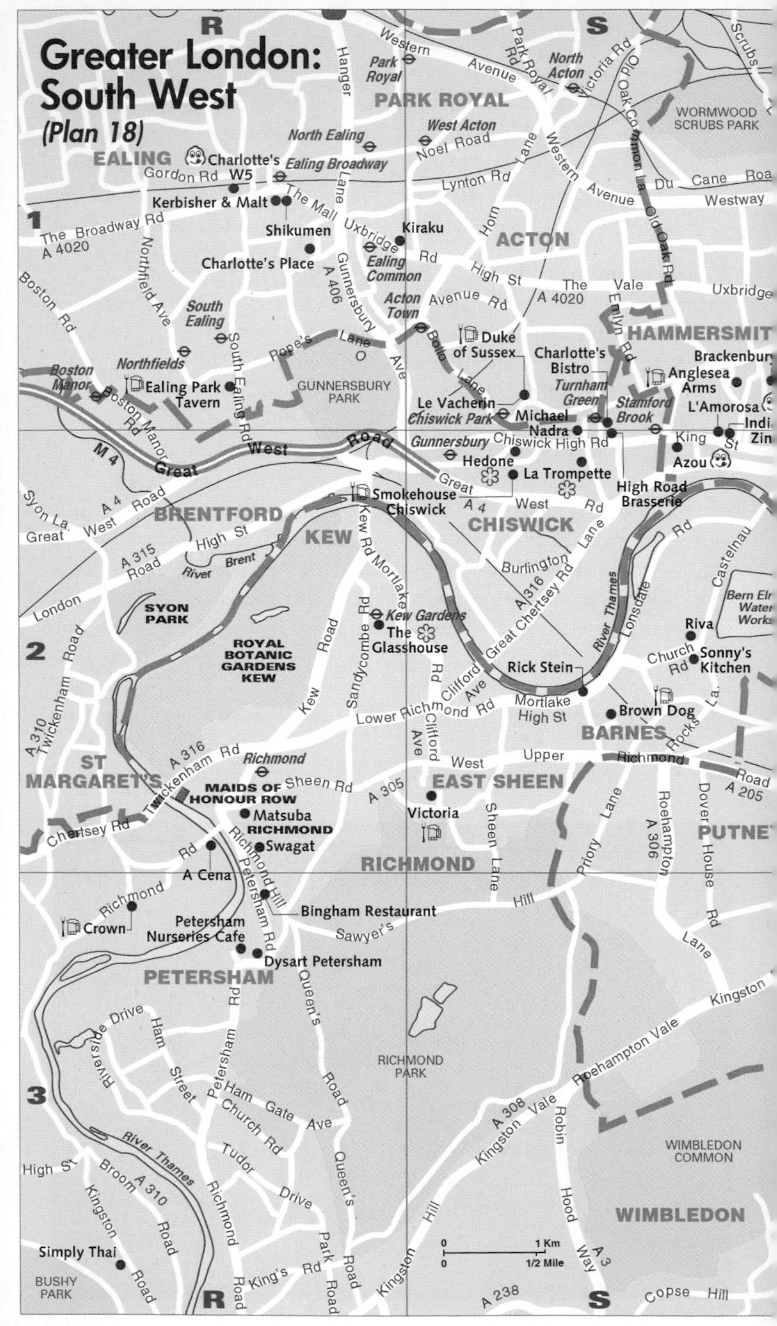

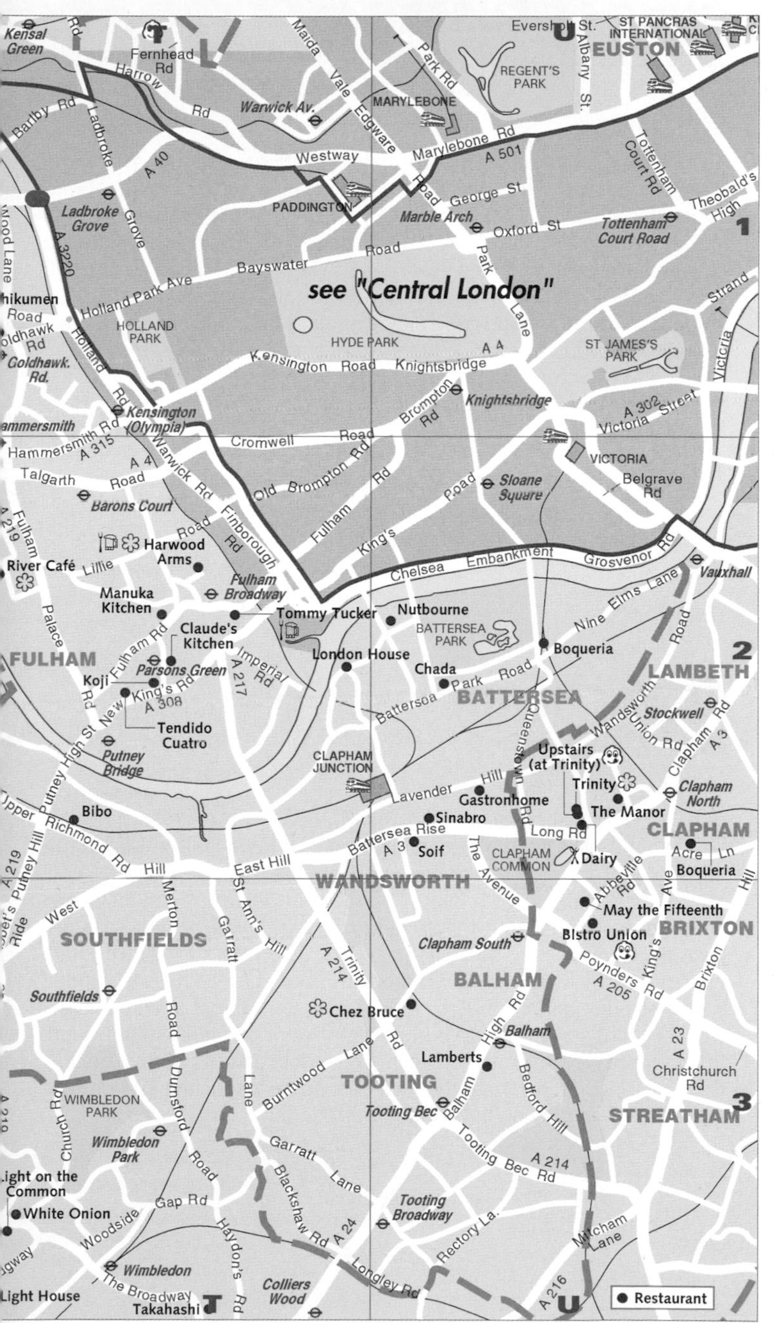

see "Central London"
EUSTON
ST PANCRAS INTERNATIONAL
REGENT'S PARK
MARYLEBONE
PADDINGTON
HYDE PARK
HOLLAND PARK
ST JAMES'S PARK
VICTORIA
BATTERSEA PARK
CLAPHAM JUNCTION
CLAPHAM COMMON
WIMBLEDON PARK
FULHAM
BATTERSEA
LAMBETH
CLAPHAM
WANDSWORTH
SOUTHFIELDS
BRIXTON
BALHAM
TOOTING
STREATHAM
Harwood Arms
River Café
Manuka Kitchen
Tommy Tucker
Nutbourne
Claude's Kitchen
London House
Chada
Boqueria
Koji
Tendido Cuatro
Upstairs (at Trinity)
Trinity
The Manor
Gastronhome
Sinabro
Bibo
Soif
Dairy
Boqueria
May the Fifteenth
Bistro Union
Chez Bruce
Lamberts
Light on the Common
White Onion
Light House
Takahashi
Restaurant
1
2
3

DUKE OF SUSSEX

Mediterranean cuisine • Pub

MAP: 18-S1

The Duke of Sussex may seem like a typical London pub, even from the front bar, but step through into the dining room and you'll find yourself in what was once a variety theatre from the time when this was a classic gin palace, complete with proscenium arch, glass ceiling and chandeliers. If that wasn't unusual enough, you could then find yourself eating cured meats or fabada, as the menu has a strong Spanish influence. Traditionalists can still get their steak pies and treacle tart but it's worth being more adventurous and trying the sardines, the paella and the crema Catalana. This is a fun, enthusiastically run and bustling pub and the kitchen's enthusiasm is palpable. On Mondays it's BYO; Sunday is quiz night.

- **Acton Green** — 75 South Par ✉ W4 5LF
  020 8742 8801 — **www**.realpubs.co.uk
  Chiswick Park.
- Carte £24/31

LE VACHERIN

French • Brasserie

XX A/C

MAP: 18-S1

Le Vacherin calls itself a bistro but, with its brown leather banquette seating, mirrors and belle époque prints, it feels more like a brasserie, and quite a smart one at that. The most important element of the operation is the appealing menu of French classics which rarely changes, largely because they don't need to but also because the regulars wouldn't allow it. The checklist includes oeufs en cocotte, escargots, confit of duck and crème brûlée. Beef is something of a speciality, whether that's the côte de boeuf, the rib-eye or the chateaubriand. Portions are sensible, flavours distinct and ingredients good. The only thing missing in terms of authenticity are some insouciant French staff and a little Piaf playing in the background.

- **Acton Green** — 76-77 South Par ✉ W4 5LF
  020 8742 2121 — **www**.levacherin.com
  Chiswick Park
- Menu £25 (weekdays) - Carte £25/53
  Closed Monday lunch

LAMBERTS

Modern British • Neighbourhood

MAP: 18-U3

Mr Lambert and his eponymous restaurant have succeeded by offering the locals exactly what they want: relaxed surroundings, hospitable service and tasty, seasonal food. The menu is updated each month and small suppliers have been sought out. The cooking is quite British in style and has a satisfying wholesomeness to it; Sunday's ribs of Galloway beef or legs of salt marsh lamb are hugely popular. Equal thought and passion have gone into the commendably priced wine list, which includes some favourites offered in 300ml decanters. Other nice touches include filtered water delivered gratis and velvety truffles brought with the coffee. The owner's enthusiasm has rubbed off on his team, for whom nothing is too much trouble.

- **Balham** — 2 Station Par, Balham High Rd. ✉ SW12 9AZ
  ✆ 020 8675 2233 — **www**.lambertsrestaurant.com
  ⊖ Balham
- Menu £17 (weekday dinner) - Carte £24/39
  Closed 25-27 December, Sunday dinner and Monday

BROWN DOG

Modern British • Pub

MAP: 18-S2

To the untrained eye, this dog can look a little forlorn, but then, if you live on one of the many residential streets adjoining it, what your local looks like from the outside is not going to be your primary concern. Mind you, this is a pub which needn't bother looking too attractive because it's concealed within a maze of terraced houses and passing trade is rare. Inside, the lived-in look gives the place a relaxed and homely feel, especially as it's accompanied by easy-going service executed with a smile. The balanced menu offers a decent range of traditional fare like venison pie or haddock fishcake, all done 'properly'; the dishes are flavoursome and the kitchen uses some lesser cuts like bavette to keep the prices down.

- **Barnes** — 28 Cross St ✉ SW13 0AP
  ✆ 020 8392 2200 — **www**.thebrowndog.co.uk
  ⊖ Barnes Bridge (Rail).
- Carte £20/40
  Closed 25 December

Ⓝ RICK STEIN

Seafood • Fashionable

MAP: 18-S2

This Victorian building was originally the stables and coach house for Barnes Council and sits in a stunning spot beside the Thames, its glass extension offering far-reaching views up and down the river. A suitable spot, perhaps, for a celebrity chef finally dipping his toe into the London dining scene, and it's certainly attracting the crowds with its classic Stein seafood and its lively atmosphere. Seats at the bar, at the counter and out on the terrace are available on a first-come-first-served basis, in part to placate the locals, while the affable staff seem to cope with the numbers well. Dishes from Stein's travels inform the menu, so expect Indonesian seafood curry or hake alla Carina alongside favourites like cod and chips with mushy peas.

- **Barnes** — Tideway Yard, 125 Mortlake High St ✉ SW14 8SN
  ✆ 020 8878 9462 — **www**.rickstein.com
- Menu £25 (weekday lunch) - Carte £26/77
  Closed 25 December - booking advisable

RIVA

Italian • Neighbourhood

MAP: 18-S2

Customer loyalty is the sine qua non of any successful restaurant; those seeking guidance on how to build it should get down to Barnes and learn from Andrea Riva. His secret is to shower so much attention on his regulars that all other diners sit imagining the day when they will be treated in the same way - when he will tell them what he's going to cook especially for them. That could be some milk-fed lamb, game, suckling pig or risotto; all expertly rendered using tip-top, seasonal ingredients. While you wait for graduation, you'll be served by a friendly young female team and still get to enjoy some gutsy, flavoursome food. Andrea is also a keen wine collector so if you can talk oenology it could improve your chances of joining the club.

- **Barnes** — 169 Church Rd. ✉ SW13 9HR
  ✆ 020 8748 0434
- Carte £33/52
  Closed 2 weeks August, Easter, Christmas-New Year, bank holidays and Saturday lunch

SONNY'S KITCHEN ꟾO

Mediterranean cuisine • Neighbourhood

MAP: 18-S2

This longstanding and much-loved neighbourhood favourite is co-owned by industry heavyweights Rebecca Mascarenhas and Philip Howard, who are both Barnes residents. The place has a bright, relaxed feel, with a slight Scandinavian edge; there's a bar and deli at the front and a striking collection of art on the walls from Rebecca's private collection. The menu is appealingly all-encompassing and the kitchen takes good ingredients, treats them with respect and keeps dishes simple and easy to eat. Bread and desserts are highlights and portions surprisingly generous - which is just as well as prices can be steep. Weekends here are especially popular, due to the brunches, roasts and Sunday night BYO, for which no corkage is charged.

- **Barnes** — 94 Church Rd ✉ SW13 0DQ
  ✆ 020 8748 0393 — **www**.sonnyskitchen.co.uk
- Menu £20 (weekday lunch) - Carte £26/38
  Closed 25-26 December, 1 January and bank holiday Mondays

BOQUERIA ꟾO

Spanish • Tapas bar

MAP: 18-U2

For their second branch, the team behind Boqueria decided against creating a straight replica of their original tapas bar in Brixton. Instead, they've made it a much smarter operation all round, which seems appropriate when you consider that this was once a bank - indeed, one of the old vaults is now used as a private dining room and another as a fridge and store room. There are also a few differences with the menu, with some dishes unique to here - the best being the classic Mallorcan dish Coca Mallorquina, and the island sausage Sobrasada. Other gems on the menu are the Catalan salad with salt cod, tuna and anchovies, served with an excellent romesco sauce; and the mini burgers with their pleasing chorizo kick.

- **Battersea** — 278 Queenstown Rd ✉ SW8 4LT
  ✆ 020 7498 8247 — **www**.boqueriatapas.com
  ⊖ Clapham Junction
- Carte £11/19
  Closed 25 December

CHADA

Thai • Friendly

XX A/C **MAP:** 18-U2

Chada opened in Battersea Park Road back in 1986 and has remained a much loved local Thai restaurant ever since. Its longevity is due in no small part to the owner, who runs it with considerable charm and who is always checking to see that her guests have everything they need. The extensive menu has been revamped a little and includes a selection of 'small eats' which represent a version of street food, albeit with a degree of refinement. Worth ordering, along with the classic soups and salads, are the steamed dumplings and the signature dish of crisp pork belly with red curry and ginger. The restaurant is bright, fresh and decorated with eye-catching Thai artwork and artefacts.

- **Battersea** — 208-210 Battersea Park Rd. ✉ SW11 4ND
  ✆ 020 7622 2209 — **www**.chadathai.com
  ⊖ Clapham Junction
- Carte £19/37
  Closed Sunday and bank holidays - (dinner only)

N GASTRONHOME

Modern French • Intimate

X **MAP:** 18-U2

This cool cat is run by two young Frenchmen - one a chef, the other a sommelier - who met whilst working at the Ritz Club and subsequently opened a pop-up together, before settling in budding Battersea. The room is small but cosy and seems to suit the set-up: Christopher proves an engaging host while Damien runs the kitchen with aplomb. Menus take a tour around the L'Hexagone, with dishes changing every two months; those who are happy to hand over the reins to the chef can opt for the 5 course 'Menu Surprise'. Dishes might be regional French in base but they come with a very modern, almost Scandic touch - light and refined, with every ingredient on the plate allowed to shine. The wine list has a French bias and offers prices right across the scale.

- **Battersea** — 59 Lavender Hill ✉ SW11 5QN
  ✆ 020 3417 5639 — **www**.gastronhome.co.uk
- Menu £24 (lunch) - Carte £45/52
  Booking essential at dinner

LONDON HOUSE

Modern British • Neighbourhood

MAP: 18-T2

Neighbourhood restaurants are not a concept generally associated with Gordon Ramsay but with London House he veered from his norm – a fact for which the locals must be truly grateful. It was always a relaxed kind of place but they've listened to their customers and now it's even more so – and all the better for it. The converted 18C coal store is a place of two halves: there's a lively bar where you can watch the sport or catch up with friends over cocktails and snacks, while the restaurant is set over several smart rooms – and there's also a lovely courtyard garden at the back. The seasonal menu is based around the classics and hearty steaks from the grill; some modern touches are added to the dishes and the component ingredients marry well.

- **Battersea** — 7-9 Battersea Sq, Battersea Village ✉ SW11 3RA
  020 7592 8545 — **www**.gordonramsayrestaurants.com/london-house
  Clapham Junction
- Menu £17 (weekday lunch) - Carte £29/47

NUTBOURNE

Modern British • Neighbourhood

MAP: 18-U2

Following the success of The Shed and Rabbit comes a third restaurant from the Gladwin brothers; this time located south of the river. Named after the family farm and vineyards in West Sussex, from where much of the produce comes, Nutbourne brings the essence of the countryside to London, with playful furnishings including the occasional stuffed boar's head. British ingredients drive the eclectic daily menu, with meats cooked on their open fire; dishes like fennel and pork chop with lovage, sunflower seed dressing and crackling; or caramelised quince, meadowsweet sponge, clementine curd, lovage and whey sorbet are hearty, wholesome and full of flavour. The wine list offers a good all-round selection; try one of the family's own bottles.

- **Battersea** — Unit 29, Ransomes Dock, 35-37 Parkgate Rd ✉ SW11 4NP
  020 7350 0555 — **www**.nutbourne-restaurant.com
- Menu £20 (weekday lunch) - Carte £25/45
  Closed Christmas, New Year, Sunday dinner and Monday - booking advisable

SINABRO ¶O

Modern cuisine • Neighbourhood

MAP: 18-U2

'Sinabro' is Korean for 'slowly but surely without noticing', and is a fitting name for Yoann Chevet's restaurant, which has established itself as part of the local dining scene. The main room feels almost kitchen-like, courtesy of a wall of stainless steel; grab a seat at the wooden counter - made by Yoann's father - then sit back and watch the show. Menus evolve constantly and give just a hint of what is to come, with descriptions such as 'salmon, pomegranate, spinach' or 'duck, polenta, peach'. Confidently prepared dishes allow quality ingredients to speak for themselves; they rely largely on classic French flavours but are modern in style. Brunch is served on Saturdays and the Tuesday-Friday lunch 'plat du jour' is particularly good value.

■ **Battersea** — 28 Battersea Rd ✉ SW11 1EE
020 3302 3120 — **www**.sinabro.co.uk
Clapham Junction

■ Carte £30/45
Closed 13-28 August, 25 December, 1 January, Sunday and Monday

SOIF ¶O

French • Neighbourhood

MAP: 18-U2

Wholesome food, an appealingly louche look and a thoughtfully compiled wine list; fair prices, a great atmosphere and delightfully natural service: there's a lot to love about this busy bistro-cum-wine-bar. Cooking is French but with regular excursions across the border into Italy, so you might find moules marinières next to burrata in the 'small plates' section, and duck rillettes as well as salame under 'charcuterie'. It comes as no surprise to find that drinks are given equal billing with the food chez Soif - in fact this restaurant doubles as a wine shop: the predominantly French list includes plenty of natural wines from artisan winemakers and there are 20 wines to choose from at shop prices on what are known as Happy Mondays.

■ **Battersea** — 27 Battersea Rise ✉ SW11 1HG
020 7223 1112 — **www**.soif.co
Clapham Junction

■ Menu £20 (weekday lunch) - Carte £29/40
Closed Christmas, New Year, Sunday dinner, Monday lunch and bank holidays - booking essential at dinner

BOQUERIA

Spanish • Tapas bar

MAP: 18-U2

Named after - and inspired by - Barcelona's famous food market, this contemporary tapas bar is a welcome addition to the neighbourhood and has quickly established a local fan-base. The menu doubles as a place mat and is a mix of recognisable classics and more adventurous offerings; it is also supplemented by specials on the blackboard. As everyone involved appears to hail from Andalucía, it makes sense to kick off with a glass of sherry. The Ibérico hams are in excellent order, the lamb medallions are full of flavour and be sure to save room for a particularly good crema Catalana. It's worth sitting at the counter as the main dining area at the back lacks a little personality. Their café next door serves coffee and churros.

■ **Brixton** — 192 Acre Ln. ✉ SW2 5UL
020 7733 4408 — **www**.boqueriatapas.com
Clapham North

■ Carte £12/25
Closed 24-27 December and 1 January - (dinner only and lunch Saturday-Sunday)

NANBAN

Japanese • Simple

MAP: 17-N2

Back in 2011, American Tim Anderson was crowned the youngest winner of BBC's MasterChef. Several years and several pop-ups later, he is now the proud owner of this ramen-bar-cum-izakaya, tucked away at the back of Brixton Market. A concrete floor and plain walls give the place an industrial feel, while cookery books and a great display of sake and shochu add colour (there's also a rather nice collection of Japanese craft beers). The intoxicating smell of chicken stock jolts the olfactory receptors into action; staff are happy to make recommendations but be aware that dishes arrive in no particular order unless you specifically ask. Food is fresh and full of flavour; the spicy, super-crispy chicken karaage will have you coming back for more.

■ **Brixton** — 426 Coldharbour Ln ✉ SW9 8LF
020 7346 0098 — **www**.nanban.co.uk
Brixton

■ Carte £19/29
Closed 25 December and Monday lunch

CHARLOTTE'S BISTRO

Modern cuisine • Neighbourhood

MAP: 18-S1

Unlike some desirable London neighbourhoods, Chiswick has always had plenty of restaurants, so locals never feel the need to venture too far from home for dinner. This little sister to nearby Ealing's Charlotte's Place provides them with another pleasantly unpretentious option. A large bar takes up most of the front section and then it's a few steps up to the bright dining room with a glass roof. The menu changes regularly and has a European accent, with dishes such as crab and celeriac tian, cod brandade, pan-fried halloumi, rolled leg of lamb and fishcakes. There's also a nice little cheese menu. Wines are listed by character and include bottles from some small producers. Service and prices are equally friendly.

- **Chiswick** — 6 Turnham Green Terr W4 1QP
  020 8742 3590 — **www**.charlottes.co.uk
  Turnham Green
- Menu £25/35
  Booking advisable

HIGH ROAD BRASSERIE

French • Fashionable

MAP: 18-S2

It's usually so busy you'll have trouble getting in the door – quite literally, sometimes, as the entrance is often crowded with evening drinkers or lunchtime pushchairs. This modern take on a brasserie certainly has the look, with its mirrors, panelling and art deco lighting; turn right for the more comfy seating. Staff are used to being busy and get the job done, although without much time for pleasantries. What is surprising is that, despite the volume of customers, the kitchen is able to deliver a good standard of accurately cooked classics including steak frites, duck confit, grilled lobster or whole sea bass, along with salads and sandwiches. The bill can rise quickly as sides are required, but there's a good value daytime menu.

- **Chiswick** — High Road House Hotel, 162 Chiswick High Rd. W4 1PR
  020 8742 7474 — **www**.highroadhouse.co.uk
  Turnham Green
- Carte £20/36
  Booking essential

HEDONE ✿

Modern cuisine • Design

XX A/C MAP: 18-S2

Michelin

FIRST COURSE: Devon crab with velvet crab consommé, hazelnut mayonnaise and Granny Smith apple. • Sweetbreads with morels and wild garlic.

MAIN COURSE: Hare à la royale. • Sea bass with textures of cauliflower and coconut.

DESSERT: Vanilla millefeuille with balsamic vinegar. • Mandarin sorbet with saffron and citrus.

Mikael Jonsson's restaurant continues to flourish but this former lawyer and food blogger turned chef is not one for complacency, so it also continues to evolve. Surprise menus of either 7 or 10 courses come with wine pairings; the content of these menus is governed by what ingredients are in their prime, and it is this passion for seeking out the best seasonal produce - be it sea bass, suckling pig or salt marsh lamb - which underpins the superlative new Nordic cooking. Watching the chefs prepare every dish from scratch in the big open kitchen, one can see the attention to detail involved and the respect with which the ingredients are treated. This results in refined, well-balanced and immeasurably satisfying dishes which show a good understanding of technique. Fish plays a key role, seasoning is judicious, and the sourdough is some of the finest you'll find in the city. The atmosphere is busy yet relaxed and service from the young team is smooth and evenly paced.

■ **Chiswick** — 301-303 Chiswick High Rd ✉ W4 4HH
✆ 020 8747 0377 — **www**.hedonerestaurant.com
⊖ Chiswick Park

■ Menu £95/135
Closed 2 weeks summer, 2 weeks Christmas-New Year, Sunday and Monday - booking essential - (dinner only and lunch Friday-Saturday) - (surprise menu only)

MICHAEL NADRA

Modern cuisine • Neighbourhood

MAP: 18-S1/2

Half way down a residential street in Chiswick sits this intimate little restaurant which has always proved a very good fit for the area. The cooking is bright, contemporary and at times quite elaborate; the influences are kept largely within Europe and the quality of the ingredients is good. The chef-owner, who must spend hours on the North Circular travelling between this restaurant and his other one in Primrose Hill, understands the importance of getting the pricing right – his six course tasting menu is not only a good way to experience the kitchen's skill and ambition but is also sensibly priced, especially when accompanied by the chosen wines. Tables are set quite close together which adds to the warm neighbourhood feel of the place.

- **Chiswick** — 6-8 Elliott Rd W4 1PE
  020 8742 0766 — **www**.restaurant-michaelnadra.co.uk
  Turnham Green
- Menu £28/39
  Closed 24-28 December, 1 January and Sunday dinner

SMOKEHOUSE CHISWICK

Traditional British • Neighbourhood

MAP: 18-S2

The success of the first Smokehouse in Canonbury meant a second was inevitable, although the owners were sensible enough to avoid making a carbon copy. The menu at this sizeable pub, which has a lovely rear garden, still centres around barbeque but it's not quite as 'in your face' as Islington - residents of Chiswick are perhaps a little more demure. The Belted Galloway burgers with pulled pork fly out of the kitchen but the winning dish is the short rib Bourguignon with creamy mash. The kitchen frequently cook a whole beast, like a Gloucester Old Spot and then make terrines and potted meats, hams and charcuterie. There are lighter dishes on offer and, if you make it to dessert, they do a mean rum and raisin rice pudding.

- **Chiswick** — 12 Sutton Ln North W4 4LD
  020 3819 6066 — **www**.smokehousechiswick.co.uk
  Chiswick Park.
- Carte £26/34
  Dinner only and lunch Friday to Sunday

LA TROMPETTE ✿

Modern British • Neighbourhood

XX · MAP: 18-S2

Michelin

FIRST COURSE: Raw bream, bonito, shimeji, shiso cress and English wasabi. • Agnolotti of suckling pig with peas, radish and aged parmesan.

MAIN COURSE: Crisp suckling pig shoulder, creamed polenta, grapes, cavolo nero and chilli. • Roast Welsh lamb with glazed aubergine, green tomatoes and Padrón peppers.

DESSERT: Banana soufflé with gingerbread and passion fruit ice cream. • Warm custard tart with yoghurt ice cream and roast cherries.

One of the reasons for the success of La Trompette is that it has always looked after its customers: when the shop next door was bought and the restaurant expanded, the owners didn't add more tables, they merely used the extra room to add more space between the existing ones. The very pleasant service team also ensure that customers keep returning – they manage the feat of making service seem effortless and the diners do their bit by creating a warm, congenial atmosphere. These days there is a greater distinction between the lunch and dinner menus. Lunch is all about great value; dishes are quite simple but just as skilfully prepared and the kitchen uses lesser known cuts and fewer luxury ingredients. At dinner the mackerel is replaced by turbot and the cooking is a tad more ambitious, but it's never over-elaborate. Another reason for La Trompette's continued success is that, despite the very accomplished cooking, it never gives the impression that it would rather be in Mayfair – it suits Chiswick and the locals clearly like having it.

- **Chiswick** — 5-7 Devonshire Rd ✉ W4 2EU
  ✆ 020 8747 1836 — **www.**latrompette.co.uk
  ⊖ Turnham Green
- Menu £35 (weekday lunch)/55
  Closed 24-26 December and 1 January - booking essential

BISTRO UNION

Modern British • Neighbourhood

MAP: 18-U3

One look at the menu and it's pretty clear that this sister to Trinity understands what it is you need to do if you want to be considered a proper neighbourhood restaurant: it does brunch every day, can do a light lunch, has an all-day children's menu and offers an appealing set dinner on a Sunday night to encourage everyone out of their houses for one last weekend hurrah. The main menu itself is also flexible, so you can drop in for some Cornish mussels or order roast chicken for two. If you are pushing the boat out, it's worth eschewing the starters in favour of the 'snacks' which could include anchovy toast or crisp sweetbreads. The appeal of the place is further enhanced by its warm atmosphere and eager, sweet-natured staff.

- **Clapham Common** — 40 Abbeville Rd ✉ SW4 9NG
  020 7042 6400 — **www**.bistrounion.co.uk
  Clapham South
- Menu £26 (weekday dinner) - Carte £25/47
  Closed 24-27 December - booking advisable

DAIRY

Creative British • Rustic

MAP: 18-U2

London's markets supplied much of the furniture and crockery, and the higgledy-piggledy look of this fun, lively restaurant adds to its charm. What one doesn't expect to find in this environment is food that is so innovative. The chef-owner's cooking is informed by his travels and his experience gleaned in some famous kitchens. His menu is driven by the ingredients - they grow their own herbs and some fruit and veg on the rooftop, and have three beehives - and all the modern techniques such as pickling and fermenting are there. The food is earthy, original and very labour intensive, but it's also easy to eat - the set menu, with some unusual drinks pairings, is the best option. It's also worth trying the pintxos bar next door.

- **Clapham Common** — 15 The Pavement ✉ SW4 0HY
  020 7622 4165 — **www**.the-dairy.co.uk
  Clapham Common
- Menu £25 (weekday lunch) - Carte £22/33
  Closed Christmas, Sunday dinner, Monday and lunch Tuesday - booking essential at dinner

THE MANOR

Creative British • Neighbourhood

MAP: 18-U2

Those who like the Dairy down the road will like The Manor - not only do they share the same ownership but they also share the same menu format and style of cuisine. It is slightly bigger here and, with its distressed looks and informal yet informed service from a delightful young team, it perfectly captures the zeitgeist. The cooking is heavily influenced by modern Scandic kitchens and first-timers should go for the tasting menu. The dishes show plenty of innovation, and modern techniques - from smoking and charring to pickling and fermenting - are used to good effect. The dishes are not just artfully presented but are surprisingly robust in flavour and the contrast in textures is one aspect that's particularly memorable.

- **Clapham Common** — 148 Clapham Manor St ✉ SW4 6BX
  ✆ 020 7720 4662 — **www**.themanorclapham.co.uk
  ⊖ Clapham Common
- Menu £30 - Carte £20/28
  Closed 21-27 December, 1 January, Sunday dinner, Tuesday lunch and Monday

MAY THE FIFTEENTH

Mediterranean cuisine • Rustic

MAP: 18-U3

It might have seemed like an odd decision to change the name when everyone knew this neighbourhood bistro as Abbeville Kitchen, but when the head chef took over he wanted to make it his own and so named it after the day he signed the forms. Gone too is the Gallic feel to the place - a lick of paint inside and out now makes you feel you're in Brighton rather than Brittany. At least the food hasn't changed - it remains gutsy and wholesome and the daily changing menu offers the option of ordering small tasting plates or a more traditional three-courser. The choice is varied - it's not often you see empanadas and Swaledale lamb on the same menu - and the prices are fair. The charcuterie boards stand out, as do dishes for two like roast chicken.

- **Clapham Common** — 47 Abbeville Rd ✉ SW4 9JX
  ✆ 020 8772 1110 — **www**.maythe15th.com
  ⊖ Clapham South
- Menu £20 (weekday lunch) - Carte £23/43
  Closed 24-27 and 1 January - bookings advisable at dinner - (dinner only and lunch Friday-Sunday)

TRINITY ✿

Modern cuisine • *Fashionable*

XX 🍽 A/C ✿ **MAP:** 18-U2

Michelin

FIRST COURSE: Tuna tartare with crab salad, avocado and pickled cucumber. • Tartare of Angus beef with smoked bone marrow, pickled mushrooms and caviar.

MAIN COURSE: Pot-roast Anjou pigeon with salt-baked celeriac and red wine salsify. • Confit wild sea trout with tomato butter sauce, salmon roe and sea kale.

DESSERT: Salted caramel custard tart. • Tarte Tatin with prune and Armagnac ice cream.

Loyalty is a two-way street and Adam Byatt's Trinity is one of those wise old neighbourhood restaurants which realised that you have to look after your regulars if you want them to keep coming back. So, unlike dining at many a West End restaurant, here you won't be encouraged to get your coat as soon as you swallow your last mouthful. The kitchen is classically trained but not hamstrung by tradition; dishes are refreshingly free from extraneous elements or unnecessary decorative flourishes - and the focus remains firmly on the primary ingredient, whether that's a perfectly cooked piece of sea bass or a succulent Iberico pork chop. This confidence extends to the desserts too - even those averse to sharing should consider ordering the tarte Tatin with prune and Armagnac ice cream for two. Service is personable and keen and the restaurant is bright and contemporary, with windows into the kitchen and out onto the small terrace. Trinity and Clapham Old Town are a perfect fit.

■ **Clapham Common** — 4 The Polygon ✉ SW4 0JG
✆ 020 7622 1199 — **www**.trinityrestaurant.co.uk
⊖ Clapham Common

■ Menu £39 (lunch) - Carte £47/63
Closed 24-30 December and 1-2 January

UPSTAIRS (AT TRINITY)

Modern British • Fashionable

MAP: 18-U2

When Adam Byatt gave his Trinity restaurant its most recent makeover he also created a separate operation upstairs. It has a more relaxed feel than downstairs, with the open-plan kitchen being the focus of the room. The food is all about sharing - about five dishes between two should be enough but as everything sounds so appealing and the prices are so reasonable, you'll be tempted to over-order. The seasonal British ingredients are used to good effect to create visually appealing dishes; they come with a Mediterranean bias and certainly deliver on flavour - be sure to end with the salted caramel tart. Wine plays a big part with the 'by the glass' selection showcasing some lesser-known names and producers.

- **Clapham Common** — 4 The Polygon ✉ SW4 0JG
  ✆ 020 3745 7227 — **www**.trinityrestaurant.co.uk
  ⊖ Clapham Common
- Carte £21/37
  Closed 24-30 December, 1-2 January, Sunday and Monday - (dinner only)

CHARLOTTE'S PLACE

Modern cuisine • Bistro

MAP: 18-R1

It's been a sweet shop, a transport café and a private club but it really found its niche as an honest and warmly run local restaurant. The ground floor offers views over the Common so is more popular at lunch; downstairs is ideal for couples who only have eyes for each other. The à la carte offers ample choice and the cooking is largely British, with smoked fish, traditional Sunday lunches and homely puddings done well; there are also one or two Mediterranean influences and the beef onglet enjoys a constant presence. There is a small cover charge but it does pay for bread and unlimited amounts of filtered water, rather than being an accountant's wheeze for squeezing more money out of the customers.

- **Ealing** — 16 St Matthew's Rd ✉ W5 3JT
  ✆ 020 8567 7541 — **www**.charlottes.co.uk
  ⊖ Ealing Common
- Menu £23/39
  Closed 26 December and 1 January

CHARLOTTE'S W5

Modern cuisine • Neighbourhood

MAP: 18-R1

This bright, buzzy restaurant occupies a previously derelict stable block and opened in 2016 to coincide with the large development of apartments which surrounds it. It's all about flexibility - you can pop in for brunch, a drink, a snack or a full meal and it stays open all day. It also manages that rare trick of being just as suited to couples on dates as it is to family gatherings. The other clever aspect is the modern European menu: every dish is available in a choice of three sizes to make sharing easier, whatever your number. Similarly, every bottle of wine is also offered by the glass or carafe. Add in a great drinks list, a charming service team and sensible prices - and there's little wonder it's proving so popular.

- **Ealing** — Dickens Yard, Longfield Ave ✉ W5 2UQ
  ✆ 020 3771 8722 — **www**.charlottes.co.uk
  ⊖ Ealing Broadway
- Menu £15 - Carte £28/32

KERBISHER & MALT

Fish and chips • Simple

MAP: 18-R1

There may have been a revolution in British cooking over the last two decades, but for many people, especially tourists, fish and chips will always be our national dish. Restaurants have been doing decent versions for years but Kerbisher & Malt represents a new wave of ethical fish and chip shops that are raising this classic dish to new heights. The fish here is fresh, sustainably sourced and cooked to order in rapeseed oil (which is then turned into biofuel); chips are made from British spuds and are fried separately; and all packaging is biodegradable. Choose your fish and a side order of thick 'Yorkshire caviar' or pickled onion rings, along with a pot of great tartare sauce. There's another branch in Hammersmith.

- **Ealing** — 53 New Broadway ✉ W5 5AH
  ✆ 020 8840 4418 — **www**.kerbisher.co.uk
  ⊖ Ealing Broadway
- Carte approx. £16
  Closed Christmas and New Year

KIRAKU

Japanese • Friendly

MAP: 18-R1

Ayumi and Erica became so frustrated with the lack of a decent local Japanese restaurant that they decided to open one themselves; and now it is not just the bourgeoning Japanese community who flock to this cute little place. It's modestly styled and brightly lit, but service is very charming. Look out for the daily changing dishes on the blackboard. Zensai, or starters, include the popular Agedashi dofu; these can then be followed by assorted skewers, noodles and rice dishes. Fish is purchased daily and their sushi now displays a more modern touch; Bara Chirashi is the house speciality. Be sure to end with matcha ice cream or green tea sponge cake. The restaurant's name means 'relax and enjoy' and it's hard not to.

- **Ealing** — 8 Station Par, Uxbridge Rd. ✉ W5 3LD
  020 8992 2848 — **www**.kiraku.co.uk
  Ealing Common
- Carte £14/40
  Closed Christmas-New Year

SHIKUMEN

Chinese • Brasserie

MAP: 18-R1

Unlike the branch in Shepherd's Bush, this Shikumen specialises exclusively in dim sum - at both lunch and dinner. The menu offers around 50 choices: you can either choose from the various sections or just go for one of the nicely balanced set menus. The star of the show is the roast pork cheung fun, although the seafood congee is also worth ordering; the rice pots, like sea bass with tofu, ensure that you won't leave hungry. Everyone should try traditional Cantonese afternoon tea at least once and here you'll find a good selection of teas to go with the dim sum and the sweet treats. The restaurant isn't quite as big as its sister but it too is located within a corporate-minded hotel and decorated in a dark and sultry style.

- **Ealing** — 26-42 Bond St ✉ W5 5AA
  020 8567 2770 — **www**.shikumen.co.uk
  Ealing Broadway
- Carte £20/50

VICTORIA

Modern British • Pub

MAP: 18-S2

Chef-owner Paul Merrett is something of a food hero in these parts: he gives cookery classes at the school next door and the ethos of his pub is, first and foremost, to serve the local community. It has a pleasant lived-in feel, with the nooks and crannies of the bars usually busy with loungers and drinkers; if you're here to eat you're better off heading for the conservatory, which overlooks their terrace. The appealing menu offers a good range of dishes and comes with a distinct Mediterranean slant, with Middle Eastern influences never far away. You can start with chickpea and basil hummus, then move on to chargrilled lemon chicken or falafel or, if you prefer something simpler, there's a well-priced selection of burgers available.

- **East Sheen** — 10 West Temple Sheen ✉ SW14 7RT
  ☎ 020 8876 4238 — **www**.thevictoria.net
  ⊖ Mortlake (Rail).
- Carte £27/47

CLAUDE'S KITCHEN

Modern cuisine • Bistro

MAP: 18-T2

The eponymous Claude has created two little operations within one converted Victorian pub. On the ground floor is 'Amuse Bouche', a champagne bar where the bubbles are sold at competitive prices, along with assorted boards of cheese or cured meats. Upstairs is a small and intimate dining room where you'll find a concise à la carte menu as well as a tasting menu with matching wines. Everything is homemade here, including the terrific bread, and the food is colourful, fresh and tasty, although Claude does have the occasional urge to drop in one or two challenging flavour combinations. Come before 7pm and the menu is available at a reduced – great value – price. Do try the delicious pomme 'Daniele' as a side – and leave room for pudding too!

- **Fulham** — 51 Parsons Green Ln ✉ SW6 4JA
  ☎ 020 3813 3223 — **www**.amusebouchelondon.com
  ⊖ Parsons Green.
- Menu £20 - Carte £29/39
  Closed Sunday - booking essential - (dinner only)

HARWOOD ARMS ✿

Modern British • Pub

MAP: 18-T2

Harwood Arms

FIRST COURSE: Cornish crab and herb muffin. • Berkshire rabbit with chestnuts, pear and ceps.

MAIN COURSE: Braised shoulder of venison, smoked bone marrow tart and beets. • Jowl of pork with bacon marmalade, cider-pickled cabbage and apple.

DESSERT: Lemon curd doughnuts with Earl Grey cream. • Strawberry and camomile trifle with lemon verbena.

It may be a very handsome pub in a smart postcode and have all its tables laid up for dining but there's nothing stuck-up or snooty about this place - in fact, the only thing that's superior is the cooking. It's British to its core, with its reassuringly concise, daily changing menu resolutely governed by our country's own seasonal produce. Cornish fish, Herdwick lamb, Cumbrian chicken and Wiltshire pork can all feature and game is a real strength of the kitchen whether it's rabbit, grouse or Hampshire muntjac. Dishes have real depth and flavours are bold and satisfying. Service is smooth and assured and comes courtesy of a young yet experienced team and the well-chosen wine list offers a particularly good choice of mature claret. If you're sitting beneath the skylight then look up and you'll spot the rooftop vegetable and herb 'garden'. As this is still a pub, you can just pop in for a drink at the bar but if you do then be sure to order some of the great bar snacks like game rissoles or a venison scotch egg.

- **Fulham** — Walham Grove ✉ SW6 1QP
  ☎ 020 7386 1847 — **www**.harwoodarms.com
  ⊖ Fulham Broadway.
- Menu £36/43
  Closed 24-27 December, 1 January and Monday lunch except bank holidays - booking essential

KOJI

Japanese • Wine bar

MAP: 18-T2

For 30 years this was called Mao Tai and served Chinese cooking; owner Mark Barnett decided to change it into his own version of a Japanese izakaya a few years ago - and it's a decision which has proved successful given the number of customers it welcomes through its doors. The front section is all bar, with a large list of cocktails and wines; at the back is a sushi counter - the best place to sit - as well as a dining area with lots of natural light and a contemporary look. The menu mixes the classic and the more modern, with tempura and dishes from the robata grill particularly popular. Food is full of flavour and the kitchen clearly know their craft, while the sweet front of house staff prove very helpful should you need guidance.

- **Fulham** — 58 New King's Rd ✉ SW6 4LS
  020 7731 2520 — **www**.koji.restaurant
  Parsons Green
- Carte £40/65
  Closed 24-26 December and Monday

MANUKA KITCHEN

Modern cuisine • Rustic

MAP: 18-T2

A chef and an ex hotel manager chanced upon this former Italian restaurant and thought it the perfect spot for a venture of their own. Using only their own funds, they subsequently created this simply furnished little place, which they run with great enthusiasm. Their aim is to provide wholesome food at keen prices without compromising on the quality of the ingredients. Tyler, the chef, is from New Zealand, as is Manuka honey which is purported to have magical powers. His menu is appealing in its variety and dishes come with plenty of punch; the crispy squid is proving a very popular choice, as is the bolognese which uses Wagyu beef. Honey does also make an occasional appearance - perhaps with the cheese or in a crème brûlée.

- **Fulham** — 510 Fulham Rd ✉ SW6 5NJ
  020 7736 7588 — **www**.manukakitchen.com
  Fulham Broadway
- Menu £15 (weekday lunch) - Carte £26/37
  Closed 25-26 December, Sunday dinner and Monday lunch

TENDIDO CUATRO

Spanish • Neighbourhood

MAP: 18-T2

Any resemblance to their other restaurant in Old Brompton Road is entirely intentional: here too the front panels burst open in summer to reveal a warm interior where vivid colours are used with wild abandon. The main difference is that, along with tapas, the speciality is the Valencian classic, paella. Using bomba rice, the choice varies from seafood to quail and chorizo; vegetarian to cuttlefish ink. They are designed for two but that assumes a more than eager appetite, especially if you've had a couple of small dishes as a run-up. The tapas is nicely varied, from refreshing baby anchovies to crisp pig's ears. Service is spirited and the room comes alive later in the evening as the locals return from work and wander over.

- **Fulham** — 108-110 New Kings Rd ✉ SW6 4LY
  ✆ 020 7371 5147 — **www**.cambiodetercio.co.uk
  ⊖ Parsons Green
- Menu £30 (lunch and early dinner) - Carte £16/41
  Closed 2 weeks Christmas

TOMMY TUCKER

Traditional British • Pub

MAP: 18-T2

Locals will remember this as The Pelican, a relatively quiet pub that would get overwhelmed whenever Chelsea were playing at home. The people behind Claude's Kitchen in nearby Parsons Green then gave it a head-to-toe revamp and the TT, as they call it, is now the sort of place everyone would want on their street. The black façade doesn't really give the right impression because inside it's bright and open-plan – the nicest part is the 'Music Room' with its sheet music wallpaper. The menu is unstructured and divided under headings of 'meat', 'fish' and 'fruit and veg', with asterisks marking the dishes available as starters. The food is rustic, earthy and satisfying and the service is thoughtful and sincere.

- **Fulham** — 22 Waterford Rd ✉ SW6 2DR
  ✆ 020 7736 1023 — **www**.thetommytucker.com
  ⊖ Fulham Broadway.
- Carte £19/39

L'AMOROSA

Italian • Neighbourhood

MAP: 18-S1

Andy Needham's name and reputation were established when he was head chef at Zafferano. He now has his own place and his considerable experience is clear to see. This is the sort of relaxed Italian restaurant we'd all like to have at the end of our street. The cooking provides a lesson in sincerity and the importance of trusting in the quality of the ingredients; the homemade pasta is always a delight and the regulars, of whom they are many already, will no doubt never allow the tiramisu to be removed from the menu. The restaurant is bright and sunny, with the best seats being those on the raised floor at the back; service is well-meaning; prices are more than fair; and the atmosphere is relaxed and unhurried.

- **Hammersmith** — 278 King St ✉ W6 0SP
  ✆ 020 8563 0300 — **www**.lamorosa.co.uk
  ⊖ Ravenscourt Park
- Menu £17 (weekday lunch) - Carte £25/39
  Closed 1 week August, 1 week Christmas, Sunday dinner, Monday and bank holidays

ANGLESEA ARMS

Modern British • Neighbourhood

MAP: 18-S1

The Anglesea Arms was one of the daddies of the gastropub movement, and for several decades has given those who live nearby an excuse never to venture too far for dinner; with its warm, laid-back atmosphere, friendly young staff - and food that's a cut above your usual pub fodder. The nicely seasonal menu gives the impression that it's written by a Brit who occasionally holidays on the Med - there are some suitably robust dishes but the kitchen is also capable of displaying a pleasing lightness of touch. Plates are never overly crowded with ingredients and modern versions of old-school desserts like rice pudding and apple crumble certainly hit the spot. The pub also offers a regularly changing selection of regional real ales.

- **Hammersmith** — 35 Wingate Rd ✉ W6 0UR
  ✆ 020 8749 1291 — **www**.angleseaarmspub.co.uk
  ⊖ Ravenscourt Park
- Carte £24/36
  Closed 24-26 December

AZOU

North African • Neighbourhood

MAP: 18-S2

You'll probably walk past the first time and not notice this unassuming little place but, once visited, you won't walk past again. Inside is all silks, lanterns and rugs but it is also very personally run; the owner will often pop out from his kitchen to offer guidance – and his advice is well worth listening to. The cooking skips across North African countries – order some Algerian olives while you choose from the wide choice of main courses. Understandably, most of the regulars come here for a tajine, especially the Constantine with its tender lamb and triple-steamed couscous. Highlights to start include the terrific baba ganoush with homemade bread and fresh briouat. It's the perfect food to share as the dishes come in large portions.

- **Hammersmith** — 375 King St W6 9NJ
  020 8563 7266 — **www.**azou.co.uk
  Stamford Brook
- Carte £21/38
  Closed 1 January and 25 December - booking essential - (dinner only)

BRACKENBURY

Mediterranean cuisine • Neighbourhood

MAP: 18-S1

The much-loved Brackenbury may have taken on slightly different guises over the years but it has always been the quintessential neighbourhood spot and that hasn't changed – you get the sense that most of the customers are locals who've walked here and that adds to the cosy, hassle-free and convivial atmosphere. When it comes to the cooking, chef-owner Humphrey Fletcher looks to Italy, then France and then the Med for inspiration; his dishes are easy to eat and satisfying, the flavours marry well and the accompanying wine list may be relatively short but is nicely balanced and sensibly priced. The front section of the restaurant is a little more relaxed; the other rooms are slightly more formally dressed.

- **Hammersmith** — 129 - 131 Brackenbury Rd W6 0BQ
  020 8741 4928 — **www.**brackenburyrestaurant.co.uk
  Ravenscourt Park
- Menu £16 (weekday lunch) - Carte £23/47
  Closed Christmas, New Year, Easter, August bank holiday, Sunday and Monday

INDIAN ZING

Indian • Neighbourhood

MAP: 18-S2

The menu tells you all you need to know: this is not your typical high street Indian restaurant. Chef-owner Manoj Vasaikar seeks inspiration from across the country and his cooking cleverly balances the traditional with the more contemporary. Evident care goes into the preparation of the fragrant dishes, which deliver many layers of flavours – lamb dishes are particularly good, as are the various breads. However, you'll see many customers giving the menu no more than a cursory glance – that's because they're regulars who know what they want before they get here, and is the reason why Karwari fish curry, lamb rogan josh and the thalis can never be taken off the menu. Service is courteous and unhurried and the room judiciously lit.

- **Hammersmith** — 236 King St. ✉ W6 0RF
  ✆ 020 8748 5959 — **www**.indianzing.co.uk
  ⊖ Ravenscourt Park
- Menu £14/27 - Carte £21/44

BIBO

Italian • Bistro

MAP: 18-T2

Few restaurateurs are as adept as Rebecca Mascarenhas in creating great neighbourhood restaurants and, with Bibo, she hit the bullseye once again. This fun Italian restaurant has all the right component parts, from an appealing environment and clued-up service to food that's well-priced and effortlessly easy to enjoy. It also ticks the accessibility box as it's somewhere you can just pop into for a drink and a plate of great nibbles. The same appealing menu is served at lunch and dinner, the British and imported Italian produce is top notch and dishes are refreshingly uncomplicated yet full of flavour. The Latin name means 'to drink', so it's no surprise that the wholly Italian wine list is also worth exploring.

- **Putney** — 146 Upper Richmond Rd ✉ SW15 2SW
  ✆ 020 8780 0592 — **www**.biborestaurant.com
  ⊖ East Putney
- Menu £17 (lunch) - Carte £30/38
  Closed 25-26 December, Sunday dinner, Monday and bank holidays

RIVER CAFÉ ✿

Italian • Fashionable

MAP: 18-T2

River Cafe

FIRST COURSE: Calamari ai ferri. • Sea bass carpaccio with marigold tomatoes, golden oregano and chilli.

MAIN COURSE: Wood-roasted Dover sole with marjoram, lemon and artichoke alla Romana. • Poached veal shin with pancetta, fresh horseradish, Swiss chard and peas.

DESSERT: Chocolate Nemesis. • Summer pudding with valpolicella.

It's more than thirty years since the River Café opened but the ethos here is still very much the same, with superlative ingredients at the centre of everything they do. The team who work here seem like one big happy family, with servers who welcome you as if into their own home and all the chefs on show in what must be one of the calmest kitchens in London. The menu is written anew for each service and bursting with authentic Italian flavours; there's a vigour and honesty to the cooking and dishes like wood-roasted Anjou pigeon with speck, celeriac and watercress, or veal shin slow-cooked in chardonnay, sage and garlic are made with top-class produce and come in hearty, rustic portions. Pasta is a must-have, as is the perennial Chocolate Nemesis; one bite of the latter and you'll understand why it never comes off the menu. This iconic restaurant's location on the banks of the Thames is as much part of the experience as the cooking – ask for a seat on the riverside terrace, or failing that, sit by the window.

- **Hammersmith** — Thames Wharf, Rainville Rd ✉ W6 9HA
  ✆ 020 7386 4200 — **www**.rivercafe.co.uk
  ⊖ Barons Court
- Carte £61/85
  Closed Christmas-New Year and Sunday dinner – booking essential

THE GLASSHOUSE ✿

Modern cuisine • Fashionable

XX A/C ✿ **MAP:** 18-R2

The Glasshouse

FIRST COURSE: Roast duck breast with charred salsify, pickled rhubarb and samphire. • Grilled mackerel with courgettes, caramelised apple and toasted sunflower seeds.

MAIN COURSE: Monkfish, Fowey mussels, sea beets, parsnips, blood orange and verjus sauce. • Loin of Welsh lamb with roast sweetbreads, sweet potato purée and summer vegetables.

DESSERT: Passion fruit meringue with coconut ice cream and caramelised mango. • Poached apricots with baklava, burnt honey dressing and Greek yogurt.

The Glasshouse is the very model of a modern neighbourhood restaurant. It sits in the heart of lovely, villagey Kew, always seems to be busy and is known for the quality and reliability of its cooking. The food is confident yet unshowy – much like the locals themselves, who are the restaurant's biggest fans – and comes with distinct Mediterranean flavours along with the occasional Asian hint. The kitchen is also using more Welsh ingredients these days, especially beef and lamb, as the chef is from north Wales. The wine list is well worth closer examination as it offers an interesting range by the glass and a particularly good selection of grower champagnes. The floor to ceiling windows create a feeling of space which cleverly distracts you from realising that actually the place is quite cramped – just don't let the staff sit you in the middle of the room as you'll feel surrounded by diners and staff rushing by. Service is eager and youthful.

- **Kew** — 14 Station Par. ✉ TW9 3PZ
  ✆ 020 8940 6777 — **www**.glasshouserestaurant.co.uk
  ⊖ Kew Gardens
- Menu £35 (weekday lunch)/70
  Closed 24-26 December and 1 January

BINGHAM RESTAURANT

Modern cuisine • Design

MAP: 18-R3

Its riverside location has always made The Bingham hotel a popular choice for a wedding but it is also known for having a very good restaurant. Start with a drink in the cocktail bar or on the balcony terrace overlooking the garden and river before heading into the comfortable dining room. The menus offer plenty of choice, with an à la carte and a market menu, but the incurably indecisive need not panic because they can go for the mystery menu and leave it all to the kitchen. The food is a blend of the modern and the classical and, pleasingly, more thought has been given to the flavours than to the embellishments. The service team, rather like the clientele, are younger than expected - which also adds to the atmosphere.

- **Richmond** – Bingham Hotel, 61-63 Petersham Rd. ✉ TW10 6UT
  ✆ 020 8940 0902 — **www**.thebingham.co.uk
  ⊖ Richmond
- Menu £17 (lunch) - Carte £30/48
  Closed Sunday dinner

DYSART PETERSHAM

Modern cuisine • Intimate

MAP: 18-R3

Overlooking Richmond Park and built in the early 1900s as part of the Arts and Crafts movement, the Dysart is named after the family who once lived in Ham House. The owners decided to run it as a restaurant rather than a pub and have created a bright and fresh space that successfully blends its period features with more contemporary design elements. Service comes with a formality that seems somewhat at odds with this environment yet the formula clearly pleases the locals. The menu is also a blend of styles - the young chef uses top-notch ingredients and his cooking comes with a classical base to which he adds subtle Asian tones to create quite refined, delicately flavoured dishes. Look out for the occasional music recital evening.

- **Richmond** — 135 Petersham Rd ✉ TW10 7AA
  ✆ 020 8940 8005 — **www**.thedysartpetersham.co.uk
- Menu £25 (weekdays) - Carte £38/75
  Closed Sunday dinner, Monday and Tuesday - booking advisable

MATSUBA

Japanese • Design

MAP: 18-R2

Matsuba is a small, family-run place that is so understated it's easy to miss - look out for the softly lit sign above the narrow façade. The interior is equally compact and low-key, with just a dozen or so tables, along with a small counter at the back with room for four more. In fact the biggest thing in the room is the menu, which offers a comprehensive tour through most recognisable points in Japanese cooking. The owners are Korean so you can also expect to see bulgogi, the Korean barbecue dish of marinated meat that comes on a sizzling plate. All the food is fresh and the ingredients are good; lunch sees some very good value set menus. The service is well-meaning and it's hard not to come away thinking kind thoughts.

- **Richmond** — 10 Red Lion St ✉ TW9 1RW
  020 8605 3513 — **www**.matsuba-restaurant.com
  ⊖ Richmond
- Menu £25/45 - Carte £30/45
  Closed 25-26 December, 1 January and Sunday

PETERSHAM NURSERIES CAFÉ

Modern cuisine • Rustic

MAP: 18-R3

On a summer's day there can be few more delightful spots for lunch than the café at Petersham Nurseries. Buy into the whole Sunday-supplement charm of the place and you'll find that, whether you're on the terrace or inside the greenhouse with its wobbly tables and soil floor, the hustle and hassle of modern life seem a world away. The cooking is a perfect match for this rural retreat: it uses the freshest of seasonal produce in unfussy, flavoursome dishes. Nothing - apart from the daily sorbet - is frozen here and fridges are nigh on empty at the end of each day. Many herbs and leaves come from their own gardens and dishes like shoulder of lamb with cime di rapa and anchovies come with a subtle Italian accent.

- **Richmond** — Church Ln (off Petersham Rd) ✉ TW10 7AB
  020 8940 5230 — **www**.petershamnurseries.com
- Carte £28/43
  Closed 24-27 December and Monday - booking essential - (lunch only)

SWAGAT ꙮ

Indian • Bistro

X A/C **MAP:** 18-R2

This likeable little Indian restaurant is run by two friends; they met while training with Oberoi hotels in India before coming to London to work in some of the capital's best Indian restaurants. One partner organises the warm, well-meaning service, while the other ensures his kitchen delivers authentic and satisfying cooking, some of which comes with north Indian influences. Dishes display a pleasing degree of lightness and subtlety so the first taste is always that of the prime ingredient rather than the spice; there's a health dividend to some of the dishes, such as sea bass with chilli and ginger; and vegetarians have plenty of choice. Add in complimentary poppadoms and chutneys and you can see why it's a hit with the locals.

- **Richmond** — 86 Hill Rise ✉ TW10 6UB
  ✆ 020 8940 7557 — **www**.swagatindiancuisine.co.uk
  ⊖ Richmond
- Menu £30 - Carte £20/32
  Closed 25 December - booking essential - (dinner only)

SHIKUMEN ꙮ

Chinese • Intimate

XX ♿ A/C **MAP:** 18-T1

One glance at the menu of this sleek-looking Cantonese restaurant and any spirits dashed by the terminal blandness of this end of Shepherd's Bush will be instantly uplifted. It offers an appealing selection of authentic dishes and makes good use of top quality ingredients like Scottish lobster and beef. The standout is the Peking duck, which needs 45 minutes' notice at busy times, and which comes in two servings: the first with pancakes; the second with rice or noodles. It's well worth coming at lunch for the handmade dim sum and that includes their Xiao Long Bao which boast an impressive 15 pleats. The name of the restaurant translates as 'stone gate' and refers to a style of house which blends Chinese and Western styles. There's a sister branch in Ealing.

- **Shepherd's Bush** — 58 Shepherd's Bush Grn ✉ W12 8QE
  ✆ 020 8749 9978 — **www**.shikumen.co.uk
  ⊖ Shepherd's Bush
- Carte £19/48
  Closed 25 December

EALING PARK TAVERN

Modern British • Trendy

MAP: 18-R1

This west London landmark, an impressive Arts and Crafts property dating from 1886, has been reborn and brought right up-to-date thanks to a splendid refurbishment from the Martin Brothers. With a panelled bar complete with stuffed animals, a bright, cavernous dining room, a suntrap terrace and the 'Long Arm Brewing Co.' at the back of the pub providing three bespoke ales (try the American IPA-OK), this is the sort of place we'd all like to live near. Service is charming and friendly and the cooking is robust yet comes with a refined edge, whether that's the freshest fish from Billingsgate, Yorkshire game in season, the chop or pie of the day, or the delightful old school puds. For larger groups, 'Feasting' menus can be arranged.

- **South Ealing** — 222 South Ealing Rd ✉ W5 4RL
  020 8758 1879 — **www**.ealingparktavern.com
  South Ealing
- Carte £22/35

SIMPLY THAI

Thai • Neighbourhood

MAP: 18-R3

Over the years, this simple Thai restaurant in the heart of suburbia has built up a loyal clientele. They describe the cooking as 'a healthy approach to eating' and there's a bewildering array of dishes to choose from; if you're struggling to decide, pick one of Patria's signature dishes. What the cooking lacks in authenticity (it's adjusted for Western tastes), it makes up for in its commendable use of British ingredients. You might find cod dumplings in green curry sauce or rack of lamb marinated with Thai spices. The budget conscious should come on a Sunday for the street food selection, while the dipping sauces, made in house, are good any day of the week. Service is friendly but don't be surprised if things slow down as the place fills up.

- **Teddington** — 196 Kingston Rd. ✉ TW11 9JD
  020 8943 9747 — **www**.simplythai-restaurant.co.uk
  Hampton Wick (Rail)
- Menu £30 (weekdays) - Carte £20/32
  Closed 25-26 December - (dinner only)

A CENA

Italian • Neighbourhood

MAP: 18-R2

The constantly evolving menu at this bigger-than-you-first-think Italian restaurant, just over Richmond Bridge, covers all parts of the country, although you can expect more of a nod to the north in the colder months when dishes become a little heartier. The cooking is fresh and tasty; pasta is most certainly a highlight and desserts, although limited in choice, are usually done well too. The front section of the restaurant can feel a little cramped and it's at the back where it all seems to be happening. The owners are not actually Italian but his mother is and she clearly exerted quite an influence because his passion and enthusiasm are obvious. They also own a nearby foodstore and butcher's.

- **Twickenham** — 418 Richmond Rd. TW1 2EB
  020 8288 0108 — **www**.acena.co.uk
  Richmond
- Menu £10 (weekday lunch) - Carte £20/45
  Closed 2 weeks August, Sunday dinner, Monday lunch and bank holidays

CROWN

Traditional British • Pub

MAP: 18-R3

Much to the delight of St Margarets residents, this fine-looking Georgian pub has been revived and revitalised. Setting the scene are an old lantern hanging above the entrance and a mosaic floor inlaid with the pub's name, while inside it feels relaxed and stylish, with parquet floors, feature fireplaces and bright colours; sit in the airy, elegant rear restaurant, with its high vaulted ceiling and garden view. There's something for everyone on the global menus, from sharing boards and classic pub dishes to Mediterranean-influenced fish stew or Asian-inspired Tom Yum Thai prawns and squid. Portions are ample and cooking fresh, tasty and reliable. Service is enthusiastic and the pretty beer garden is popular with drinkers and diners alike.

- **Twickenham** — 174 Richmond Rd, St Margarets TW1 2NH
  020 8892 5896 — **www**.crowntwickenham.co.uk
  St Margarets (Rail).
- Carte £23/43
  Closed 26 December

CHEZ BRUCE ✿

French • Brasserie

MAP: 18-U3

Chez Bruce

FIRST COURSE: Tuna tartare with spiced onions, lime and coriander. • Charred hispi cabbage with whipped parmesan, artichoke, truffle and hazelnut.

MAIN COURSE: Barbary duck breast with wild garlic butter and asparagus. • Grilled Shetland salmon with new potatoes, artichoke barigoule and rouille.

DESSERT: Lemon and mascarpone Swiss roll with Yorkshire rhubarb. • Crème brûlée.

Chez Bruce has had a successful formula for many years and epitomises all that is wonderful about neighbourhood restaurants, even having to extend into the adjacent deli a few years back in order to satisfy the demand for a table. What keeps customers keen is its flavoursome and uncomplicated food, its sensible prices, the sprightly service from a charming team and the buzzing yet easy-going atmosphere. Matthew Christmas is the head man in the kitchen, having worked closely with owner Bruce Poole for many years. His cooking provides an object lesson in the importance of flavours and balance: dishes are assured, the plate is never too crowded and natural flavours are to the fore. The base is largely classical French but comes with Mediterranean tones, so expect to find words like parfait, pastilla, brandade and confit on the menu, which lists around seven dishes per course. The wine list is a work of art; the cheese trolley is always worth exploring; and coffee comes with shortbread at lunch and terrific palmiers at dinner.

- **Wandsworth** — 2 Bellevue Rd ✉ SW17 7EG
  ✆ 020 8672 0114 — **www**.chezbruce.co.uk
  ⊖ Tooting Bec
- Menu £35/55
  Closed 24-26 December and 1 January - booking essential

LIGHT HOUSE

Mediterranean cuisine • Neighbourhood

MAP: 18-T3

A neighbourhood favourite, the Light House offers Mediterranean cooking in smart, comfortable surroundings, with a light and spacious feel. While they do offer the occasional Thai dish, it is in Italy where the majority of the menu and the kitchen's strengths lie, with a roll-call of favourites that include tagliatelle, gnocchi, saltimbocca and panna cotta. The food is wholesome and confident, with plenty of bold flavours; puddings are a highlight and prices at lunch and in the early evening are attractive, which ensures that it is often very busy. The result is that the young team can sometimes struggle to keep up, but they remain admirably calm and cheery. As this was once a shop selling lights and fittings, it is fittingly well lit.

- **Wimbledon** — 75-77 Ridgway ✉ SW19 4ST
  020 8944 6338 — **www**.lighthousewimbledon.com
  Wimbledon
- Menu £17 (weekdays) - Carte £26/42
  Closed 25-26 December, 1 January and Sunday dinner

LIGHT ON THE COMMON

Traditional British • Neighbourhood

MAP: 18-T3

One of the signs of success for a neighbourhood restaurant is when it's used by regulars throughout the day; this sister to Light House is a case in point, with locals popping in for a coffee or a snack as often as booking a table for a three course meal. Things kick off at breakfast with an extensive menu offering everything from bircher muesli or pancakes to salt beef hash or a full English. Lunch sees an equally wide choice, with starters, salads and sandwiches available alongside dishes like fish pie or a rare breed burger; dinner broadens things further, and the set dinner menu, available Monday–Thursday, offers great value for money. Add in friendly staff and a bright, modern backdrop and you can see why it's a hit.

- **Wimbledon** — 48 High St ✉ SW19 5AX
  020 8946 3031 — **www**.lightwimbledon.co.uk
  Wimbledon
- Menu £23 (weekdays) - Carte £23/33
  Closed 25 December and Sunday dinner

TAKAHASHI ꟷ

Japanese • Friendly

MAP: 18-T3

Eponymous chef-owner Nobuhisa Takahashi spent 14 years at Nobu restaurants in Tokyo, London and Cape Town, and his experience is plain to see in dishes like black cod miso and salmon carpaccio with yuzu salsa. This sweet, unadorned spot is far from a Nobu facsimile, however, and the judicious use of Mediterranean ingredients and its 'tapas' menu sections show that this is a broad-minded kitchen with a creative bent. Dishes offer up pure, delicate flavours; the sushi and sashimi are a must, as are signature dishes Portobello mushroom ajillo and crispy pork belly with aubergine miso. Taka's charming wife Yuko runs the service with a very personal touch. If you are not sure what to order then ask her advice - or go for one of the two tasting menus.

- **Wimbledon** — 228 Merton Rd ✉ SW19 1EQ
  ✆ 020 8540 3041 — **www**.takahashi-restaurant.co.uk
  ⊖ South Wimbledon
- Menu £20/40 - Carte £22/47
  Closed Monday and Tuesday - booking essential - (dinner only and lunch Saturday-Sunday)

WHITE ONION

Modern cuisine • Bistro

MAP: 18-T3

The relaxed atmosphere that exists within the deep blue walls of this bistro deluxe makes it incredibly easy to feel at home here - this is the sort of restaurant every high street could do with having. There's a handsome marble-topped bar at the entrance, modern artwork hanging on the walls and a young serving team who are attentive and professional without undue pomp. Everything from the bread to the ice cream is homemade and the flavoursome French cooking has a classical base and clever modern touches. Don't miss the terrine of ox cheek and ham hock or the monkfish rolled in crispy potatoes. The set lunch menu offers great value for money and the wine list is carefully chosen, with a terrific selection by the glass and carafe.

- **Wimbledon** — 67 High St ✉ SW19 5EE
  ✆ 020 8947 8278 — **www**.thewhiteonion.co.uk
  ⊖ Wimbledon
- Menu £23 (lunch) - Carte dinner £29/48
  Closed first 2 weeks August, 25 December-4 January, Monday, lunch Tuesday-Wednesday and Sunday dinner

T. Hanslien/Loop Images/Photononstop

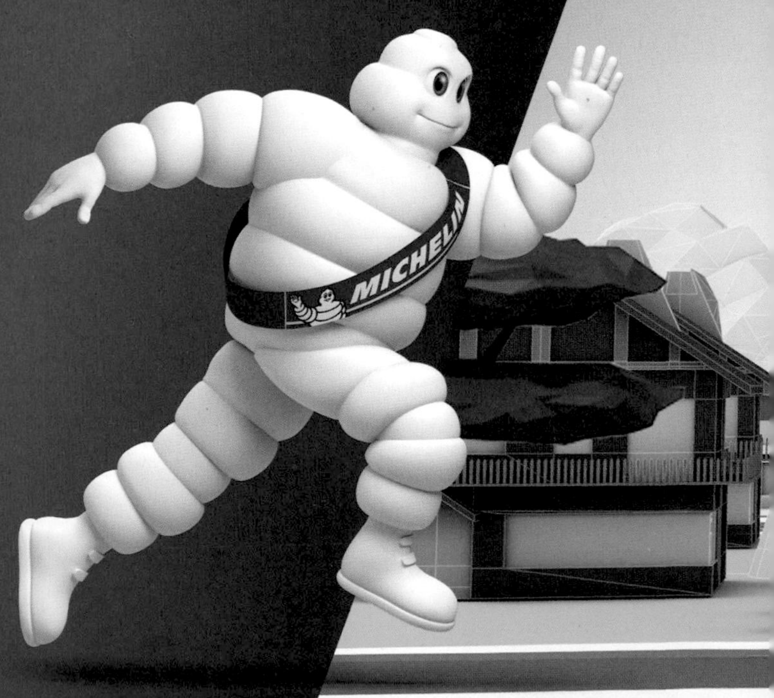
MICHELIN

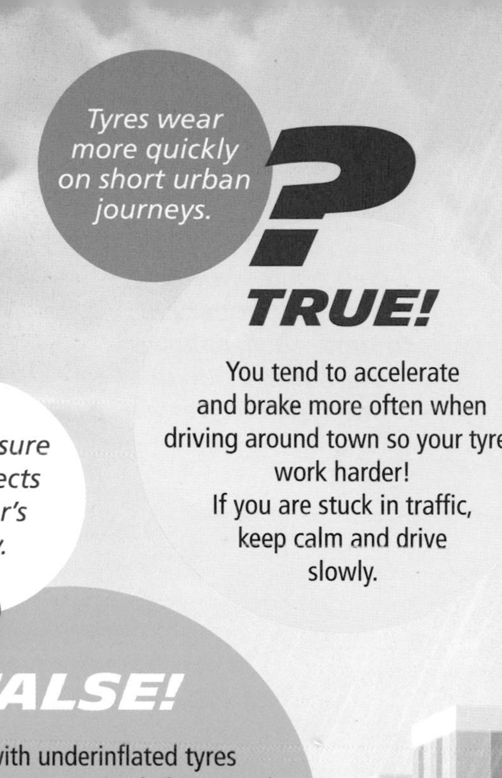

Tyres wear more quickly on short urban journeys.

TRUE!

You tend to accelerate and brake more often when driving around town so your tyres work harder!
If you are stuck in traffic, keep calm and drive slowly.

Tyre pressure only affects your car's safety.

FALSE!

Driving with underinflated tyres (0.5 bar below recommended pressure) doesn't just impact handling and fuel consumption, it will shave 8,000 km off tyre lifespan.
Make sure you check tyre pressure about once a month and before you go on holiday or a long journey.

If you only encounter **winter weather from time to time** - sudden showers, snowfall or black ice - **one type of tyre** will do the job.
?
TRUE!
The revolutionary **MICHELIN CrossClimate** - the very first summer tyre with winter certification - is a practical solution to keep you on the road whatever the weather.

*Fitting **2 winter tyres** on my car guarantees maximum safety.*
?
FALSE!
In the winter, especially when temperatures drop below 7°C, to ensure better road holding, all four tyres should be identical and fitted at the same time.
2 WINTER TYRES ONLY = risk of compromised road holding.
4 WINTER TYRES = safer handling when cornering, driving downhill and braking.
If you regularly encounter rain, snow or black ice, choose a **MICHELIN Alpin tyre**. This range offers you sharp handling plus a comfortable ride to safely face the challenge of winter driving.
MICHELIN

MICHELIN IS COMMITTED

▶ *MICHELIN IS* ***GLOBAL LEADER IN FUEL-EFFICIENT TYRES*** *FOR LIGHT VEHICLES.*

▶ ***EDUCATING OF YOUNGSTERS IN ROAD SAFETY,***
NOT FORGETTING TWO-WHEELERS. LOCAL ROAD SAFETY CAMPAIGNS WERE RUN IN ***16 COUNTRIES*** *IN 2015.*

QUIZ

1 TYRES ARE BLACK SO WHY IS THE MICHELIN MAN WHITE?

Back in 1898 when the Michelin Man was first created from a stack of tyres, they were made of natural rubber, cotton and sulphur and were therefore light-coloured. The composition of tyres did not change until after the First World War when carbon black was introduced. But the Michelin Man kept his colour!

2 FOR HOW LONG HAS MICHELIN BEEN GUIDING TRAVELLERS?

Since 1900. When the MICHELIN guide was published at the turn of the century, it was claimed that it would last for a hundred years. It's still around today and remains a reference with new editions and online restaurant listings in a number of countries.

3 WHEN WAS THE "BIB GOURMAND" INTRODUCED IN THE MICHELIN GUIDE?

The symbol was created in 1997 but as early as 1954 the MICHELIN guide was recommending "exceptional good food at moderate prices". Today, it features on the MICHELIN Restaurants website and app.

If you want to enjoy a fun day out and find out more about Michelin, why not visit the l'Aventure Michelin museum and shop in Clermont-Ferrand, France:

www.laventuremichelin.com

Michelin

INDEXES

ekash/iStock (bottom) • gilaxia/iStock (top)

ALPHABETICAL LIST OF RESTAURANTS

A

B

C

H

I

J

K

L

M

P

T

U

V

W

Y-Z

STARRED RESTAURANTS

✿✿✿

✿✿

✿

BIB GOURMAND

H

J

K

L

M

P

S

T

U-W

RESTAURANTS BY CUISINE TYPE

ARGENTINIAN

ASIAN

AUSTRIAN

BARBECUE

BASQUE

CHINESE

CLASSIC CUISINE

CREATIVE

CREATIVE BRITISH

CREATIVE FRENCH

CREOLE

FISH AND CHIPS

FRENCH

GREEK

INDIAN

ITALIAN

JAPANESE

KOREAN

LEBANESE

MEATS AND GRILLS

MEDITERRANEAN CUISINE

MEXICAN

MIDDLE EASTERN

MODERN BRITISH

MODERN FRENCH

MODERN CUISINE

MOROCCAN

NORTH AFRICAN

NORTH AMERICAN

PERUVIAN

POLISH

PORTUGUESE

PROVENÇAL

SCANDINAVIAN

SCOTTISH

SEAFOOD

SOUTH INDIAN

SPANISH

THAI

TRADITIONAL BRITISH

TRADITIONAL CUISINE

TURKISH

VEGETARIAN

WORLD CUISINE

THE BEST PUBS

RESTAURANTS WITH OUTSIDE DINING

L

M

N-O

P

RESTAURANTS OPEN FOR BREAKFAST

INDEX OF MAPS

CENTRAL LONDON

GREATER LONDON

Ruislip Gardens
2
9
South Harrow
South Ruislip
Sudbury Hill
Northolt
Sudbury Town
Greenford
Alperton
Perivale
Park Royal
Hanger Lane
North Ealing
1
7
South Kenton
North Wembley
WEMBLEY CENTRAL
Stonebridge Park
Harlesden
WILLESDEN JUNCTION
Northwick Park
Preston Road
6
Kingsbury
WEMBLEY PARK
Neasden
Dollis Hill
Willesden Green
Kilburn
Finchley Road & Frognal
8
Brent Cross
Golders Green
Hampstead
Hampstead Heath
Brondesbury Park
Brondesbury
Kensal Rise
WEST HAMPSTEAD
FINCHLEY ROAD
Swiss Cottage
Belsize Park
Chalk Farm
Kilburn High Road
Kensal Green
Queen's Park
Kilburn Park
South Hampstead
St. John's Wood
Mornington Crescent
Maida Vale
Warwick Avenue
Marylebone
Edgware Road
BAKER STREET
Great Portland Street
2
4
EALING BROADWAY
West Acton
North Acton
Ladbroke Grove
Westbourne Park
Royal Oak
Bayswater
PADDINGTON
Queensway
EDGWARE ROAD
Regent's Park
WARREN ST
BOND ST.
Ealing Common
Acton Central
East Acton
WHITE CITY
WOOD LANE
Latimer Road
South Acton
Holland Park
NOTTING HILL GATE
Lancaster Gate
Marble Arch
OXFORD CIRCUS
Shepherd's Bush Market
SHEPHERD'S BUSH
GREEN PARK
ACTON TOWN
Goldhawk Road
HIGH STREET KENSINGTON
PICCADILLY CIRCUS
South Ealing
Chiswick Park
Turnham Green
KENSINGTON (OLYMPIA)
Hyde Park Corner
CHARING CROSS
Northfields
Knightsbridge
Boston Manor
Stamford Brook
5
3
Gloucester Road
Sloane Square
WESTMINSTER
Osterley
Ravenscourt Park
Hounslow West
Hounslow East
HAMMERSMITH
West Kensington
EARL'S COURT
VICTORIA
St. James's Park
Hatton Cross
Hounslow Central
Barons Court
SOUTH KENSINGTON
HEATHROW TERMINALS 1,2,3
Gunnersbury
WEST BROMPTON
Pimlico
9
River Thames
HEATHROW TERMINAL 5
HEATHROW TERMINAL 4
Fulham Broadway
Imperial Wharf
Vauxhall
Parsons Green
Kew Gardens
Putney Bridge
Wandsworth Road
CLAPHAM HIGH STREET
CLAPHAM JUNCTION
4
4
CLAPHAM NORTH
RICHMOND
East Putney
Clapham South
LONDON TRANSPORT
1 BAKERLOO
2 CENTRAL
3 CIRCLE
4 DISTRICT
5 HAMMER & CITY
6 JUBILEE

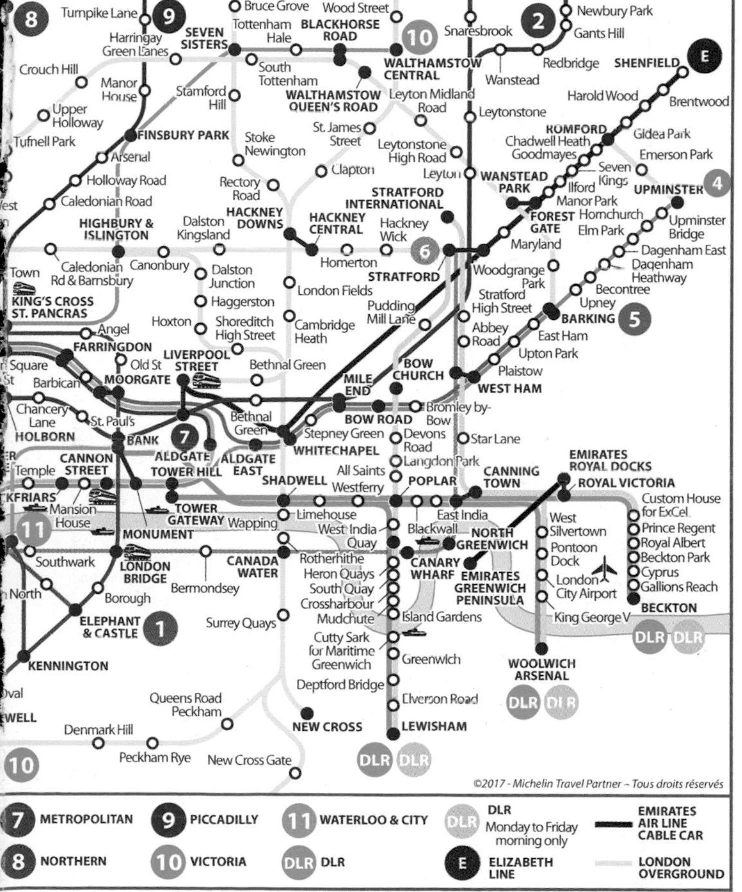

8
Turnpike Lane
9
Bruce Grove
Wood Street
Newbury Park
Tottenham Hale
BLACKHORSE ROAD
10
Snaresbrook
2
Gants Hill
Harringay Green Lanes
SEVEN SISTERS
SHENFIELD
E
Crouch Hill
South Tottenham
WALTHAMSTOW CENTRAL
Wanstead
Redbridge
Manor House
Stamford Hill
WALTHAMSTOW QUEEN'S ROAD
Leyton Midland Road
Harold Wood
Brentwood
Upper Holloway
Leytonstone
Tufnell Park
FINSBURY PARK
Stoke Newington
St. James Street
ROMFORD
Gidea Park
Arsenal
Leytonstone High Road
Chadwell Heath
Goodmayes
Emerson Park
Holloway Road
Clapton
Leyton
WANSTEAD PARK
Seven Kings
Rectory Road
Ilford
UPMINSTER
4
Caledonian Road
STRATFORD INTERNATIONAL
Manor Park
HIGHBURY & ISLINGTON
Dalston Kingsland
HACKNEY DOWNS
HACKNEY CENTRAL
Hackney Wick
FOREST GATE
Hornchurch
Upminster Bridge
Elm Park
Maryland
Dagenham East
6
Homerton
Caledonian Rd & Barnsbury
Canonbury
Dalston Junction
STRATFORD
Woodgrange Park
Dagenham Heathway
Town
Becontree
KING'S CROSS ST. PANCRAS
London Fields
Stratford High Street
Upney
Haggerston
Pudding Mill Lane
BARKING
5
Hoxton
Shoreditch High Street
Cambridge Heath
Abbey Road
East Ham
Angel
FARRINGDON
LIVERPOOL STREET
Upton Park
Old St
Bethnal Green
BOW CHURCH
Plaistow
Square
Barbican
MOORGATE
MILE END
WEST HAM
Chancery Lane
St. Paul's
Bethnal Green
BOW ROAD
Bromley by-Bow
HOLBORN
BANK
7
Stepney Green
Devons Road
Star Lane
ALDGATE
ALDGATE EAST
WHITECHAPEL
Langdon Park
EMIRATES ROYAL DOCKS
Temple
CANNON STREET
TOWER HILL
SHADWELL
All Saints
POPLAR
CANNING TOWN
ROYAL VICTORIA
Westferry
KFRIARS
Mansion House
TOWER GATEWAY
Limehouse
East India
Custom House for ExCel
11
Wapping
West India Quay
Blackwall
West Silvertown
Prince Regent
MONUMENT
NORTH GREENWICH
Royal Albert
Pontoon Dock
Southwark
LONDON BRIDGE
CANADA WATER
Rotherhithe
Beckton Park
CANARY WHARF
EMIRATES GREENWICH PENINSULA
Heron Quays
Cyprus
London City Airport
Gallions Reach
North
Borough
Bermondsey
South Quay
Crossharbour
BECKTON
Surrey Quays
Mudchute
Island Gardens
King George V
ELEPHANT & CASTLE
1
DLR
Cutty Sark for Maritime Greenwich
KENNINGTON
Greenwich
WOOLWICH ARSENAL
Deptford Bridge
Oval
Queens Road Peckham
Elverson Road
WELL
NEW CROSS
LEWISHAM
Denmark Hill
Peckham Rye
New Cross Gate
10
©2017 - Michelin Travel Partner – Tous droits réservés
7 METROPOLITAN
9 PICCADILLY
11 WATERLOO & CITY
DLR Monday to Friday morning only
EMIRATES AIR LINE CABLE CAR
8 NORTHERN
10 VICTORIA
DLR DLR
E ELIZABETH LINE
LONDON OVERGROUND

MICHELIN TRAVEL PARTNER

Société par actions simplifiées au capital de 11 288 880 EUR

27 Cours de l'Ile Seguin - 92100 Boulogne Billancourt (France)

R.C.S. Nanterre 433 677 721

Dépôt légal 09-2017

Printed in Italy - August 2017
Printed on paper from sustainably managed forests

Compogravure : Nord Compo à Villeneuve d'Ascq (France)
Impression et Finition : Printer trento (Italie)

Our editorial team has taken the greatest care in writing this guide and checking the information in it. However, practical information (prices, addresses, telephone numbers, internet addresses, etc.) is subject to frequent change and such information should therefore be used for guidance only. It is possible that some of the information in this guide may not be accurate or exhaustive as at the date of publication. We therefore accept no liability in regard to such information.